Understanding
the Russians

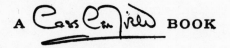 A CassCanfield BOOK

HARPER & ROW, PUBLISHERS

NEW YORK, EVANSTON, AND LONDON

FOY D. KOHLER

Understanding the Russians

A CITIZEN'S PRIMER

Grateful acknowledgment is made for permission to reprint the following excerpts:

From *Journey for Our Time* by Astolphe de Custine, translated by Phyllis Penn Kohler. Copyright, 1951, by Phyllis Penn Kohler. Published by Henry Regnery Company, Chicago. Reprinted by permission of the translator.

From *Khrushchev and Stalin's Ghost,* by Bertram D. Wolfe; published by Praeger Publishers, Inc., New York, 1957. © 1957 by Bertram D. Wolfe. Reprinted by permission of the Publishers.

FIRST EDITION

LIBRARY OF CONGRESS CATALOG CARD NUMBER: 73-108940

FOR PHYLLIS

CONTENTS

Preface, ix

Introduction, xiii

CHAPTER I   The Soviet Scene: Geography and Historical Background, 1

CHAPTER II   The Revolutions of 1917: The Bolsheviks—What Lenin Did to Marx, 17

CHAPTER III   Stalin and the Making of the Soviet System, 46

CHAPTER IV   World War II: Its Impact and Consequences, 64

CHAPTER V   Postwar Reversion to Orthodoxy: Origins of the Cold War, 87

CHAPTER VI   The Khrushchev Era, 106

CHAPTER VII   Post-Khrushchev Leadership and
                 Policies, 132

CHAPTER VIII   The Communist Monolith:
                 How It Was Achieved and
                 How It Operated, 160

CHAPTER IX   The Fracturing of the Communist
                 Monolith: The Sino-Soviet Conflict
                 and Its Consequences, 186

CHAPTER X   The Fractured Monolith: Picking Up
                 the Pieces, 218

CHAPTER XI   Foundations and Instruments of
                 Soviet Policy, 242

CHAPTER XII   U.S.–Soviet Confrontations after
                 World War II and the Development
                 of U.S. Policy, 272

CHAPTER XIII   Germany and Berlin: A Problem in
                 Crisis Management, 304

CHAPTER XIV   Cuba and the Soviet Problem in Latin
                 America, 340

CHAPTER XV   Vietnam: A War of National
                 Liberation?, 366

CHAPTER XVI   The Middle East: Area of Potential
                 Confrontation, 398

                 Epilogue, 413

                 Index, 427

Preface

Though I am now starting my third year of academic life at the University of Miami, I would not profess that this book is a "scholarly" work. I suppose it is inevitable that after more than thirty-six years in the Foreign Service of the United States I am and will probably remain more a professional diplomat than an academician. A professional diplomat is a dabbler in all the academic disciplines, a master of none; but he is supposed nowadays to be a master of synthesis. Diplomacy in our era is no longer a matter of dealing with a handful of courtiers, of influencing a sovereign. It bears only a remote resemblance to the glamorous picture of personal intrigue emerging from old histories and romantic novels and exciting spy stories. Modern diplomacy is rather a continuing and exhaustive study of whole societies and of their interrelationships. It requires knowledge of the history and culture, of the political, economic, techno- logical and social forces at work in the society in which the diplomat resides. It requires careful evaluation of the direction in which these forces will move within that society, and of the effect their movement will have on relations between that society and other societies, especially his own.

What are the diplomat's sources? More specifically, what are the sources of the observations and views expressed in this book? They are literally myriad, including notably:

· Personal observation during nearly seven years of resi- dence and travel in the Soviet Union, first from February, 1947, to July, 1949, then from September, 1962, to November, 1966, plus shorter visits in 1959, 1968 and 1969.

· Thousands of conversations with Soviet citizens, from members of the Kremlin leadership to university rectors in Moscow and elsewhere, to a factory manager in Sverdlovsk, to a port captain in the Soviet Far East, to an aged peasant woman waiting for a Volga ferry.

· Hundreds of hours of participating in negotiations with Soviet officials, both bilaterally and multilaterally, in diverse forums.

· Endless discussions with my own American diplomatic colleagues, journalists and outside experts on Russia and the Soviet Union—and similar exchanges of views and opinions with experts and diplomats of other countries.

· Reading the Soviet press and other current publications for a quarter of a century.

· Listening day after day, year after year to Soviet radio and television.

· Seeing and hearing hundreds of Russian plays, operas, ballets and concerts.

· Going through the general readers of the seven-year Soviet primary school (comparable to the old McGuffey *Readers* in the United States).

· My own eclectic library in English, French and Russian,

ranging from serious political and historical studies through the
Russian classics and modern Soviet novels, to scores of local
guidebooks about places visited throughout the Soviet Union.

Consequently, for what I know of Russia and the Soviet
Union and of American relations with that society, I owe much
to many. But I find it generally impossible to sort out the various
sources and to identify them in detailed footnotes. They are not
filed that way in my own mind and my own mental computer-
retriever system is not so programed. Indeed, I am somewhat
apprehensive that I may seem to present as my own ideas which
someone else may consider his own. I do not do so consciously
or intentionally except where I have explicitly quoted a source. I
do quote at some length from the American edition of the letters
of the Marquis de Custine, edited, translated and published by
my wife some years ago under the title *Journey for Our Time*. I
also quote a particularly pithy passage from *Khrushchev and
Stalin's Ghost* by my old friend and associate Bertram D. Wolfe,
on whose wise guidance, both written and oral, I have relied for
a score of years. My friend Tom Whitney, the other Toledo
(Ohio) product who went to Moscow, has long been a guide to
Russian writing and writers, both in personal discussions and in
his book *The New Writing in Russia*. Benjamin Gitlow's *I Confess* has provided invaluable material about the attitudes and
aspirations—and disillusionment—of the early American Communists. I have also leaned heavily on and quoted from Lazar
Pistrak's pioneering biography of Khrushchev, *The Grand Tactician: Khrushchev's Rise to Power*, and on David Shub's *Lenin*.
Both Leon Trotsky's *Stalin* and Svetlana Alliluyeva's two books,
Twenty Letters to a Friend and *Only One Year*, have contributed, from very different points of view, to my understanding of
Stalin. Alexander Werth, who "was there" until after I first went
to Moscow, has helped me to pull into focus the tumultuous
events of *Russia at War*. An unpublished study by my Foreign
Service colleague, John Ausland, a member of the "Berlin Task
Force," has served to remind me of many aspects of the long
Berlin crisis from 1948 through 1962.

I could go on and on in acknowledging the contributions to

my own education on Russian and Soviet affairs—by Loy Henderson, the key man in the embassy in Moscow during the 1930s though never ambassador, by my associates and ambassadorial predecessors and successors, George Kennan, Charles Bohlen, Llewellyn Thompson and Jacob Beam, and by my younger colleagues in the Foreign Service who now head and staff our embassies throughout Eastern Europe and the key posts dealing with European affairs in the State Department.

Most of the material in this book was first pulled together in the form of lectures to my classes at the University of Miami. Portions were included and summarized in three lectures I delivered at the School of Advanced International Studies of Johns Hopkins University in Washington in the spring of 1968, in a series honoring the memory of my late friend and chief, Secretary of State Christian Herter. I have updated and revised it— and, I hope, improved it—in the light of the penetrating and challenging questions asked by my students and by the distinguished audiences at the Herter lectures.

I am grateful to my associates at the Center for Advanced International Studies of the University—Dr. Mose L. Harvey, Dr. Leon Gouré, Mr. Vladimir Prokofieff—for reading the original material and making indispensable corrections and useful suggestions. The patience and efficiency of my assistants here at the Center—Dr. Margarita M. Pelleyá and Mrs. Florence F. W. Coey (who was also with us in Moscow)—in filing, typing, proofreading, correcting, suggesting, are beyond praise.

My wife, a real professional and partner through thirty-five years of Foreign Service and now university life, continued to make her usual major contributions and to bear with my disposition through this exercise.

I judge that it is conventional for an author to assert that the final responsibility for his work is all his own, so I do.

Village of Tequesta
January, 1970

Introduction

I first went to Moscow at the end of World War II by my own application, mainly because years of study and many long discussions with my colleagues who had served there had given me no satisfactory concept of what Russia and the Russians were really like. So—even though it was said at that time that anyone who actually asked to go to Moscow should have his head examined—I simply felt I had to see it for myself, and ended up by living there for the better part of seven years.

During these years of study, observation and residence in the Soviet Union, it was increasingly borne in on me that there are a few rather simple, fundamental factors which anyone who wants to understand the Soviet Union must get into his head and keep there.

Americans and other Westerners are frequently confused because practically every source paints Russia in different colors, from the brightest red to the most somber black. Some of this results from predispositions and political motivations, of course, but even visitors of good, objective intentions can and do bring back a wide variety of differing reports. There is a basic reason for this. The Soviet Union is a land of contradictions—contrasts between the old and the new, frequently juxtaposed, or between the accomplishments of advanced science and the poverty of everyday life; disharmony between the professed ideology and the real aspirations of the Soviet citizen; and differences between what the Soviets say and what they really believe, or between what they say and what they actually do. The Soviet Government, with its rigid controls, can and does mobilize the best of its limited scientific and technological resources, both human and material, for priority projects; it is thus capable of accomplishing outstanding feats, as evidenced by Soviet development of missiles and space vehicles. However, it soon becomes apparent to those who live there and observe the society that the country is starved for the vast range of applied technology characteristic of Western societies, from nylon stockings to superhighways. The mechanization and automation of so much of our working and leisure life are largely absent in the Soviet Union. One cannot help being struck by the remarkable contrast of a society which produces better cosmonauts than mechanics, more sophisticated electronics than plumbing, better "Sputniks" than automobiles. Most observers come to a kind of rough estimate that in most fields of general industrial and professional development the Soviet Union is up to twenty-five years behind the West. The lag in the villages— the collective farms—is even greater. Here the scene is comparable to the American Midwest some fifty years ago. There is the same lack of amenities, of labor-saving devices, of roads and vehicles, of fertilizers and of scientific methods of breeding, planting and cultivation of both livestock and crops.

The second factor can be summarized in the warning:

"Don't think this society started just fifty years ago." So much of what is said and done, so many of the attitudes people hold, can be traced back to the myths and the traditions and the experiences of Russia's long and turbulent history. An example is the profound antipathy which the Russian feels toward the Chinese. This certainly does not arise from a differing interpretation of Communist ideology or even from the struggle for power and influence between the two countries within the Communist world. Rather, it is an ingrained prejudice which goes back to the Mongol-Tatar invasion, seven centuries ago, and Tatar occupation and despoliation of the Russian lands for the next three centuries.

We are frequently discouraged by the apparent political apathy of the Soviet population and its acquiescence in the regime's totalitarian controls and attempts to manipulate the populace toward its own power ends. We should remember that the Russians and the other peoples living in the Soviet Union have been subjected to long conditioning in tyranny and despotism under Czarist rule. Indeed, it was only in the last half of the last century that the Russians began to glimpse the possibility of a freer life. It is a tragedy of history that the democratic forces involved in the "February Revolution," which overthrew the Czar, were too weak to sustain their cause; and that the Bolshevik Revolution in October, 1917, in fact turned back toward the old practices.

It is often said that Russians resemble Americans. There is much truth in this. We have both been shaped by living in a tough continental environment and by struggling for survival against a hard and hostile climate. This has made the Russian a rugged, virile person, whom one gets to like—wary, but wanting to be sociable, imaginative, isolated but curious, ever-seeking and seldom finding an escape from the harsh realities of life. However, there are some fundamental differences in our heritage, often reflected in hard-to-understand attitudes toward government, or secrecy, or sportsmanship, or a variety of subjects.

It is useful to recall that the beginning of constitutional government in the West, with the granting of Magna Carta in England in the thirteenth century, roughly coincided with the

Tatar conquest and destruction of the fledgling Russian state at Kiev. Then for half a thousand years, while the Western world was progressing under the stimuli of the Renaissance, the Reformation, the Age of Discovery and the Industrial Revolution, the Russian people were held in a condition of ignorance and in social and economic slavery, first by the Mongol conquerors and then by a succession of Czars. We take for granted —indeed, we are scarcely conscious of—what these great historical events mean in terms of the character formation and general political and social development and outlook of peoples in the Western world. Our respect for the individual and our idea of the state as the servant come from classical Greece and Rome. Our sense of honorable and chivalrous competition derives from the gallant exploits of the Crusades—concepts acquired automatically from our parents and teachers, from reading the stories of Greek heroes and of King Arthur and his knights of the Round Table. Our traditions of individual initiative and independence stem from the Age of Discovery and from the exploration and settlement of the world's frontiers. We simply inherit this outlook and consider it quite natural that our Constitution contains provisions protecting the rights, the legitimate activities and the property of the individual.

But while all these basic concepts were taking root in the Western world, the Russians tilled lands they could not own, were not allowed to move from the soil and were wholly isolated from the rest of the world. Western influences began to reach and have a real impact on Russia only after the American and French revolutions, and particularly after the Napoleonic invasions. They stimulated a magnificent flowering of Russian culture and of Russian political thought—comparable to the age of Shakespeare and Bacon in England three centuries earlier— which blended this Western heritage and Russian tradition. Pushkin, Lermontov, Krylov, Gogol, Belinsky, Herzen, Dostoyevsky, Chekhov, Tolstoy—these great masters of the nineteenth-century enlightenment continue to supply the basic spiritual nourishment of the Russian peoples. Beside their works the output of regimented Soviet writers falls flat indeed. When the Soviet Union was faced with a life-or-death struggle against

Nazi Germany, Stalin rallied the population to an heroic effort of resistance, not in defense of Communism but in defense of the fatherland—not in the name of Marx and Lenin but in the name of the great writers, musicians and scientists of the period of cultural flowering, and of the great national heroes of Russian history: Alexander Nevsky, who routed the Swedes and the Livonian knights in 1242; Dmitri Donskoy, who defeated the Tatars in 1380; Minin and Pozharsky, who fought off the Poles in the seventeenth century; and Suvorov and Kutuzov, who led the Russian forces against Napoleon.

The third basic factor to keep in mind is the fact that the Soviet Union is ruled by a minority political organization which seized and has maintained a monopoly of political power. According to its own figures, the Communist Party of the Soviet Union has a membership of about fourteen million, or roughly 5 percent of the population. More than a century ago, the Russian revolutionary writer, Alexander Herzen, predicted that "a communist revolution in Russia would be the Czarist aristocracy turned upside down." This is almost visibly true, and the ordinary Russian citizen still thinks in terms of "we" (the people) and "they" (the rulers). But there is a fundamental difference. The Czars had their source of legitimacy in the accepted doctrine of the Divine Right of Kings. The Bolsheviks are obliged to justify their "right to rule" by proclaiming and acting in the name of a new theology, Marxism-Leninism— materialistic in concept, authoritarian in practice, messianic in spirit—which asserts as a matter of historical inevitability that their system is destined to rule the world. This ideology regards man as the instrument of the state rather than the state as the instrument of man—and in turn regards the state as the instrument of a self-chosen and self-imposed Communist elite. And the political system, based on this ideology and on what Lenin called "democratic centralism," makes no provision for legitimate succession to leadership. Thus, when a leader disappears from the scene—whether as a result of death, as in the case of Lenin or Stalin, or as a result of conspiracy, as in the case of Khrushchev—there must inevitably be a struggle for individual power among the principal potential claimants to the succession. There is of course an initial huddling together in a so-called "collective leadership" to preserve the system itself, on which all depend. However, the dynamics compel toward the emergence of a "boss" of the Communist Party, which holds the monopoly of political power. Moreover, as time passes and the *élan* of revolution fades, the succession process leads to what Bertram Wolfe calls "the law of diminishing dictatorships." Not only the organs of political, economic and social direction, but the Party itself become vast, entrenched bureaucracies, the members of which are preoccupied, not with creating something new but with jockeying for personal position within the established system. That system is thus no longer capable of producing a new Lenin or a new Stalin or even a new Khrushchev.

Now a final basic factor. The Soviet Union stretches out over a vast land area more than double that of the United States. It is true that much of this area is barren or lies in an unfavorable Arctic climate. However, much of it is simply underpopulated and undeveloped, and there is great need for development capital. The Soviet population totals about 240 million inhabitants or some 18 percent more than our own. There is a simple arithmetical formula which was the source of most of Khrushchev's troubles and will be a source of troubles for his successors for a long time to come. The Soviet Government tries to rival the United States in military and space programs, on which it is estimated to spend about 80 percent as much as we do. And it tries to do this on a total Gross National Product valued at $412 billion, against our GNP of $835 billion. These figures are for 1968; future figures will be higher on both sides, but will have about the same relationship. Someday something will have to give.

The best advice I received when I was about to leave Washington to undertake my new professorial career at the University of Miami came from a colleague who had reversed this process, by coming into government after many years of teaching. He told me the story of another government official who had left Washington to go to a university. This predecessor of mine had met his first class, made his first lecture—then suddenly realized he had shot his whole wad, stated all his conclusions and had nothing left to say.

I have rather violated my colleague's advice by setting forth in this introduction the foregoing considerations about the Soviet Union, but I hope that the reader of this volume will want to know how and why I reached these conclusions. And I hope that in the following pages he will find an adequate explanation as to why I consider these factors critical to understanding what the Russians are like and why the Soviet leaders behave as they do.

CHAPTER I

The Soviet Scene: Geography and Historical Background

The Soviet Union today covers over a sixth of the earth's land surface—a vast, flat, sprawling domain that extends for nearly 6,000 miles from west to east and as much as 3,000 miles from north to south. Its 8.7 million square miles make it more than twice the size of the United States. I have traveled over most of the territory. But it was only after I had crossed Siberia and found myself in the Maritime Provinces, washed by the waters of the Pacific, that I realized the full extent of its reach. Sitting in Nakhodka, the commercial port which is being built near the forbidden naval-base city of Vladivostok, it was borne in on us that we were beyond—to the east of—China and Southeast Asia. My wife and I sat in our miserable hotel room and listened to the radio in the medium-wave bands broadcast directly from Japan to the south. Also to the south of us, we realized for the first time, were the Philippines, and a direct line farther south would pass through the middle of Australia.

For the most part the Soviet land is an open plain, without natural frontiers, occupying the heart of the Eurasian land mass. The flatness of the whole stretch from the Baltic to the Pacific is broken only slightly by the Ural Mountain chain, the historic dividing line between Europe and Asia. But this is not much of a break, for the Urals are relatively low hills, averaging about fifteen hundred feet in height, not even comparable to our own Eastern Appalachians. Only in the south and southeast is the land protected by the high ranges of the Caucasus and Elbrus mountains, the Hindu Kush and, bordering China, the Tien Shan and Altai. Even this protective chain is broken by the Caspian Sea and its related passes into Iran, through which flowed the medieval China silk-trade routes and an endless succession of Mongol-Tatar invaders. On the western border, in the lowlands adjoining Poland, some protection is afforded by the great marshes. These bothered Napoleon in 1812 and Hitler's forces more than a century later.

The Arctic Circle slices through the northern fringe of this vast territory. In the high northwest corner of the Soviet Union, around the Kola Peninsula and the Far Northern port of Murmansk, which became famous as the terminus of the Lend-Lease supply route during World War II, the climate is somewhat modified by the remnants of the Gulf Stream which flows off our Florida coast, then on to the North Atlantic and finally the Arctic. With the occasional help of ice breakers during the winter, Murmansk can be kept open the year round. To the east, however, all along the Arctic Ocean toward Alaska, navigation is possible with the help of ice breakers only a few months each year. The adjoining land is subject to permafrost; that is, the ground is always frozen. Agriculture is practically impossible and even the construction of buildings is barely feasible. Below this tundra are the great forests, stretching for thousands and thousands of miles, thick and almost unending: silver birches, pines and firs—then firs, pines and silver birches without end.

The landscape has an almost haunting quality. I can well understand how a Russian comes to love this native scene, all green in the summer, snow-white with evergreen decoration in the winter. Farther to the south on the European side, the forests thin out in the Ukraine—which literally means "border-land" in Russian—to release great tracts of rich black soil for agriculture. This great black-soil region of the Ukraine was regarded in the last century as the bread basket of Europe. Indeed, even in this century, this bread basket was the main objective of Hitler's wild ambitions. To the east, across the Caspian Sea, and to the south of Siberia proper, moisture is lacking. In this area, Kazakhstan and Central Asia, the forests give way to the steppes and then to desert.

The most pronounced characteristic of the Russian physical scene is the rivers. They have also been one of the major determinants of Russian history and development. Here a real distinction exists between European Russia and Siberia. On the European side of the Urals the main rivers—the Dnieper, the Don, the Volga—originate in the great reservoirs of marshland lying to the west of Moscow. They flow generally from north to south, the first two emptying into the Black Sea and the Volga into the Caspian. These rivers were the main roads of Russian history. At various points, particularly near their sources, they come close enough together so that even in ancient times it was easy to find portages, and light boats could be carried or tugged from one water system to another. The rivers thus provided the basic traffic system. They served traders, and they served invaders. Today these portages have been largely substituted by interlocking canals. Thus there was, from the earliest times, a great water route through the Russian lands that came close to linking the Atlantic Ocean and the Baltic Sea with the Black Sea and the Mediterranean. The early Scandinavian Vikings came into Russia through the Baltic, then by way of the Dvina to the Dnieper, where they were instrumental in founding the first great Russian capital in Kiev. Later the road-portage link between the Neva and the Volga led to the founding of Novgorod the Great, now a town in the backwash but once the greatest merchant city in Russia. In due course Moscow grew to domi-

nant importance, in large degree because she controlled the
headwaters of the various river systems.

The great rivers of Siberia, contrary to the case in European Russia, nearly all originate to the south, in the hills of
Central Asia, and flow northward to the Arctic. This fact tends
to limit their usefulness, but they did have their role in the
period of Russian colonial expansion toward the east in the last
century. This colonial advance through the virgin forests—the
taiga—and almost unpopulated territory of Siberia tended to be
an advance from one river system to another until Russians
finally reached the great ocean in the east. Stalin's quondam
Foreign Minister, Andrei Vyshinsky, used to boast that the
Soviet Union was going to use its new-found control of atomic
explosions to reverse these rivers and irrigate the deserts of
Central Asia. The idea did not seem too farfetched, since the Ob
and the Irtysh, for example, drop only six hundred-odd feet in
their twelve-hundred-mile journey north to the Arctic Ocean.
However, as with so many such Soviet boasts, nothing more has
been heard of this project for some twenty years.

The second principal physical characteristic of the Russian
scene is the endless hinterland of forests, which stretch out
from and between the river systems. In them, the Russian
peasantry found both livelihood and shelter from the invading
nomads coming from the east. In this dark, almost impenetrable
environment, the Russian peasant could never know what menace of man or beast might spring out on him from behind any
tree. It was this life in the forests that developed the constant
wariness which is still the chief characteristic of the Great
Russian peasant. It also made its impress on his spirit. A whole
world of fancies and musings absorbed him, especially during
the long nights of the long winters. These are reflected and
carried on from generation to generation in Russian folk tales
and folk songs, many of which have provided the themes for
more modern writers of fairy tales, novels, poetry and even
opera and ballet. One of the first great Russian writers, Viktor
Krylov, spent his life articulating and beautifying this rich
heritage of folklore.

And finally there is the climate, harsh and continental—

long months of bitter cold and heavy snow cover. We shared the feelings of all Russians when the long winter came at last to an end, with the melting of the snows and the deep ice cover of the rivers, and the appearance of the first spring flowers. It was a messy, muddy season, but the sense of relief was unmistakable and irresistible. As Sir Bernard Pares put it in his *History of Russia:* "To the Russian peasant it can seem no mere fiction that death is followed by Resurrection; and Easter, like so many feast days that mark in his calendar the changes of the seasons, seems indeed, also, a great feast of nature." The struggle against the hostile elements is indeed never-ending, and the Russians take it seriously. They fight the snow as it comes down and get it out of the way before it can overwhelm them. They heat their houses well. In country villages the peasants have a kind of clay stove on top of which they sleep. I may add that cleanliness is not one of the important factors in fighting the cold. We used to say that the Russian villager would sew himself in his clothes in the fall and not remove them till spring. And I must say this practice gives the air in the village teahouse or club a certain piquant odor.

This tough environment and rough climate have made and still make life for the Russian a matter of survival of the fittest. The development of industries, the building of railroads crossing the great rivers, the advent of oil and electricity, instead of wood, as fuel—all these factors have modified the influence of the physical environment to some extent—but only to a limited extent. The weather remains harsh as ever, the forbidding expanses of marsh and forest and plain are little altered.

I will leave it to the anthropologists to sort out in detail, if they can, the endless movements of tribes across the great Eurasian land mass in search of food and safety. These migrations have left very little trace, since the only building materials used were perishable animal skins and wood. However, these vast movements of people certainly characterized the early centuries of our era; and one can suppose that by the fifth or sixth centuries many settlements had taken place, notably along the high western banks of the great rivers and in the shelter of the deep forests lining their branches and tributaries. Along with the settlements of the Slavonic tribes there were certainly also settlements and trading establishments of the more advanced and civilized Vikings, who came into Russia through the Baltic. In any case, Russian history, as such, would really start with the formation of the principality of Kiev—Kievsky Rus—under the authority and rule of a single large princely family of Viking origin. This principality gradually extended its sway over large areas of what are now the Ukraine and Russia proper. It traded widely and had relationships with other principalities throughout the then known world. The story is told that in the tenth century the ruling Prince Vladimir Svyatoslav, seeking an instrument which would impose some organization and discipline on his pagan subjects, shopped around in the religious field. After looking at Rome, Mecca and other centers, he decided that the Eastern Orthodox religion of Byzantium would be the best bet. So he made his decision, organized a skeleton priesthood and one bright Sunday morning in the spring of 988 mobilized the entire population of Kiev and marched them down and into the river, from which they emerged baptized Christians. We have often stood on the heights over the Dnieper, alongside a carefully preserved statue of the Great Prince Vladimir, looking, with him, down on the majestic Dnieper, scene of this mass baptism. Thus, a thousand years ago, the concept of the Church as an instrument of state power was introduced onto the Russian scene.

This first political organization—Russian Kiev—lasted for the better part of four centuries. Kiev became a big and beautiful city, adorned with splendid churches. Their basic architecture was inspired by the great cathedrals of Byzantium, but it was embellished with bold new forms springing from the fantasies of the Slavic imagination. Kiev became prosperous. It traded not only with Byzantium but with Western Europe. It became a spiritual and cultural center. The Orthodox religion took hold. The beauty and majesty of the Eastern ritual provided that escape from the harsh realities of his rugged environment which the Russian sought. The priests and monks became the custodians and chroniclers of the traditions and the history of the Slavs. Kiev's icons rivaled those of Byzantium itself. They set the pattern of Russian art for centuries to come. Then, in 1240, Kiev was overwhelmed by the Mongol-Tatar force of Batu (grandson of Genghis) Khan, and practically wiped off the face of the map. The great city was reduced to a few hundred houses.

These early Viking-Russian rulers of Kievsky Rus dispersed in different directions. The senior branch of the family set up a new national center in the backwoods of Moscow, a town less than a century old and so unimportant at that time that it attracted little attention from the Tatar invaders. Moscow did not attempt the heroic but fatal resistance which Kiev had put up against the Mongols. Instead, the Muscovites made a vassal peace with the conquering hordes and thus survived. The Moscow aristocracy gradually built up its wealth and accumulated real strength. The wills of the successor grand princes of Moscow had a great deal to do with this. While other branches of the great princely family were parceling out their domains among their different children, the Moscow branch increasingly tended to leave the predominant portion to the eldest. Moscow was also favored by its geographic position, as we noted earlier. Hidden away in the watershed, the town was a good refuge when the Mongol-Tatar domination was at its height. By carefully paying tribute to the Tatar overlords, Moscow was long able to remain at peace with them and its population grew as people from other areas came there for security. Similarly, Moscow was able to provide security for the Church and a safe residence for its head, the Metropolitan. He served the autocracy well and supported its aim of eventually freeing the nation from the "heathen" yoke.

Lacking interest or experience in government, and pleased with the servility of the Moscow princes, the Tatar Khans in due course entrusted to Moscow the collection of their general tributes from all the Russian lands and made the Grand Prince of Moscow judge of the disputes between other Russian princes. Many of these, appreciating their own weakness against the great growth of Moscow's wealth and power, entered her service. One of them, Dmitri Donskoy—Dmitri of the Don—built up a league of princes which challenged the Tatars and actually beat them badly, but not decisively, in a great battle at Kulikovo, on the banks of the Don. That was in 1380. Finally, in 1480, Ivan III refused to pay the usual tribute to the Great Khan Ahmed and uneasily awaited the Tatar onslaught. But this time there was no fighting. Both sides avoided engagements. The Tatar's Golden Horde broke up and did not return. The long years of spadework had united Russia behind Moscow, while the factions and divisions were now on the other side, among the many heirs of Genghis Khan. While the various Tatar factions thereafter continued to attack and harass the Moscow aristocracy, Moscow had, in fact, become the most united and powerful force on this Eurasian land mass and was even able in her turn to advance on Asia.

Aside from the continuing harassment of the Tatars, Moscow was now challenged on the west by the Poles and a struggle ensued which was to last in one form or another for centuries and which is probably not yet at an end. In order to meet these challenges on both sides, the Moscow princes devised a system of granting fiefs to military officers who served at the same time both as army commanders and as managers on the land. They were given complete authority over the local peasants. Thus grew up serfdom, which was to become the main theme in the history of the Russian people. There was some peasant resistance. Many of the more enterprising serfs, seeking to escape the taxes imposed on them by the squires and the obligatory recruiting, migrated to the border lands where control was looser and where they could sell their services as soldiers in the continuing war with the Tatars. Bands of these migrants founded the association and eventually the settlements of the Cossacks in the region of the Don River, taking their name from the Turkic word "*kazak*"—a "rebel" or, by extension, "free man."

In trying to stop this migration from the center, Moscow found useful not only the grant of authority to the squires or boyars, but also a peasant institution which had existed in Russia as far back as history can trace. This was the village commune—in Russian *mir*—based on a community of labor. In view of the inhospitable agricultural condition of the Russian lands, the necessity for joining forces to clear tracts of forests and the fact that the soil underneath was of variable quality, peasant communities concluded that organized cooperation was essential and that the cleared land would have to be divided into strips of varying productivity to avoid inequality in the rewards for their common labor. The Moscow government came to realize that if it collected its taxes from the village commune as a whole, which was easier anyway, the village assembly would have strong reasons for stopping migration so that a heavier tax burden would not fall on those who remained at home.

The evils of the developing ruling system of Muscovy came to a head in the mad, savage reign of Ivan IV, called Ivan the Terrible. When he died in 1584, he left the country in chaos. There followed the "Time of Trouble," when one class after another rose up against the rest, the slaves and the boyars, the middle gentry and the Cossacks. The Poles established themselves in the Kremlin and tried to impose a new sovereign on Russia. A part of this terrible period is celebrated in song in the magnificent opera of Mussorgsky, *Boris Godunov*. At last, in desperation, Russian Church leaders took the lead in forming a great national coalition which drove the Poles from Moscow and then elected as Czar a young member of the Romanov family. Thus, in 1613, began the last dynasty. It was to come to a bloody end more than three centuries later when in 1917 Czar Nicholas II and his entire family were wiped out in the Ural city of Yekaterinburg, now known as Sverdlovsk.

During the "Time of Trouble," the serfs had scattered in all directions, even out into Siberia, which was vigorously explored and partly settled during that period. However, as soon as the Romanov dynasty was established, the nobles demanded that their workers be returned. Enormous man hunts were organized and the bulk of the wanderers was found. A register was set up of the whole population, which tied to the soil not only the existing serfs but all those who would be born of them. Thus from 1649 the social pattern of the rulers and their henchmen, on one side, and of the slave mass of the population, on the other, was set in concrete. From then on the aristocracy tended more and more to separate itself from the mass of the Russian people, even to breed itself apart by widespread intermarriage with Europeans. This was especially true after Peter the Great in 1703 built a new capital—St. Petersburg—on the shores of the Baltic and forced Russia into Europe.

Peter was a tremendous man, physically and mentally. He created most of the institutions which characterized Czarist Russia to its end and left his imprint on everything. Much of his influence remains even today. He created the Russian Army and Navy. He forced all the gentry into a rigid hierarchy of state service with no distinction of birth, only of rank (in Russian *chin;* government functionaries are still *chinovniki*). He created the first Russian industry by imperial decree, appointing the directors of factories and allotting so many peasant souls to obligatory labor. He imposed a network of indirect taxation, covering everything from birth to death. He regulated social gatherings. He built up a huge and cumbrous administrative machine. Finally, after he had himself destroyed his only son, he died heirless. The result was that he was succeeded by a number of bad sovereigns, half of them foreign, enthroned by a series of palace revolutions. Whether or not it was his intention, however, he left behind an organized autocracy with a semi-military-rank structure and a sort of self-perpetuating bureaucracy.

The longer one lives in modern Russia, the more one realizes the fallacy of trying to understand this country with the misconception that it started just fifty years ago. The point was brought home to us first and with lasting force in Moscow in 1948, when we discovered the writings of the Marquis de Custine. We owed this discovery to the "find" in a secondhand bookshop of a copy of an abridged edition of his writings in Russian which the Soviet regime had itself put out in 1930 and subsequently suppressed. Since Custine had written his penetrating work in 1839, the Communists apparently believed these selected excerpts would be useful in the continuing campaign to discredit the former Czarist autocracy. But it was clear that the new rulers in the Kremlin had soon discovered that Soviet readers were finding Custine's observations as revealing with respect to Stalin's regime as to the despotism of Czar Nicholas I a century earlier.

Following the lead of our fortuitous tip, we turned to the original French version of Custine's letters about Russia. We read his observations with unending astonishment, repeating over and over to ourselves: "But this couldn't have been written a century and a quarter ago; it had to be written last week!"

Astolphe de Custine went to Russia in the wake of the civil turmoil in France following the French Revolution and the fall of Napoleon. He was the counterpart, as regards Russia, of that other great French observer, Alexis de Tocqueville, who in the same period came to the United States to write a similarly classic and imperishable work about *Democracy in America*. Custine's letters served to bring the Soviet Union into perspective for us in Moscow better than any of our previous readings and studies.

After our return from our first stay in Moscow my wife did a one-volume English-language version of Custine, selected from the original four-volume work, which was published in 1951 under the title *Journey for Our Time*. Here are a few of the parallels between Custine's observations in 1839 and our own experiences in 1946 to 1949 which the late General Bedell Smith and I pulled together for his introduction to the American edition.

My own position and that of my staff as foreign diplomats in the Soviet Union showed little variation from that of our predecessors accredited to the Czarist court a century before. In both eras one finds the same restrictions, the same surveillance, the same suspicion. Custine can say: "The diplomatic corps and Westerners in general have always been considered by this Government, with its Byzantine spirit, and by Russia as a whole, as malevolent and jealous spies." A century later Soviet Major General Sarayev, a member of the wartime Soviet Military Mission in Washington, admits to us quite frankly that all foreign officials "are considered potential spies." The handicaps which this attitude and its corollary practices place on Western diplomacy could not be better described than in Custine's words: "If better diplomats are found among the Russians than among highly civilized peoples, it is because our papers warn them of everything that happens and everything that is contemplated in our countries. Instead of disguising our weaknesses with prudence, we reveal them with vehemence every morning;

whereas the Russians' Byzantine policy, working in the shadow, carefully conceals from us all that is thought, done and feared in their country. We proceed in broad daylight; they advance under cover: the game is one-sided."

A change in nomenclature has not altered the character of Russia's rulers or of its institutions. Whether it is Stalin or the Czar, it is still "the little father" of the Russian people and it is still merciless despotism. Here is the Marquis' description: "The Russian Government is the discipline of the camp substituted for the civic order—it is a state of siege become the normal state of society." Even the Czarist *tchin,* that "military order applied to an entire society," has been revived and applied to civilian functions. During the period of my stay in Moscow, entire ministries and entire industries were actually being put into para-military uniform, ranging from the employees of the Ministry of Finance to the entire personnel of the mining industry, down to the lowliest miner. The privileged class is today as remote from the mass of citizens as was Nicholas' court. The rank and position of the individual derives from the new Soviet "Czar" as surely as it did in the days of Nicholas I or in the days of Peter the Great. The ruler continues to be the most powerful and least accessible of all the world's sovereigns. Cut off from his own people as well as from foreigners by the forbidding Kremlin walls, the army of police assigned to guard him, and the deep secrecy maintained concerning his personal life, Stalin is to most Russians merely a name and a symbol. But like his Czarist predecessors, he is omnipresent, dominating the lives and thoughts of his subjects in every city, village, and hamlet across one-sixth of the world's surface. In Custine's words: "All must strive scrupulously to obey the thought of the sovereign; his mind alone determines the destiny of all."

The great arranged fêtes which enable the people to participate in the glory of the ruler still take place. One inevitably compares the Fête of Peterhof so vividly described by the Marquis with the colossal mass parades in the Soviet Union today. Twice a year Nicholas opened his court to chosen representatives from all classes who were permitted to pay him homage. Twice a year chosen representatives from all classes are permitted to pay homage to Stalin. As Custine says: "In this language of the oppressed, interpreted by the oppressor, permissions are obligatory." Thus on May Day and on the anniversary of the so-called October Revolution "spontaneous demonstrations" take place in Moscow's Red Square. More than a million souls who have received "permission" and who have stood in line for hours awaiting their turn to demonstrate their zeal for the Little Father, all bedecked in colorful regalia, bearing pennants and flowers, silent and somber, file past Stalin and his suite. This spectacle always evoked in us Custine's sentiment at Peterhof: "I have never seen anything lovelier for the eye or sadder for the mind. . . ." But this magnificent and costly show is open only to those participating and to invited guests, including, as in Custine's day, the foreign diplomats. The streets are cleared for blocks around and heavily policed. This is not a spectacle for the masses as it would be in any other country; it is rather another instrument of absolute and arbitrary rule.

During my assignment to Moscow the history of events as recent as World War II was gradually rewritten under our eyes. When I went to the Soviet Union in 1946 there still remained some of the aura of our wartime alliance. By the time I left in 1949 one would have thought from reading the Soviet press that the Western Powers had been the allies not of the Soviet Union but of Hitler, and that their evil designs had been similarly foiled. Our Marquis waxed indignant over comparable phenomena in Czarist Russia and cogently described the practice: "Russian despotism not only counts ideas and sentiments for nothing but remakes facts; it wages war on evidence and triumphs in the battle."

Another story with numerous modern parallels is Custine's account of the troubles of a French citizen who had been overheard expressing his disapproval of Russian despotism before he had even arrived in Russia. The arrest in the middle of the night, the incommunicado imprisonment, the refusal of any explanation, the final expulsion from the country after the intervention of the ambassador—how many times have I been involved in such cases. A change of names, a change of dates and Custine's story would have served as a report on the treatment accorded the American journalist, Anna Louise Strong, despite her previous years of service to Communist propaganda.

Finally, how pat from Stalin's lips would come the statement of Czar Nicholas I to our Marquis: "One does not know me very well when one criticizes me for my ambition. Far from seeking to extend our territory, I would like to be able to draw the populations of all of Russia closer around me. It is solely over misery and barbarism that I wish to make conquests: to ameliorate the lot of the Russians, this would be better than to aggrandize myself."

These examples may suffice to demonstrate that the analogy

between Russia of 1839 and the Soviet Union today is so striking that one must pinch himself to recall that Custine was writing more than a hundred years ago. The exercise of sovereignty through fear, the omnipresence of the secret police, the operation of the bureaucracy, the absence of personal and public liberty, the uprooting and banishment to Siberia of whole populations, the repression of nonconformist artistic endeavor, the sudden imposition of drastic monetary reforms, the subjugation of the Church, the conquest of foreign lands; above all, the secrecy, deceit and hypocrisy—all these and hundreds of other phenomena are historic as well as actual.

To appreciate the relative state of political and social life and evolution in the Russia Custine describes, it is useful to recall that it was only twenty-five years after the beginning of constitutional government in the West—with the granting of Magna Carta in England—that the fledgling Russian state at Kiev was overrun and despoiled by the Tatar hordes. Thereafter, while the Western world was progressing under the stimuli of the Renaissance, the Reformation, the Age of Exploration and Discovery, all Russia was held in a state of subjection and isolation from these developments. Indeed, Russia was to remain isolated from Western influences almost entirely until Peter built his window to the West at St. Petersburg at the beginning of the eighteenth century. Even then the light was feeble and did not reach the great mass of the Russian population living in serfdom. Even Peter, in his later days, tended to turn away from Europe and to look inward, defending his empire against the onslaughts of Charles XII of Sweden from the west, while himself trying to extend his domain to the south at the expense of the Ottoman Turks. Western influences really began to have an impact on Russia only after the American and French revolutions. They were imported in wholesale quantities in the minds and in the knapsacks of the officers and of the 600,000 men in Napoleon's invading army; then again by the returning Russian officers and soldiers who participated in the occupation of France after Napoleon's downfall. Two years before the Marquis de Custine visited Russia, Alexander Pushkin—who did for Russian language and literature what Shake-

speare had done for English language and literature more than
two centuries earlier—had met his untimely end in a duel. It
was, of course, too soon for Custine or anyone else to appreciate
Pushkin's lasting influence; nor could he foresee the magnificent
flowering of Russian culture and political philosophy which
would follow after Pushkin in the Russia of the nineteenth
century. In this "golden age" Russia produced masters of literature, drama, music and arts. Turgenev, Gogol, Dostoyevsky,
Tolstoy, Gorky, Chekhov, Herzen, Tchaikovsky, Rimsky-Korsakov
—none of these great figures had left his impress on Russian
society when Custine wrote. Along with this period of cultural
enlightenment, there developed in Russia during the latter part
of the last century a really progressive revolutionary movement.

I should point out also that there has been some easement
and evolution of the situation since the death of Stalin and that
some of the comparisons between 1839 and 1949 would not fit
so exactly today as they did twenty years ago. The real tragedy
of Stalin's era is that he did try to turn the clock back a full
century and to nullify the great gains of the Russian people
during this long period of progress and evolution.

The point I really want to underscore is the importance not
only of the environment but also of history in molding the
Russian of today. Despite the talk of the new Soviet era and the
new Soviet man, the Soviets have always had some recourse to
and are proud of their history, their historical traditions and
their historical figures. Even in Stalin's day—and, indeed, in
Lenin's before that—the relics of the past were preserved from
wanton destruction by being called "the people's property." The
preservation of the Kremlin is an example. There are thousands
of other historic monuments, and the movement to restore and
preserve them is ever-growing. The great Soviet movie producer
of the Lenin-Stalin era, Sergei Eisenstein, achieved his fame
mainly by producing historical movies about Alexander Nevsky,
the Russian Prince who threw back the Swedes and Livonian
knights seven centuries ago, and about Ivan the Terrible. The re-
pertories of such major theaters as Moscow's Bolshoi and Leningrad's Kirov—when they do not deal purely in fairy tales—tend
to turn to such historic themes as Borodin's *Prince Igor*, Mussorg-

sky's *Boris Godunov* or Glinka's *A Life for the Czar,* now called simply *Ivan Susanin.* And all over the country, more and more churches and aristocratic estates are being restored and pre-served—not as working institutions, of course, but as museums and reminders to the Russians of their own past.

CHAPTER II

The Revolutions of 1917: The Bolsheviks—
What Lenin Did to Marx

There was not one straight, broad road to revolution in Russia. There were, instead, many obscure paths through a veritable jungle of capricious rulers, an irresponsible aristocracy, political discontent, police suppression, bureaucratic incompetence, cultural ferment, soaring ambitions, frustrated hopes and finally sheer desperation. If the going was difficult along the great rivers and the blazed forest trails of early Russian history, it becomes really tough through the disordered growth of the nineteenth century. But perhaps if I explore these overgrown paths separately, I can show how they eventually come together and lead to a common destination—the violent overthrow of the monarchy and aristocracy which had ruled Russia for many centuries.

The writers have left the most visible trail. I have already noted that the great ferment of political and social thought in the West which had led to the American and French revolutions had started to reach Russia more or less simultaneously with these great events. At that time French was not only the language of diplomacy but was widely regarded as the language of real culture. It was widely used by the Russian aristocracy even in their daily lives, in preference to Russian, which was regarded as the language of the servants and serfs. Toward the end of the eighteenth century the works of a good many Western writers began to be imported into Russia, both in their original languages and in Russian translations. This was particularly true of the advanced French writers and thinkers like Rousseau, Voltaire and Montesquieu. The latter's *Spirit of Laws*, with its theme of the separation of powers between the executive, the legislative and the judicial, had a considerable impact—apparently not appreciated by the authorities—in bringing into question the absolutism of the Czar's rule in Russia. Works in other languages were translated, too. Among the English imports, for example, were the essays of Sir Francis Bacon, John Locke and Jeremy Bentham and Blackstone's *Commentaries on the Laws of England.* Several members of the Russian gentry studied in Glasgow under Adam Smith, and his *Wealth of Nations* appeared in Russian early in the nineteenth century. There were some American thinkers and writers available also, notably Ben Franklin and Alexander Hamilton. Ben Franklin's *Poor Richard's Almanac,* interestingly enough, was translated into Russian from the French. I doubt if the language sounded much like Ben Franklin by the time it went through this process, but I guess the basic ideas probably survived. Lord Byron's poetry and the ideas which led him to be the heroic and dramatic champion of Greek independence from the Ottoman Turks were to have a great influence on the father of Russian language and literature, Alexander Pushkin.

Practically all the great writers of the Russian flowering in the nineteenth century and at the beginning of the twentieth century were repeatedly in trouble with the official Czarist censorship. This was a section of the Czar's secret police which operated under the euphemistic title of the "Third Division of the Imperial Chancery." Many of the works of the Russian enlightenment are simply romantic or imaginative and a great contribution to world literature. However, even when the authors avoided political references which would get them into trouble with the censors, their work still carried a sense of civilized values, of social rights and wrongs. They tended to exalt the worth of the individual.

Despite the fact that Pushkin had been born and raised in the court at the Czar's summer palace outside St. Petersburg, he was the first of the great writers to feel the iron hand of authority. In 1820, when he was only twenty-one years of age, he was exiled to southern Russia for having published an *Ode to Liberty*. Impressed by some of the freer forms of life he found in the Caucasus Mountains, he managed a few years later to get by the censors his work *The Gypsies,* imbued with a feeling of frustrated yearning for freedom. Shocked and grieved by Pushkin's premature death in a senseless duel in 1837, Lermontov poured out his feelings in his *Ode on the Death of a Poet.* He, in turn, was exiled to the Caucasus. Lermontov was even more impressed by the beauties of the scenery and the life of the mountaineers than Pushkin, and his attempt to describe all this—notably in his *A Hero of Our Time*—turned him toward realism. In this way Lermontov became a sort of transition between the romanticism of Pushkin and the satirical realism of Gogol. Gogol himself seemed to be able to manage his business with the censors somewhat better, perhaps because he knew they did not have a sense of humor. His fantastic story of cynical dealing in the *Dead Souls* of serfs who had died but whose names had not yet been removed from the official register, and his ridiculing of the gentry in his *Inspector General,* laid bare the social order for all to see. Somewhat later, around mid-century, and in his quieter way, Turgenev, with his *Sportsman's Sketches* of the horror of life on the Russsian land, struck a telling blow at serfdom. Turgenev was a personal friend of that great, contradictory, ever-searching master of language, Leo Tolstoy. Tolstoy's genius confounded the censors, but did not save him from his own conscience. In his personal life

Tolstoy was always concerned about the problem of serfs. Being of the aristocracy himself, he had inherited a good number of them. First, when he was a very young man, he tried unsuccessfully to establish a school to educate them. Later, in 1859, he tried to free his serfs, but the serfs suspected his motives so this didn't work either. The great mid-century dramatist, Alexander Ostrovsky, was another who felt the heavy hand of authority. When he published his first play, *Bankrupt,* in 1847, he was dismissed from his job in the government service and the play was banned from the stage.

At about the same time, that tortured genius, Feodor Dostoyevsky, appeared on the literary scene. His first work, dealing with the lot of the downtrodden, *Poor Folk,* had a great success. This was due in part to the extravagant praises of the influential and respected critic Vissarion Belinsky, whose literary criticism was a convenient means of expressing strong political views. However, before Dostoyevsky's writing career could progress much further he was arrested in 1849 for political activities and condemned to death. He was reprieved at the last minute and his sentence was commuted to four years at hard labor in Siberia (vividly described in his novel *The House of the Dead*), followed by forced service in the army. He was finally permitted to return to St. Petersburg in 1859. From then until his death in 1881, he produced a series of great novels which pictured with vivid intensity the turbulent, charged atmosphere of the times.

In the latter part of the nineteenth century the dramatist Anton Chekhov made his contribution to the development of social dissent and discontent by his brilliant portrayals of the dullness and stagnation of Russian life under the Czars. Maxim Gorky, the first of the great writers who himself came up from *The Lower Depths,* had an even greater impact with his brutally realistic portrayal of the human dregs at the bottom of Russian society. He actively participated in the Revolution of 1905, then escaped abroad and finally returned to Russia only after the Revolution of 1917.

A path somewhat to the left of that made by the great writers was trod by a series of colorful individuals who were closer to being real revolutionaries, or at least political agitators, than they were writers. Most of them did write prolifically, but their product was mainly social essays, political tracts and outright revolutionary propaganda, rather than great literature. In a sense they were the Tom Paines of the coming Russian revolutions. However, while Tom Paine was able to operate freely in pre-Revolutionary America, these Russian radicals were unable to do so in Czarist society, and they spent most of their lives abroad, smuggling their works back into the country where collaborators received, reproduced and distributed them widely through underground channels.

The greatest of these radicals was Alexander Herzen. Born in 1812, the year of Napoleon's invasion of Russia, he lived until 1870. His last name, Herzen, meaning in German "of the heart," reflects his origin. He was the illegitimate son of Ivan Yakovlev, member of a wealthy family of the old Moscow nobility, and of Louise Haag, a German girl whom Ivan—who was not the marrying type—had seduced and brought back to Russia as his mistress. The uncertainty of his social status—or, as he himself later put it, the humiliations and insults of his upbringing—certainly had to do with the molding of Herzen's attitudes toward life and society. It is understandable that the first revolutionary outbreak in modern Russian history, the unsuccessful rising of the "Decembrists," in 1825, made a great impression on him. In his early teens, a student at the University of Moscow, Herzen and his friend and fellow student, Nikolai Ogarëv, stood side by side on the hills outside of Moscow and solemnly swore to give their lives to the service of the sacred cause for which the "Decembrists" had suffered.

This event which played such a decisive role in Herzen's life should be explained briefly. After the downfall of Napoleon, Czar Alexander I and the other shaken monarchs of Europe had moved to repair the havoc created by Napoleon throughout Europe and to restore the "old order" to firm foundations. To this end, in 1815 they summoned the Great Congress of Vienna. I shall not go into this fascinating meeting here. Suffice it to say that the arrangements made at the Congress did restore a kind of superficial political stability in Europe which was to last for some time. However, these political arrangements could not stop the continued flow of ideas emanating from the French Revolution and spread by Napoleon's forces.

The post-Napoleonic confusion in Russia created an opportunity for the formation of numerous revolutionary and patriotic societies. Many members of these societies were army officers, who had had contact with Napoleon's forces in Russia or who had participated in the occupation of France—thus seeing with their own eyes a different world and being exposed to new ideas. The occasion of the succession of Alexander I, who was childless, by his unpopular brother Nicholas provided an opportunity for action. These army officers were able to persuade several regiments in St. Petersburg to refuse their oath of allegiance to Nicholas and to demand that his elder brother, Constantine, be made emperor and that a constitution be granted. The rebels were crushed by artillery fire. Five of their leaders were hanged and scores of others were exiled for life to Siberia. This, parenthetically, marked the beginning of the reign of the Nicholas I about whom Custine wrote.

True to their oath, Herzen and Ogarëv became active in spreading "advanced" ideas among their contemporaries and fellow students. In 1834, at the age of twenty-two, Herzen and a number of his associates were arrested for "conspiracy." All received heavy sentences. After some nine months' imprisonment, Herzen was banished to the distant provincial capital of Vyatka, in the Ural Mountains. Some three years later he was allowed to return to Moscow, but the constraints of the Czar's secret police were too much for him to bear. Finally, in 1847, he was able to wangle passports from the Russian authorities and, with his family, emigrated first to Paris, then to London. Herzen's friend Ogarëv had more trouble getting his passports, but finally in 1856 he, too, succeeded and with his family joined the Herzens in London. In 1857 the two of them began publishing—first in London, later in Switzerland—a serious sociopolitical journal which they called Kolokol—The Bell. Although The Bell was officially banned in Russia, it managed to reach the country and circulated there in considerable quantities. It is even said that Czar Alexander II, who succeeded Nicholas, read it regularly. After the so-called "emancipation" of the serfs in

Russia in 1861, Herzen's articles turned increasingly toward a consideration of the Russian village commune as the pattern for social development in the future. These articles had a great influence, and, in fact, the agrarian approach became a basic creed for practically all of the non-Marxist socialists.

Living in exile in Europe from 1847 to 1870, Herzen, with Ogarëv and others who collected around him, became the focal point of the Russian resistance in exile. He attracted and was joined by many strange characters. One of these was the born anarchist Mikhail Bakunin, who, in 1878, became active in the First Communist International, organized by Marx and Engels. In this society Bakunin—expansive, unreasoning and unreasonable—insisted on preaching his doctrine of "anarchism, collectivism and atheism." He tangled with the more orderly Karl Marx and in 1872 was expelled from the organization. Another was the nihilist Sergei Nechaev, who was a real case of truth being stranger than fiction. In due course, he was to become the hero—or perhaps I should say the villain—of Dostoyevsky's great novel *The Possessed*. Dostoyevsky's fantastic and gripping story is, in fact, a reasonable biography of this fanatical character.

In 1868, at the age of twenty-one, Nechaev was a teacher of divinity in St. Petersburg at a time when student circles there were seething with revolutionary ideas. Finding himself subjected to repeated police interrogation and constant police observation, he acquired a false passport and disappeared to join Bakunin and others of the Herzen group in Switzerland. A year later he returned to Moscow to engage in the conspiratorial organization of the students there. A basic principle of Nechaev's method of organization was complete obedience to the leader by all members. When after a few months he suspected one of the students—a certain Ivanov—of wavering, he arranged a plot involving the other members of the organization to murder the student in cold blood as an example of "revolutionary discipline." This savage act shocked not only the Czarist authorities but Russian society in general. Nechaev again disappeared, presumably again to Switzerland. Agents of the Czarist secret police were sent there to look for him. However, although they were able to infiltrate the exile revolutionary groups without being suspected, Nechaev was never found. This was one of the earliest recorded cases of interpenetration between the secret police and the revolutionaries which was to become characteristic of the evolving political scene in Russia.

During the mid-nineteenth century the European powers, and Russia in particular, were preoccupied with the so-called "Eastern question," that is, the question of who would succeed to the estates of the weakening and decaying Ottoman Turkish Empire in Constantinople. France and Russia were vying for control of the "Holy Places" in Palestine. When the Ottoman Sultan in 1852 awarded this custody to France, Russia responded by occupying that part of the Ottoman Empire which later became Rumania. This move triggered the Crimean War, in which Turkey, England, France and Sardinia all teamed up against the Russians and sent forces into the Crimea, which Russia had earlier taken from the Turks. The ensuing hostilities are notable mainly for inspiring Alfred Lord Tennyson's famous poem "The Charge of the Light Brigade" and Florence Nightingale, the founder of modern nursing. The result, however, was a great and humiliating defeat for the Russians, which weakened the power of the Czar. Nicholas I died before the war ended, and it can be supposed that he was just as glad not to live to suffer the consequences of this humiliation.

In fact, the Crimean disaster encouraged the Russian progressives to demand and obtain from Czar Alexander II a *ukaz* freeing the serfs, then over a third of the total population, and laying down certain conditions under which these freed serfs might acquire title to land. These conditions proved to be too onerous to be met by most of the freedmen. Writing about the emancipation some years after its promulgation, Karl Marx's associate, Friedrich Engels, described the results this way: "At the time of the redistribution of land in exchange for freedom for personal services, the state not only robbed the peasants of most of the land, but also of the best land, which was transferred to the nobles; in addition, the peasant had to pay for the poorest land the price of the best." Later the American envoy, Andrew Dickson White, said in a report to the State Department: "I do not deny the greatness and nobleness of Alexander II and the services of the men he called to his aid; but I lived in Russia both before and since that reform, and feel obliged to testify that thus far its main purpose has been so thwarted by reactionaries that there is as yet little if any practical difference between the conditions of the Russian peasant before and since obtaining his freedom."

The activities of secret revolutionary and patriotic societies in Russia following the Napoleonic era and the influence of the Russian "progressives" in persuading the new Czar, Alexander II, to issue his emancipation proclamation were landmarks along the third path toward revolution in Russia, namely, political developments inside the country. As we have seen, no open and organized activity was possible under Nicholas I, and this continued to be the situation well into the latter half of the nineteenth century; even a student discussion group was regarded as a "conspiracy" against the throne and exposed its participants to the direst consequences, as in the case of Alexander Herzen. But secret groups continued to flourish, to reflect the growing social unrest and to discuss remedies. Some radical writers even continued to try to cope with the censors inside the country, the most notable being Nikolai Chernyshevsky. Although he spent over twenty-five years in prison or in Siberian exile, Chernyshevsky left behind a collection of materialistic, socialistic writings which were later to have a major influence on the thinking of Lenin and make their author an enduring Bolshevik hero.

It is clear that attitudes, even of members of the court and of the governing bureaucracy, were being influenced by the vivid portrayals of the evils and injustices of Russian life flowing from the pens of the great writers and by the outright revolutionary propaganda produced and circulated by underground organizations and networks. After Alexander II was persuaded to act in 1861, he followed the emancipation of the serfs with a whole series of other reforms. These included an easing of the censorship, greater freedom of movement inside the country and abroad for Russians, greater freedom to travel around Russia for foreigners, the introduction of trial by jury and the establishment of a certain measure of local rule by elective district councils known as zemstvos. In the seventies, almost spontaneously, thousands of young men and women started a "movement to the people," seeking to help implement the reforms or to stir sentiment for more reform. Most of them, in all good will, went to the villages and tried to settle down as teachers, doctors, nurses, booksellers; like Tolstoy in his attempts to "do good," they usually encountered a dubious reception from the suspicious peasantry. Others went out as conspirators, plotting against the life of particularly odious officials. In due course, the conspiratorial type tended to group itself into an organization called the Narodnaya Volya, "Will of the People," which was finally to be responsible for the assassination of "Czar-reformer" Alexander II. The other type, more evolutionary in their aims, grouped themselves in an organization called "The Black Partition." The members of this group were later to become the first Marxists in Russia, calling themselves "Social Democrats" and establishing links with the other Marxist parties arising in Europe. Inside Russia they concentrated on proselytizing and organizing the relatively small but rapidly growing industrial population. As we shall see later, the Social Democrats themselves tended to divide into fractional groups on the basis of theoretical differences.

After the assassination of Alexander II in 1881, the Narodnaya Volya was stamped out; its remnants reorganized into the non-Marxist party of Social Revolutionaries. They continued to work among the peasantry, mainly in a practical way; but until the end of free political life in Russia after the 1917 Revolution, they continued to harbor in their midst an underground terrorist organization. I well remember how anxious Chairman Khrushchev was, when he came to see me the morning after the assassination of President Kennedy, to make clear to me that the Communist Party of the Soviet Union—like the Social Democrats from whom they descended—did not believe in political terrorism and assassination. But I am getting ahead of my story. In connection with the assassination of Alexander II, the anonymous Executive Committee of the Narodnaya Volya had issued an ultimatum offering peace to the monarchy in exchange for a constitution. After some vacillation, the new Czar, Alexander III, answered with a harsh negative. He canceled the moderate constitutional project which the dead Czar had been about to publish, multiplied the police, enlisted spies, closed the feeble liberal newspapers, purged the libraries, established new controls of professors and curricula, reduced the power of the zemstvos, prohibited student organizations and in general tightened all the screws.

Still another path through the revolutionary jungle leads to the Ulyanov family, one of whom is better known to us as Lenin. Lenin's father was an earnest, diligent government employee who had been able, thanks to sacrifices by his modest family, to obtain an education at the high school in his home town of Astrakhan, and at the University of Kazan. His family was basically Russian but with some Tatar blood evidenced in the high cheekbones, flat nose and slanting eyes both of the father and of Lenin himself. Lenin's mother came from slightly higher on the social scale, being the daughter of a medical doctor and small landowner of the province of Kazan. Her mother came from one of the German colonies on the Volga, and she was raised more in the German than in the Russian tradition. Father Ilya Ulyanov had taught school in Penza and Nizhni Novgorod for some years when he was offered a promotion in the form of appointment as inspector of schools in the provincial capital of Simbirsk on the Volga. It was here, in this provincial capital—now renamed Ulyanovsk—that Vladimir Ilyich (meaning son of Ilya) Ulyanov was born on April 22, 1870. He was the third child in the family, having an elder brother, Alexander, and a sister, Anna. It was a quiet, serious, well-behaved and respected family of the lower gentry. Even Leon Trotsky, in his study of the youth of Lenin, was unable to discover any apparent reasons why the Ulyanov boys should have developed revolutionary tendencies.

Alexander was the first to do so. He went to St. Petersburg in 1883 to enter the university. At that time student activities were at a low ebb as a result of the police crackdown following the assassination of Alexander II two years before. Alexander let himself be drawn into a small conspiratorial group of seven students who were then studying Karl Marx's *Capital*—which had just been introduced clandestinely into the universities— and plotting very amateurishly to revive the terrorist activities of the defunct Narodnaya Volya. Since he was studying science, Alexander became the chemist of the group, able to manufacture dynamite. To make a long story short, three of the members were picked up by the Czar's police on the main street of St. Petersburg, quite by accident, with one of Alexander's homemade bombs in their possession. In the face of the squealing of some of his colleagues at the trial, Alexander turned noble and tried to assume full responsibility himself. It was all very juvenile, but Alexander and four of his comrades were hanged. The real importance of the matter was to be its effect on Alexander's younger brother.

The death of Alexander made Vladimir the head of a family now ostracized by a fear-ridden society, and opened an unbridgeable gulf between him and the regime that had taken his brother's life. In due course his reaction was to make him a man apart, even among his associates in the socialist movement. In all Simbirsk society the only one who befriended the Ulyanov family was the director of the high school from which Vladimir was about to graduate. By one of those strange quirks of fate, this man was Feodor Kerensky, the father of Alexander Kerensky, whose provisional revolutionary government was to be toppled by Lenin in 1917. Father Kerensky even helped Vladimir to enter the University of Kazan; but the name Ulyanov was now a dangerous one and Vladimir was soon expelled from the university and ordered to leave Kazan, simply for attending a general students' meeting which had addressed a petition to the university administration. For the next few years, while repeatedly trying to gain readmission to the university, Vladimir Ilyich lived with his mother and sister, studying languages and law feverishly on his own, and reading through every library in the province. After five years, at the age of twenty-two, he managed to get a certificate to practice law and found employment with a politically liberal lawyer in the Volga River port of Samara.

Meanwhile, despite everything, Russia was moving rapidly

toward industrialization, and liberal elements began to be concerned not only about the lot of the peasantry but about the conditions of the working man—the new proletariat coming into the major cities. In 1883 a few veterans of the Narodnaya Volya organization under the leadership of Georgi Plekhanov, a brilliant intellectual, organized the first Russian Marxist or Social Democratic organization under the name of "Emancipation of Labor." This group, living mostly in exile, published a number of studies subjecting to "Marxist" criticism the Populist—that is, Narodnik—dogma, which held that the peasant was the driving force of revolution in Russia, that the possibility of noncapitalist development existed in the country, and that the tactic of individual terror was an acceptable method of revolution. These studies found their way back into Russia, and indeed all the way to the young lawyer in far-off Samara. They led him from populism to Marxism. Vladimir Ilyich now absorbed the works of Karl Marx and was soon writing papers applying Marxist theory to Russian problems and to the realities of Russian life. These were passed surreptitiously from hand to hand of chosen comrades to read. One of them even reached a certain lady, a Marxist intellectual and schoolteacher in St. Petersburg named Nadezhda Krupskaya, who was to become the author's wife and lifelong collaborator.

Vladimir Ilyich soon became convinced that the proletariat in the industrial towns would be the driving force of the struggle against Czarism, decided to make revolution his profession and, to this end, to leave the backwash of the Volga as soon as possible and move to the center of events. He managed to get to St. Petersburg toward the end of 1893. Within a few months he had met and teamed up with Krupskaya and was zealously writing elaborate treatises on the political questions of the day. These were reproduced and circulated and read throughout the underground study groups in the capital. Self-confident, articulate, devastating in verbal attack on any opponent, he soon achieved a commanding position among the Marxists in St. Petersburg.

The Czarist police were not displeased by the growing conflict between the Populists—the Narodniks—and the Marxists. They even let Ulyanov have a passport to spend a few months in Western Europe in the spring of 1895. In Geneva he met and impressed his mentor, Plekhanov, and others, and on his return smuggled some of their literature back into Russia in the false bottom of his trunk. Taking courage from the seeming restraint of the police, the Petersburg group planned to launch a major underground publication that autumn, to be called *The Workers' Cause*. All their plans were reported to the police by a member of the group who was actually an *agent provocateur*, so Vladimir Ilyich spent the next two years in prison. However, he was able to continue his writing there; and during three subsequent years of exile in Siberia, he redoubled his efforts. He even made a certain amount of money by selling to a wealthy "liberal" publisher who befriended the Marxists the manuscript of a work on *The Development of Capitalism in Russia*. Within a year, Krupskaya, too, had been arrested, and managed to join Vladimir Ilyich in his Siberian exile.

After his release from Siberia in the year 1900—alone, Krupskaya still having a year to go—and another arrest for visiting "forbidden" St. Petersburg, Vladimir Ilyich again went to see Plekhanov in Switzerland, this time illegally. He was anxious to start a "Marxist" newspaper, but found that a split had already developed among the Russian Social Democrats abroad. Despite the obstacles, he managed to get the project organized, with his wife as the secretary, or agent, inside Russia. Younger than most of the exiles—he was thirty-one, against Plekhanov's forty-five—Lenin soon dominated the project. In the first issue of the new publication, named *Iskra—The Spark*—he authored the lead article: "Urgent Tasks of Our Movement." The basic idea in it was momentous for the future history of Russia; he argued that the labor movement, left to itself, would become "petty and inevitably bourgeois" and that this movement must therefore be led by a "vanguard" consisting of people who "devote to the revolution not only their spare evenings, but the whole of their lives." Shortly afterward, Vladimir Ilyich, who had now begun consistently to use the Party pen name of Lenin, developed his theories of how to organize this "vanguard" in 1902 in a book entitled *What Is to Be Done?* The theory was truly Russian, in that it was built upon the tradition of the Narodniks and other extremists of the past: conspiracy, centralism, hierarchy, obedience and life dedication. In it, Lenin attacked practically all other elements of the revolutionary movement in Russia: the peasant socialists, the Marxist "economists," the Marxist "revisionists" and the labor organizations.

Indeed, the socialist movement was now split into many factions, both inside and outside Russia. After much maneuvering by all factions, a "Unification Congress" was arranged. About fifty delegates met in Brussels in July, 1903. Leaving doctrinal disputes mainly to others, Lenin concentrated on trying to create a tight, centrally directed organization he could control, using as the basis of his strength members of the board and agents of the paper *Iskra*. On one controversial point, thanks to the walkout of some of the opponents he had attacked and the abstention of others, he got a small majority of the votes—in Russian *bolshinstvo*. He immediately seized upon this to give his group the name of "majority-ites"—in Russian *Bolsheviki*, or, as we Anglicize the term, "Bolsheviks." Strangely enough, his opponents in the temporary minority—*menshinstvo* —accepted the designation of "minority-ites," *Mensheviki*, or, as we say, "Mensheviks." And although Lenin was to be more often in the minority than in the majority, as the Russian socialist movement developed, he clung to the psychological advantage of professing to speak in the name of the majority. Indeed, at this very Congress, in spite of his one-shot victory on a secondary point, other votes ousted him from control of his cherished instrument, the journal *Iskra*. When he tried to mount a counterattack, he was censured by his fellow members of the Central Committee.

Meanwhile, as Lenin continued to scheme to gain control of the Social Democratic movement and as a weak Czar dozed in his St. Petersburg palaces, great things were happening in Russia. The Industrial Revolution was in full swing, under the guidance of Sergei Witte, a commoner who had risen from railway station agent to directorship of the railways, then to Minister of Communications, then Minister of Finance. Railways were being built all over the country, as far as the Pacific

Ocean. In the decade from 1890 to 1900 Russia's rate of growth in the production of iron, steel, coal, oil and cotton reached levels as high as those ever attained by any developing country, including the United States. The working class in the big cities was growing stormily as peasants flocked from the countryside into the new industrial enterprises. With this came trade unions and a rising demand for liberal reforms. In a sense, this development justified Lenin's earlier prognosis. But Lenin was not there to lead; others were doing that. There seemed to be no real lack of money for political activity—emerging industrialists and even some of the wealthy nobles were contributing substantial sums to the growing trade-union movements and to progressive political organizations. Even in the bureaucracy there were different attitudes toward these organizations, some apparently believing that they might provide channels of government influence and control, others fearing them as a menace to the system.

Once again, as in the case of the Crimean War in the mid-nineteenth century, outside events were to play a hand in this evolutionary game. Russian expansion to the east and its ambitions in Manchuria and other parts of the decadent Chinese Empire in the north, as well as in Korea, brought Russia into conflict with the Japanese, who were aggressively expanding onto the Asian mainland from their island base in the east. The Czar's government refused a Japanese offer to negotiate an agreement dividing the area into spheres of influence, apparently believing Japan was no match for Russia and that war and a Russian victory would deflect the growing threat of internal troubles. In February, 1904, the Japanese attacked, without a declaration of war, and in the ensuing year of hostilities, to the astonishment of the whole world, defeated Russian land armies in Manchuria and destroyed the Russian fleet. It is interesting to note that Lenin and most other Marxist revolutionaries, presumably including Stalin, were defeatists in this war, hoping that a Czarist setback would promote their cause. However, forty years later, after the Soviet Union had participated as our ally in the defeat of the Japanese in World War II, Stalin had a very different version. In an "Address to the People" published in *Pravda* on September 3, 1945, he said:

When Japan began her aggression against our country, as is well known, Russia suffered then and there a defeat caused by Japan—but this defeat of the Russian armies of 1904–1905 left sad memories in the minds of the people. It laid upon our country a black spot. Our people believed and expected that there would come a day when Japan would be beaten and this spot wiped out. We, the members of the older generation, have nostalgically waited forty years for that day. And now the day has come. Today, Japan recognizes herself defeated and has signed an unconditional surrender.

In fact, the disaster did weaken the Czar and give a lift to the revolutionaries. The next act was to feature a young priest named Father Gapon, a former prison chaplain. Father Gapon had, with a certain police tolerance, become active and achieved a position of leadership with the workers, particularly the workers in a large locomotive factory in St. Petersburg. When the factory management turned down some modest requests by the union and fired a member of the union's central committee, the workers urged Father Gapon to take them directly to the "dear Father Czar," so that they might humbly lay their troubles at his feet. So a march was organized, and on January 22, 1905, some 200,000 men, women and children set out for the Winter Palace, singing over and over again as they walked along "God Save the Czar." But the Czar was not there; he and his family had taken off for the countryside. Instead, his troops were there. They descended upon the marchers and fired at close range. Men, women and children fell. Several hundred were killed, more wounded. It was, indeed, as it was to be known in Russian history, a "Bloody Sunday."

Abroad, the exiles were in a state of great excitement. Lenin called a new congress, to meet in London in April. "The congress must be simple," he wrote, "like a war council—and small in numbers, like a war council. It is a congress to organize war." But only the Bolsheviks came. The Mensheviks, who were now a great majority, especially inside Russia, held their own congress and redoubled their activities in St. Petersburg. After a summer of seething resentment, the St. Petersburg workers in October, 1905, organized a great and unprecedented general strike. In connection with the strike, the Mensheviks organized a "Council of Working Men's Representatives." Here I must explain that the Russian word for council is *soviet*. Thus the basic institution that was to figure so largely in Lenin's takeover in 1917 and to give its name to the whole country was originally a Menshevik creation. Even then, however, Lenin was quick to see the great potential of such an organization. In November, 1905, he wrote: "Politically one ought to consider the Soviet as the germ of the provisional revolutionary government." Lenin wrote this in Stockholm on his way back to Russia. Like many of the exiles, he sensed the great turnover to be in the immediate offing and wanted to get in on the act.

Meanwhile, on the advice of men like Witte (who had been made Prime Minister), Czar Nicholas II on October 30 had announced the establishment of a representative elective assembly—called the Duma—the granting of civil liberties and of a constitution. The Workers Council—the Soviet—lost no time in taking direct action to implement the practical aspects of the Czar's manifesto—freedom to assemble, freedom to organize and strike and freedom of speech and press. They won their battle with the Czar's censors, for example, by simply having the printers' union refuse to set in type any newspaper which submitted its copy to the government for approval. By the end of the year, however, the strike was over and much of the steam had gone out of the participants. The government felt strong enough to strike back and began by arresting the leadership of the St. Petersburg Soviet. This did not include a single Bolshevik, though it did include one Leon Trotsky, then the acting secretary of the Soviet, who was later to become a Bolshevik. On his way to exile in Siberia, after fifteen months in prison, Trotsky managed a daring escape and was able to beat his way across Russia and into Finland. Like Lenin, he was not to return to Russia until the next upheaval in 1917.

The events of 1905 temporarily brought the theoretical squabbling to an end as Mensheviks, Bolsheviks and other splinter groups got together under the stress of war and defeat. They decided to abolish their individual factions and to merge. To this end, new unification congresses were held—in Stockholm in 1906 and in London in 1907. The executive board elected in Stockholm consisted of seven Mensheviks and three Bolsheviks. By the following year Lenin had obtained the support of a number of splinter groups so that the board this time consisted of five Bolsheviks, four Mensheviks and two each from the Polish and Latvian parties and the Jewish Bund. Lenin finally had a plurality again, if not a majority, but this was not a secure position and, moreover, serious fissures were still visible under the wallpaper. Consequently, despite the original merger decision, Lenin carefully held his own group together. Meanwhile, all these parties on the left, as well as the extremists on the right, had decided to boycott the elections of representatives to the Duma. The elections were a surprise to the extremists on both sides. In their absence, the peasantry voted in massive numbers for the most advanced and liberal candidates available—for Constitutional Democrats, for individual Social Democrats who ran in defiance of Party instructions, and for peasants and agrarian intellectuals in general. The Constitutional Democrats—popularly known as Kadets from the initials KD—won 190 seats; and a group of laborites calling themselves *Trudoviki* —from *trud,* meaning labor—won 94. The two moderate parties thus had a clear majority of the total 490 seats.

After Witte had seen the country through the uprising, the Czar, feeling strong enough to revert to reactionary rule, dismissed him from the premiership in May, 1906. When, two months later, the first Duma voted to take up the land question—one of the forbidden subjects—the Czar dissolved it and called for new elections. Less than a year later the new Premier, Peter Stolypin, dissolved the second Duma, using as a pretext some hostile statements made at the Social Democratic Unity Congress in London. Then, prior to the elections for a third Duma, the government by simple *ukaz* altered the electoral laws, cutting the value of the peasants' vote by half, that of labor by a third—and thus stacking the deck so that the new Duma was heavy with landowners, priests, nationalists and other conservatives and the progressive opposition was cut to a minority. Lenin was later to take a page out of Stolypin's book when, in 1918, he made a worker's vote equal to that of five peasants.

Stolypin was indeed a worthy opponent for the radicals. He believed that the trouble with the emancipation act of 1861 was that it had preserved the peasant commune—the *mir*—instead of setting up a class of individual proprietors and thus creating a conservative, property-minded class such as the Marxists had wrongly imagined the Russian peasant already was. In fact, between 1907 and 1914, under the Stolypin land-reform laws, two million peasant families seceded from the village *mir* and became individual landowners. In an article published in 1909, Lenin himself wrote: "The Stolypin 'constitution' and Stolypin's agrarian policy mark a new stage in the break-up of the old, semipatriarchal, semifeudal Czarism, a new step toward its transformation into a bourgeois monarchy." Stolypin's far-reaching reforms might well have been successful if their implementation and effectiveness had not been disrupted by his assassination in 1911 and the subsequent outbreak of World War I in 1914.

I shall not go into the causes and course of this first great world conflagration, except to the extent it bears on the fate of Russia and some of the Russians I have been talking about. In the early stages Russia, England, France, Belgium, Serbia and Japan were joined together in a great alliance, which the United States finally entered some three years later. On the other side were the so-called Central Powers, Germany and Austria-Hungary, which were joined by the Ottoman Empire. In July, 1914, Russia ordered general mobilization, and on August 1 Germany declared war. The Russians had some initial successes on the Eastern front in Prussia, Poland and Austria-Hungary, but were gradually driven back with great losses and bogged down in Russian territory. In 1916 the Russians mounted a massive counteroffensive, but this had collapsed by the end of the year with the loss of over a million men, and the Russians were thrust back even farther. Again the great Russian armies, which included the bulk of the adult male population, sat on the defensive, in the most appalling conditions. Guns were lacking, ammunition was lacking, shelter was lacking, clothing was lacking, food was lacking, and so was everything else. Disease, discontent and, increasingly, dissent were rampant. The Czar's autocracy had once again, as in the Russo-Japanese War of 1905, shown itself incapable of organizing, supplying and maintaining—much less of inspiring—a massive modern military effort.

As the front crumpled, so did the government back in Petrograd (the German-sounding Petersburg having been russified). The process was aggravated by the intrigues and machinations of the Empress and her mentor, the mad monk Rasputin, behind the back of a feeble, frustrated Czar Nicholas II, who had gone off to the military headquarters. And the shortages and privations prevailing on the military front now hit the home front. Without fuel transport broke down. The cities throughout Russia soon faced a critical lack of bread and meat and fat. Food riots broke out. The Duma, which operated under very restricted authority, as I mentioned earlier, was powerless to influence events. It did, of course, discuss conditions in the country, the imperative need for change, even the irresponsible and capricious conduct of the Empress. After having been suspended for a while, because of what the Czar himself called "hard speeches," it was reconvoked on February 27, 1917. At the opening session, the man who had shown himself the most courageously outspoken member, Alexander Kerensky, leader of the labor party—the *Trudoviki*—declared: "There are people who assert that the ministers are at fault. Not so. The country now realizes that the ministers are but fleeting shadows. The country can clearly see who sends them here. To prevent a catastrophe the Czar himself must be removed, by force if there is no other way." Meanwhile, riots and demonstrations were increasing, as were strikes. On March 11 the president of the Duma warned the Emperor at military headquarters: "The situation is serious. The capital is in a state of anarchy. The government is paralyzed; the transport service has broken down; the food and fuel supplies are completely disorganized. Discontent is general and on the increase. There is wild shooting in the streets; troops are firing at each other. It is urgent that someone enjoying the confidence of the country be entrusted with the formation of a new government. There must be no delay. Hesitation is fatal."

The Czar replied: "Dissolve the Duma." The next day the Duma assembled in the midst of a general strike of factories, universities and schools and of wild street demonstrations. Despite Kerensky's urging, the representatives proved not courageous enough to defy the Czar's dissolution decree. However, on this same day, the workers of the Petrograd factories organized a Soviet of Workers' Deputies, modeled after the Petrograd Soviet of 1905. They elected the leader of the Social Democratic Duma delegation as chairman and Kerensky as vice-chairman. A general meeting of workers' representatives was called for that very evening. When it met, not only workers' representatives showed up, but also representatives of many regiments of the Czar's Army. They had been ordered to Petrograd to suppress the bread riots but had refused to fire on the demonstrators and instead had turned these demonstrations into a revolution. They were admitted to the organization, and the assembly now became the Soviet of Workers' and Soldiers' Deputies. In the confusion Kerensky managed to reassemble the Duma and to persuade a majority to elect a provisional committee, headed by Prince Lvov as Prime Minister, to take over the reins of government.

Aroused by the news from the capital, the Czar set out from headquarters to Petrograd, thinking that his authority would rally the troops and restore the situation. He got only halfway when his train was stopped. After two days of hesitation, during which he received reports making clear that the whole country was behind the revolution, he signed an abdication in favor of Grand Duke Michael. However, Nicholas' action was too late. The Soviet refused to recognize the continuation of the dynasty and the Grand Duke himself refused the succession.

The Petrograd Soviet of Workers' and Soldiers' Deputies was now the most important body in Russia, but it did recognize the authority of the Duma's Provisional Government on the basis of an agreed program. This program provided full and immediate amnesty for all political prisoners and exiles; freedom of speech, press, assembly and strikes; the abolition of all class, group and religious restrictions; the election of a constituent assembly by universal secret ballot to determine the form of government and adopt a constitution for Russia; the replacement of the police by a national militia, subject to the local authorities; democratic election of officials for municipalities and townships; the retention in Petersburg, fully armed, of the military units that had taken part in the revolution; and the extension of civil liberties to the soldiers, who would be subject to military discipline only while in the performance of duty.

Although Kerensky was the only laborite or socialist in the Provisional Government, which was otherwise essentially bourgeois, he stood out because he also represented the Soviet, in which a majority of the members of the Executive Committee were Mensheviks and Social Revolutionaries. Kerensky was thus the link uniting the moderates of the Duma and the radicals of the Soviet. He traveled around the country calling for support for the Provisional Government, and in good measure received that support. However, the problems were overwhelming. Not only was the country in a state of chaos, but Russia was still at war. The Western Allies were doing everything possible to keep Russia at war, even though German and Austrian armies were encamped on great parts of its territory and the Russian forces opposing them were rapidly dwindling as conscripts by the thousands simply took off for home.

While these momentous events were taking place, most of the Bolshevik leaders were either abroad or in Siberian exile. Disappointed with the collapse of the Revolution of 1905 and fearing rearrest by the Czar's secret police, Lenin and Krupskaya had returned in 1907 to a bleak and isolated existence in Western Europe. He carefully followed the news from Russia, including the records of proceedings of the Duma, and continued to write his articles and books, including his magnum opus, *Imperialism, the Highest Stage of Capitalism*. During these ten years, particularly after the outbreak of World War I, he had organized several meetings of his followers in Switzerland and in Austria-Hungary. The war had, in fact, practically destroyed the international socialist movement. Lenin had been shocked and incredulous as one European party after another rallied to the cause of its own national government, even participating in voting giant war credits to support its respective national cause. He broke with practically all his old associates during this period and on this point, with the exception of his hard-line personal followers. On November 1, 1914, he had published an article on "The War and Russian Social-Democracy" which declared in part:

The proletarian international has not perished and will not perish. The working masses will overcome all obstacles and create a new international. The present triumph of opportunism will be short-lived. The greater the sacrifices the war imposes, the clearer it will become to the working masses that the opportunists have betrayed the workers' cause and that the weapons must be turned against the governments and the bourgeoisie of every country. Turning the present imperialist war into a civil war is the only correct proletarian slogan.

But while Lenin became estranged, during this period, from his older Marxist associates, many of his writings did manage to get circulated inside Russia and his hard line was popular and influential, particularly among the Petrograd workers. When Lenin and his fellow exiles heard the unexpected news of the revolution in Russia and of the political amnesty decreed by the Provisional Government, they had but one thought: to get back to Russia as fast as possible. This was not without its problems in war-torn Europe. But the enemy, the Germans, came to Lenin's rescue by giving him and his colleagues a special train across Germany to Sweden and Finland. Knowing the Bolshevik opposition to the war, they thought that Lenin's presence in the country would hasten the Russian exit from the war and the release of German forces for use on the Western front. And despite the dubious circumstances of their return, Lenin and his party were greeted by a massive welcome organized by his followers when they arrived at the Finland Station in Petrograd on April 16, 1917.

After telling the crowd at the station that world revolution was just around the corner, Lenin proceeded immediately to Bolshevik headquarters, which had been set up in one of the Czar's palaces. After listening to the reports of his lieutenants, he rose and attacked them bitterly for having supported the Provisional Government during his absence in Switzerland. "No support for the Provisional Government," he decreed to his stunned followers. The next day, at a general Social Democratic conference, Lenin repeated his uncompromising line, thus putting a quick end to any hope of unity among the various Social Democratic factions. Two days later, in his famous "April Theses," published in the Bolshevik organ *Pravda*, he expressed support for the Soviet of Workers' and Soldiers' Deputies, as against the Provisional Goverment, and proposed that his Bolshevik faction, in order to emphasize its complete break with the past, change its name to the "Communist Party." Despite a storm of criticisms, protests and opposition, even within the Bolshevik ranks, Lenin's fierce will, biting eloquence and grim determination prevailed. The main resolutions of the All-Russian Bolshevik Party Conference which met May 7–12 followed the line of Lenin's "April Theses." Few of his own followers then realized that Lenin's slogan, "All power to the Soviets," concealed a deliberate campaign by propaganda, maneuver and manipulation to gain control of those Soviets and use them for Bolshevik purposes. He succeeded. In this feverish atmosphere the demoralized troops at the front, workers in the cities and the hungry villagers responded to Lenin's cries for immediate peace, bread and land, rather than to the moderate socialists, who were urging patience and persistence in continuing the war until a democratic peace could be negotiated and promising broad social and economic reforms thereafter.

A debate between Lenin and Kerensky, at the All-Russian Congress of the Soviets in Petrograd on June 17, brought into dramatic relief the dualism inherent in Russian revolutionary socialism since the earliest days. Arrayed on one side were Kerensky's followers: Mensheviks, Social Democrats and Social Revolutionaries, heirs of the traditions of the Decembrists, of the "People's Will," of Herzen and of the imported democratic rationalism of Western Europe. On the other side were Lenin's new Bolshevik followers, the impatient soldiers and peasants who, whether they knew it or not, were the spiritual grandchildren of the early peasant rebels and of Nechaev and Bakunin.

Taking the platform first, Lenin declared: "It is not a question of promising reforms—these are empty words—but of taking the step we need to take now." He went on to say that his party was ready to take all power into its own hands at any minute, to expose war profiteers, to arrest "fifty or one hundred" of the biggest capitalists, to announce to all nations: "We regard all capitalists as robbers . . . the French capitalists, the English capitalists, all of them. . . . If Russia were a revolutionary democracy," he concluded, "not merely in word but in deed, it would proceed to further the revolution and not compromise with the capitalists."

Kerensky replied. After reviewing and rebutting Lenin's remarks, he said: "I dare say that it is likely that citizen Lenin has forgotten what Marxism is. He cannot call himself a socialist, because socialism nowhere recommends the settling of questions of economic war, of the war of classes in their economic relations, the question of economic reorganization of the state, by arresting people, as is done by Asiatic despots. . . . You, Bolsheviks, recommend childish prescriptions: 'Arrest, kill, destroy.' What are you, socialists or the police of the old regime?"

The battle continued with its ups and downs all through the summer. The Kerensky government was obliged to fend off the attacks, demonstrations and threats not only of the Bolsheviks but also of an impatient high military command, which was threatening to oust the Provisional Government and establish military rule to restore order. After an abortive uprising in July, the Provisional Government ordered Lenin's arrest, but he escaped and went into hiding in Finland. Then in August the Commander in Chief, General Lavr Kornilov, actually started to march on the capital, but Kerensky was able to mobilize sufficient force in Petrograd to fend him off. At this point Lenin wrote to his Central Committee:

The Kornilov revolt is an extremely unexpected and downright unbelievably sharp turn in events. Like every sharp turn, it calls for revision and change of tactics. . . . We will fight and are fighting Kornilov, just as Kerensky's troops are. But we do not support

Kerensky; on the contrary, we expose his weakness and vacillations . . . we must campaign against Kerensky not so much directly as indirectly, that is, by demanding a most active, energetic and truly revolutionary war against Kornilov. The development of that war alone can lead us to power, but of this we must speak as little as possible in our propaganda (all the time remembering that even tomorrow events may put the power into our hands, and then we shall not relinquish it).

On September 27 Kerensky, trying, in spite of all the harassment, to meet his original commitments to the Soviet, organized a provisional parliament to function until elections could be held for a constituent assembly on the following November 25. From Finland, Lenin ordered the Bolsheviks to abstain. Even in this temporary exile, he continued to write prolifically and to exhort his followers to greater efforts as what he considered the critical moment approached. Some of the basic conclusions he reached during this period are reflected in a pamphlet called *Can the Bolsheviks Retain State Power?* In it he argued that if the Czar could rule Russia with 130,000 members of the nobility and landed gentry, then the Bolshevik Party with 240,000 members was at least as strong. Shortly after, toward the end of October, he returned surreptitiously to Petrograd to organize the takeover. The main instrument was to be a Revolutionary Military Committee of the Petrograd Soviet under Leon Trotsky, with a commissar appointed for every army unit in the capital and its environs. On November 7* the Bolshevik forces struck, quickly taking over the Winter Palace and most of the government buildings. Kerensky escaped, but

---

* A Soviet decree early in 1918 adopted the Gregorian calendar, introduced by Pope Gregory XIII in 1582 and adopted centuries earlier by all Western countries except Russia, which had continued to adhere to the Julian, or Old Style, calendar. The effect was a forward adjustment of Russian historical dates by thirteen days. Thus, while the anniversary of the Bolshevik seizure of power is celebrated on November 7, this event took place, according to the Julian calendar then in force in Russia, on October 25, 1917, and continues to be called the "October Revolution" or "Great October." Similarly, the events leading to the overthrow of the Czar early in March, 1917 (New Style), are referred to as the "February Revolution."

most of the Provisional Government was arrested. Lenin was in power.

Having followed all these trails leading over the course of a century to revolution in Russia, we have seen that conflicting groups who invoked the name of Marx had the most disparate and contradictory attitudes. Perhaps we should now take a brief look at Karl Marx himself. He lived from 1818 to 1883. A heavily bearded, ponderous, nineteenth-century, German professorial type, he is usually described as a social philosopher and radical leader. After years of studying in London he produced his major work, *Capital* (in the original German *Das Kapital*). I think the least we can say for him is that somewhat belatedly he described the evils of the early Industrial Revolution in England more graphically and more effectively than any other person. His prejudices and limitations, however, led him to the conclusion that these evils were incurable by any means other than revolutionary upheaval. In his view there would be an increasing monopolization of capital as the new industrialists drained off the "surplus value" of the products created by working men using machines. To maximize his profits, the industralist would increasingly grind down the level of the workers. Class lines would become sharper, and an explosive situation would develop in which violent overturn would become inevitable. Now, as a matter of fact, the voluminous materials which Marx used for his analyses came mainly from British parliamentary studies, prepared as the basis for corrective legislation to cure the evils and improve the conditions in an early industrial society—such as the restraint of monopoly, the establishment of decent standards for working conditions and hours of labor, the right of labor to organize and the establishment of a progressive tax system. In fact, reforms were well under way in England by the time *Das Kapital* appeared in print in 1867.

As a political agitator and prophet, Marx was uniformly unsuccessful and wrong in his analyses. When Marx and his collaborator, Engels, issued their *Communist Manifesto*, at the time of the civil disturbances and uprisings in Europe in 1848, he thought the Communist revolution on a vast scale was already at hand all over Western Europe. And thereafter, until the end of his life, whenever there was any political flurry on the continent, he just as inaccurately proclaimed that the "inevitable" day had arrived. In any case, Marx conceived of his theories as applicable not to a backward state like Russia but only to states in which the Industrial Revolution had already taken place and a large proletarian working class had developed. In correspondence with an early Russian Marxist, he even replied negatively to the question as to whether he could fit the Russian village commune, the *mir,* into the concepts set forth in *Das Kapital,* saying that his book had spoken of the "historical inevitability of the English road only in the lands of Western Europe."

In all his writings, Marx simply developed a theory of the inevitability of revolution. He had almost nothing to say about what would happen after that revolution, beyond the vague predictions that man would "work in accordance with his ability and consume in accordance with his needs" and that the state as such would "wither away." The furthest he went in this direction was in a piece published in 1875, called *Criticism of the Gotha Program,* in which he said: "Between the capitalist and the communist society lies the period of the revolutionary transformation of the one into the other. To this corresponds a political transition period in which the state can be nothing else but the revolutionary dictatorship of the proletariat."

During his long years in exile, Lenin wrote prolifically, using Marx as a springboard to launch himself into a sea of ideas which reflected—and could only reflect—his own Russian background and upbringing. As Bertram Wolfe puts it: "One hears on American campuses the 'Marxist theory of the State,' when more often what is meant is the Leninist theory of the State; or the 'Marxist theory of Imperialism' when what is meant is the Leninist theory of Imperialism." This is a mistake not made inside the Soviet Union today. I have been trying to remember whether I ever heard a Soviet official or Soviet citizen quote Marx to me. I can't think of a single instance. But Lenin—yes: "As Lenin said . . ." "As Lenin taught us. . . ." And nine times out of ten the quote which follows is one you feel sure would make Marx turn over in his grave.

CHAPTER III

Stalin and the Making of the Soviet System

In his thinking and his writing, Lenin—like Marx before him—
had not unnaturally concentrated on the questions of the conditions and methods for seizing power, and given relatively little
attention to what happens afterward. But after the success of
his *coup d'état* against the provisional revolutionary government
on November 7, 1917, the first problem was the formation of a
new government. In his autobiography Trotsky tells the story of
his discussion with Lenin as to what its members should be
called.

"Anything but ministers—that is a vile, hackneyed word,"
said Lenin.

"We might call them commissars, but there are too many

commissars," suggested Trotsky, "—perhaps Supreme Commissars?"

"No, 'Supreme' does not sound well either."

"What about People's Commissars?"

"People's Commissars? . . . Well, that might do, I think," replied Lenin, "—and the government as a whole?"

"A Soviet, of course—the Soviet of People's Commissars."

"The Soviet of People's Commissars? That's splendid, savors powerfully of revolution!" said Lenin.

The following day a meeting of the "All-Russian Congress of Soviets" passed a decree establishing the first Soviet Government. The decree did not immediately burn all bridges; it referred to the new government as provisional "until the Constituent Assembly is convened." The Congress of Soviets that day also passed a decree, on which Lenin had worked through the night, expropriating all landed estates. Such expropriation had been the program not of the Bolsheviks but of the Social Revolutionaries. Lenin explained to his followers: "We must identify ourselves with the peasants, with their wishes—we never intended to give a monopoly over the peasants to the Social Revolutionaries." On the same day, Lenin and Trotsky in their respective new capacities as Chairman of the Soviet of People's Commissars and Commissar of Foreign Affairs issued an appeal for peace negotiations to end the war.

Issuing edict after edict in the ensuing days, Lenin contemptuously rejected approaches for unity from other leftist parties, even arranging police harassment of former associates—including his original mentor, Plekhanov—who dared to question the government's moves. To one old associate he explained: "It is a question of creating a socialist state. It isn't a question of Russia at all. I spit on Russia. This is merely one phase through which we must pass on the way to world revolution."

Having repeatedly and publicly questioned Kerensky's good intentions regarding the Constituent Assembly, Lenin apparently felt constrained to allow the scheduled elections to be held, as scheduled, on November 25. Thirty-six million Russians went to the polls. Despite the power position of the Bolsheviks, only nine million voted for them. Twenty-one million voted for the Social Revolutionaries, who thus elected 370 or a clear majority of the total 707 deputies. The Bolsheviks had 175, the pro-Lenin Left Socialists 40, the Mensheviks 16 and the Constitutional Democrats 17, while 80-odd were representatives of national minority groups. The outcome was an immediate psychological blow and a critical potential threat. But Lenin did not flinch. When the new Assembly met on January 16, 1918, he first tried to ride roughshod over it in the name of the Soviet of Workers' and Soldiers' Deputies, then dissolved it. Privately he told Trotsky: "We made a mistake in not postponing the calling of the Constituent Assembly. We acted very incautiously. But it came out for the best. The dissolution of the Constituent Assembly by the Soviet Government means a complete and frank liquidation of the idea of democracy by the idea of dictatorship."

Meanwhile, as the weeks and months passed, the new government issued one decree after another: curbing the press; establishing workers' control in the factories; nationalizing first the banks and later the sugar and oil industries; establishing state control over all enterprises with more than ten employees; creating a state monopoly of foreign trade; finally, prohibiting private trade internally.

However, all this was more easily decreed than done. The Bolsheviks had easily enough established control over Moscow and other major cities of European Russia, though ever-increasing terror was essential to maintain that control. Elsewhere chaos and conflict reigned, and the confusion was confounded by Allied efforts to keep Russia in the war and thus prevent the transfer of the German forces in Eastern Europe to the Western front. It was in connection with this effort that President Wilson, on January 8, 1918, proclaimed his famous Fourteen Points for a peace settlement. These went a long way—with their pledges of open negotiations, no annexations, self-determination of peoples, specifically including Russia, and the like—toward meeting the goals set forth in the appeal for peace negotiations Lenin and Trotsky had themselves issued on the first morning of their assumption of power. But the Wilsonian prose had no effect. The Bolshevik regime had already opened negotiations with the Germans; and in March, 1918, despite opposition within his own ranks, as well as from Russia's allies, Lenin bought an end to hostilities with Germany at the heavy price of the Treaty of Brest-Litovsk. Under its provisions, Russian forces were obliged to withdraw from Finland, Poland and the Baltic States and to leave the Germans in occupation of the Ukraine—where an independent government had been established—and of other territories in the South, including the oil fields of the Caucasus.

Preoccupied with the desperate struggle on the Western front, the Allies were indecisive and halfhearted in their further actions with respect to Russia. After Brest-Litovsk the British landed several thousand Allied troops at Murmansk and Archangel in the North, to prevent war supplies from falling into German hands. In August similar landings were made by Japanese, then British, French and American contingents, in Vladivostok in the Far East and by the French at Odessa in the South, on the Black Sea. Meanwhile, a Czechoslovak force of about thirty thousand men, which had been fighting on the Eastern front and was trying to get around to the west, had bogged down in the middle of Siberia and taken control of the region. All these forces gave some support and assistance to the Russian "White Armies," led mainly by Czarist officers, in their struggle against the Reds. There was no concerted Allied policy or concerted Allied effort to overthrow the Bolsheviks; nor, indeed, even any coordination between the various contingents. However, this intervention was later to be built up by the Soviet regime into a story of massive imperialist intervention in the Civil War—and this myth remains a part of the official ideology to this day.

In March, 1918, Lenin had moved his government out of Petrograd and into the Kremlin in Moscow. From here he and Trotsky directed the Civil War effort for another three years before it could be said that Soviet power was secure. As the Red forces advanced, the Cheka, common name for the "All-Russian Extraordinary Commission for Repression of the Counterrevolution and Sabotage," was given a free hand in "liquidating the bourgeoisie," with powers of summary arrest, trial and execution. Czar Nicholas II and his family were executed in Yekaterinburg (Sverdlovsk) on July 16, 1918, as the Civil War raged in the Urals region. Shortly afterward, on August 30, Lenin was wounded by a would-be assassin—a Social Revolutionary girl agent named Fanny Kaplan—and five hundred prominent figures of the old regime were shot that very night. Thereafter, the "Red Terror" was on in earnest, and the Cheka's victims among the middle class and richer peasants, called kulaks, were soon numbered in the thousands.

Besides the "Red Terror," deprivation and starvation were also taking a great toll. Under the so-called "War Communism" decrees the economic life of the country practically came to a stop. Production fell to fractions of prewar levels, and in 1921 a great famine in the Ukraine further aggravated the situation. It was at that time that the Hoover Relief Commission played a great helping role in keeping much of the population alive. Officially nothing is said about this nowadays, but one still runs into older Russians who remember this American relief effort with deep gratitude. The effort was limited, however, relative to the all-encompassing scope of the economic catastrophe. A series of peasant revolts broke out in central Russia, and strikes were spreading in the cities. In the former capital of Petrograd hungry workers were looting the warehouses.

The climax came on March 1, 1921, when the sailors of the Kronstadt Island fortress off Petrograd, the very unit that had marched on Lenin's behalf against Kerensky in 1917, revolted against him. Mass meetings of the garrison passed resolutions demanding: new elections to the Soviet by secret ballot; the restoration of freedom of speech, press and assembly; abolition of Communist political agents in the army and navy; withdrawal of grain-requisitioning squads and re-establishment of a free market for the peasants. The mutiny was liquidated in the bloodiest possible way, with the use of the Cheka and selected army units; the Kronstadt garrison was practically wiped out. However, Lenin sensed that it was time to retreat. On March 15, before the guns of Kronstadt had been finally silenced, he presented to the Tenth Congress of the Bolshevik Party his "new economic policy," which he frankly described as a type of "state capitalism." Under it the state retained control of basic industries and transportation, as well as foreign trade. However, agriculture and small industry were permitted to return to private enterprise. The new policy even allowed the granting of economic concessions to foreign capitalists and businessmen. It is interesting to note in passing that a number of Americans took advantage of these provisions. Among these were Averell Harriman, who participated in a manganese-mining concession in the Caucasus, which he had the foresight to liquidate before Stalin came to power; and Armand Hammer, who built and operated a pencil factory in Moscow—still in existence—in return for which he received enough Romanov art and jewels to open the now well-known Hammer Galleries in New York City. The new economic policy not only eased the immediate crisis but, in fact, started a general, gradual restoration of production and was to continue until 1928.

Toward the end of 1921, Lenin's health began to fail. He frequently complained of headaches and developed spells of dizziness. He started taking things easier, retaining the main decisions but delegating more work to his lieutenants, particularly Trotsky, the Commissar of War, Joseph Stalin, who had been elected General Secretary of the Party, and Grigory Zinoviev, head of the Petrograd Soviet and of the Communist International. After two strokes in 1922 Lenin sensed his approaching death and prepared a "political testament" dealing with the problem of his succession. In it he expressed the opinion that Trotsky and Stalin were the two most able leaders in the Central Committee and the fear that there might be rivalry and a split between them. He thought that Trotsky was too preoccupied with purely administrative affairs. Stalin, he said, was "too rude" to exercise the "enormous power" which he had "concentrated in his hands" as General Secretary of the Party. He therefore recommended that Stalin be replaced in that office. Lenin lingered on feebly for another year and died on January 20, 1924. His embalmed remains are today on view in an enormous red granite mausoleum in Red Square.

Stalin saw to it that Lenin's political testament was not published in the U.S.S.R. During the next thirty years, in fact, it

was he who would pick up and institutionalize Lenin's beginnings, bringing Russia to a state of totalitarian, despotic control
that would have been the envy of Czar Nicholas I, or even Ivan
the Terrible. But first Stalin had to dispose of some rivals, in
particular Leon Trotsky, and to consolidate his power.

Who was Stalin? To this day, no one can fully answer that
question. His own rare references to his early life are laconic
and contradictory and the official accounts were so frequently
rewritten as to be highly misleading. However, much research
has been done and the basic facts are clear enough. He was
born December 21, 1879, as Joseph Vissarionovich Dzhuga-
shvili, in the high Caucasus Mountain town of Gori, near Tiflis,
capital of the Russian province of Georgia, once a proud,
independent kingdom. His father, Vissarion, was a poor village
cobbler of peasant origin who died when Joseph was eleven. His
mother Yekaterina, daughter of a serf, was an illiterate and
deeply religious woman who took in washing to make ends meet
and to help her only remaining son—the previous three had
died in infancy—get an education and become a priest. After
six years at a parish school in his native village, Joseph entered
the Georgian Orthodox Theological Seminary in Tiflis, which he
attended from September 1, 1894, to July 20, 1899, according to
a brass plaque which can still be found on the façade of the
building, now used for other purposes. The circumstances of his
leaving before graduation are obscure. However, it is clear that
he read "forbidden books," including Karl Marx, and engaged in
political activities during his stay at the seminary; and it is
generally believed that he was expelled for these reasons. Indeed, by his own account, he entered the Marxist revolutionary
movement in 1898, while still in the school, and became a
political agitator among the Tiflis railway workers. Then, after
his departure from the seminary, he shifted his efforts to the
factory workers in the nearby towns of Batum and Baku.

Stalin began appearing in Czarist police records at this
time and spent varying periods in prison or in Siberia, from
which he usually—and rather suspiciously—managed to escape. He apparently became an early admirer of Lenin and
Lenin's writings, and claims to have had an exchange of corre-

spondence with Lenin in 1903, after the Social Democrats had split into Bolshevik and Menshevik wings. He did not meet Lenin until the Bolshevik Party Congress in Finland in 1905 and then at a few subsequent conferences—but apparently as a sort of fringe member from far-off Transcaucasia. There is no record of his having played any leading role in the Revolution of 1905. However, during this early period, in addition to his agitational work, he did become a kind of specialist in organizing robberies of banks and government payrolls to supply the Bolshevik treasury.

In his private life, Stalin married a non-Party Georgian girl, who bore him a son, Jacob, before leaving him a widower not many years later. He was to marry for a second time only after he was established in Moscow in 1919. His second wife, Nadya Alliluyeva, the daughter of a Party colleague in Tiflis, was much younger than Stalin. She bore him two children, Vasili and Svetlana. Nadya died in 1932, after a quarrel with Stalin about some aspects of his harsh rule. Some say Stalin murdered her in a fit of rage. Others say that she committed suicide. Her own daughter believes the latter version. Nadya Alliluyeva Stalina was buried with the elite in the cemetery of the old Novodevichy Monastery, and the white marble likeness which Stalin had erected there—whether out of repentance or pure grief—is one of Moscow's loveliest monuments.

After the suppression of the Revolution of 1905, there was an ebb in the tide of revolution. Lenin himself returned to Switzerland, in a state of despondency. However, back in Transcaucasia, Stalin seems to have gone on with his organizing work on behalf of the Bolsheviks, with continued success. As he himself described his subsequent career:

I remember the years 1905–1907, when at the desire of the Party I was drawn into the work at Baku. Two years of revolutionary work among the oil workers made me a practical fighter and a practical leader. I learned for the first time what the leadership of great masses of workmen really meant. I became a journeyman of the revolution. I remember 1917, when by the decision of the Party, after prison and deportation, I was drawn into St. Petersburg. There,

among the Russian workers, in close contact with the great educator
of the proletariat throughout the world, Comrade Lenin, in the storm
of the mighty struggle between the proletariat and the bourgeoisie
during the world war, I learned for the first time to understand what
it meant to be one of the leaders of the great working class party.
There, in Russia [as opposed to Transcaucasia], under Lenin's
direction, I became a master workman in revolution.

Trotsky, his enemy, described Stalin's development somewhat differently but not without respect:

Koba [Stalin] was the committee man par excellence. . . .
Lacking the personal qualities which would have enabled him to
influence the masses directly, he clung with redoubled tenacity to the
political apparatus. The Committee became for him the axis of his
universe—the Tiflis, the Baku, the Caucasian, before it became the
Central Committee. In time his attachment to the Party machine was
to develop with extraordinary strength; the committee man became
the super-*apparatchik*, the General Secretary, the chief and very
personification of the bureaucracy . . . the centralized political apparatus was for him the essence of Bolshevism.

In fact, in anticipation of Lenin's death and in the period
following that death, Stalin made one alliance after another
calculated to strengthen his own position and to weaken that of
Trotsky. After first defeating Trotsky in alliance with the left-
wingers, Stalin at the Fourteenth Party Congress in April, 1925,
shifted to the right. On the eve of the Congress Stalin had made
his famous speech expounding the theory of "Socialism in One
Country"—proclaiming the theory of the self-sufficiency of the
Soviet revolution. This was not only a rejection of Trotsky's
concept of "permanent revolution," but also a real departure
from Leninist internationalism, although Stalin did his best to
gloss over and even suppress any mention of this latter point.
By this time he had also used his position as General Secretary
to abolish freedom of expression inside the Party and to transform it into a "monolithic" body. Then, in 1928–29, after he had
succeeded in expelling Trotsky and his own former left-wing
colleagues from the Party, Stalin in turn moved against his new
right-wing associates. Unabashedly reversing himself, he

adopted the domestic program previously sponsored by the left-wingers and began to industrialize the U.S.S.R. and to collectivize agriculture with a speed and ruthlessness which horrified even the original advocates of these policies. In 1929 he expelled Trotsky from the Soviet Union and forced all opposition leaders, right and left, to surrender and to "recant." He had now become the undisputed master of the country.

Launching the first of his Five-Year Plans for industrialization in 1928, Stalin harked back to one of his predecessors, saying: "When Peter the Great, having to deal with the more advanced countries of the West, began feverishly to build factories and workshops in order to supply his armies, none of the old classes could successfully solve the problem of overcoming the backwardness of the country." And, indeed, with his iron grip Stalin could do better. Personal consumption was held to minimal levels. The peasants were forced to deliver foodstuffs for absurdly low prices. The industrial effort was combined with the forced collectivization of agriculture and the liquidation of the rich peasants, the kulaks, who had received their lands under the Stolypin agricultural program or under Lenin's decrees confiscating great estates and establishing the "new economic policy." Forced labor was the keynote, as millions of kulaks and their families were deported from their native villages to the new industrial plants and to labor camps, where they were set to work at unskilled labor for mere subsistence rations.

In addition to this forced displacement of population, there were the slave-labor camps for political opponents of the regime and so-called "class-hostile elements." This system had been set up by a Soviet Government decree as early as May, 1919, but was vastly developed by Stalin. He organized, under the control of the police, the Main Administration of Labor Camps, known by its Russian initials as GULAG. GULAG used its prisoners in the construction of highways and railways, in mining, stone quarrying, gravel- and stone-crushing, digging vast canal projects and the like. These camps were mainly in regions such as northern Siberia and the Kazakh Desert, where the climate was too severe for normal colonization and the work under primitive conditions too arduous to attract voluntary labor. Estimates as to the total of political prisoners in such camps vary but in the 1930s and again after World War II ran up to fifteen million persons. The cost in human and material terms was appalling, but the program accomplished its main purpose of creating an essential economic infrastructure.

Under Stalin's dictatorship there was a marked reversion in social life also, back toward traditional Russian standards. The experimentalism, the easy morality, the depreciation of the Russian past, began to disappear. The introduction of incentive pay, the granting of privileges and high incomes to the bureaucracy, army and police officers and industrial executives, led to great discrepancies between the incomes of the elite and of the masses of workers. Strict discipline was reintroduced into the schools, with marks and examinations and uniforms for students. Tuition was reinstated for secondary and higher education. Divorce was made difficult and abortions were made illegal. The censorship bore down on literary and cultural life. As the population entered its second generation under the Soviet system, discriminations against those who could not prove themselves to be of worker or peasant origin were abandoned, if only for the good reason that the sons and daughters of the Soviet elite could not so describe themselves.

To give his rule a façade and to divert world attention from his internal repression, Stalin introduced a new Constitution in 1936. That Constitution proclaims the U.S.S.R. to be a "Socialist" state based on the Soviets of Workers' Deputies, symbolizing the "dictatorship of the proletariat." Labor is declared to be a "duty and matter of honor of every able-bodied citizen on the principle: 'He who doesn't work, doesn't eat' "; and the basic "principle of socialism" is described as: "From each in accordance with his ability, to each in accordance with his work." Much of the section on the basic rights of the citizen—freedom of speech, of press, of assembly and demonstration—might have been written by our own founding fathers. The joker is the article which subjects all those provisions of that Constitution to the monopoly of political power in the hands of the single and only authorized political organization, the Communist Party.

We should pause briefly to note that the Bolshevik rulers have adopted the name "socialism" for their state power and for the present epoch in Soviet history, which is defined as a period of transition from capitalism to Communism. Theoretically, it is only after "the building of Communism" that Marx's concept of "to each in accordance with his need" can be realized. Little is heard about Marx's corollary concept that in that future period of abundance and euphoria "the state will wither away"; on the contrary, Party literature has increasingly tended to emphasize that its role as vanguard leader will increase as the society approaches the era of Communism. In any case, the Soviet use of the term "socialism" should not be confused with "democratic socialism" as practiced in some countries of Western Europe, e.g., Great Britain or Sweden; or as advocated by those who call themselves "socialists"—as opposed to "Communists"—here in the United States. Western "socialists" seek economic and social reforms by evolutionary and parliamentary means in free societies, without the violent overthrow of existing political institutions and their replacement by a so-called "dictatorship of the proletariat" accompanied by the suppression or liquidation of political opposition.

The structure of political power in the Soviet Union rests on four pillars: the Communist Party, especially its centralized leadership; the government bureaucracy; the armed forces; and the political police. The road to the top in the Soviet Union has always been through the Party. However, once on top the leader can manipulate the Party and the other elements of power in various ways to consolidate and maintain his authority. Lenin used the Party itself as an instrument of internal power, with help from the police, and with the bureaucracy and armed forces neutralized. Stalin increasingly used the political police as his chosen instrument. Indeed, he used the police terror not only to manipulate the masses of the population but even to control the Party itself. In a series of spectacular purges in the mid-1930s, Stalin proceeded to eliminate from the Party every conceivable rival or potential threat to him personally or to the regime. This included practically all the "Old Bolsheviks," some fifty of whom were induced to confess treason and sabotage in a series of show trials staged in 1936, 1937 and 1938. It also included seven top marshals and generals, the leaders of the Red Army and thousands of lower-ranking officers. Executions during the great purges are estimated at about one million people, and perhaps double that number are thought to have perished in the prison camps.

The political or secret police is, indeed, one of the oldest and most fearful of Russian institutions. Founded by Ivan the Terrible, this organization was known throughout Czarist days as the Okhrana. It was replaced after the Revolution by the Cheka. Since that time it has gone through a number of changes of names: in 1922 it became the United General Political Administration or OGPU; in 1934 the People's Commissariat for Internal Affairs or NKVD; then Ministry of State Security or MGB. After 1954 it was known as the Committee for State Security, or KGB, and then in 1968 a Ministry of Internal Affairs, or MVD, was superimposed. However, to this day older Russian citizens are likely to talk of the secret police under the old Czarist name of Okhrana. Historically, as we have seen, there was much interpenetration between the secret police and revolutionary societies, and there are theories that Stalin himself was a double agent. In any case, he greatly strengthened the police institution, issuing decrees in 1934 and 1937 authorizing the political police to conduct trials or pass sentences without trials, and for this purpose to set up a special judicial and punishment department within the NKVD.

In his operation of the Communist Party system, Stalin reduced the euphemistic term "democratic centralism" to its ultimate absurdity. Lenin had frequently consulted his colleagues in the leadership of the Party and had given the rank and file some sense of participation, even though he really made every important decision himself. During Lenin's lifetime there had, in fact, been thirteen congresses of the Communist Party of the Soviet Union, the last taking place in January, 1924. In principle, these *congresses* were held every second year, with a smaller *conference* being called between the more formal congresses so that there was at least one large-scale meeting of representatives of the Party from all over the country once every year. After Lenin's death the schedule was held to for a few years, the Fourteenth Congress taking place in 1925 and the Fifteenth in 1927. Then, as Stalin was busy liquidating Trotsky and other opponents, the intervals between congresses became longer, the Sixteenth being held in 1930 after a lag of three years, and the Seventeenth in 1934 after a lag of four years. At this Seventeenth Congress a Central Committee of seventy-one members was elected. Then came the great purges of 1936–38. By the time the Eighteenth Congress was convened in 1939, only seventeen members of the Central Committee of 1934 had survived to be re-elected by this Congress. The next Congress, the Nineteenth, would not take place until thirteen years later, in October, 1952, more than seven years after the conclusion of World War II, and after the postwar purges which took place in 1947–49.

Now let us turn briefly to the foreign relations of the Soviet regime. The principal excuse for Allied intervention in Russia during the Revolution had been the protection of Allied armaments and other war supplies from falling into the hands of the Germans. After the German defeat in November, 1918, there was no longer a reason to maintain the troops on Russian soil, nor indeed was there any popular support for this in the Allied countries, and they were gradually withdrawn. The German collapse also meant the end of the German occupation of Russian territories in the west, but the Soviets were obliged to carry on warfare in this sector—against the new Polish regime—until March, 1921.

Peace with the Germans having been established by the Treaty of Versailles, the Supreme Allied Council turned its attention to the economic reconstruction in Europe. To this end it summoned a conference in Genoa in April, 1922, to include not only the Allied Powers but the Central Powers as well. The United States refused to attend on the grounds that it would be impossible to keep the conference from dealing with political questions and that the economic recovery of Russia depended less on international action than on the internal policy of the Soviet Government. The conference came to nothing, mainly because of French and Belgian insistence that the Soviets recognize and undertake to repay the huge loans which had been made to the Czar before the Revolution. The Soviet Foreign Minister not only refused to reconsider the Soviet repudiation of these debts but used the demand as an excuse to make a number of propaganda speeches. Moreover, outside the formal conference, he scored a real success. Meeting separately with the German delegation at the nearby Italian city of Rapallo, he concluded a treaty with them by which both countries reciprocally renounced all claims to war indemnities, and Germany renounced any compensation for nationalized properties taken from German subjects in Russia "provided that the Soviet Government does not satisfy similar claims of other states." Diplomatic, consular and economic relations were re-established between the two countries.

Rapallo broke the ice. Despite their resentment of the mounting activities of the new Communist International, the British extended recognition to the Soviet Government in February, 1924; and by the end of the following year all the great powers except the United States had established diplomatic relations. In this period, under Lenin's guidance, the Soviets established friendly relations with their southern neighbors, Turkey, Persia and Afghanistan, detached Outer Mongolia from China and set it up as an allegedly independent republic. Then they went on to reassert, to the annoyance of the British, Russian interest and influence in China itself.

During the Wilson administration the United States withheld recognition as a matter of principle, stated by Secretary of State Bainbridge Colby: "We cannot recognize, hold official relations with, or give friendly reception to the agents of a government which is determined and bound to conspire against our institutions." During the ensuing Republican administrations this position of principle was supplemented by demands for satisfaction in the matter of Czarist debts and settlement of the claims of American nationals as conditions of recognition. But when Franklin Roosevelt became President, in the middle of the great depression, he proceeded to recognize the Soviet Government, and diplomatic relations were established in 1934. On the question of principle, he got from the Soviet Foreign Minister, Maxim Litvinov, a pious pledge of noninterference in American internal affairs and some assurances on the rights of American citizens in the Soviet Union, but he dropped the claims for payment of debts. In fact, the absence of official relations had not prevented the development of a considerable range of private activities. As industrialization got under way, thousands of American technicians were employed by the Soviet Government, and American firms such as General Electric and Ford participated in the construction and equipping of industrial enterprises and hydroelectric projects.

During the first fifteen-odd years of the Soviet regime, its foreign policy posture was one of harsh hostility toward the West. Stalin's internal policy of "socialism in one country" had its foreign policy counterpart in the slogan, "the menace of capitalist encirclement." This hostile policy began to shift as Hitler rose to power in Germany with his openly militaristic aggressive plans. The Soviet Union finally joined the League of Nations in September, 1934, and in that forum its Foreign Minister, Litvinov, repeatedly advocated the ideas that peace was indivisible and that security must be organized on a collective basis. Toward that end the Soviet Government concluded military alliances with France and Czechoslovakia and pacts of nonaggression with its Western neighbors—Poland, Finland and the Baltic Republics of Latvia, Lithuania and Estonia. Extreme revolutionary demands were dropped, and both internal and external propaganda with respect to the West, and particularly the Western European countries, was greatly softened. Communist parties sought to organize "united fronts" with the European socialists and other leftist groups. Diplomatic soundings were taken with the British and the French about the possibilities of bringing about a common front against Germany, but years of Soviet promotion of revolution in the Western democracies and the propagation of the Communist doctrine that "imperialist" wars were both inevitable and desirable to pave the way toward world revolution had left a residue of deep suspicion and distrust. Consequently, instead of joining in a common front, the British and French, without American objection, excluded Russia when in September, 1938, they entered the Munich agreement with Germany, appeasing Hitler by approving the sacrifice to him of a large part of Czechoslovakia. Indeed, until Hitler made it clear that his chief target was the Soviet Union, Stalin himself seemed not greatly to fear Nazi developments in Germany. During this period there was clearly an unexpressed hope on both the Western and Russian sides that Hitler would direct his aggression against the other.

I never met Stalin personally. I used to see him from time to time, mainly atop Lenin's tomb reviewing the May Day or November 7 parades, or, rarely, at other ceremonies. I frequently saw him on the movie screen—there was no TV then— and for the two and a half years I was in Moscow during his reign you could not pick up a newspaper or magazine without seeing his picture. And I heard him occasionally on the radio, pronouncing dull, dogmatic discourses in a Russian marked by a heavy Georgian accent. Even my boss, Ambassador Bedell Smith, saw Stalin only a few times during his three-year stay in Moscow. Remoteness and aloofness were Stalin's style, like that of the Czars who had preceded him. He had no personal magnetism or eloquence, either of hand or of tongue. But Stalin was a master organizer, a man with a gift for putting his unconditional supporters into key places in the Party machine, a manipulator of men who knew how to use their every weakness for his own purposes. In the biography he was writing when Stalin's long arm reached out to murder him in exile in Mexico, in 1940, Leon Trotsky wrote: "Stalin represents an utterly exceptional phenomenon. He seized power even before the masses had learned to distinguish his face among the others when they marched past the leaders of the Revolution in the traditional Red Square parades. He is neither a thinker, a writer nor an orator. He took possession of power not with the aid of personal qualities but with the aid of an impersonal machine. And it was not he who created the machine but the machine that created him."

The question thus arises as to who created the machine, and I think the answer must clearly be—Lenin. Throughout his revolutionary activity and again after he came to power, Lenin had consistently sought to create a small, tight organization that he could personally control. While he had maintained a façade of consultation and democratic practices, we have seen that he did not hesitate to override his followers even when they were almost unanimously against him, as in the case of their initial support of the Kerensky Provisional Government. Indeed, Leon Trotsky, in 1904, before he had become Lenin's principal partner, had prophetically foreseen that the machine Lenin was creating would breed personal dictatorship. He wrote then: "The organization of the Party will take the place of the Party itself; the Central Committee will take the place of the organization; and finally, the dictator will take the place of the Central Committe." It might thus be said that Stalin's role was not initiation but completion. As Ivan the Terrible had brought the Czarist autocracy to the wildest extremes of despotism, so had Stalin done with Communism.

CHAPTER IV

World War II: Its Impact and Consequences

Americans tend to forget that the United States "sat out" the
prewar diplomatic maneuvers and the first years of World War
II. Hamstrung by neutrality legislation, Washington was playing
no positive role in world affairs. Weak governments in Great
Britain and France, still reeling from the economic depression,
militarily unprepared, distrustful of Russian overtures for cooperation, were unable to cope with the demagogue-dictator who
had mobilized Germany under the slogans of anti-Semitism and
anti-Bolshevism and declared his intention to create a new
German Empire in Europe itself. As Hitler successively took
over the Rhineland, the Saar and Austria, Western Europe
seemed mesmerized into inactivity. When Hitler turned next
toward Czechoslovakia, Britain and France finally acted, not to

stop but to appease him. At Munich, in September, 1938, the British and French Prime Ministers agreed to press the Prague Government to cede to Germany Czechoslovakia's Sudetenland province and to accept Hitler's assurance that he had no further territorial demands. Six months later, in March, 1939, Nazi forces proceeded to take over the entire country.

Even as they did so, Hitler's propaganda machine was carrying on a violent campaign against the Poles and thus making it clear that Poland was the next target. This gave a new dimension to the European picture. The Poles and the Russians had been at war off and on for centuries. In the seventeenth century the Poles, then strong, had actually occupied Moscow and installed a Polish puppet on the throne of the Czars. As the Russians grew stronger and the Poles weaker during the next two centuries, Poland had been three times partitioned between Russia and Germany. Then Lenin's most stubborn foe after he took power was Poland, with which hostilities continued from 1918 to 1921. Consequently, in their unenviable geographical position, the Poles in the 1930s considered the Soviet Union hardly less a menace to Poland's existence and freedom than Germany. All in all, the situation was complicated enough to make the maneuvers of the next two years one of the most bizarre chapters in the annals of diplomatic history.

On the heels of Hitler's takeover of Czechoslovakia in March, 1939, Litvinov proposed to the Western European democracies that a conference be convened in Bucharest to consider common policies. The British rejected this as "premature," and proposed instead that, in the event of further moves by Hitler, the British, French, Poles and Soviets should "consult." A few weeks later, in a gallant if "quixotic" gesture, Britain unilaterally extended guarantees to Poland and Rumania—then invited the Soviet Union to follow her example. Instead of accepting the British invitation, the Soviets on April 17 proposed to Britain and France the formation of a "triple alliance" against Hitler, at the same time suggesting that the British and French Foreign Ministers visit Moscow to discuss the proposal.

As the British dallied, the Russians reshuffled the cards. On May 3 Moscow announced that Litvinov had been replaced as

Commissar of Foreign Affairs by Vyacheslav Molotov, who also remained Chairman of the Soviet of People's Commissars—or, in other words, Prime Minister of the Soviet Union. A few days later the British finally sent a temporizing reply to the Litvinov proposal, and in mid-June they dispatched to Moscow for conversations not the British Foreign Secretary but a high Foreign Office professional, William Strang. He was later joined by a middle-level military mission, and discussions and negotiations continued inconclusively throughout the summer of 1939. When the Soviet military negotiator, Marshal Kliment Voroshilov, put forward concrete military plans calling for Soviet military intervention in Poland in the event of a Hitler attack, the Poles refused, wanting to limit the Soviet role to the provision of material and technical aid. Voroshilov then broke off the negotiations.

It is clear in retrospect that the Soviets had decided that nothing short of a binding treaty of alliance between Britain, France and the Soviet Union would satisfy them; otherwise they would reserve their freedom to maneuver. It is also clear that the replacement of Litvinov by Molotov meant that Stalin had decided that such a treaty would not be forthcoming and that the Soviets would explore the possibilities of an arrangement with the Germans. This process started immediately after Molotov took over the handling of foreign affairs—and while it was done secretly, we now know all the details from German documents captured by our forces during the war. After a round of hinting and diplomatic sparring by both sides, the German Ambassador in Moscow, Count Werner von der Schulenberg, on August 15 told Molotov that the German Government considered that all problems from the Baltic to the Balkans could be settled and that the Western democracies were the natural enemies both of Germany and of the Soviet Union. "Since war may come soon," he continued, "immediate clarification is desirable." He said that German Foreign Minister Joachim von Ribbentrop was prepared to come immediately to Moscow. In the next few days there ensued a flurry of diplomatic exchanges, with the Germans presenting a draft nonaggression pact and the Russians presenting a counterdraft. Stressing the need for haste, Hitler in a letter to Stalin on August 20 accepted the Soviet draft, and von Ribbentrop proceeded to Moscow. On August 23 the non-aggression pact was signed and published to a stunned world. What was not published was a secret protocol drawing a dividing line for spheres of influence from Lithuania through the middle of Poland and giving the Soviet side a vague sort of primary interest in Southeastern Europe. On September 1 Hitler's war machine rolled into western Poland. On September 3 Britain and France declared war on Germany. The Soviets had now deflected the direction of Hitler's attack toward the West. And in practice they tried to keep it that way, faithfully making enormous deliveries of oil and other needed raw materials to Germany. At the same time, however, they tried to reinsure their security by extending their borders and their influence.

By September 9 Hitler's forces had overrun western Poland up to the agreed line of demarcation. A week later the Red Army invaded from the east and in a few days had occupied eastern Poland, capturing some 68,000 Polish officers and men. The pretext given was the need to protect the Belorussian and Ukrainian minorities in the territory. On the heels of this move the Russians demanded and received from the independent Baltic states of Estonia, Latvia and Lithuania the cession of military, air and naval bases.

At the end of the month, on Soviet invitation, Ribbentrop again visited Moscow, and on September 28 he and Molotov signed and published the following declaration:

Having signed today an agreement which finally settles the problems that had arisen from the disintegration of the Polish state and having thus laid the solid foundations for a lasting peace in Eastern Europe, the Soviet and German governments declare that the liquidation of the war between Germany on the one hand and Great Britain and France on the other would be in the interest of all nations. If, however, the endeavors of both governments remain fruitless, this will only show that Great Britain and France will bear the responsibility for continuing the war. If this war is to continue, the governments of Germany and the Soviet Union will consult each other on the necessary measures to be taken.

In his speech on this occasion, Molotov revealed that the Kremlin had levied demands on Finland for the cession of a strip of Finnish territory northwest of Leningrad and for a naval base on the Gulf of Finland. The Finns, he regretted, were being difficult. A month later the Red Army attacked Russia's small neighbor. But this was no pushover. The Finns resisted heroically and left nearly fifty thousand Russians dead on the battlefield before they were finally overwhelmed by sheer numbers the following March. Molotov again explained, in a speech to the Supreme Soviet on March 29, 1940. He claimed that "Already by 1939 Finland, and especially the Karelian Isthmus, had been converted into a *place d'armes* ready for an attack by third powers on the Soviet Union." He said that the peace treaty, under which Finland had ceded large slices of its territory to the Soviet Union, "properly insures the safety of Leningrad and of Murmansk and the Murmansk railway." Murmansk, as I pointed out earlier, is the only ice-free port of the Soviet Union in the North which communicates with the West.

Later that spring the Germans overran Scandinavia and Western Europe, entering Paris on June 14, 1940. A few days later the Red Army occupied the Baltic Republics and the northern and eastern provinces of Rumania, known as Bessarabia and the Bukovina. Despite some emerging difference of interests, especially in Finland and the Balkans, Soviet-German collaboration continued during this period in accordance at least with the letter, if not the spirit, of their agreement. In November, 1940, Molotov visited Berlin at German invitation. In these conversations it became apparent that the two parties did not share an identical view as to the shape of the future world each wanted. Hitler and Ribbentrop claimed that the British were as good as finished and that the main problem was the division of the British Empire; they tried to divert Soviet attention toward India. Indeed, in an air-raid shelter into which their meeting had been forced by British bombers, Ribbentrop actually handed to Molotov a draft of an agreement which would turn the so-called "Axis Pact" between Germany, Italy and Japan into a four-power pact under which the three Axis Powers would recognize the "present"—that is, expanded—frontiers of the Soviet Union, while Soviet "territorial aspirations" were defined as lying "in the direction of the Indian Ocean." Molotov was stony-faced as only Molotov can be, and noncommittal. After his return to Moscow and consultation with Stalin, Molotov on November 26 handed to the German Ambassador a statement saying that the Soviet Government was prepared to accept the draft four-power pact "subject to the following conditions":

1. Provided that the German troops are immediately withdrawn from Finland, which, under the compact of 1939, belongs to the Soviet Union's sphere of influence. At the same time, the Soviet Union undertakes to insure peaceful relations with Finland and to protect German economic interests in Finland (export of lumber and nickel).
2. Provided that within the next few months the security of the Soviet Union in the Straits [that is, the Turkish Straits] is assured by the conclusion of a mutual assistance pact between the Soviet Union and Bulgaria, which geographically is situated inside the security zone of the Black Sea boundaries of the Soviet Union, and by the establishment of a base for land and naval forces of the U.S.S.R. within range of the Bosporus and the Dardanelles by means of a long-term lease.
3. Provided that the area south of Batum and Baku in the general direction of the Persian Gulf is recognized as the center of the aspirations of the Soviet Union.
4. Provided that Japan renounces her rights to concessions for coal and oil in Northern Sakhalin.

I have quoted these provisos in full because they are important points of reference. They define the "aspirations" not only of the Soviet Government in 1940, but of the Czar's Government before that, and of Soviet governments today and in the future.

On the surface, Soviet-German collaboration continued, with the Russian side delivering millions of tons of products helpful to the German war effort: grain, cotton, oil, timber, manganese and chromium. But despite Soviet inquiries and expressions of "surprise," the Germans did not reply to Molotov's memorandum. On May 6, 1941, in an unprecedented move, Stalin took over as Chairman of the Council of People's Commissars, leaving Molotov with only the Foreign Affairs portfolio. The German Ambassador to Moscow reported to Berlin that he thought Stalin had done this because he wanted to continue good relations with Germany and felt that he could handle this question best himself. However, the shift was to no avail; we now know that on December 18, 1940, frustrated by continuing British resistance and probably influenced in part by his negative reaction to the Molotov provisos, Hitler had issued his top-secret orders for "Operation Barbarossa." In this he directed that "the German armed forces must be prepared to crush Soviet Russia in a quick campaign even before the conclusion of the war against England." And indeed, having accumulated vast forces and material in Eastern Europe during the spring, Hitler struck in the early morning hours of June 22.

On that same day it fell again to Molotov to make the announcement to the Soviet people. After stating the simple facts he said: "This unheard-of attack upon our country is perfidy unparalleled in the history of civilized nations. . . . The attack upon our country was perpetrated despite the fact that during the entire period of the operation of the treaty of nonaggression the German Government could not find grounds for a single complaint to the U.S.S.R. concerning observance of the treaty." Within twenty-four hours Molotov was followed on the airwaves by the hard-pressed British Prime Minister, Winston Churchill, who declared:

No one has been a more consistent opponent of Communism than I have for the last twenty-four years. I will not unsay a word that I have spoken about it. But all this fades away before the spectacle which is now unfolding. . . . Any man or state who fights on against Nazidom will have our aid. Any man or state who marches with Hitler is our foe. That is our policy and that is our declaration. It follows, therefore, that we shall give whatever help we can to Russia and the Russian people.

The Acting Secretary of State of the United States, Sumner Welles, issued a statement similar in substance but more cautious in tone, since we were not yet officially at war. In it he reiterated American opposition to dictatorships both Nazi and

Communist but declared that the immediate issue was whether Hitler's plan for universal conquest could be "successfully halted and defeated." "Consequently," he concluded, "any defense against Hitlerism, any rallying of the forces opposing Hitlerism, from whatever source these forces may spring, will hasten the eventual downfall of the present German leaders, and will therefore redound to the benefit of our own defense and security."

Twelve days later, on July 3, Stalin finally spoke. This was not the General Secretary of the Communist Party speaking, nor even the Chairman of the Council of Commissars of the Soviet Union. It was the head of the Russian nation, appealing to his people in unprecedented terms: "Comrades, citizens, brothers, and sisters, men of our army and navy! I am addressing you, my dear friends!" He continued:

How could it have happened that our glorious Red Amy surrendered a number of our cities and districts to the Fascist armies? Is it really true that the German-Fascist troops are invincible, as is ceaselessly trumpeted by boastful Fascist propaganda? Of course not! History shows that there are no invincible armies and never have been. Napoleon's army was considered invincible but it was beaten successively by Russian, English and German armies. Kaiser Wilhelm's German Army in the period of the first imperialist war was also considered invincible but it was beaten several times by Russian and Anglo-French forces and was finally smashed by the Anglo-French forces. The same must be said of Hitler's German-Fascist army today.

Stalin went on to explain that the initial German successes had resulted from perfidy and surprise. He pointed out that the Treaty of Nonaggression was designed solely to maintain the peace and that it had given the Soviet Union a year and a half to prepare its forces to "repulse Fascist Germany should she risk an attack on our country despite the pact." He said that by tearing up the pact and attacking the U.S.S.R. Fascist Germany had gained a certain advantageous position for its troops for a short period but had lost politically by exposing itself in the eyes of the entire world as a bloodthirsty aggressor. On the conduct of the war he said:

We must wage a ruthless fight against all disorganizers of the rear, deserters, panicmongers and rumormongers; we must exterminate spies, diversionists and enemy parachuters. . . . In case of the forced retreat of Red Army units, all rolling stock must be evacuated, the enemy must not be left a single engine, a single railway car, not a single pound of grain or a gallon of fuel. Collective farmers must drive off all their cattle and turn over their grain to the safekeeping of the state authorities for transportation to the rear. All valuable property . . . which cannot be withdrawn must be destroyed without fail. In areas occupied by the enemy, guerrilla units mounted and on foot must be formed, diversionist groups must be organized to combat the enemy troops, to foment guerrilla warfare everywhere, to blow up bridges and roads, to damage telephone and telegraph lines, to set fire to forests, stores and transports. . . . In this war of liberation we shall not be alone. . . . In this connection, the historic utterance of the British Prime Minister, Mr. Churchill, regarding aid to the Soviet Union and the declaration of the United States Government signifying its readiness to render aid to our country, which can evoke a feeling of gratitude in the hearts of our peoples of the Soviet Union, are fully comprehensible and symptomatic.

In fact, the Soviet Government started immediately a colossal transplantation of industry out of the European part of the Soviet Union threatened by invasion. It was a stupendous operation. Between July and November, 1941, over 1,500 industrial enterprises, including 1,360 large war plants, had been moved to the east—to the Volga area, to the Urals, to western Siberia, to Kazakhstan and Central Asia, along with most of the workers to go with the machines.

But the Germans rolled on. In a few months Leningrad was surrounded and was to undergo an epic siege and famine which decimated its population; nevertheless, it held. In mid-October the Germans were within forty miles of Moscow, and it seemed that the capital might momentarily fall. The diplomatic corps and many government departments were evacuated, and tens of thousands of Russians managed to flee to the east. Nevertheless, with every remaining man, woman or child mobilized not only to dig trenches but to bear guns, Moscow, too, held. On November 6, 1941, the traditional Revolutionary Day meeting was held in one of the large subway stations. Stalin again spoke, in

the name of what was now called "The Great Fatherland War."
He admitted Soviet casualties of nearly two million in these few
months and made his first appeal for the opening of a second
front in Western Europe. After calling the Nazis "wild beasts,"
he made another significant appeal to Russian national pride:

And it is these people without honor or conscience, these people
with the morality of animals who have the effrontery to call for the
extermination of the great Russian nation—the nation of Plekhanov
and Lenin, of Belinsky and Chernyshevsky, of Pushkin and Tolstoy,
of Gorky and Chekhov, of Glinka and Tchaikovsky, of Sechenov and
Pavlov, of Suvorov and Kutuzov.

The next day, in the same driving snow that had helped
stop the Germans outside Moscow, he addressed the armed
forces parading in Red Square in similar terms, declaring:

The enslaved peoples of Europe are looking upon you as their
liberators. Be worthy of this great mission! The war you are waging
is a war of liberation, a just war. May you be inspired in this war by
the heroic figures of our great ancestors, Alexander Nevsky, Dmitri
Donskoy, Minin and Pozharsky, Alexander Suvorov, Mikhail Kutuzov!

All in all, Stalin had come almost full circle from the Communist internationalism of Lenin and Trotsky, with his invoca-
tion of Russia's great writers and musicians and scientists and
its great national heroes: Alexander Nevsky, who had routed the
Teutonic knights in 1242; Dmitri Donskoy, who defeated the
Tatars in 1380; Minin and Pozharsky, who fought the Polish
invaders in the seventeenth century; and Suvorov and Kutuzov,
who led the forces against Napoleon. Great efforts were made to
spread Stalin's "Holy Russia" speech throughout the country by
radio and propaganda leaflets, even into the occupied territories.
There is no doubt that his remarks, made at the time and in the
circumstances they were, had a great effect in lifting popular
morale and stimulating determination in defense of "the fatherland."

Great Britain and the United States had moved rapidly to
implement their public declarations of support. A British military mission immediately proceeded to Moscow, and on July 12
a British-Soviet Treaty of Mutual Assistance was signed. At the

end of July President Roosevelt sent his close adviser, Harry Hopkins, to Moscow; he held a series of conversations with Stalin and Molotov. Stalin told Hopkins he thought that the front would be "solidified not later than October 1" and added that if the United States would give the Soviets "aircraft, guns and ammunition, we can fight for three or four years." Despite the gloomy prognosis of the American military attachés stationed in Moscow, Hopkins was impressed and arranged for a full-fledged American-British-Soviet conference in Moscow at the end of September to have a detailed look at Soviet needs in the light of the military situation then prevailing and the future outlook. This conference was held on schedule, with Averell Harriman representing the United States; it led to the initiation of a truly gigantic American Lend-Lease program.

As the war went on, Stalin continued to move in the direction of national and traditional policies. On October 9, 1941, a government *ukaz* abolished the institution of political commissars in the Red Army and established a single professional military command, with the political commissar reduced to being the commander's "deputy in the political field." The next steps were toward reconciliation with the Orthodox Church and the exploitation of the Church's influence, particularly among the mass of the peasantry, in stimulating the war effort, as well as in improving the Soviet image abroad. The reconciliation was at first informal but nevertheless effective; it was formalized by the conclusion of a sort of "concordat" in 1943 which allowed the Metropolitans to elect a Patriarch and to re-establish the Holy Synod as the organ of ecclesiastical government. The Patriarchate then was allowed to resume publication of its journal, which had been suspended in 1936, to own property and to open a number of theological seminaries and academies.

Another move toward traditionalism was the attempt to revive and exploit the old Pan-Slavic movement of the previous century. In August, 1941, a first "all-Slav" meeting was organized in Moscow. Much was made of the German war on "Slavdom," and the meeting called on all the Slav peoples to wage a holy war against Germany; the appeal was signed by "representatives of the peoples of Russia, Belorussia, the

Ukraine, Poland, Czechoslovakia, Yugoslavia and Bulgaria." Although this move was to encounter difficulties arising out of differences among the Slavic governments—particularly the Soviet Union and Poland—further meetings were held during the course of the war and much propaganda was issued.

The crowning gesture came on May 22, 1943, when the Presidium of the Executive Committee of the Communist International adopted a resolution dissolving the organization. Stalin explained the move to a Reuter's correspondent a few days later, saying:

It showed up the Nazi lie that Moscow intended to interfere with allies of other states or to "bolshevize" them. It also facilitated the work of all patriots for uniting all the progressive forces, regardless of party allegiance and political policy. It was particularly timely just when the fascist beast was exerting his last reserves of strength that the freedom-loving nations should organize a common onslaught on him, and so save all nations from the fascist yoke.

While this gesture was psychologically useful with the Soviet Union's new allies, especially Great Britain and the United States, it may be noted that the members of the Presidium who signed the resolution were all Communist exiles from their own European countries who were living in the Soviet Union—and who continued to live in the Soviet Union until they could return to Communist Party or government activities in their own countries after the war.

Meanwhile, American Lend-Lease supplies and equipment were flowing into the Soviet Union in truly colossal quantities. President Roosevelt had set up an interim credit of $1 billion after Harry Hopkins' visit to Moscow in July, 1941. This had been vastly increased after the Harriman mission in September–October of that year, and by the end of the war the total value of aid had reached something over $11 billion. The volume was great enough to fill 2,660 ships and weighed over 17 million metric tons. Half of this was military equipment, including over 7,000 tanks and nearly 15,000 aircraft, some 9,000 antiaircraft guns and 130,000 machine guns, as well as nearly 600 naval craft. It also included a number of complete industrial projects such as oil refineries, tire factories and aluminum and pipe-fabricating mills.

On the political side, the United States and Britain had in September, 1941, secured the adherence in principle of the Soviet Union to the Atlantic Charter drawn up by Churchill and Roosevelt at their mid-Atlantic meeting of August 14, 1941. This statement declared, in brief summary, that:

1. The two nations would seek no territorial aggrandizement.
2. No territorial changes would be made except through the freely expressed wishes of the peoples concerned.
3. Sovereign rights and self-government would be restored to those who had been forcibly deprived of them.
4. All states would have access to the trade and the raw materials of the world.
5. All nations would collaborate to bring about improved labor standards, economic advancement and social security for all.
6. A peace would be established to assure for all men in all lands freedom from fear and want.
7. The seas should be free to all.
8. The use of force would be abandoned and all nations which threatened or committed aggression would be disarmed.

These aims were formalized in a so-called Declaration of the United Nations on January 1, 1942, when twenty-six states allied against Hitler also pledged themselves to continue their joint war effort and not to make peace separately. The Soviet Union was included among those signatories. Then, at a conference of American, British and Soviet Foreign Ministers in Moscow in October, 1943, Secretary Cordell Hull, with Anthony Eden's support, got Molotov to accept a four-power—U.S., United Kingdom, U.S.S.R. and China—declaration of war aims, including the establishment of an international organization following the war to replace the defunct League of Nations set up after World War I. The Soviets were reluctant to accept the signature of the Chinese Government on this document but finally consented. The following year representatives of these four countries met at Dumbarton Oaks in Washington and drafted specific proposals for a charter for the new organization.

The Moscow conference of foreign ministers was the first of a series of tripartite meetings of the same kind. I shall not go into them in any detail. Generally speaking, they took up questions of war cooperation, with little cooperation forthcoming from the Soviet side. Later they dealt increasingly with political problems since, as military victory approached, the political dilemmas and disagreements over the postwar settlement sharpened. At a level above the CFMs—as we came to call them— were the three summit meetings of the heads of government: at Teheran in October, 1943; at Yalta in February, 1945; and at Potsdam, outside Berlin, in July, 1945. It should be noted that these summit meetings were all held either on the border of the Soviet Union, in the Soviet Union or in Soviet-occupied territory. There was nothing accidental about this. It was at Soviet insistence. While the pretext was that the location was determined by considerations of security and by the fact that Stalin as the Commander in Chief could not be far from his post, there is no doubt that this insistence was calculated to enhance Soviet prestige—by leaving an image of the West coming to the Soviets, rather than of the Soviets going to the West.

In all these meetings of the foreign ministers and the heads of government—and, indeed, in all the various operating organizations set up among the Allies—the Soviets displayed an enviable singleness and tenacity of purpose. It became increasingly clear that, apart from their immediate aim of getting the second front established, the Soviets were set on assuring themselves of the retention, after the war, of all the territories they had seized in Eastern Europe during the period of their collaboration with Hitler and, in addition, as many as possible of the objectives that Molotov had set forth in his memorandum of November 26, 1940, to Ribbentrop and Hitler. As they pursued these aims, the principal political disagreements which arose with the Western Allies related to Eastern Europe, and especially to Poland.

In its mortal peril after the German attack, the Soviet Government concluded an agreement on July 30, 1941, with the Polish Government-in-Exile in London, providing for the re-establishment of diplomatic relations and pledging mutual assistance against Hitlerite Germany. The Soviet Government specifically recognized the "Soviet-German treaties of 1939 as to territorial changes in Poland as having lost their validity." The Soviet side also granted amnesty to all Polish citizens then detained on Soviet territory, either as prisoners of war or on other grounds, and gave its consent to the formation in the Soviet Union of a Polish army under a commander appointed by the Polish Government-in-Exile. The implementation of this agreement was to put a continuous strain not only on Soviet-Polish relations but on relations within the alliance. At the time of the partition of Poland between Germany and Russia in 1939, several hundred thousand Poles had been taken prisoner or deported by the Russians; others had simply fled to the east, and there were Poles scattered literally all over the Soviet Union. According to Polish intelligence, some sixty thousand prisoners of war, including some twelve to fifteen thousand officers, were known to have been held, until the spring of 1940, at three specific camps in Soviet-occupied eastern Poland. But when Polish General Wladyslaw Anders arrived in the Soviet Union to re-establish a Polish army, no trace could be found of these officers. Despite unallayed suspicions on this question, and continuing political frictions, General Anders did manage to mobilize many thousands of Poles and to take them out through Iran to fight on the Western front.

The Russians were probably just as glad to see them go, for they had other plans, designed to lead to the establishment of a "friendly government" of Poland under Soviet influence and control. To this end they set up a Union of Polish Patriots headed by a Polish-born Soviet citizen, the wife of a Deputy Commissar of Foreign Affairs of the Soviet Union, and participated in by a number of Polish Communists and Soviet sympathizers, including many Jews who had suffered from anti-Semitism in prewar Poland. The captive Union was aided in publishing a newspaper and even in setting up a Polish division, named for the Polish national hero, Kościuszko, to fight with the Red Army.

Then came a bombshell.

In mid-April, 1943, the Germans announced that they had found several mass graves in the Katyn Forest near Smolensk containing the bodies of thousands of Polish officers. The Germans set up a much-publicized Committee of Inquiry, including some neutral members, which investigated and "proved" that these Polish officers had been shot by the Soviet authorities in the Smolensk area in the spring of 1940. When the Polish Government-in-Exile requested an impartial investigation by the International Red Cross, the Soviet Union immediately stigmatized this as a hostile attitude and broke diplomatic relations. After the liberation of the area in the fall of 1943, the Soviets set up their own committee, which in turn "proved" that the Germans had massacred the Polish officers in 1941. A Select Committee of the American Congress which examined the evidence in 1952 concluded that "the Soviet NKVD committed the mass murders as a calculated plot to eliminate all Polish leaders who subsequently would have opposed the Soviet's plans for communizing Poland." The Nuremberg war crimes tribunal found the Soviet evidence on the Katyn massacres much too thin to justify an indictment of the Germans.

In July, 1944, the Soviet Government created, as successor to the Union of Polish Patriots, a so-called Polish Committee of National Liberation, which was to become the core of the postwar Communist regime in Poland. Under British and American pressure, Stalin allowed the head of the London-based Polish Government to come to Moscow to confer with the new Committee, but their conversations were fruitless.

Another tragedy was about to befall. On August 1, as the Red Army was approaching Warsaw, the Poles in the capital rose against the Germans under the leadership of the Polish underground army directed by the Polish Government in London. But as the bloody battle progressed inside the city, the Soviet offensive halted. When the British and Americans wanted to drop supplies into the city from the air, the Soviet Government refused to allow these aircraft to land on Russian fields, since it did "not wish to associate itself either directly or indirectly with the adventure of Warsaw." Churchill and Roosevelt, greatly agitated, jointly appealed to Stalin, saying, "We are thinking of world opinion if anti-Nazi forces in Warsaw are in effect abandoned." Stalin still said "no." Finally, on October 2, the remaining Poles gave up to the Germans; 300,000 of them had perished. When the Red Army finally entered Warsaw, in January, 1945, more than nine-tenths of the city had been destroyed. The Moscow-organized Polish Committee of National Liberation took charge of what remained.

The final act of the Polish tragedy was to come in early 1945, after the Soviet forces had overrun all Poland. What was left of the Polish underground army and underground government after the Warsaw uprising was continuing to operate under the authority of the Polish Government-in-Exile in London. Stalin decided to decapitate the organization. The commanding general and fifteen other leaders were invited to meet a number of Russian officers, ostensibly to discuss the Yalta decisions on Poland and a *modus vivendi*. The meetings were a trap; all sixteen were arrested and taken to Moscow. When Churchill inquired about them, Stalin replied that they were charged with subversive activities behind the lines of the Red Army. London and Washington were greatly disturbed. President Truman asked the late President Roosevelt's man Friday, Harry Hopkins, himself a dying man, to undertake a new mission to Moscow. Hopkins told Stalin that in the last six weeks deterioration of American public opinion had been so serious as to affect adversely the relations between the two countries. He said this public opinion was affected by specific incidents—referring, of course, to the arrest of the Poles—and that "Poland had become a symbol of our ability to work out problems with the Soviet Union." Stalin would not budge on the arrest of the Poles, though Hopkins' efforts were probably responsible for getting them prison sentences, ranging up to ten years, instead of death. Hopkins' efforts also brought about agreement to admit a number of the London Poles into the Polish cabinet in Warsaw, and a so-called Government of National Unity was finally set up in June, after further hard negotiations which took place in Moscow. The Communists were in the key positions, and it would only be a few years before they took over completely.

Similar though less spectacular dramas were taking place in other parts of Eastern Europe. As the Red Army advanced, it carried in its baggage many of the members of the Executive

Committee of the Communist International who had voted to dissolve the organization in 1943, as well as many less prominent figures in the international Communist apparatus. The Baltic Republics were "liberated" and reclaimed for the Soviet Union in the fall of 1944. The NKVD came in on the heels of the Red Army and soon started the flow of Estonian, Latvian and Lithuanian "bourgeoisie" toward Siberia. The deportations were to amount to many tens of thousands within the next few years. In September an armistice was concluded with Finland; in deference to Western interest and sympathy with the Finnish people, the country was left politically independent but of course was in an extremely weak position vis-à-vis its great neighbor.

By the time the three heads of government met at Yalta in February, 1945, the Red Army controlled most of Eastern Europe, with Communist puppet governments installed in Rumania, Bulgaria and Hungary. Tito's partisans dominated the political scene in Yugoslavia. In the Far East, despite some major victories, what looked like a long road to Tokyo still lay ahead. At Yalta there was relatively little argument over the treatment of Germany. Unconditional surrender and an Allied Control Council to serve as a coordinating and policy organ for all Germany; allocation of zones of occupation in the country and sectors in Berlin to the three powers; and the basic principles regarding reparation arrangements—all these points were quickly agreed upon. Agreement was also reached on the proposed United Nations Charter, including the "veto" formula, in return for which Stalin received two extra voting memberships for the Ukraine and Belorussia. Churchill and our ailing President Roosevelt tried strenuously, but without success, to influence Soviet policy and moderate Soviet activities in Eastern Europe, especially in Poland. Secret agreement was reached on the side for the Soviets to enter the war against Japan three months after the defeat of Germany, subject to certain conditions, namely, the preservation of the *status quo* in Outer Mongolia, return of southern Sakhalin to Russia, internationalization of the port of Dairen, Soviet annexation of the Kurile Islands and the restoration to the Soviet Union of former Czarist

Russian rights in Manchuria. These stipulations were later accepted by China—under considerable American pressure—and incorporated into the Sino-Soviet Treaty of Friendship and Alliance signed on August 14, 1945.

A number of side effects of the war were to have a considerable influence on Soviet internal and external policies after the war and to create some problems inside the country which have still not been solved. As the massive Soviet armies moved into Eastern and Central Europe, millions of Russian officers and soldiers saw countries where housing conditions were much better than in Russia, where farms were more prosperous-looking and where there was still something to be bought in the shops. There is no doubt that these soldiers were affected by their contact with this better way of life. A series of articles in *Pravda*, in the fall of 1944, addressed itself to the men of the armed forces, trying to debunk with words what these men had seen with their own eyes: "We shall pass through many foreign countries yet," said *Pravda*. "Soldiers! Your eyes will often be dazzled; but do not be deceived by these outward signs of their so-called civilization! Remember, real culture is that which you carry with you."

Then there was the problem of the liberated areas in the Soviet Union itself, especially in the Ukraine. Here there had been widespread collaboration between the population and the Nazi invaders. Most observers, in fact, agree that if Hitler had instructed his forces to behave with restraint and understanding and had cultivated local tendencies toward national separatism, he could have won the population over to his side. Instead, he destroyed his chances by establishing a Nazi "superman" occupation regime and treating the local population as subhuman. Despite this, he left behind a revived nationalist sentiment and a widespread hope in the liberated territories, and even inside the army, with its millions of peasant conscripts, that the collective farm—or kolkhoz—system would be changed. The Party was worried about all this, and the Party magazine *Bolshevik* in its issue of October, 1944, dealt with the subject, saying in part:

The enemy has spread the poison of racialist theories in these areas, inciting Ukrainians against Russians, Belorussians against Lithuanians, Estonians against Russians, etc. The Nazi invaders have also inflamed private property instincts among these peoples. They liquidated the kolkhozes, distributed the land. . . . The Party organizations must intensify their work, especially in the rural areas of the Ukraine. They must remember that until this German-Ukrainian nationalism is completely weeded out, the restoration of the Ukrainian economy and national culture is impossible.

Another problem had arisen in the Communist Party itself. As a war measure, presumably considered an encouragement and incentive to the populace, admission to the Party had been greatly relaxed at the beginning of the war, particularly for the members of the armed forces. Between 1941 and 1944 some six million new members were admitted. The armed forces newspaper *Red Star* dealt with this subject in September, 1944:

The ideological training of members is now more necessary than ever. The Party organizations in the army have done much in this respect—but not enough. The Army's Party organizations largely consist of young Party members and are being replenished by more young men who have been tested as brave soldiers but who politically are insufficiently experienced. . . . Secondly, the front now runs through territories outside our borders. To find his way about in these new conditions, a Communist needs a sound ideological equipment more than ever.

Then there was the question of the return of the prisoners of war in German hands. These also numbered in the millions. In general, contrary to Western practice, the official Soviet attitude toward these men was that in allowing themselves to be captured they had not done their duty to the end—and that they were at least equivalent to deserters if not actually traitors. In addition, there were the millions of forced laborers who had been taken to Germany, particularly from the Ukraine; they, too, were regarded as deeply contaminated by their residence, however unwilling, in a bourgeois society and thus as subject to weeding out and to isolation from the communities of their origin. Even more extreme was the case of the tens of thousands who had joined armed units of the Soviet national groups which had been organized in Germany and actually participated in the fighting on the German side. Moscow sought to lay hands on these in order to liquidate anti-Soviet elements abroad and to inflict what it considered suitable punishment.

As victory came into sight, an even more fundamental problem arose. During the war the Communist Party had been glad enough to identify itself with the armed forces who were doing the fighting for "the fatherland"; but with the end of hostilities it was essential that the Party regain its identity and its ruling role, without rivalry from the army as a separate institution or instrument of political power.

Finally, the Soviet war losses were truly staggering. It is estimated that the Soviet Union lost in one way or another over twenty million people, including at least seven million soldiers. Some three million of this seven million are believed to have died in German captivity. Several million civilians perished under the German occupation, including about two million Jews who were massacred, and many thousands of the Soviet partisan fighters. Over a million people died in the besieged city of Leningrad alone, mainly of just plain starvation. Scores of cities and literally thousands of villages were completely destroyed. There was certainly not a family in the Soviet Union which was not directly affected, and their memories have been kept alive by a continuing stream of stories, novels and plays recreating the horrors and sacrifices of the war. It is small wonder that those of us who have lived amongst them have no doubt about the sincerity of the ordinary Soviet citizen's fervent desire for peace.

Toward the end of the war the Soviet Government did meet two commitments that it had made to the Western Allies.

The first was active participation in the United Nations Conference on International Organization which met in San Francisco from April 25 to June 26, 1945, on which date the United Nations Charter was signed. The United States had been particularly insistent on this. President Roosevelt and especially Secretary of State Cordell Hull were Wilsonians. They, and many members of Congress, both Democratic and Republican, in a sense represented the American guilt complex arising out of the Senate's rejection, thirty years before, of United States participation in the League of Nations set up after World War I. The Soviets were represented by a large and strong delegation headed by Foreign Affairs Commissar Molotov. It was, in fact, in San Francisco that I first saw and met many of the Soviet officials with whom I would be dealing frequently in years to come. Most of the major problems connected with the provisions of the Charter had been settled in advance at the conferences of foreign ministers and heads of government. Consequently, while there were a few flurries and minor differences to be ironed out in San Francisco, there were no major negotiating crises between the Soviet Government and its Western Allies.

Some people, after reading the eloquent statement of noble aims in the Preamble to the Charter, have questioned American eagerness to get the Soviets to subscribe to another fine statement at the very time they were violently flouting similar vows to which they had originally subscribed in the Atlantic Charter and the United Nations Declaration of January, 1942. This can, of course, be debated. However, on balance, most of us who have worked in the Soviet field feel that there is some hope that one day the Russian people will demand that some content be given to these forms and formulae of *real* democracy to which the Soviet regime has from time to time professed adherence.

The other commitment was participation in the final phases of the war against Japan. After amassing overwhelming military forces along the Korean and Chinese borders, the Soviet Government made a formal—if *pro forma*—declaration of war and launched an attack on August 8, 1945. Just two weeks later, on August 22, Stalin announced the surrender of the Japanese Kwantung Army. The Soviets had used airborne troops extensively, particularly to occupy the ports of Dairen and Port Arthur, where they feared the Americans might land before they could get there. Even after the formal surrender, the Soviet forces continued to penetrate into northern Korea and to occupy southern Sakhalin and the Kurile Islands. They captured nearly 600,000 Japanese prisoners, including 148 generals. They also seized enormous stores of Japanese military hardware and ammunition.

It must be said that the Soviets had managed to go very far toward the attainment of their original objectives. The question legitimately arises as to how this could have happened. I must say in all frankness that one of the reasons was the incredible ignorance, especially in the United States, about the nature of the Soviet Communist regime and its aims in the world. Aside from this, there is something in the American character that seems to impel us, if we have to cooperate with someone, not only to overlook his faults but actually to like him. The propaganda that was turned loose in the United States during the war years to popularize our Soviet allies went to truly incredible extremes. One of the most nauseating was the movie made on the basis of Ambassador Joseph Davies' book, *Mission to Moscow*. President Roosevelt fully shared these weaknesses. Even worse, he also had the illusion that his own personality could bring "Uncle Joe" around to cooperation with the West not only during the war but afterward. His efforts were like dropping water on granite. And at Yalta, mortally ailing, he was certainly no match for the wily and astute Stalin.

In any case, once we were in the war, the only way the Russians could have been stopped from seizing the Eastern European countries and eastern Germany would have been for us to have got there first. Churchill, in fact, had proposed early on that the Western second front be established through the Balkans, having precisely this contingency in mind, I am sure. He even put the project forward at Teheran, where it was stiffly opposed by Stalin; and while the long argument there was carried on in purely military terms, it is clear that Stalin recognized Churchill's political motives. On the other hand, the United States military—and even some of the British—felt strongly that purely military considerations dictated landings across the Channel in France. President Roosevelt supported them—and so it was done. As to the Far East, our military pessimistically estimated that the war with Japan would be long and costly in American lives. They considered that it would be worth a high price to induce the Soviets to come in. Many of our diplomatic professionals, knowing Soviet aims and ambitions, were arguing that, far from paying the Russians to come in, one couldn't pay them enough to keep them out. And in the end it is clear that the Japanese would have capitulated even if the Russians had not come in at all.

CHAPTER V

Postwar Reversion to Orthodoxy:
Origins of the Cold War

In July, 1945, on the heels of the Nazi surrender, the title of
Moscow's principal international propaganda organ—a weekly
magazine published in multiple languages—was changed from
War and the Working Class to *New Times*, a title which it still
carries. I recall that observers at the time had the impression
that the new title was half of an expression—"New times, new
tasks"—that Lenin had once used in introducing a policy shift
in revolutionary days, but I have not been able to locate the
precise quotation.

On February 9, 1946, about six months after the capitulation of Japan, Stalin made a so-called "pre-election" speech in
Moscow. He reiterated the Marxist view that wars are an "inevitable result of the development of world economic and social

political forces on the basis of modern monopoly capitalism."
The Second World War was thus not "a casual occurrence," he
continued, but "the entry of the Soviet Union into the war
against the Axis states could only enhance, and indeed did
enhance, its anti-Fascist and liberation character." Stalin then
posed the question: "And so what are the results of the war?"
He answered himself:

We concluded the war with complete victory over the enemies.
That is the chief result of the war. But that result is too general and
we cannot stop at that. . . . Our victory means, first of all, that our
Soviet social order has triumphed. . . .

Second, our victory means that our Soviet State system has
triumphed, that our multilateral Soviet State has stood all the trials
of war and has proved its vitality. . . .

Third, our victory means that the Soviet armed forces have
triumphed, that our Red Army has triumphed, that the Red Army
bore up heroically under all the trials of war, utterly routed the
armies of our enemies and came out of the war as a victor. [Voice
from the floor: "Under the leadership of Comrade Stalin!" All rise—
stormy, prolonged applause, rising to an ovation.]

Now a few words about the Communist Party's plans of work
for the immediate future. As is known, these plans are set forth in
the new Five-Year Plan which is shortly to be endorsed. The principal aims of the new Five-Year Plan are to rehabilitate the ravished
areas of the country, to restore the prewar level in industry and
agriculture, and then to surpass this level. . . . I have no doubt that
if we give our scientists proper assistance they will be able in the
near future not only to overtake but to surpass the achievements of
science beyond the boundaries of our country.

As regards plans for a longer period ahead, the Party means to
organize a new mighty upsurge in the national economy, which
would allow us to increase our industrial production, for example,
three times over as compared with the prewar period. . . . Only
under such conditions can we consider that our homeland will be
guaranteed against all possible accidents. That will take three more
Five-Year Plans, I should think, if not more. But it can be done and
we must do it.

While the world press did not appreciate the full significance of this statement at the time, its import was clear to the
Western Allied governments. They realized that it was a Soviet

renunciation of the wartime alliance and reversion to Communist orthodoxy—and thus an official confirmation of the course the Soviet Union had already started to follow in its policy and its activities. Indeed, it recalled to them Stalin's earlier formulation of Moscow's basic international concept, in an interview with an American labor delegation on September 9, 1927, when he had said:

. . . In the further progress of development of the international revolution, two world centers will be formed: the socialist center, attracting to itself all the countries gravitating toward socialism, and the capitalist center, attracting to itself all the countries gravitating toward capitalism. The fight between these two centers for the conquest of world economy will decide the fate of capitalism and Communism throughout the whole world.

Commenting on the international situation to the State Department two years later, when I was Chargé d'Affaires at the American Embassy in Moscow, I introduced my report with these observations:

At the end of World War II, the Soviet Union stood at a crossroads. The U.S.S.R. had gained not only awed respect as a major power but also acceptability and a great reservoir of good will among practically all the peoples of the world. She might well have lived in peaceful possession of her wartime conquest and gains, to a great extent the gift of her grateful and trusting allies. Had she chosen to play the international game cooperatively, these would today be essentially little less than what she now possesses and they could have been securely held in a calm and peaceful world.

Instead, the Soviet Government chose the opposite course—that of doubly ensuring and heavily exploiting its gains, of rejecting and antagonizing its wartime allies, of preparing the Soviet peoples for further conflict and of redoubling efforts to increase the scientific and industrial war potential of the U.S.S.R. Wartime cooperation with the capitalist West now receives no mention, efforts of Soviet propaganda writers on this period being devoted entirely to painting a war history picture in which the Western Allies, in particular the United States, were utilizing every opportunity to prepare positions for a third world war against the Soviet Union and the countries of the "people's democracies." While the continued existence of capitalist states is cited as a danger requiring the maintenance of the

Soviet State apparatus, the old concept of capitalist encirclement, no longer worthy of the Soviet giant, has been gradually allowed to lapse. It has been replaced by the Communist concept of the development of "two world centers," as described by Stalin, and the theme of "time is on our side" is frequently mentioned. In other words, the picture of a world divided into "two camps," which Stalin in 1927 drew for the future, he today considers to have arrived.

The deliberate choice which the Soviet leaders made after the end of World War II has in fact resulted in the creation of the two hostile centers predicted by Lenin and Stalin. It can only mean that the Kremlin has chosen to launch "the struggle between these two centers" which is "to decide the fate of capitalism and Communism throughout the whole world."

Why, then, did Stalin deliberately make such a decision?

The answer lies, in the first instance, in the question of "legitimacy." It is important always to remember that Bolshevik rule in the Soviet Union constitutes a monopoly of political power in the hands of a minority, by the Bolsheviks' own admission and definition. Even today membership in the Communist Party is limited to about fourteen million people, or around 5 percent of the population. After the war, despite the wartime inflation of membership, the percentage was even lower. Since time immemorial it has been regarded as essential that every sovereign justify his "right to rule." In the days of monarchies, including Czarist rule in Russia, "legitimacy" stemmed from the accepted doctrine of the "Divine Right of Kings." In our Western democracies, legitimacy flows from the will of the people, as expressed in the freely adopted constitutions and free choice, through secret elections, of those who govern. In the case of the Communist countries, legitimacy is based on Marxist-Leninist-Stalinist doctrine, which justifies "the dictatorship of the proletariat" in the name of the "inevitable world revolution" against capitalism and imperialism. If the capitalist and imperialist states were no longer the mortal enemy to be struggled against and overthrown, then there would be no justification for the continued maintenance of the single Communist Party system and for depriving the Soviet people of the right freely to choose their own leaders.

Apart from the theoretical question of restoring the legitimacy of his rule, Stalin faced a lot of practical problems which had to be solved in order to re-establish the primacy of the Party and the iron control which the dictatorship had exercised before the war. The army had developed into a kind of semiautonomous political institution and its Commander in Chief, Marshal Georgi Zhukov, the defender of Moscow and Stalingrad and the conqueror of Berlin, had become a national hero. He was certainly second to no one in the Soviet Union, except perhaps Stalin, in popularity and prestige. The millions in the armed forces had been exposed to the "corrupting influence" of the European world, and Stalin could not have failed to remember the lesson of the subversive activities in the Czar's armies after the defeat of Napoleon a century and a quarter before. Millions of others who had been taken to the West as prisoners or slave laborers had caught the same moral ferment from their contact with foreign countries. Then there were those who under German occupation had regained their lands and learned again about the benefits of private trade. Moreover, Stalin and the Party were undoubtedly taken aback by the eagerness with which the population at large had embraced the wartime return to traditionalism and nationalism. Finally, just from his personal point of view, Stalin could no longer feel the need of comparison with his historic predecessors like Peter the Great. He himself was now the greatest conqueror in all Russian history. All in all, there was a ferment abroad, stirring a vague yearning for freedom and a new curiosity about the outside world.

On the international plane, it might be said that the final summit conference at Potsdam was less the last act in the history of cooperation within the wartime alliance than the first act in the long "Cold War" already beginning between its Eastern and Western members. Stalin and Molotov led the Soviet delegation. Churchill and Eden headed the British delegation from July 17 to 28, when they were replaced by Prime Minister Clement Attlee and Foreign Secretary Ernest Bevin, who had come to power as a result of the British general elections. For the United States it was a new President, Harry Truman, and a new

Secretary of State, James Byrnes. In any event, the atmosphere was very different from that which had prevailed at Teheran and Yalta. Military problems had been replaced on the agenda by political questions. The United States and British delegations charged that the Soviet policies being pursued in Eastern Europe—in Poland, Rumania, Hungary and Bulgaria—were in direct violation of the Yalta "Declaration on Liberated Europe." The United States strenuously objected to recognizing the puppet regimes in Bulgaria, Hungary and Rumania. The Russians countered with similar charges about British and American activities in Greece and in Trieste.

On the main problem—Germany—there was agreement on essential administrative measures, including the establishment and operation of the Allied Control Council for all Germany, and on certain principles relating to the "demilitarization, denazification and democratization" of the country, but there was no agreement as to what these great words meant. Seeking to maximize their war reparations, the Soviets sought central machinery for this purpose which would give them access to the industrially rich valley of the Ruhr River, located in the Western zones of occupation. This was rejected by the West, and it was then agreed that the bulk of Soviet reparations should be taken from the Soviet's own Eastern Zone of occupation and from German properties seized throughout Eastern Europe. This decision in effect negated the concept of dealing with Germany as a whole and amounted to a first step toward a partition of the country along the boundaries between the Western zones of occupation and the Soviet Zone. A formalized Council of Foreign Ministers was set up to deal with the question of the preparation of peace treaties with Germany and the other enemy countries.

It was at the end of the Potsdam Conference that President Truman told Stalin privately about the American development of the atom bomb, just a few days before the first one was dropped on Hiroshima. In his book, *Russia at War*, Alexander Werth reports that on the following day, August 7, Stalin summoned to the Kremlin the five leading Russian atomic scientists and ordered them "to catch up with the United States in the minimum time, regardless of cost." The head of the secret police, Lavrenti Beria, was put in charge of all the laboratories and industries which were to produce the Soviet bomb. We now know that Beria, in fact, did much more than just prod the scientists and workers. His secret police, by startlingly successful penetrations of the American atomic center at Los Alamos and subversion of scientists who had actually worked there, laid their hands on most of the basic plans and designs for an atomic bomb. And we now know that this was a major factor in enabling the Soviets, contrary to our estimates and expectations, to explode their first bombs as early as August, 1949.

Even before Potsdam was over, serious differences had started to arise with respect to the implementation of the Yalta agreement for the return of displaced persons—prisoners of war, slave laborers and others—to their countries of origin. We had believed we were talking about facilitating the return to the Soviet Union of Soviet nationals who *desired* to return, plus, of course, such individuals as might be charged specifically with war crimes. After serious incidents arose in which Soviet displaced persons violently resisted repatriation—a few even committed suicide—the American military authorities were given orders to repatriate nobody forcibly except actual war criminals, since it was entirely contrary to our principles to force the return of individuals who did not wish to go or who felt they would suffer for their political opinions. These orders directly contradicted the Soviet concept of the relation of the citizen to the state, which declared (in the 1947 published edition of the *Criminal Code of the Russian Federation*): "The refusal of a citizen of the U.S.S.R. . . . to return within the borders of the U.S.S.R. is to be regarded as flight into the camp of the foes of the working class and peasantry and to be classified as treason." Such persons, the Code continued, "are outlawed" and went on: "Outlawing involves the confiscation of all the property of the outlaw and the shooting of the outlaw within 24 hours after his identification." Another article (58-1c) of the Criminal Code added that "adult members of the traitor's family . . . are subject to deprivation of voting rights and exile to remote regions of Siberia." Consequently, the Soviet authorities protested this American action as an unfriendly and even hostile act.

A whole series of other developments on the international scene reflected more and more Stalin's directive to dissociate the U.S.S.R. from its wartime Allies and his determination to expand the limits of Soviet empire and influence to the maximum.

I became intimately involved in one of the first developments, in my capacity as Assistant Chief of the old Division of Near Eastern Affairs, which at that time included Greece and Turkey. Greek monarchists and republicans had been squabbling and the King of Greece had not returned to Greece after its liberation. Early in 1945 the Greek Government appealed to the four principal Allies to supervise elections which would determine the direction of political evolution in postwar Greece. The British, French and Americans accepted, but, despite our urging, Moscow rejected the invitation. We realized that this was designed to lay the basis for Russian charges, later, that the Allies had imposed a solution in Greece. Consequently, we were particularly careful to organize our observation of these elections in a way that would effectively forestall such charges. We set up some five hundred tripartite observation teams in jeeps and had their operations scientifically plotted by the most experienced experts in polling and public-opinion sampling we could find in our three countries. On the heels of the actual election, on March 31, 1946, we were able to get out promptly such a detailed, documented and convincing report on the honesty and regularity of the proceedings that we, in fact, frustrated in advance the Soviet propaganda.

At about the same time, in the summer of 1945, after a hostile propaganda campaign, the Soviet Government brought forth the demands on Turkey that had been foreseen in the Molotov memorandum to Hitler's Foreign Minister Ribbentrop on November 26, 1940. Moscow demanded that the Turks agree to a revision of the Montreux Convention on the Turkish Straits —connecting the Black Sea and the Mediterranean—by giving the Soviet Union a base and a share in the defense of the straits; and to the cession to the Soviet Union of two old Turkish provinces lying on the Soviet border, Kars and Ardahan. After some playing for time and consultation, the Turks rejected both demands with British and American support.

It was Soviet support of guerrilla warfare in Greece, following their refusal to participate in the observation of the Greek elections, and their hostility toward Turkey, that led to the Truman Doctrine of March 12, 1947. In his message to Congress on that date, requesting legislative authority to grant economic and military aid to the two countries, President Truman declared:

I believe that we must assist free peoples to work out their own destinies in their own way. . . . We cannot allow changes in the *status quo* in violation of the Charter of the United Nations by such methods as coercion, or by such subterfuges as political infiltration. In helping free and independent nations to maintain their freedom, the United States will be giving effect to the principles of the Charter of the United Nations.

The requested legislation was promptly passed.

The Truman Doctrine was the first formal, official declaration that the United States was prepared to accept the Soviet challenge and to "contain" the Soviet drive for expansion of its territories or influence. The challenges were to continue and the confrontations they engendered were to become more and more serious, with very few breathing spells in between.

However, Stalin's Cold War was waged not only abroad but also against his subjects in the Soviet Union. The lengths to which he went in those postwar years to weed out every suspect element of the population and to isolate the Russians from any foreign contact or any foreign news were truly beyond belief. Even living in the midst of it all, we found it hard to realize that what we were witnessing was real and not just the product of our own nightmares.

When my wife and I sailed on the Swedish ship *Gripsholm* in January, 1947, we found aboard a dozen or more Soviet citizens who had been members of the Soviet delegation to the third meeting of the Council of Foreign Ministers, held in New York at the end of 1946. This had been a relatively successful meeting, which had reached agreement on the text of peace treaties with Italy, Rumania, Bulgaria, Hungary and Finland. In the relaxed and secure atmosphere of the boat, our Soviet fellow travelers were congenial and we spent much time together. After we got to Moscow, we invited them to come to drink and dine with us. We had not a single response. A couple of months later, when I went to sessions of the fourth meeting of the CFM, taking place there in Moscow, I did see most of them again— but mainly from a distance. They fled as I approached, professing not to hear my friendly greeting. It was then borne in on me, for the first time, that back on their home territory they dared not be seen talking with me and thus be obliged to explain how they had come to know me.

However, the aura of the wartime alliance had not yet entirely dissipated. The word had not yet flowed down to non-official Russians. In that first year we came to know a number of the ballet and theater people and writers, and many of them came regularly to the Sunday night movies we arranged at the embassy residence. But the clamps were being screwed down.

On June 10, 1947, the press published a decree of the Supreme Soviet entitled "On Liability for Divulging State Secrets and for Losing Documents Containing State Secrets." This decree provided for sentences of up to twenty years in corrective labor camps for the accidental or unintentional revelation—that is, "in cases where this cannot be described as treason or espionage"—of any information considered to be a "state secret." And the nature of a "state secret" was described in fantastic detail. Since the mentality which could produce such a document is beyond the understanding—or even imagination— of most Americans, I quote the decree at what may seem to be considerable length but is, in fact, a highly abridged version:

Information of a Military Character

1. Organization, numbers, location, state of preparedness, armament, military training, material and financial security, mobilization and operational plans for armed forces (or any unit thereof).
2. Composition, extent, condition, location and purpose of state stores of all types, of state material and food reserves as well as reserves of manpower subject to mobilization. . . .

3. Mobilization and operational plans, calculations, projects and measures . . . on lines of state administration, industry, transport, communications and all other branches of national economy (as a whole and for individual departments, undertakings and territories).

4. Location, equipment, financial and industrial plans, condition, productive capacity, nomenclature and extent of production in war industry as well as other industry engaged in filling military orders.

5. Discoveries, inventions and improvements, research and experimental work in the field of technical and other means of defense.

6. Documents, papers and publications relating to defense.

Information of an Economic Character

7. Information which the Council of Ministers decides should be kept secret: on industry as a whole and in its various branches, on agriculture, trade and means of communication.

8. State of monetary reserves, information on current balance of payments and plans for financial operations of the U.S.S.R. Information on location and method of storing and transporting precious metals belonging to the state reserve, foreign currency and banknotes.

9. Plans and planning proposals relative to import and export of different types of goods; state of exportable reserves of various goods.

10. Geological reserves and production of nonferrous and rare metals and earths.

Information on Discoveries, Inventions and Improvements of a Nonmilitary Character

11. Discoveries, inventions, technical improvements, research and experimental work in all branches of science, technology and national economy.

Other Information

12. Information relative to negotiations and agreements between the U.S.S.R. and foreign states as well as to any other measures in the field of foreign policy and foreign trade not contained in officially published data.

Neither for the foreigners nor for Russians was there much left to talk about after the publication of this decree. Ninety percent of the information that most governments in the West publish about themselves and the state of their societies was strictly taboo. It was literally to skate on thin ice even to talk about the weather, since this had a bearing on such forbidden subjects as agricultural production.

In January, 1948, the *Official Gazette* of the Supreme Soviet published a decree designed to cut off all the informal official contacts which had grown up during the war. It prescribed that "relations of state institutions of the U.S.S.R. and their officials with institutions and officials of foreign states will be effected through the Ministry of Foreign Affairs of the U.S.S.R. . . . Relations in any other form may take place only if directly laid down in a law or in an international treaty." This latter provision was obviously intended to take care of Soviet representation at the United Nations. I might also note that Stalin in 1946 had dropped the titles of "Commissars" and "Commissariat" and replaced them by "Minister" and "Ministry," the very bourgeois titles Lenin had found to be "vile and hackneyed." At the same time, he had prescribed uniforms for the employees of most ministries, from diplomats right down to the coal miners, thus enhancing the impression of a garrison state. But the import of the decree was clearly not lost even on the population at large. This was particularly true after the publication in April of an interpretative article by the Prosecutor General of the U.S.S.R.—the official who had run the purge trials. It was addressed to local prosecutors throughout the country and said, in part:

Taking into consideration the chief, decisive tasks facing the Soviet State and, first of all, the task of the fulfillment of the postwar Five-Year Plan, the activity of the prosecuting institutions should be directed toward: a resolute intensification of the struggle against misappropriation of state and public property; every possible strengthening of state discipline; combating violations of military duty, labor discipline and discipline in transport; combating other grave crimes, such as speculation, bribery, robbery, production of home-brew, etc. . . . Resolute struggle against cases of divulging state secrets and all kinds of violations of the duty of the Soviet citizen connected with loss of vigilance and with obsequiousness to things foreign . . .

From 1946 to 1948 the government conducted a great crackdown on the intelligentsia, known to history as the *Zhdanovshchina,* from the name of the Politburo member, Andrei Zhdanov, who headed the operation. In the press and in public meetings, writers, authors, dramatists, actors, composers, were accused of "formalism" or "cosmopolitanism" or "bourgeois tendencies." The victims either groveled and recanted publicly, or they disappeared into the Siberian labor camps. Others were disappearing, too, without such public show, including quite a few of our Russian contacts and of our Russian employees at the embassy, especially those who had American relatives or a claim to American citizenship. If we went to look for them, we found their rooms closed with a police—MGB—seal and no one in the vicinity willing to say a word. If we inquired at the Foreign Ministry, we were told that the relationship between the Soviet Government and the Soviet citizen was no business of a foreigner; this was an internal affair. Secret police frame-ups were repeatedly staged against our American employees. These attempts were recurrent features of the scene, and everyone had to be constantly on the alert. We had been in Moscow only a few months when my wife went out for a visit in Western Europe. Within an hour after my return from accompanying her to the airport, the telephone rang and I found a sort of honey-blond voice inviting me to a party—and this in spite of the fact that telephone numbers themselves were considered classified information and that there had been no telephone book published in Moscow since the late 1930s. Despite all our precautions and warnings to the staff, we lost two members to this kind of entrapment.

Then there was the question of travel inside the Soviet Union. Restrictions on travel by foreign officials had been allowed to lapse during the war and had not been formally reimposed. However, we found that it was becoming impossible to get tickets on public transportation to go practically anywhere. We even made a sort of game of it. We would assign a member of the staff to go every day, regularly, to the railway station and to the travel bureau—called Intourist—to try to buy tickets for a given destination. The Russian employees at these agencies played the game, too. They invented the most fantastic excuses for not being able to supply tickets, in spite of the fact that they knew our officers had already seen them sell tickets to Russians standing in the queue ahead of them and would see them selling to others behind them. After about a month, our officer would skip a day and return the next day. Then he would be greeted with the most effusive speeches: "Oh, what a shame that you didn't come yesterday: for the first time in a month I could have taken care of you." However, during this period we *could* go as far as our private automobiles would take us and bring us back, since there was no way to obtain gasoline along the roads. Frequently, the police would escort us, but all the same we managed to have some very revealing journeys within a radius of a hundred-odd miles out of Moscow itself. Even within this radius, we saw some of the labor camps and prisoners working on such projects as laying pipelines and cables, mostly supplied under Lend-Lease and bearing American trademarks. We even ran into some German scientists who had been imported for the production of rockets.

It is a typically Russian paradox that travel opened up only after official travel restrictions were promulgated late in 1948. Two-thirds of the country was banned to foreigners, but a third of the Soviet Union is still a lot of territory. And after the rules were published, the little ticket agent knew that he would not get in trouble if he sold you a ticket to a permitted destination. However, they caught us on the more intimate type of automobile travel we had been doing around Moscow; such travel was now prohibited to foreigners beyond a twenty-five-mile radius from the center of the city.

By the time we left the Soviet Union, in the summer of 1949, the only Russians we were able to see, except on purely official occasions, were those who worked for us in one capacity or another, such as language teachers, domestic servants or laborers. Of course, they simultaneously kept close tab on us for the Soviet secret police. This was a well-recognized arrangement on both sides. We tried to cooperate with the servants by letting them know where we were going and whom we were inviting, so they could devote more of their attention to us and less to their other masters. This isolation of foreigners continued until after Stalin's death, with a few other official harassments thrown in for good measure. Just before I left, in 1949, the Soviet Government initiated a massive jamming operation against the Voice of America and other free-world broadcasts. Then, in 1951, it declared Ambassador George Kennan *persona non grata,* after he had been in the Soviet Union only a few months, in reprisal for some critical remarks he had made to correspondents at the Berlin airport. Finally, in 1952, it ordered the removal of the American and British Embassy offices from their locations overlooking the Kremlin to more remote sites.

But however harassed the foreigner might feel in Moscow, he realized that the Soviet citizenry were faring much worse and his heart bled for them. In addition to the mandatory internal passport, which tied all citizens to their place of abode, the "labor book" was reintroduced, tying the bearer to his place of employment and recording his every tardiness or failure to meet his assigned quotas of work. A new decree prohibited marriages between Soviet citizens and foreigners; it was, of course, applied retroactively, making it impossible for many Russians who had legitimately married British and American spouses during the war to leave the country until after the death of Stalin.

Overnight, on November 16–17, 1947, a monetary reform was clamped on, which wiped out the savings of everyone, particularly the peasants who had been allowed some latitude during the war and immediate postwar years in selling their produce in free markets. Ten rubles, whether in cash or in banks, had to be turned over for one new one. Rationing was in effect, and the rations were meager. When the rationing was discontinued at the end of 1947, with great fanfare, the situation got even worse. There were, in fact, practically no goods to buy, and the move simply meant that people had to get up earlier and spend more hours in the endless queues which were a feature of postwar Moscow.

By the time we arrived in Moscow we had already learned

of the drastic treatment being accorded the returning prisoners and slave laborers and even members of the armed forces returning from the West. The minimum was a prolonged "brainwashing"; the maximum was death. The bulk of these people spent time in labor camps, followed by forced residence in remote parts of Siberia or Central Asia. When we visited these distant areas in 1965, we met some who had never been back to their places of origin; by the time they were free to do so under Khrushchev, they were no longer interested; they had lost their family ties.

We also learned on that first arrival of the blow which had fallen, after the turn of the tide in the war, on two "autonomous states"—the Crimean Tatar and the Chechen Republics—whose conduct during the war had not been to the liking of the Kremlin. These small national entities had been utterly obliterated by the mass arrest and deportation of their entire populations. (Later we learned other national groups had suffered the same fate.) A similar operation went on while we were in Moscow. On June 15, 1949, at 2 A.M., as is the custom, the MVD descended in force on the inhabitants of the Caucasus border region. Every inhabitant of Greek, Iranian, Turkish or Armenian origin, whether or not he was a Soviet citizen, was given two hours to pack his essential possessions preparatory to leaving. After this, he was loaded into an MVD truck, taken to the nearest railroad line, herded with sixty-nine other deportees into a small Russian cattle car and started on a long voyage eastward toward an unknown destination. The deportees, who numbered in the tens of thousands, included thousands of loyal Soviet citizens, many of whom had been repeatedly decorated for heroism in the war. Great Russians were not included, even though they might be the husband or wife or other close relative of the deportees whose foreign origin had brought them a vote of lack of confidence and a grim fate from the all-powerful rulers in Moscow. The great purge of the "bourgeois cosmopolitans" among Soviet teachers, writers, scientists and other intellectuals during the winter of 1948–49 was similarly directed mainly toward the removal of a non-Russian element in the population, namely the Jews, to whom is ascribed a separate nationality even though they do not inhabit a separate national territory. (Few Jews live in the so-called Jewish Autonomous Oblast, a kind of wildwoods ghetto set up by Stalin in 1928 in Far Eastern Siberia.)

General Bedell Smith tells of a conversation he had with Marshal Vasili Sokolovsky when he was General Eisenhower's Chief of Staff and the Marshal was commander of Soviet forces in Germany. General Smith spoke critically of the methods of political repression which the Communists were already employing in the occupied areas of Central Europe. Marshal Sokolovsky looked at him with surprise and said: "I don't see why you should criticize. We aren't doing anything there that we don't do at home." And indeed, as General Smith discovered when he came to Moscow as Ambassador, the practice is no secret. The official Communist periodical *Bolshevik* in its issue of April, 1947, spelled it out this way:

> The Soviet State determines the behavior and activity of Soviet citizens in various ways. It educates its Soviet people in a spirit of Communist morality, of the system which introduces a series of legal norms regulating the life of the population, imposing interdictions, establishing encouragements, naming a punishment for the violation of these norms. The Soviet State stands guard over these legal norms with all its power. The conduct and activity of the Soviet people is also determined by the force of a public opinion which is created by the activity of numerous public organizations. In creating public opinion, the decisive role is played by the Communist Party and the Soviet State, which, through various media, formulate public opinion and educate the workers in a spirit of socialist awareness.

From my personal observations of the origins of the Cold War, the only confusion left in my mind is some uncertainty as to whether Stalin's principal target was his former allies abroad or his own subjects at home.

But it is only since my return from my second tour in Moscow, at the end of 1966, that I have gradually become aware that what seemed to me a clear picture is being clouded by an overlay of historiographic confusion. Some half-dozen books have appeared in recent years, and more continue to appear, which seek to revise the generally accepted view of the Cold

War as the American response to Soviet expansion, an unsought and unwelcomed development in international affairs. The general implication of these works is that a war-weary and war-weakened Russia was bound to seek cooperation with the West, but that the hostility of Western leaders toward Communism made it impossible for them to understand this fact and thus to act in a way which would have prevented the Cold War.

Supporting the general thesis, these "revisionists" put forward a number of concrete propositions. One argued that the abrupt termination of Lend-Lease in August, 1945, and American failure to act on a Soviet suggestion that we lend them $2 billion for postwar reconstruction left Stalin little choice but to act essentially as he did. Now Lend-Lease was strictly a wartime instrument, and it was terminated after the war not just for the Soviet Union but for all our other allies as well. The action may well have been too abrupt, but it was not discriminatory. Moreover, goods already in the pipeline were allowed to go forward, and in the case of the Soviet Union this included nearly $300 million worth of goods of utility in the civilian economy. In the conditions prevailing at the time it could hardly have been expected that any American administration could justify the lending of $2 billion of the taxpayers' money to a government which had already made amply clear its hostile intentions. However, immediately after the war, we did contribute about $250 million worth of aid, *gratis*, to the devastated regions of the Soviet Union through UNRRA—the United Nations Relief and Rehabilitation Administration. And when we launched our massive European recovery program in mid-1947, it was not we but the Russians themselves who ruled the Soviet Union and its Eastern European satellites out of the benefits of the Marshall Plan.

Another "revisionist" says that "the Cold War cannot be understood simply as an American response to a Soviet challenge, but rather as the insidious interaction of mutual suspicions, blame for which must be shared by all." Now, as a matter of fact, I think that these mutual suspicions were responsible for much of the aggravation of the Cold War, but I cannot accept that they were responsible for its origins.

Still another "revisionist" asserts that after the United

States acquired the atomic bomb, American diplomats tried to take back what they had implicitly conceded at Yalta, with respect to Eastern Europe. As I said in my report to the State Department back in 1948, which I quoted earlier, the Soviet Union could have retained all its essential positions in Eastern Europe without conflict with its wartime allies. All Moscow really had to do, for example, was to behave toward Poland, Rumania, Hungary and Bulgaria as it did toward Finland. It was Stalin's insistence on installing his own Communist puppets and establishing totalitarian political systems without the consent of the people that produced the friction.

Finally, one "revisionist" maintains that American policy in the early years of the Cold War must be seen as part of a larger pattern of American globalism reaching as far back as 1898. This thesis would seem to be one of American "capitalist imperialism" dating back to the Spanish-American War. Without defending our adolescent foray into the world at that time—it's not really defensible—the facts of history simply don't support the corollary conclusion. The tragedy of the history of the first forty years of this century was rather the American retreat into isolationism and neutrality and its failure even to make a good try at helping to prevent World Wars I and II.

One could go on listing and rebutting these revisionist propositions piecemeal, but it hardly seems necessary or worthwhile. In the last analysis, they all share one basic and mortal defect. This is their authors' ignorance of the other half of the equation—the nature of the Soviet system, and in particular the necessity of "legitimacy" for Communist minority rule in the Soviet Union. These revisionist writers have thus been unable to understand the inexorable compulsions that caused Stalin to make the decisions he did make in the conduct not only of foreign but also of domestic affairs.

CHAPTER VI

The Khrushchev Era

Unlike Lenin, who had a long lingering illness before he died, Stalin's death was unexpected. Just two months before, he had announced the discovery of a so-called "Doctors' Plot." A group of Kremlin physicians had been arrested and soon confessed not only to having poisoned the late Andrei Zhdanov and another Politburo member, both of whom had earlier been supposed to have died natural deaths, but also to be engaged in the slow poisoning of some of the top military commanders. Zhdanov was the man who had conducted the purge of the intellectuals which began in 1946. He had at that time, and up to his death in 1948, also been considered as the most likely heir apparent to Stalin—that is, by everyone except perhaps Stalin himself. Far from preparing for his succession, Stalin had given the appearance of expecting to rule forever and had continued carefully to balance off one of his henchmen against the other. In fact, it was generally believed that the announcement of the "Doctors' Plot" in January, 1953, was only the opening gun in another round of purges.

Then came the news that "during the night of March 1–2 Comrade Stalin suffered a hemorrhage of the brain." Three days later and some six hours after the event, came the announcement of Stalin's death on March 5, 1953. It was signed by all the members of the Party's top leadership. It was an extraordinary document. After eulogizing Stalin as "Lenin's comrade-in-arms and the inspired continuer of Lenin's cause, the wise teacher and leader of the Party and the peoples" it went on in a tone of alarm:

Our task is to guard the steel-like and monolithic unity of the Party as the apple of our eye. . . . High political vigilance, irreconcilability and stalwartness in the struggle against inner and outer foes . . . The most important task of the Party and the government is to insure uninterrupted and correct leadership. . . . The greatest unity of leadership and the prevention of any kind of disorder and panic . . .

These are indeed strange words, and words highly revealing as to the nature of the Communist system, to us in the West, who are accustomed to a legitimate, constitutional ordering of such matters.

In a system where there is no constitutional or other accepted arrangement, the question of succession can only be determined by a naked struggle for power, as we saw in the case of Stalin's succession to Lenin. However, in circumstances such as those of Stalin's death, the first reaction of the principal potential rivals for succession to power has to be—and was—to huddle together and present at least an outward façade of unity in order to protect the system itself, on which they all depend. Stalin had neglected and even debased the top organs of the Party, and operated as an individual despot. Indeed, at the Nineteenth Party Congress in 1952 Stalin had abolished the Politburo and replaced it with a large and formalist "Presidium" of twenty-five members; he had also expanded the Secretariat of the Party to ten members. The government, too, had become a sort of amorphous organization under Stalin.

With surprising speed, the leading heirs agreed on new and tighter arrangements, both within the Party and within the government. The designation of Presidium—instead of Politburo—was retained, but its membership was cut back to ten. The Secretariat was reduced to five members. The head of the government, that is, Chairman of the Council of Ministers, was to have four first deputies and one just plain deputy.

In these first drawings, Georgi Malenkov ostensibly came out on top, inheriting not only the chairmanship of the Council of Ministers but also the ranking secretaryship of the Party. On the government side, his first deputies were, in hierarchical order:

- Lavrenti Beria, who was also restored as Minister of Internal Affairs (MVD)
- Vyacheslav Molotov, who was also restored to the post of Foreign Minister
- Nikolai Bulganin, who also took over the Ministry of Defense
- Lazar Kaganovich, who supervised the industrial sector.

Anastas Mikoyan was the unnumbered Deputy Prime Minister and also handled the Ministry of Trade. Old Red Army Marshal Voroshilov was given the chairmanship of the Presidium of the Supreme Soviet, an honorific post but one which is considered technically chief of state—that is, equivalent to King or President. And to give some popularity to the new leadership, Marshal Zhukov was recalled from his provincial exile and made First Deputy Minister of Defense.

The group also decided on the funeral arrangements. Khrushchev was to be chairman of the affair, calling on Malenkov, Beria and Molotov, in that order, to deliver the funeral orations.

Malenkov had been the most visible rival to Zhdanov as heir apparent, and this was evidently the reason for his initial primacy. However, he was fenced in, on the government side, by Beria and the battery of deputy prime ministers and, on the

Party side, by Khrushchev, who had two of his cohorts with him in the five-man Secretariat while Malenkov had only one hench-man. Malenkov's position soon began to crumble. On March 10, the day after Stalin's funeral, the Party's newspaper *Pravda* re-published a three-year-old photograph from which other leading personalities had been blocked out in order to show Malenkov standing alone with Stalin and Mao Tse-tung. Just how it was maneuvered, no one knows—except maybe Khrushchev—but this pictorial evidence of Malenkov's ambitions and pretensions was probably a factor in his being compelled within the next few days "to request" his release from his duties as Secretary of the Party. Thus, shortly after Stalin's disappearance from the scene, we have a picture of four separate contenders sitting atop the four pillars supporting Bolshevik power: Malenkov in con-trol of the government bureaucracy, Beria of the police, Zhukov (nominally under Bulganin) of the armed forces and Khru-shchev of the Party. The question was who would topple whom and straddle all the pillars.

Beria lasted one hundred days. He had promptly started to purge the secret police throughout the country and to make sure that his own trusted appointees were in the key slots. He had also started to cultivate the national minorities. Among other activities, he had initiated a purge in the Ukrainian Party and governmental apparatus which led to the ouster of some of Khrushchev's henchmen in that republic. While he sought firm control of the police apparatus as essential for his own protec-tion, his colleagues felt increasingly menaced as they saw this dread instrument of Stalin's rule grow stronger and stronger in Beria's hand. So in late June they arrested him. A *Pravda* edi-torial on July 10 threw the whole book of charges at him. He was accused: of using the MVD organs against the Party and its leadership and against the government, by selecting workers for his ministry for their "personal loyalty to himself"; of under-mining the collective farms and creating difficulties in the country's food supply; of undermining the multinational Soviet state by activating "bourgeois-national" elements in the Union republics; even of becoming "a hireling of foreign imperialists," with whom he allegedly plotted to restore capitalism. The article declared that "It is necessary to check systematically and un-remittingly the activity of the Ministry of Internal Affairs. This is not only the right but the direct duty of Party organizations."

The liquidation of Beria was not an easy operation. It re-quired the cooperation of Marshal Zhukov in supplying army tanks and trusted military personnel, since the MVD itself con-trolled the internal-security and frontier defense troops, com-posed of hundreds of thousands of men, including at least fourteen well-armed divisions.

About five months later, in December, 1953, the Soviet press announced that Beria and several of his co-conspirators had been tried—essentially on the charges listed in the *Pravda* article—and sentenced to death; and that the sentences had been carried out. However, Khrushchev later told a visitor from the French Socialist Party that Beria had been shot immediately after his arrest, there in the Kremlin, in the presence of the entire Party leadership. Khrushchev is reported to have de-scribed the affair this way: ". . . we found ourselves in a difficult position. Evidence for his consignment to a court we still did not have, yet to leave him at liberty was impossible. We came to the unanimous decision that the only correct measure for the defense of the Revolution was to shoot him immediately. This decision was adopted by us, and carried out on the spot. But we felt much easier when, some time after his condemna-tion, we received sufficient and irrefutable evidence of his guilt."

Malenkov's strategy was to strengthen the government apparatus, protecting it against encroachments by the Party, while trying to weaken the power of the Party Secretariat and to keep the Party's Central Committee uninfluential, as it had become in Stalin's days, at least until he could add more bureaucrats to it. Khrushchev, modeling his strategy on that used by Stalin in the 1920s, countered by installing his own adherents throughout the Party apparatus, particularly as lead-ers of the regional Party organizations, appointing to these positions many who had been associated with him in his earlier work in the Ukraine and in Moscow. Within the Presidium, Khrushchev countered Malenkov's governmental programs, notably his effort to centralize economic administration. While Malenkov favored increased reliance on experts and intensive cultivation in agriculture, Khrushchev proposed a crash program in the virgin and reclaimed lands to achieve a quick increase in grain production. When Malenkov attempted to improve supplies of consumer goods rapidly, Khrushchev charged him with retarding the essential growth of heavy industry. After the Soviets mastered the hydrogen bomb in 1953, Malenkov took the position that war had now become so dangerous that it required a negotiated settlement of the Cold War. Khrushchev countered that thermonuclear weapons rather increased the danger of a surprise attack, and called for increased defense spending and vigorous conduct of the Cold War.

By these tactics Khrushchev gained the support of the Stalinist conservatives—Molotov, Kaganovich, Bulganin and Voroshilov. They had been alarmed by Malenkov's initial bid for full power after Stalin's death, and were also concerned by his subsequent effort to establish new courses in domestic and foreign policies. So on February 8, 1955, less than two years after Stalin passed from the scene, Malenkov, outmaneuvered and outvoted in the Party Presidium, publicly confessed his "guilt and responsibility for the unsatisfactory state of affairs in agriculture" and his "insufficient experience in local work . . . and in the direct guidance of individual branches of the national economy." Again "at his own request," he was relieved of the chairmanship of the Council of Ministers and made Minister of Electric Power Stations. Khrushchev proposed Bulganin as successor, and so he became. Some time later it was announced that Malenkov had been removed from his ministerial post and made director of a power station in Central Asia. For the next dozen years he completely disappeared, but I now hear he has been seen back in Moscow, apparently a retired, finished old man.

After this performance, some of the conservatives who had supported Khrushchev against Malenkov began to realize that they, like Frankenstein, were helping to create a monster who threatened their own positions. So they reversed their course and set out to try to strengthen the government, i.e., the Council of Ministers, and to limit Khrushchev's authority as First Secretary of the Party. Khrushchev handily won the first round against them, and in July, 1955, strengthened his position by bringing more of his supporters into the Party Presidium and into an enlarged Central Committee Secretariat. On the heels of this initial victory, Khrushchev issued a call for the Twentieth Party Congress, to be held in Moscow the following February. This was half a year earlier than required by the new Party statutes, which had been amended to provide for Party congresses once every four years. By the time the Congress was held, Khrushchev had managed to get his own man, one Dudorov, placed as Minister of the Interior and to prepare a slate for elections to the new Central Committee of the Party in which 113, or 44 percent of the total membership of 255, were "new"—that is to say, Khrushchev's nominees.

The Congress itself was a one-man show. Khrushchev made the opening and closing addresses. He made the official report, in which he borrowed from the deposed Malenkov and developed further the line of "peaceful coexistence" between capitalist and Communist powers. He also revised Communist doctrine to proclaim the noninevitability of war and to accept the possibility of "separate roads to socialism" for the various Communist countries. And he made his famous "secret speech" denouncing Stalin, the text of which was to be released to an astounded world by the United States State Department a few months later, on June 4, 1956.

Despite Khrushchev's domination of the Twentieth Congress, the opposition had not given up, and its maneuvers continued. Just over a year later they managed to outvote him in the Party Presidium and demanded his resignation. He refused to accept the Presidium decision, arguing—and making it stick —that it was the Central Committee which had elected him and which alone could withdraw his mandate. Since he had already filled that body with his own supporters, Khrushchev won handsomely. This was in June, 1957. Under Khrushchev's influence, the Central Committee then went on to denounce and expel from all Party posts the so-called "anti-Party group"—meaning "anti-Khrushchev" group—of Malenkov, Kaganovich, Molotov and Shepilov. Dmitri Shepilov had been Khrushchev's own nominee to replace Molotov as Foreign Minister but had inexplicably joined the opposition. Shortly after, Molotov was sent to Outer Mongolia as Ambassador, and the other three were exiled to minor provincial posts. Khrushchev was now in a position to fill the vacancies in the top Presidium with his own appointees. By October, Khrushchev felt strong enough to charge Marshal Zhukov with "Napoleonic tendencies" and have the Central Committee oust the Marshal from its membership and from the Presidium.

Who was this "Grand Tactician," as he was called by Lazar Pistrak, his first English-language biographer?

Nikita Sergeyevich Khrushchev was born on April 17, 1894, in Kalinovka, a village in southwestern Russia near the Ukrainian border and the coal mines of the Don River basin. His extraction seems to have been mainly Russian, though there well may have been some Ukrainian or Polish admixture. His early life was undoubtedly grim. "I began working when I learned to walk," he has said. "Till the age of fifteen I tended pigs, then sheep, and then the landlord's cows." He seems to have had a smattering of elementary schooling in the village parochial school, where the subjects taught were described as: "Law of God, church songs, Russian reading and writing, elementary knowledge of arithmetic and elementary information on the history of the Church and of the Fatherland." Nikita's father, Sergei, was one of the first generation of poor peasants who left the land, after the emancipation of the serfs, to become industrial laborers. Sergei went to the nearby town of Yuzovka and was employed as a miner at a British-owned iron works. When Nikita was fifteen, that is, in 1909, his father brought him to Yuzovka and got him a job in a Belgian-owned metallurgical plant to learn the trade of fitter. Here he was to remain and work for a good many years to come. He seems to have escaped the mobilization for the Czar's armies during World War I, thanks to his occupation as fitter. Such mechanics were very rare in Russia at that time and considered hard to replace. And even the many official biographies later published did not portray him as playing any role in the 1917 Revolution. Sometime during the revolutionary period, however, he does seem to have come under the influence of Lazar Kaganovich and to have joined Kaganovich's budding Bolshevik organization in Yuzovka, and to have seen some service with the Red Army. After the Civil War, he returned to Yuzovka, apparently under Party instructions to mobilize the miners to increase production. Meanwhile, Khrushchev had been married to a first wife, who, after bearing him a son and daughter, perished in the great famine of 1921.

Ambition seems to have started stirring in Khrushchev at about this time, together with a realization that if he wanted to get ahead in the Party machine he would have to have more education. So in 1922, at the age of twenty-eight, he entered one of the evening school "workers' faculties" which had been set up by the Bolshevik regime. In his three years at the workers' school Khrushchev became secretary of the Party cell and developed into a full-fledged political agitator. When Lenin died in 1924, Khrushchev seems to have guessed right and to have tied his star to the Stalinist kite, for he began to rise rapidly in the Party hierarchy. By 1926 he was recorded as a delegate to the All-Ukrainian Party Congress, making fiery speeches demanding punishment of Stalin's opposition. In 1927 he was promoted to Party work in the Ukrainian metropolis of Kiev. Meanwhile, in 1924, Khrushchev had married his second and present wife, Nina Petrovna. From later conversations with them, my wife and I had the impression that she had been one of his teachers in the workers' school at Yuzovka and that she had been a great influence in stimulating him to continued self-improvement and to advancement in Party work.

In 1929 Khrushchev received an assignment as a student at the Party's Industrial Academy in Moscow. He was apparently sent there to do more than study, however, for he was soon reported to be active in purging the academy of Stalin's opponents. And he seems to have done his work well there, because in 1931 he was made First Secretary of the Party organization in one of the important districts of Moscow. By 1935 he had become First Secretary of both the Moscow city and provincial Party committees and a junior (candidate) member of the top-level Politburo. On the occasion of this promotion the Party newspaper *Pravda* referred to him as "an outstanding representative of the postrevolutionary generation of Party workers educated by Stalin." This was the period of Stalin's great purges. Khrushchev is on record with many speeches at this time, referring to Stalin as the "genius of humanity" and "great leader"—in Russian *vozhd*—a word which is the precise equivalent of *duce* in Italian, the term used for Mussolini, and of *führer* in German, the title accorded Hitler. He fervently supported the terror and the verdicts of the purge trials against, in his own words at the time, "the vile, base, Trotskyite degenerates." Again and again, he called for "vigilance against the enemies of the people," that is, suspected or potential opponents of Stalin. "Let the enemies know," he cried, "that no matter how deep down they may sit in their burrows, we will uncover and annihilate them, and reduce to dust every last one of them, and scatter them to the four winds so that not even a trace will remain." But Khrushchev must have performed services more material than public oratory during the purges, for in 1938 Stalin sent him back to the Ukraine to "deal the final blow" to these so-called "enemies of the people" in that region. Within a year, 163 of the 166-man membership of the Ukrainian Party's Central Committee had been liquidated, and Khrushchev was promoted to full membership of the Politburo.

Then came World War II. Khrushchev was not a member of Stalin's inner war cabinet—the State Defense Committee—but he was a member of the "military committee," and served as a kind of roving political commissar on the front in the Ukrainian sector. In 1939 he played a major role in the occupation of eastern Poland, the deportation of suspect elements of the local Polish population to Siberia and the purge of the Polish Communist Party in those territories. After the Nazi attack, he worked with the major military headquarters in his territory and was active in applying the "scorched earth" directives and in organizing "partisan" resistance behind the enemy lines. For these activities he received the rank of lieutenant general and a chestful of awards. After the Nazi retreat the following year, Khrushchev became both Chairman of the Council of Ministers and First Secretary of the Party in the Ukraine.

Here he faced truly colossal tasks: of rehabilitating the longest-occupied and most devastated region in the Soviet Union; of suppressing nationalist and separatist tendencies revived by the Nazis; of recollectivizing the land the Nazis had distributed back to the peasants; and of restoring the primacy of the Communist Party. At one point, in 1946, he had a serious setback. Apparently as a result of intrigues by Malenkov and other rivals back in Moscow, he was subjected to official Politburo criticism for alleged deficiencies in "ideological work" and in the restoration of agricultural production in the Ukraine. His old fellow townsman, Lazar Kaganovich, was sent down to Kiev to replace Khrushchev as First Secretary. However, in less than a year Khrushchev had managed to regain his footing and his Party position, and Kaganovich returned to Moscow. (Kaganovich, who had helped and protected Khrushchev in Yuzovka, then in Moscow, now in the Ukraine, is the same man whom Khrushchev later accused of hideous crimes and had expelled from the Party as a member of the "anti-Party group.") In December, 1949, Stalin recalled Khrushchev to Moscow as a Secretary of the All-Union Central Committee of the Party, nominally to be in charge of the Party's agricultural work but politically to be a counterweight to Malenkov, and, with Malenkov, to provide a counterweight to Beria. The stage was then set for the drama in which Khrushchev dislodged his rivals one by one from the other pillars of Soviet power and ended up on top not only of the Party but also of the government, the police and the armed forces.

We came to know Khrushchev and his wife well over a period of something more than five years, from July, 1959, when I accompanied Vice President Nixon to the Soviet Union and participated in many hours of talk between them; through Khrushchev's visit to the United States in September of that year when my wife and I, along with the Cabot Lodges and others, escorted him and his wife and party for two weeks around the United States; and until he fell from power in October, 1964, after I had been Ambassador in Moscow for more than two years. I remember pictures of him taken in the 1930s when he was supervising the building of Moscow's subways. He was already bald but reasonably well built by Russian standards. By the time I came to know him personally, he was fat and had developed such an enormous paunch that he was nearly as broad as he was tall and waddled like a duck when he walked. He was a very short man, maybe five feet three inches. To me he came to be the embodiment of the almost untranslatable Russian adjective *khitryi*. It is usually applied, not without a certain respect and appreciation, to the Russian peasant. According to the dictionary it means sly, cunning, artful, intricate or wily. But it really means more than this; it also means unscrupulous, smart, clever, quick-witted. Roll all these adjectives into one and you have the *khitryi* Khrushchev—a bootlicker or a bully as circumstances required, a demagogue and opportunist always. He also had, just to complicate his character, a colossal inferiority complex—because of his origins, because he was not an Old Bolshevik and just because he was a Russian—and, typically, this inferiority complex was more often than not manifested in assertions of superiority. He had an inexhaustible store of Russian proverbs and folk tales and an unrivaled vocabulary of the unprintable, earthy expressions in which the Russian language is so rich.

Khrushchev had certainly read less of Marx and Lenin—though probably not of Stalin—than I, and yet he was a kind of "true believer," as Eric Hoffer uses the term. I used to think that he must say to himself every night before he went to bed that the system which had enabled him—a poor shepherd boy—to mount to the throne of the Czars had to be right. He had done more than his share of Stalin's dirty work of cruel, ruthless oppression and bloody purges. Yet he somehow remained a common man with a common touch, and when he came to power, he was the first ruler in Russian history who actively sought popularity. One could detect in conversation with him that he was not unaware—and, indeed, seemed to take satisfaction in the fact—that some of his acts would inevitably influence the evolution of Russian society toward greater humanism.

Khrushchev was also a sort of "man in a hurry," maybe because he was already sixty-two when he reached the height that Stalin had attained in his late forties; consequently, he was sometimes impetuous or even reckless—though, as we have already seen in connection with his Ukrainian setback and near-overturn by his Presidium colleagues in 1957, he was adept at regaining his footing.

Bertram Wolfe has an apt and pithy description of Khrushchev's behavior in these first years after Stalin's death in his book *Khrushchev and Stalin's Ghost.*

The belief that *knowledge is power* having been reversed under totalitarianism to read *power is knowledge*—Nikita Sergeyevich Khrushchev now began to exhibit mastery in every field. He told architects how to design buildings; builders how to use concrete, steel, pre-fab units and other materials; managers how to apply technology to industry; urban youth where to invest their energy and enthusiasm; farmers where corn must, should and would have to grow, why the range must be ploughed up, why cotton growing regions should eat rice instead of potatoes; milkmaids how many times a day a cow should be milked; artists what the proportions are in which sincerity and party spirit should be mixed to produce a proper work of art.

At the same time, Khrushchev became the authority on foreign affairs. With Bulganin, and sometimes with Mikoyan, or Shepilov, or Furtseva, he went to Warsaw and Prague, to China, Yugoslavia, Geneva, East Germany, India, Burma and Afghanistan in his pre-Congress buildup. He has since been to England, and to Yugoslavia once more, and has several times hinted that he would like to visit the United States.

On these trips he ignored the Foreign Minister, reducing Molotov to a mere head of chancery. He showed a readiness to speak off the cuff, to combine rude threats and sharp-tongued jests with lip service to "peaceful coexistence." From Geneva, where the Soviet Government had pledged itself to give serious consideration to all-German free elections, he went straight to East Germany to assure its Communist rulers that those who expected him to abandon any Communist positions (not the least of which was a belief in controlled elections) could "wait until the crayfish whistles on the mountain top." While touring India, Burma and Afghanistan he engaged in the crudest anti-British propaganda that had been heard since Lenin's day. "Had the British contributed a single thing in Asia?" he asked, and answered, "No, they were gangsters in the full sense of the word." When he was getting ready for his trip to England, he repeated his "gangster" statement with the bland assurance that there was "nothing in it which could offend Britain or the British people or the British Government." He told India that he supported its claims on Kashmir; Afghanistan that he supported its claims on Pushtunistan, to be carved out of Pakistan; and to the Pakistan Government he gave a four-paragraph lecture on the might of the Soviet hydrogen bomb, beginning, "We do not want to frighten anybody," and ending, "we are certain that the people of Pakistan will realize what an invidious position their country has placed itself in and will draw the right conclusions." In England he openly threatened the British political leaders and then their leaders in trade with the speed of Moscow's jet planes and the accessibility of England to "ballistic intercontinental missiles which cover such distances in several minutes." While Zhukov and Bulganin continued a polite exchange of notes with Eisenhower, Khrushchev called the President's open-skies proposal, "little different from espionage," then added rudely: "We do not like people to look into our bedroom." The sharp jests and homely figures of speech are a welcome relief from Stalin's intolerable dullness, but he yields nothing in rudeness or bellicose tone. These incautious, off-the-cuff utterances show how little he troubles to consult with the "collective leadership." It is the self-confident voice of authority.

Khrushchev did get his bid to visit the United States and many other parts of the world. The reasons for these many journeys abroad were ostensibly political, the promotion of so-called "peaceful coexistence" and the selling of Communism. But I have a feeling that the impetus in large part derived from the unbounded curiosity of almost every Russian—and Khrushchev was typical in this respect—about the outside world.

The secret speech which Khrushchev delivered on the night of February 24–25, 1956, to the 1,436 delegates assembled in the Kremlin for the Twentieth Congress of the Communist Party of the Soviet Union was not intended for publication and has never been published in the Soviet Union. However, most Soviet citizens learned about it promptly through the domestic "grapevine" and more fully, after its publication, through foreign radios; and much of the content of the speech did come out publicly in further speeches made at the Twenty-second Party Congress a few years later. The version published in the West was prepared "for the information of foreign Communists" and may, therefore, be somewhat softened and expurgated. Even so, it is one of the most startling and extraordinary indictments of individual despotism in all the annals of human history. I cannot go into the scores of cases of murder, repression, terror, torture, falsification, genocide, recounted in the sixty-odd pages of the published document, but the following excerpts suggest the general content and flavor:

. . . it is impermissible and foreign to the spirit of Marxism-Leninism to elevate one person, to transform him into a superman possessing supernatural characteristics, akin to those of a god. Such a man supposedly knows everything, sees everything, thinks for everyone, can do anything, is infallible in his behavior. Such a belief about a man, and specifically about Stalin, was cultivated among us for many years. . . . Stalin acted . . . by imposing his concepts and demanding absolute submission to his opinion. Whoever opposed this concept or tried to prove his viewpoint and the correctness of his position was doomed to removal from the leading collective and to subsequent moral and physical annihilation. . . . Stalin originated the concept "enemy of the people." This term automatically rendered it unnecessary that the ideological errors of a man or men engaged in a controversy be proven . . . the only proof of guilt used, against all norms of current legal science, was the "confession" of the accused himself; and, as subsequent probing proved, "confessions" were acquired through physical pressures against the accused . . . he abandoned the method of ideological struggle for that of administrative violence, mass repressions and terror. . . . Mass arrests and deportations of many thousands of people, execution without trial and without normal investigation created conditions of insecurity, fear and even desperation. . . . Stalin, using his unlimited power, allowed himself many abuses, acting in the name of the Central Committee, not asking for the opinion of the Committee members nor even of the members of the Central Committee's Political Bureau . . . many Party, Soviet and economic activists, who were branded in 1937–1938 as "enemies," were actually never enemies, spies, wreckers, etc., but were always honest Communists; they were only so stigmatized and, often, no longer able to bear barbaric tortures, they charged themselves (at the order of the investigative judges-falsifiers) with all kinds of grave and unlikely crimes . . . of the 139 members and candidates of the Party's Central Committee who were elected at the 17th Congress, 98 persons, i.e., 70 per cent, were arrested and shot (mostly in 1937–1938). . . . The same fate met . . . also the majority of the delegates to the 17th Party Congress. Of 1,966 delegates . . . 1,108 persons were arrested on charges of anti-revolutionary crimes, i.e., decidedly more than a majority. . . .

The vicious practice was condoned of having the NKVD prepare lists of persons whose cases were under the jurisdiction of the Military Collegium and whose sentences were prepared in advance. Yezhov would send these lists to Stalin personally for his approval of the proposed punishment. In 1937–1938, 383 such lists containing the names of many thousands of Party, Soviet, Komsomol, Army and economic workers were sent to Stalin. He approved these lists.

A large part of these cases are being voided because they were baseless and falsified . . . from 1954 to the present time the Military Collegium of the Supreme Court has rehabilitated 7,679 persons, many of whom were rehabilitated posthumously. . . .

Stalin was a very distrustful man, sickly suspicious; we know this from our work with him. . . . Possessing unlimited power, he indulged in great willfulness and choked a person morally and physically. A situation was created where one could not express one's own will. . . .

The power accumulated in the hands of one person, Stalin, led to serious consequences during the Great Patriotic War. . . . Stalin put forward the thesis that the tragedy which our nation experienced in the first part of the war was the result of the "unexpected" attack of the Germans against the Soviet Union. But, comrades, this is completely untrue. . . .

Many facts from the prewar period clearly showed that Hitler was going all out to begin a war against the Soviet state. . . . Despite . . . grave warnings, the necessary steps were not taken to prepare the country properly for defense and to prevent it from being caught unawares. . . . Very grievous consequences . . . followed Stalin's annihilation of many military commanders and political workers during 1937–1941 because of his suspiciousness and through slanderous accusations. . . . The policy of large-scale repression against the military cadres led also to undermined military discipline, because for several years officers of all ranks and even soldiers in the party and Komsomol cells were taught to "unmask" their superiors as hidden enemies. . . . All this brought about the situation which existed at the beginning of the war and which was the great threat to our Fatherland . . . due to the faulty methods of directing the nation and the party by Stalin himself. . . .

Stalin considered that he never erred, that he was always right. He never acknowledged to anyone that he made any mistake, large or small, despite the fact that he made not a few mistakes in the matter of theory and in his practical activity.

. . . the mass deportation from their native places of whole nations, together with all Communists and Komsomols without any exception . . . was not dictated by any military considerations . . . no man of common sense can grasp how it is possible to make whole nations responsible for inimical activity, including women, children, old people . . . to use mass repression against them, and to expose them to misery and suffering for the hostile acts of individual persons or groups of persons. . . .

Stalin became even more capricious, irritable and brutal; in particular his suspicion grew. His persecution mania reached unbelievable dimensions. . . . Let us also recall the "affair of the doctor-plotters." . . . Stalin . . . issued orders to arrest a group of eminent Soviet medical specialists. . . . Stalin personally called the investigative judge, gave him instructions, advised him on which investigative methods should be used; these methods were simple— beat, beat and, once again, beat. Shortly after the doctors were arrested, we members of the Political Bureau received protocols with the doctors' confessions of guilt. . . . When we examined this "case" after Stalin's death, we found it to be fabricated from beginning to end. . . .

The cult of the individual acquired such monstrous size chiefly because Stalin himself, using all conceivable methods, supported the glorification of his own person . . . the impression was created that Stalin always played the main role, as if everywhere and always Stalin had suggested to Lenin what to do and how to do it. . . . Stalin never traveled anywhere, did not meet city and kolkhoz workers. . . . He knew the country and agriculture only from films. And these films had dressed up and beautified the existing situation. . . .

Why did Khrushchev—a creature of Stalin—make such a speech? Nobody quite knows the answer to this question, perhaps not even Khrushchev himself. However, a number of factors certainly entered into the decision:

First, the temptation to blame a predecessor for past crimes and to try to dissociate oneself from responsibility.

Second, by implication, the opportunity to excuse oneself

in advance for not being able to solve the problems the predecessor left behind.

Third, the need to appease the as yet unarticulated but very
real anti-Stalinism which had risen throughout the country after
the easing of the police oppression and terror.

Fourth, the demand of the army for the vindication of the
honor of the thousands of officers who had been liquidated as
traitors.

Fifth, the danger that if Khrushchev did not take the lead,
one of his rivals might; indeed, the speech was adroitly slanted
to imply the involvement of his principal opponents in Stalin's
crimes.

Finally, the necessity of quieting his associates' alarm
about his own rise to power on the Stalin pattern.

Whatever the precise reasons, or mix of reasons, the
speech and the ensuing de-Stalinization campaign—or campaign against "the cult of personality," as it was euphemistically
called within the Soviet Union—shook Soviet society to its
depths and started currents flowing which still have not been
and probably cannot be reversed. It also shook the Communist
world and launched a debate on the nature of relations between
Communist parties which is still continuing. On June 16, 1956,
shortly after the State Department released the text, Italian
Communist leader Palmiro Togliatti advanced the notion of
"polycentrism" for the world Communist movement. Riots
erupted in Poland and were followed in October by the overturn
of the Stalinist leadership of the Polish Communist Party. In
that same month a bloody revolt took place in Hungary which
could only be crushed by the use of Soviet armed forces.

I sometimes have the impression that, despite Khrushchev's unparalleled ability in party infighting and his boastful
bombast, he was appalled and rather frustrated by the enormity
of the problems that faced him as the No. 1 man in the great
Soviet Union. I used to say that he reminded me of some of the
Secretaries of State I had seen come and go in my day. They
come in full of hope and determination to create a bright new
world. Then they soon realize that they control a relatively small
part of that world and that they are up against some immutable

facts and unsolvable problems. In their disappointment, they seize upon the one thing they can do. They reorganize the State Department. I have been through it many times.

Khrushchev's reaction to some of his problems was rather similar. The country had still not recovered from the ravages of war and the sixth Five-Year Plan was limping badly. On March 3, 1957, he abolished the central All-Union industrial and economic ministries, and set up one hundred-odd regional Councils of the National Economy, called in short Sovnarkhoz. Functionaries of the ministries, who had enjoyed the prestige and amenities of living in the capital, were scattered to these provincial centers, to their very great disgruntlement. After the fall of Malenkov, Khrushchev had, in fact, gone ahead with his plans to plow up the so-called virgin lands—the great open plains—and for some years these areas did contribute to a real increase in grain production. However, as many expected, these lands developed "dust-bowl" characteristics. By the early 1960s production was falling off rapidly. So in November, 1962, Khrushchev decided to reorganize the Party, too. He directed that the Party organization be split into industrial and agricultural branches, to supervise and be responsible for these two principal sectors of the national economy. Most of the Party hacks were, of course, simply political propagandists and didn't really fit into either branch. So there was considerable disgruntlement in the Party as well as in the government.

On the social plane, the atmosphere began to ease after the death of Stalin, and particularly after the liquidation of Beria and consequent downgrading of the police and relaxation of the terror. The process was most visible in the field of arts and letters. Novelist, essayist and pamphleteer Ilya Ehrenburg was the first to crack the ice with his short novel *The Thaw*. He had done more than his share of sycophantic propaganda for Stalin, but seemed to be able to smell upcoming changes in the weather. He probably also had a feeling of guilt and of the need to atone for some of his past sins. In any case, *The Thaw* was startling and daring for its time. His characters talked freely of the seamy side of life under Stalin and spoke hopefully of what might come, namely, change. The novel was attacked, but

Ehrenburg got by without sanctions. Others were encouraged. Literary critics began to talk about the absence of lyricism in contemporary poetry, to call for sincerity in writing and even to attack the system of writing to the Party's order.

The real breakthrough came in 1956 after Khrushchev's secret speech denouncing Stalin. Lyric poetry appeared—some by the long-suppressed old-timers like Akhmatova, Pasternak and Tvardovsky, some by a group of new young poets, like Yevtushenko, Rozhdestvensky, Voznesensky and Akhmadulina. A flood of stories vividly described the bad living conditions of the Soviet peoples, particularly in the countryside, and began criticizing the dishonesty and insincerity of the bureaucracy. A high point was Dudintsev's novel *Not by Bread Alone*, attacking the Party controllers and bureaucrats of science and industry. It aroused a storm of controversy and discussion and brought down the wrath of the Party on Dudintsev, who would not be able to publish again for some years. However, the novel brought matters to a new stage. Battle lines formed even among the writers themselves: the liberals headed by Ehrenburg, Paustovsky and Tvardovsky and including most of the younger and more advanced writers; the Stalinists or dogmatists by a Stalinist sycophant, one Vsevolod Kochetov. The fight centered around control of the Writers Union and of the literary magazines. There were ups and downs in the struggle, with the liberals generally controlling the magazine *Novy Mir—New World—* and the dogmatists *Oktyabr—October*.

In 1957 Boris Pasternak's great novel, *Doctor Zhivago,* was published abroad. It won international acclaim, including, not long afterward, the award of the Nobel prize in literature. This brought about a crisis. Under official pressure, Pasternak turned down the award and begged not to be expelled from Russia, saying that this would be for him "the equivalent of death." He was, in fact, permitted to remain in his dacha in the suburbs of Moscow, but not to publish, until his death only two years later —an event possibly hastened by his bitter experiences with Soviet officialdom.

In May, 1959, the Party leadership met with the Congress of Writers in Moscow. To almost everyone's surprise, Khrushchev—perhaps having had second thoughts in the light of the Pasternak affair—was reasonably tolerant, saying in effect that the writers should run their own affairs and bother the government and Party somewhat less. So the flow of honest, liberal writing continued, along with the controversy and the battle among the writers themselves. Imaginative, romantic, individualistic tales flowed from the pens of writers like Kazakov, Nagibin, Kuznetsov and Tendryakov—plays of a similar nature from Arbuzov, Aleschin, Radzinsky and others. Yevtushenko published his famous poems: *Babi Yar*, about the massacre of the Jews in Kiev, and *Stalin's Heirs*, a dramatic warning that Stalin's ghost was still loose in the Soviet Union—both full of political meaning. Aksenov's *Ticket to the Stars* and Rozov's scenario, *ABC*, dealt frankly with the question of the restlessness and disorientation of Soviet youth. A remarkable collection of stories and poems published under the title *Pages from Tarusa* was a real reaffirmation of the Russian literary tradition, of the liberal heritage of the Russian enlightenment.

Then, in the November, 1962, issue of *Novy Mir*, came Alexander Solzhenitsyn's *One Day in the Life of Ivan Denisovich*, describing in graphic if grizzly detail the life of a political prisoner in one of Stalin's hard-labor concentration camps. It was truly epochal in Soviet literature. At first it was received enthusiastically by the press, and it was even said that Khrushchev himself had approved its publication. However, the story came as a bombshell in Party circles; and if Khrushchev did approve it, it would seem he was persuaded to change his mind. On December 7, 1962, came the crackdown. The campaign started with a visit by Khrushchev to a modern art exhibit in Moscow, where he let loose a violent, profane and threatening diatribe against a few abstractionists exhibiting there. Next day the Party newspaper *Pravda* broadened the scope of the offensive to include literature and music. Shortly afterward, the intelligentsia were called together and dressed down in Khrushchev's presence by Leonid Ilyichev, the Party Secretary in charge of cultural and ideological affairs. It was probably not just coincidence that this campaign was launched at the time when Khrushchev was having a lot of other troubles, including problems with agriculture and industry at home and his serious setback in the Cuba missile crisis.

In any event, it was interesting and encouraging to those of us who had been there earlier to compare Stalin's crackdown and Khrushchev's. In 1947–48 the victims either recanted and groveled before the regime or disappeared. In 1963 a very few admitted small errors, but many resisted and even spoke back, both at the meeting with Ilyichev and in the form of a signed appeal to Khrushchev to permit all trends in the arts. Those who were not courageous enough to speak out at least tended to engage in what we called "a conspiracy of silence." Tvardovsky remained editor of the *Novy Mir,* and by and large the other "liberals" also retained their employment and—perhaps with some self-censorship—continued to publish.

The ferment was, of course, not limited to the writers and artists and musicians. It extended to all fields, and particularly to the youth. They had no memory of the Revolution and even very little of the disasters of the war. They listened to foreign radios; and, particularly after a break in the political clouds brought an end to the jamming in June, 1963, the Voice of America and the BBC became Russian institutions. Young Russians heard about the mods in England, and the beatniks in the United States and they developed their own breed—the *stilyagi* with tight pants, long coats and long haircuts. They listened to jazz from the West and built whole libraries of tape recordings; then they swung and they twisted. Stories and plays began to appear about the "generation gap."

The ferment was greatly stimulated also by the official exchange programs with the West. We concluded our first one in 1958, under the labored title "Agreement on Exchanges in the Scientific, Technical, Educational, Cultural and Other Fields." Despite the political ups and downs in Soviet-American relations, successive agreements have been concluded every two years since. These agreements generally provide one hundred-odd projects per year involving about a thousand participants on each side, not counting the members of performing-arts groups. Other Western countries have followed our example, so that the total movement back and forth between West and East has now grown to significant dimensions.

The question arises why the Soviets accepted such "subversive" arrangements. Even Khrushchev was reported to have said to one of the abstractionists, "They say you like to associate with foreigners. A lot of them are our enemies, don't forget!" I think the primary reason, from an official point of view, was that the Kremlin leadership realized that if it wanted to progress it needed Western scientific and technological information and education. We were able to use their interest in this sphere to make them pay the price of extending the agreements into the field of the humanities. Then, politically, it was difficult for Khrushchev to profess a policy of "peaceful coexistence" and at the same time to keep the Soviet Union hermetically sealed off, as it had been under Stalin. Besides, he was setting a vulnerable example himself with all his travels, and pressures built up for him to allow others to see the outside world, too. I even had Russians come to me, when they knew that new exchange-agreement negotiations were coming up, and say that they had been unable to persuade their own authorities to include a project in their field in the Soviet proposals; so they asked me to include such a project in our proposals. Naturally, I obliged.

Just as the intellectuals had started to probe for possible changes in domestic policies after Stalin's death, so did the Western foreign ministries start to probe for changes in foreign policies. And we found that there were some new possibilities— not because Soviet long-range aims had changed, but because the principal rivals for power, Malenkov and Khrushchev, wanted time to concentrate on their struggle. Khrushchev was to tell us later that he had had long arguments with Molotov about the desirability of modifying some of the Stalinist positions and easing the international situation. And, in fact, there was some easement.

In July, 1953, the Korean armistice negotiations, which had been dragging on for three years while hostilities continued, were brought to a conclusion. At the beginning of 1954, after a lapse of nearly five years, a meeting of the quadripartite Council of Foreign Ministers was arranged to take place in Berlin.

Molotov represented the Soviet Union, and not much progress was made on the main issues. On his return to the United States, late in February, Secretary of State John Foster Dulles reported: "As far as Europe is concerned, we brought Mr. Molotov to show Russia's hand. It was seen as a hand that held fast to everything it had, including Eastern Germany and Eastern Austria, and also sought to grab more." However, the meeting did discuss and pave the way for a settlement in Indochina. In the following July, at a Geneva Conference under the co-chairmanship of Great Britain and the Soviet Union, agreements were reached for the cessation of hostilities in Vietnam, Cambodia and Laos. While in Berlin Molotov had insisted on linking an Austrian peace treaty to settlement of the whole German question, the Soviet position was suddenly reversed in the spring of 1955—Khrushchev claimed this was because he had finally prevailed over Molotov. So the Austrian State Treaty was signed on May 15 after eight years of negotiations. Austria committed itself to a policy of nonalignment with either bloc, and in return the Great Powers undertook to recognize and guarantee Austria's neutral status. The treaty was regarded as an important development, since it marked the first voluntary postwar withdrawal of the Soviet Union from an established position in the center of Europe. Moscow was making other conciliatory moves in the same period, including renunciation of the Stalinist claims against Turkey, settlement of its differences with Iran and increased and more amicable participation in the United Nations, including its specialized agencies and economic commissions.

The stage was thus set for the summit meeting which took place in Geneva in July, 1955. President Eisenhower was there for the United States, Prime Minister Eden for Britain and Premier Edgar Faure for France, along with their foreign ministers and advisers. Marshal Bulganin was the titular head of the Soviet delegation, since he had succeeded Malenkov as Chairman of the Council of Ministers and thus "head of government," the previous February. But Party Secretary Khrushchev was there, too, asserting himself with authority despite his nongovernmental status; and so was Molotov, as Foreign

Minister, and President Eisenhower's wartime associate, Marshal Zhukov, as Defense Minister. Molotov and Zhukov were soon to disappear from the scene, but the "B & K" traveling marionette act was to be a feature show until March 27, 1958, when Khrushchev, tired of having his puppet outrank him in international diplomatic protocol, ousted Bulganin on the charge of association with the "anti-Party group" and took over the top governmental position himself. Nothing was settled at Geneva, but on the other hand there were no disastrous clashes. The heads of government ended their consultations with a formal directive to their foreign ministers to meet again and continue negotiations on Germany, European security, disarmament and increased exchanges of peoples and information. The foreign ministers did meet at Geneva the following October–November but again without any concrete results. Secretary Dulles came back to report that the Soviets would not accept either free elections in Germany, or inspection and control of disarmament measures, or a free exchange of ideas.

Everything was set back the following year by the Soviet intervention in the Polish uprising and violent suppression of the revolt in Hungary, and by the complications arising out of the Suez Canal crisis and the British-French-Israeli attack on Egypt.

Then, on October 5, 1957, the Soviet Union introduced the Missile Age by launching the first artificial earth satellite, Sputnik I, to be followed just over a year later by the first moon shot, Lunik I. We were now in for a long period of Soviet Sputnik diplomacy, as Khrushchev set out to try to translate the Soviet Union's new prestige and new power potential into concrete political and even territorial gains. The effort was to end only in October, 1962, in the Cuba missile crisis.

As the gods willed it, I was assigned back to the State Department to take charge of Soviet and European affairs in February, 1958, just a month before Khrushchev took over the prime ministry from Bulganin and launched his Sputnik diplomacy in earnest. As I look back, I wonder how I lived through it all: the massive diplomatic correspondence, the propaganda and counterpropaganda, the politico-military decisions, the endless meetings with the Allies on one side and the Soviets on the other, the visits to the United States of Soviet Deputy Prime Ministers Anastas Mikoyan, Dmitri Polyansky and Frol Kozlov, and then of Khrushchev himself, the visit of Vice President Nixon to the Soviet Union, the U-2 affair and the abortive summit conference in Paris. By the time it was over, Khrushchev had been faced down in Berlin and Cuba and the Soviets were beginning to believe that the "missile gap" was on their side, not ours. Besides, a new element had entered the picture, in the form of Moscow's raging conflict with Peking. I was by that time established as United States Ambassador in Moscow, and I found that we could now do some business, at least on the smaller questions, if we could not hope to settle the larger ones. In 1963–64 we concluded the Nuclear Test Ban Treaty; negotiated and signed a bilateral consular convention; established a "hot line" for crisis communications between the White House and the Kremlin; concluded agreements for cooperation in the desalination of water and the exchange of satellite weather information by direct telegraphic line between the two capitals; revived and reconfirmed the agreement for the establishment of civil airlines between Moscow and New York; and extended our exchanges to include new projects in the fields of outer space and of peaceful uses of atomic energy.

The ink was scarcely dry on all these documents when new complications arose, in the form of a dramatic change of rulers in the Soviet Union.

CHAPTER VII

Post-Khrushchev Leadership and Policies

Khrushchev was out of Moscow a great deal during the spring
and summer of 1964, making official visits to the United Arab
Republic, to Scandinavia, to Poland and to Czechoslovakia and
doing much touring and talking around the Soviet Union itself.
He returned to the capital in September to act as host for a
number of foreign delegations—the President of India, the
Prime Minister of the United Arab Republic, the Communist
Deputy Prime Minister of Laos and the President of Indonesia.
We diplomats saw him a number of times in connection with
these latter events. He had been driving himself hard, and we
agreed he was showing the strain.

On Tuesday, October 13, in announcing the launching of
Voskhod the previous day, *Pravda* reported that Khrushchev and

Mikoyan had talked by telephone from Sochi with the three cosmonauts before their take-off, and that Presidium Chairman Leonid Brezhnev had talked with them from Moscow. (This added conversation was something new and, at the time, mildly intriguing.) It appears that Mikoyan had been sent down by the Presidium, which had been in session since Monday under the chairmanship of senior Party Secretary Suslov, to suggest to Khrushchev that he return and join their meeting. This we did not know at the time. We did learn the next day, Wednesday, October 14, from a foreign visitor who had seen him at the resort Tuesday morning, about Khrushchev's abrupt return to Moscow, apparently in some agitation. We were also intrigued that day by the fact that *Pravda,* in announcing the safe landing of the cosmonauts, did not report Khrushchev (or any other leader) as giving them the usual ritualistic welcome and praise by telephone. We did know, too, from the unusual collection of official cars assembled around Party headquarters, that some unannounced Party gathering was going on that day and the next day, Thursday, October 15. Rumors began to fly thick and fast, reaching a high point at an Afghan Embassy reception Thursday afternoon. When I arrived there, I found the Western diplomats huddled and whispering together in one room, the Communist diplomats doing the same in another, while the Soviet officials were gathered around the buffet dinner table, eating and drinking but not talking at all. This struck me as a poor way to communicate between East and West, so I walked up to the Soviet group at the table. A member of the Presidium was the principal guest of honor. I greeted him with the remark: "Great events." He looked at me, astounded, hesitated a moment, then assured me that nothing fundamental would change. I was then certain that Khrushchev was out, but I professed confusion, saying that I was referring to the successful conclusion of the mission of the spaceship Voskhod.

At midnight of that day, Thursday, October 15, the Soviet news agency Tass published a communiqué confirming that a meeting of the plenum of the Central Committee had taken place on October 14 and stating: "The Plenum of the Central Committee of the Communist Party of the Soviet Union approved the request of Comrade N. S. Khrushchev to be relieved of his responsibilities as First Secretary of the Central Committee, Member of the Presidium of the Central Committee and Chairman of the Council of Ministers of the U.S.S.R. in connection with his advancing age and the worsening state of his health. The Plenum of the Central Committee chose as First Secretary of the Central Committee Comrade L. I. Brezhnev." It was announced simultaneously that the Presidium of the Supreme Soviet of the U.S.S.R. had met that morning and named Alexei Nikolayevich Kosygin to replace Khrushchev as Chairman of the Council of Ministers.

We were told later that when Khrushchev met with his Presidium associates and heard their demand for his resignation he launched into a violent tirade and that a long and bitter argument ensued. Finally, as he had done when the Presidium outvoted him in 1957, he refused to accept the verdict of the Presidium and demanded a decision by the full Central Committee. This demand had been foreseen and arranged for. The full Central Committee was already in session and overwhelmingly endorsed the demands of the Presidium. It was a slick conspiracy. It soon became clear that the top leadership of both the armed forces and the secret police had been brought into the operation. On the military side, this was evident from the marked attention now paid to the Minister of Defense, Marshal Rodion Malinovsky, and to the budgetary and equipment requirements of the armed forces; then shortly afterward by the promotion of the head of the armed forces political department, General Alexei Yepishev, from candidate to full membership in the Central Committee. On the police side, the head of the KGB, Alexander Shelepin, was promoted to full membership in the Presidium of the Central Committee of the Party; and his successor, Vladimir Semichastny, was, like General Yepishev, promoted from candidate to full member of the Central Committee.

These changes were made at another Plenum of the Central Committee, held on November 16. That meeting also approved some other changes, including the addition of two other members to the Presidium. It relieved Frol Kozlov from his post as Party Secretary. Kozlov had for some time been Khrushchev's heir apparent, but he had been incapacitated by a stroke the year before and would soon die. Finally, it ousted Khrushchev's son-in-law from membership in the Central Committee for serious "mistakes in his work." On the substantive side, the Plenum decreed the abolition of Khrushchev's organizational reform, which had split the Party apparatus into industrial and agricultural branches, and restored the Party to its previous monolithic shape.

We diplomats saw the collected members of the new leadership first on Monday, October 19, when they gave a belated reception at the Kremlin for the Voskhod cosmonauts, then again at the National Holiday reception on November 7. Meanwhile, on October 23, I had my first talk with the new Chairman of the Council of Ministers, Mr. Kosygin, which was to be followed by many more over the next couple of years.

I said at the time of his ouster that I never expected to see Khrushchev again in my life, and I would repeat that today. A few correspondents have seen and photographed him on the rare occasions when he comes into Moscow to do his obligatory duty as a Soviet citizen of dropping his single Party ballot into a ballot box. To my knowledge, he has not once been mentioned by name in the Soviet press since the day of the announcement of his ouster. He is referred to occasionally, indirectly, when the Soviet leadership or the Soviet press speak of the "inadmissibility" of "subjectivism," or of "arbitrariness," or of "boastfulness." Everyone who knows how to read the Soviet press knows they are speaking of Khrushchev, but otherwise he is—to use the famous expression of George Orwell in his book *Nineteen Eighty-Four*—an "un-person." Some time before Khrushchev's downfall, the Institute of History had been directed to prepare a revised textbook on *The History of the U.S.S.R. in the Epoch of Socialism*. According to the vital statistics required to appear on all printed matter, the manuscript was turned in on June 13, 1964, but was not authorized for publication until December 3. One may be sure that the original manuscript was designed to glorify Khrushchev and his role and that his name must have appeared on nearly every page. But when the book finally appeared in print, he was mentioned only three times, then more or less in passing: first, in a list of Party leaders assigned to military duty at the beginning of the war; second, as a member of the Military Council at Stalingrad; and third, as becoming First Secretary of the Central Committee after Stalin's death. He is not mentioned at all in connection with the Twentieth, Twenty-first and Twenty-second Congresses of the Party, despite the fact that they were practically one-man shows. And the Soviet student would not know from this history that Khrushchev was ever the Chairman of the Council of Ministers of the Soviet Union. Four years later, a new basic textbook on the *History of the Communist Party of the Soviet Union,* published in October, 1968, for the instruction of Party members, went the 1964 *History of the U.S.S.R.* one better. Khrushchev is not mentioned a single time.

As I have pointed out, a number of Khrushchev's actions had been building up cumulative grievances against him: his decentralization of economic management, his splitting of the Party organization, the disasters in agriculture, his failures in Berlin and Cuba, and his ever-growing tendency to freewheel without consulting his associates. There were some additional factors. The controversy as to what to do about agriculture was continuing, and Khrushchev had summoned a Central Committee meeting for November, 1964. He had admitted in a public speech in August that "some comrades" were unhappy about the preparations for this meeting. In midsummer, without consulting his colleagues, he had sent his son-in-law, *Izvestiya* editor Alexei Adzhubei, on an exploratory junket to West Germany. Both in private conversation and in inspired press articles, Khrushchev had been creating the impression that he was planning a rapprochement with Bonn on the lines of the deal which Lenin's Foreign Minister had concluded with defeated Germany at Rapallo after the First World War. This not only worried his associates but was a matter of vital concern to the Kremlin's puppet ruler of East Germany, Walter Ulbricht. There was also growing uneasiness at the top levels about Khrushchev's handling of the conflict with Mao Tse-tung. He had already summoned an international Communist Party conference to meet in Moscow in December, with the obvious intent of preparing to excommunicate China from the world movement. Finally, he had clearly become overconfident, spending less and less time in Moscow and leaving the running of the Party and the government to his lieutenants.

A few footnotes might be added to the story. We used to say, in Stalin's day, that there was only one exit from the Politburo, namely, death. Since then, except for Beria, obliteration of the personality has replaced physical liquidation. Also, Khrushchev's insistence in 1957 and again in 1964 on decisions by the full Central Committee had somewhat enhanced the authority of that body as the custodian of Party sovereignty and thus slightly broadened the base of Party rule. Finally, it is ironical and a little tragic that, while people sobbed at Stalin's death, no tears were shed for this first ruler in all Russian history who actively sought public support and popularity.

So once again—for the third time in nearly fifty years—there was the problem of succession in a political system which makes no provision for succession. Once again there was an uneasy so-called "collective leadership" in a system the dynamics of which virtually force the emergence of a "boss" of the Communist Party, which holds the monopoly of political power. At the time of their takeover, the senior members of the present leadership were mostly in their early sixties, or about ten years younger than Khrushchev; the next layer were in their early fifties, or about twenty years younger. Thus the Soviet Union is in a second- and third-generation situation, where all the members of the leadership are purely products of the Party and government apparatus and none had personal experience in the Revolution or the Civil War or even in the first exciting, if grim, stages of the development of the system.

Consequently, the new leadership consists of rather colorless and reserved individuals. No one stands out as a dominant figure either in power or personality, and life in Moscow has become much duller than it was with Khrushchev. Leonid Brezhnev, who emerged as a sort of "first among equals," First Secretary of the Party, was born in 1906 in the Ukraine, but is of Russian stock. He was educated first in the late twenties in a technical agricultural school, then in the mid-thirties went back to school and graduated as a metallurgical engineer. He joined the Party in 1931 and became active in Party work in the Ukraine a few years later. During the war he was a political commissar with the armed forces and remained mainly in political work with the military until 1953, rising to the rank of lieutenant general. In the early 1950s he was First Secretary of the Moldavian Party, that is, the local Party boss in the state created out of the territories taken over from Rumania, and in the mid-fifties performed the same function in Kazakhstan, during the period when the virgin lands were being plowed up for growing grain. Since 1956 he has been a secretary in the central Party apparatus, except for the four years 1960–64 when he served in the titular position of Chairman of the Presidium of the Supreme Soviet. During his time in this "Presidential" capacity, Brezhnev was accessible to "capitalist" as well as "Communist" diplomats and made a number of official visits outside the Communist orbit to selected Asian and African nations, notably India, Iran, Afghanistan, Morocco, Ghana and the Sudan, but never traveled to the West. Since his elevation to First Secretary of the Party, he has withdrawn from the diplomatic scene and limited his movements to the Communist camp.

I had a long exchange of views with him shortly after my arrival in 1962, was his table neighbor at occasional official dinners and exchanged pleasantries with him at many receptions. He was always superficially affable, but never had anything to say that sent me flying back to the embassy to cable Washington—or, indeed, that I had not already read in my morning *Pravda*. Something under six feet in height, Brezhnev is a rather handsome man, with an abundant crop of black hair. He likes to dress well and I used to say that he "must have the best tailor in Moscow." He had a heart attack a few years ago, but—according to his wife and to her anxiety—he has defied the doctor's orders to stop drinking and to discontinue his chain-smoking.

Kosygin took over the government. He was born in Leningrad in 1904 and graduated from the textile institute in that city. He joined the Party in 1927 when he was working as a

teacher in Siberia, where he was active in the cooperative movement and in economic planning for that area. In the mid-thirties
he returned to Leningrad as a manager of textile plants, then
gradually rose to the top as an industrial manager and specialist
in economic management and planning inside the government,
holding such jobs as Minister of the Textile Industry, Minister
of Finance, Minister of Light and Food Industries, Chairman of
the State Planning Commission, then Deputy Chairman of the
Council of Ministers of the Soviet Union. As a result of this
training and experience, Kosygin is a relatively sophisticated
person whose horizons are not cut off by the blinders of purely
Party work. He is, of course, a believer, and I cannot say I
thought I shook him much in a long discussion we once had
about the relative merits of the Communist and the free enterprise systems. However, he studies his lessons and always has
his facts, or at least his version of the facts, at his fingertips. He
is familiar with Western economic and managerial practices
and has visited major Western countries, including the United
States. In sum, Kosygin is an able and experienced economist
and industrial manager, and a good bureaucrat.

Nikolai Viktorovich Podgorny, third member of the top
triumvirate, is Ukrainian. Born in 1903, he joined the Party in
1930 and finished his studies at the Kiev Technological Institute
of the Food Industry in 1931. Thereafter he worked in a number
of sugar plants and then in Ukrainian government departments
dealing with the food industry. He began to rise in Party work in
the Ukraine only about 1950. Khrushchev made him a member
of the Presidium of the Central Committee and brought him to
Moscow in 1958. In the post-Khrushchev reshuffle, he replaced
Brezhnev as Chairman of the Presidium of the Supreme Soviet
or nominal "President" of the Soviet Union. Rough-hewn and
folksy, he tends to talk in clichés.

Marshal Malinovsky had been chosen by Khrushchev to
replace Zhukov as Minister of Defense in 1957. A hard-bitten
old soldier, born in 1898, and a sort of political "neutral" inside
the Party, he was kept on. He died in 1967 and was replaced by
Marshal Andrei Grechko, some five years younger.

The man who came out of the reshuffle with the most striking accretion of position and power was one of the younger members, Alexander Shelepin. Already, thanks to Khrushchev, a secretary of the Central Committee, Deputy Prime Minister and head of the Party-State Control Committee, he was now, at the age of forty-six, promoted to full membership in the Presidium. A Russian, born in 1918, he became a full member of the Party in 1940. By that time he was already a "political guide" with the Red Army in Finland. His subsequent career was entirely in the youth organization, the Komsomol, of which he became head in 1952. In this capacity, he was responsible for the mobilization of hundreds of thousands of Soviet youth, in the mid-fifties for the development of the virgin lands in Kazakhstan and for settlement in Siberia and the Far Eastern provinces of the U.S.S.R. In 1958 Khrushchev put him in charge of the secret police, the KGB. He represents what may be a "new breed" of full-time professional Party workers from early youth—tough, militant and ambitious. In moving up to the Presidium, Shelepin was able to place one of his own close associates in the Komsomol at the head of the KGB, Vladimir Semichastny, who also received a Party promotion. Moreover, Shelepin had other lieutenants placed around in various strategic posts, all graduates of the Komsomol organization. These included the First Secretary of the important Moscow Party organization and the head of the State Committee for Cultural Relations with Foreign Countries.

Maneuvering and jockeying for position within the new leadership has, of course, gone on from the beginning, and Brezhnev has visibly enhanced his position at the expense of Kosygin and Podgorny. Indeed, in the 1968 edition of the basic manual on Party history, Brezhnev's pronouncements are cited twenty-odd times and he is second only to Lenin as Party oracle. Kosygin is mentioned only once in the book, and Podgorny not at all. Apparently, however, the triumvirate—or troika, to use the familiar Russian term—soon realized the danger to them of Shelepin and his group. And when one of Shelepin's cronies dared to criticize the leadership's handling of the Arab-Israeli crisis in June, 1967, Shelepin was relieved of all his Party functions except membership in the Presidium, and of his government post as Deputy Prime Minister, and made head of the trade-union organization. His associates, including Semichastny, were similarly ousted and given posts of little importance. The youth organization was subsequently given an oldline Party boss—instead of a graduate of the Komsomol apparatus—and has been brought under tighter control of the central Party. Aside from this matter of self-protection against the ambitions of younger members, other forces impelling the top figures to maintain some unity and collectivity are probably greater today than they have been in previous succession crises: in the international field, the conflict with China and its effect on the world Communist movement; in the domestic field, the enormity and complexity of the unsolved economic problems Khrushchev left behind and the weakening of the Party's position as a result of the decline of ideology.

Among the domestic problems a simple arithmetical formula was the source of most of Khrushchev's troubles and will be a source of troubles for his successors for a long time to come. The Soviet Union tries to rival the United States in military and space programs, and it tries to do this on a total Gross National Product valued at $412 billion, against our GNP of $835 billion. Allocation of scarce resources is thus an unending headache to the Kremlin leadership. While the Soviet Government can and does mobilize the best of its human and material resources for priority objectives, this has inevitably resulted in an imbalance in the economy as a whole and especially in a tremendous lag in the application of modern technology to the consumer-goods and agricultural sectors.

In Stalin's day the command system of economy worked reasonably well, though with great inefficiency because of the use of forced labor and the duplication of supervision by the government and Party bureaucracy; we used to say that it took one to work and one to watch for each job. Yet the priorities were so simple: create a heavy-industry base—more oil, more coal, more electric power stations, more iron, more steel, more heavy machines and machine tools. Everything was ordered by number, everything was evaluated by number. Only quantity counted. All investment funds went to these priority projects.

The peasantry was milked for food and raw materials and the consumer left to fend for himself.

But inevitably, as the basic industrial plant was built up— and particularly after it was restored following the war—the economy automatically got more complex and difficult to manage. Besides, as I noted earlier, the population had learned, during and after the war, that life not only could be but in fact was much better outside. People began to demand more for themselves—better food, better clothing, better shelter. The Soviet leadership was up against a "revolution of rising expectations." Khrushchev's decentralization of the economic management to economic councils in more than a hundred separate regions further complicated the problem. Each locality would plan its pet projects for industrial development and submit these plans to the central authorities for the allocation of investment funds, much as various departments of the U.S. Federal Government submit to the Bureau of the Budget their claims for their share of the budgetary pie. These claims always added up to more than was available. Since the various vested interests involved had come to be important in the political scheme of things, the tendency developed for the central authorities, instead of discriminating between regions and projects, simply to cut back all claimants a given percentage. The result was that instead of weeding out projects of lesser priority the local sponsors would simply stretch them out. Thus investment funds would be tied up for years on end before production started. We could travel all over the Soviet Union and see with our own eyes: just started, half-built, two-thirds-built plants on which construction had been suspended for lack of funds; or stores of imported machinery left outside to rust and deteriorate, so that it would be obsolete or inoperative when the plant was finally built to house it.

Another phenomenon was beginning to occur under the command economy system. Since a factory manager's rating and pay, and bonuses for his workers, depended exclusively on his success in meeting quantitative quotas or "norms" of production, he had no concern whatsoever for either quality or variety in his product. So as production increased generally, during the fifties and early sixties, literally billions of rubles' worth of shoddy merchandise began to accumulate—so shoddy that it could not even be sold to the underprivileged Soviet consumer. It actually took reduced-price sales to get rid of the stuff.

By the time I went back to Moscow in 1962 cautious debate had already started in the economic journals about the desirability of reform and improvement in economic management. The initial proponents were such economists as Yevsey Liberman and Vadim Trapeznikov, both of whom had obviously had their eyes on the experimentation with a "socialist" market economy being tried in Yugoslavia. It became clear that competent administrators like Kosygin realized that something had to be done, that some free-market factors had to be introduced to make the system operate more automatically and more efficiently. It also became clear that any moves in this direction would be opposed by vested interests, who had achieved very satisfactory positions under the old system, and by many bureaucrats, who feared they would be dislocated from their various planning and control jobs.

One of the concrete steps the new leadership took was to dismantle the regional economic councils set up by Khrushchev and to restore the central ministries. This was done in October, 1965. Meanwhile, in December, 1964, Kosygin had outlined to the Supreme Soviet, as a part of the new leadership's program, proposals for economic reform, under which sales and profit indexes would be substituted for quantitative norms of production, and direct contractual relations would be permitted between producer and retail distributor. In September, 1965, he developed these proposals somewhat further at a Central Committee Plenum. But his proposals have been repeatedly watered down to meet the resistance of opponents and are still regarded as experimental in nature.

Such economic reform in the Soviet Union does indeed raise some fundamental questions. If the manager of an industrial installation is to be judged and if he and his workers are to be paid on a basis of sales and profits, then there must be some way to measure the plant's real cost of production. This requires an appraisal of the state's actual investment in the plant, and provision for repayment to the state of its investment, together with interest on the capital, terms repugnant to Marxist-Leninist-Stalinist economic theory. There must also be some rational market factors controlling the prices the industrial manager has to pay for the raw materials and power he uses. There must also be some reasonable relationship between the prices he charges for his products and consumer demands for his and other products, on the one hand, and his real costs of production, on the other. But the price structure in the Soviet Union has always been purely arbitrary, centrally determined and weighted to favor heavy industry and to facilitate capital accumulation by the state. In 1967–68 the Kosygin Government undertook a revision of the wholesale price structure to bring it more into line with the world's standards, but it is still an arbitrary and centrally prescribed list.

If the manager is to be judged on the basis of sales and profits, then he must be able to operate his plant efficiently and to seek constant improvement in the productivity of his labor. This means he must be able to hire and fire workers, and this, in turn, raises the specter of unemployment. Of course, the Soviet Union has always boasted that it has no unemployment—that unemployment is unknown in a Communist state. This boast has, in fact, been almost true; it has been accomplished by the simple process of a central allocation of wage funds and labor quotas to enterprises. Most observers would agree that this full employment has been achieved at a cost of about 30 percent underemployment or "featherbedding." But even though administrators like Kosygin know that the Soviet Union must increase its efficiency, and especially its labor productivity, if it is ever to satisfy the mounting demands of its population or to compete in today's world, there is great reluctance in the ruling party to face up to this reality.

Finally, a really fundamental problem arises. If management is given the authority and the autonomy that real economic reform requires, what then becomes of Communist Party control? It is obvious that this question has taken the economic issue right into the Politburo, the highest Party level, and that the debate continues. Nevertheless, the experiment in applying cost-accounting and sales and profit indexes has now been extended to most industrial plants, and management has become a powerful element in the society. There will be slipping and sliding and further compromise, but I believe some reform will gradually come about. I should stress that the reform will affect only methods of management and not the basic principle of state ownership of all means of production.

While there has been a considerable movement of population into the cities and industrial complexes, as in all industrializing countries, about a third of the adult labor force, or nearly forty million people, remain in the agricultural sector, on about two million square miles of arable land and pasture. These forty million produce only 75 percent as much as is produced by five million American farmers, but it should be added in the same breath that these American farmers use four times as much fertilizer and four times as many tractors. One remarkable and significant phenomenon should be noted. Agriculture in the Soviet Union is organized in state farms, called sovkhozes, and collective farms, called kolkhozes. However, the peasants are allotted individual private plots for their own production and use, running up to about an acre in size, and are allowed to keep limited numbers of livestock. These private plots constitute about 3.3 percent of the total sown area. However, except for grains, these private plots produce a third of the total agricultural product of the Soviet Union. There is much "soldiering," underemployment and, particularly during the long winter months, even idleness on the state and collective farms. But there is no lack of attention to the private plots and to the chickens and turkeys and pigs and cows they support. If you travel through the countryside on Sundays, you find the landscape dotted with workers busy as beavers on their own plots.

In its first years Khrushchev's campaign to plow up the virgin lands in lower Siberia and upper Kazakhstan paid off with about a 50 percent increase in grain production; but after 1958 production actually started to decline, as these lands began to develop dust-bowl characteristics, as we noted earlier. A bad year in 1962 was followed by a real crop failure in 1963, with the result that the Soviet Government had to spend nearly $2 billion—a large proportion of its gold and foreign exchange reserves—for twenty-odd million tons of foreign wheat to provide bread for its people. The disaster was certainly an important factor in Khrushchev's ouster.

Naturally enough, the new leadership turned first to this critical agricultural problem, and in March, 1965, adopted a serious and sensible Five-Year Agricultural Reform Program. It provided for agricultural investments over that period amounting to 71 billion rubles, or about $80 billion at the official exchange rate, mainly for agricultural machinery and for increased production and use of fertilizers. Quotas for obligatory delivery of agricultural products to the state were reduced to more reasonable levels, and premium prices were offered for over-quota deliveries. Farm managers were authorized to pay bonuses to workers from the proceeds of these sales of over-quota production, and a minimum annual wage was established for farm labor. At the same time, prices in state stores in the villages were equalized with those in the cities—this ended a device of Stalin's for milking the peasantry by charging them half again to double as much as the city dweller paid for the same item. A year later, in May, 1966, this program was supplemented by a Ten-Year Program of Land Reclamation and Irrigation Projects in the European and southern areas of the country, where the climate is more dependable than in Kazakhstan. The virgin lands were to be de-emphasized and through rotational planting allowed to regain their stability and fertility.

The new program seemed to get off to a good start, but God helped the new leadership even more by providing favorable weather. After an average crop in 1965, a really bumper crop came along in 1966, with wheat production rising to 85 million tons against a recent average of about 65. This was enough to allow the state to create ample reserves—and, ironically, enough to imperil the basic program. I remember our embassy staff discussions at the time of the introduction of the reforms. We all agreed the plan was good if consistently implemented and carried through to the end. I said, however, that I was perfectly sure that in deciding to allocate these substantial funds to agricultural investment out of their stringently limited resources, the leadership had not made the other half of that decision, that is, out of whose pocket these funds would come. And indeed, after the bumper crop of 1966, other vested interests began clamoring for a reduction in these agricultural investments and allocation of the funds to them.

This dispute was first revealed by Dmitri Polyansky in the Party magazine *Kommunist* in the fall of 1967. Polyansky is the member of the Politburo who supervises the agricultural sector; and even in the midst of the harmony which was supposed to prevail for the celebration of the Fiftieth Anniversary of the U.S.S.R. he complained vehemently against those who were thus threatening the agricultural program. Despite his protests, pressures for diversion of funds from agriculture have continued, as satisfactory—though not bumper—crops were harvested in 1967, 1968 and 1969. State investments have, in fact, fallen considerably below the levels planned in 1965, and it remains to be seen how matters will come out in the end. Agriculture has from the beginning been the most neglected and one of the most controversial aspects of the Soviet economy. Only in recent years have the abler members of the leadership begun to appreciate that a backward agriculture is a serious drag on the economy as a whole, and even has a serious retarding effect on the growth of industry itself.

If you were to go to the Soviet Union today, you would consider it a society very different from our own. It is indeed still a controlled society. You would find that there were police microphones in your hotel room and in most other places where you might meet with Soviet citizens. You would realize that your telephone was tapped and your mail censored. You would find that the public newsstands have nothing but Soviet publications plus a few Communist journals from abroad. You would not see our official Russian-language magazine *Amerika*, distributed under the exchange program, for the good reason that its entire authorized issue (unfortunately, only fifty thousand copies) is snapped up within minutes of delivery to the kiosks, usually on an under-the-counter basis. You would come to realize that your every movement was recorded and presumably reported by most of the people with whom you came in contact—from your Intourist guide to the chauffeur of your taxi to the doorkeeper of the hotel. You would see police everywhere, even at outposts along country roads.

But one has to have lived in the Soviet Union in Stalin's day to appreciate that, despite the efforts of the present leadership to turn the clock back, today's atmosphere still does not compare with the total police terror and the fear pervading the atmosphere at that time. One has to realize, too, that the Russians have been conditioned for centuries to accept controls that to us would be intolerable. I used to discuss at length with a Russian intellectual friend the differences between our societies. The one point I could never get him to accept was the fact that we are not required to carry an internal passport, in which is recorded the holder's authorized place of residence and in which is registered his every move, with a police stamp to confirm it. My friend simply couldn't see how our society could operate without at least this much information about the citizens' whereabouts being in the hands of the authorities. Stalin's "labor book" has, however, been abandoned. When Khrushchev suggested in 1963 that it be reintroduced to improve labor discipline, the idea was received with such evident hostility that it was simply allowed to drop.

The ferment leading to manifestations of greater independence and defiance of authority in recent years is still continuing and is likely to continue, despite efforts at repression. The new Soviet leadership has tried to reassert stricter control, and has cautiously begun a partial rehabilitation of Stalin, a "re-Stalinization." The process started in July, 1965, with a decree against so-called "hooliganism," designed to control nonconformists among the population, and particularly the youth, who were tending to ape some of the more extreme youthful elements in the West. Since then the Kremlin has gone on, step by step, toward imposing tighter "discipline." In April, 1968, as worries about the "democratization" process in Czechoslovakia were added to mounting domestic concerns, the Central Committee of the Party launched a great new "ideological" revival campaign to try to pull the population back into the Party line and to warn them against the dangers of Western bourgeois ideas.

On the intellectual front, the new leadership has in general avoided broad frontal attacks on the artists and writers. It has, however, moved in hard on a succession of individual cases. One of the first, with some interesting aspects, was that of the Russian-Greek writer Valery Tarsis. After he had produced and submitted a number of manuscripts of a rebellious nature, he was committed to detention in an insane asylum. This seems to have been intended as a means of avoiding the onus of sentencing a writer to prison or to labor camps for his ideas. Proper legal forms were followed, and the result of the process was a court finding that Tarsis was mentally incompetent and consequently, under Soviet law, not responsible for his acts. Thus the authorities had rather estopped themselves from taking more drastic action against him, when in 1965 Tarsis managed to get a couple of his manuscripts to the West and have them published there—after which they were of course reported back into the Soviet Union by foreign radio broadcast services. The authorities got off this hook in the Tarsis case when his British publishers invited him to visit them. Contrary to usual practice, they promptly issued him a passport; then after he had arrived in London, the Presidium of the Supreme Soviet deprived him of his Soviet citizenship and so excluded him from returning to the Soviet Union.

In December, 1965, two other Soviet writers, Andrei Sinyavsky and Yuli Daniel, were arrested for similarly sending manuscripts surreptitiously out of the country for publication. They had not previously been declared insane, so they were tried and in February, 1966, were sentenced, respectively, to seven and five years of hard labor. Some care was exercised to put the charges on a technical-legal basis: first, violation of Soviet law by failing to submit their material through regular censorship channels; and second, circulation of "anti-Soviet slander" abroad. These fine distinctions were, however, lost on the world press and general public, to whom the trial represented simply a repression of freedom of thought and expression. The Sinyavsky-Daniel case was to have immediate reactions and a continuing sequel. Youthful friends and supporters actually organized a public demonstration in Pushkin Square shortly after the arrests. Subsequently, these supporters produced a full record of the trial, including the victims' vigorous defense, which was both circulated inside the country and disseminated abroad. All this led to the arrest of the writers Alexander Ginsburg and Yuri Galanskov and two others as the principal culprits. These four were, in their turn, tried and convicted, receiving varying sentences to prison and exile early in 1968. Many prominent writers had already started a campaign of protest against the arrest and sentencing of Sinyavsky and Daniel, mainly in the form of letters and petitions to the Soviet authorities and debates inside the Party-controlled Writers Union. The second arrests evoked another round of debates and petitions signed by additional intellectuals, including a number of the younger scientists.

These activities encouraged others to protest on their own account. In May of 1967 Alexander Solzhenitsyn, the brilliant author of *One Day in the Life of Ivan Denisovich,* addressed a letter to the Writers Union consitituting a long and violent diatribe against the official censorship and calling on the Union actively to seek the abolition of that censorship. Despite public criticism, he did not cease his efforts. When the manuscripts of his two new novels, *The First Circle* and *Cancer Ward,* reached the West and were published here more than a year later, he again addressed the Union. He denied that he had authorized their publication abroad but at the same time protested the refusal of the Soviet authorities to allow publication of these works in the Soviet Union, without the major modifications "from an ideological point of view" the censorship had required.

Meanwhile, in August of 1967, the Secretariat of the Writers Union canceled a poetry-reading trip of the poet Andrei Voznesensky to the United States, informing the American sponsors that he was ill, without even consulting him. So Voznesensky joined the hue and cry, and his protest, like all the others, managed to get reproduced and circulated inside the Soviet Union and smuggled to the outside.

In October of 1968 another group which had been heavily involved in the previous protests was put on trial and given sentences comparable to those meted out to the first two. This group included the grandson of Stalin's pre–World War II Foreign Minister, Maxim Litvinov, and the wife of Yuli Daniel, one of the writers convicted in the first of these trials. The immediate charge in this instance was an attempted demonstration in Red Square to protest the invasion of Czechoslovakia. This third trial led to a new wave of protests and petitions by intellectuals, charging that this series of repressions constituted a violation of the civil-rights provisions of the Soviet Constitution.

Although the scientific community, because of its major contribution to the Soviet power potential, had previously been generally immune from persecution, the fact that many of its young members joined in the protests led the authorities to extend the heavy hand in their direction also. A few were ousted from Party membership and others were criticized in public print for their apolitical attitudes and failure to respect the Party line.

A high point on the scientific side was reached by the circulation inside the Soviet Union and publication in the West in mid-1968 of an essay, "Progress, Coexistence and Intellectual Freedom," by the eminent young Soviet physicist, Dr. Andrei Sakharov, generally considered to be the father of the Soviet hydrogen bomb. In this paper Dr. Sakharov analyzes a wide range of world problems, including overpopulation; racial, political and economic exploitation; the developments in Czechoslovakia; the threat to intellectual freedom under the Communist regimes; and the necessity for cooperation between the United States and the Soviet Union as the world's two superpowers. But while the Soviet leadership has struck at some of the lesser scientific figures involved in protests, it has so far not dared to move against this towering scientist to whom it is so beholden.

While most members of the Soviet intelligentsia have remained in Russia, protesting when possible or just "writing for the drawer," there has been a steady trickle to the West of escapees who could no longer bear the increasingly oppressive atmosphere—a popular actor in 1965, a minor poet in 1966, a successful film director in 1967, a noted scientist and a well-known writer, Mikhail Dyomin, called the Jack London of contemporary Soviet literature, in 1968. Then in July, 1969, came the defection of the outstanding young novelist, Anatoly V. Kuznetsov, author of the novel *Babi Yar,* about the fate of Kiev's Jews under the Nazis, which inspired Yevtushenko's better-known poem on the same subject. In exile in England, Kuznetsov has published dramatic revelations about the mutilation of his manuscripts by the Soviet censorship and his harassment by the secret police, along with the complicated story of his pretended collaboration with the police and his professed intent to write a work about "Lenin in England" in order to escape. Since this ostensible collaboration had put him in good odor with the authorities, he was denounced with a double passion. The Writers Union expelled him "for betraying the fatherland, betraying the cause of socialism, and for political and moral double-dealing." A "Judas," wrote his former editor, who had "once and for all excluded [himself] from the roll of Soviet and Russian writers." "Low and underhand treachery," echoed the youth newspaper, *Komsomolskaya Pravda,* "not only marked by its unexpectedness and cunning, but sickening above all because of the cynicism . . ."

It is unfortunately clear that the regime's repressive campaign has had some real effect. Gifted writers like Solzhenitsyn and Dudintsev have not been able to get their new works published in the Soviet Union since Khrushchev's day. The output of other promising authors has noticeably lost its sparkle, as they obviously engage in self-censorship or turn to safe subjects. It has been years since a work published in Moscow burst out onto the world literary scene. Conservative, Party-line hacks have strengthened their positions, particularly in the Writers Union, and their media (notably *Oktyabr* and *Ogonyok*) have redoubled their attacks on the progressives, whose journal, *Novy Mir,* and its editor, Tvardovsky, are practically in a state of siege.

On a somewhat different plane, the extent of the disaffection toward Communist ideology, even among the second generation, was dramatically underscored by the refusal of Stalin's daughter to return to the Soviet Union from a visit to India and her decision to remain in the West. I was then back in the Department as Deputy Under Secretary of State for Political Affairs. This was, of course, a difficult case for us to handle without disowning the American tradition of asylum, on the one hand, or creating undue complications in our relations with the Soviet Union, on the other. However, Svetlana Alliluyeva was in possession of a valid Soviet passport. At her own request, she was given a visitor's visa for entry into the United States. We kept the Soviet Government fully informed of our actions in the matter, and the Soviet news agency *Tass* was obliged to issue an unprecedented statement acknowledging that she was abroad of her own volition and that her plans were up to her—this announcement must have startled all Soviet readers who read it in *Pravda* on March 13, 1967. Later, KGB agents spread stories about "mental instability," tried to defame her character and even tried to peddle doctored "Svetlana" manuscripts in Western Europe. However, their efforts were of little avail against her obvious self-possession and transparent honesty in her public appearances in the United States. And her accounts of the evolution of her own thinking away from Communism, and even toward religion, in her books *Twenty Letters to a Friend* and *Only One Year,* are striking testimony about the forces at work in Soviet society. Since the U.S.S.R. revoked her citizenship early in 1970, she is free to remain here permanently or go elsewhere, as she herself may decide.

When I returned to the Soviet Union in 1962, I was astonished by the sterility of Communist propaganda and indoctrination materials. These consist mainly of so-called "leading articles" in the major papers, especially *Pravda* and *Izvestiya,* and in the official Party periodicals. I found myself reading, literally word for word, the same clichés, the same "boiler plate" that I had read fifteen years before, in Stalin's day—formulations which had really no relationship to what had gone on meanwhile or was then going on, either in the world or in the Soviet Union itself. When I tried to discuss this question with

Russian friends, they were in turn astonished—astonished that I had bothered to read such stuff. They made it clear that they didn't.

The decline of ideology was nowhere more apparent than in the two big Party events of recent years, the Twenty-third Party Congress and the celebrations of the Fiftieth Anniversary of the Revolution.

The Congress took place in April, 1966, in the shiny new six-thousand-seat Kremlin Palace of Congresses. We were of course not allowed to be present, but the papers were expanded to publish most of the goings-on, and long excerpts of the meetings themselves were shown on television. The Congress lasted a full week, despite the fact that there was little business to do. The acts of the Presidium and Central Committee since the last Congress were unanimously ratified by a show of hands and without discussion. A gesture was made toward re-Staliniza-tion by approving the restoration of the titles of General Secre-tary, instead of First Secretary, of the Party and of Politburo, instead of Presidium, to the top leadership of the Party's Central Committee. And directives for the next Five-Year Plan were heard and approved. But the Congress was in the main a marathon of speech-making. Speech followed speech followed speech from early morning until late at night, day after day. Most of them were mainly repetition or rehash of the same propaganda we had been reading for years in the controlled press. There was considerable concern expressed about the waywardness of youth and the generation gap, and in this connection references were made to the subversive influence of foreign broadcasts and of the exchange programs with foreign countries. The boastfulness of the Khrushchev era was gone, and there was practically no repetition of his standard asser-tions about the Soviet Union's overtaking and surpassing the United States economically. There wasn't a revolutionary spark in the house, and if there had been, there was nothing to ignite. The tone was something like that of a DAR convention, except that most of the speakers were men and that they were the rulers of a great country. The Congress was, in short, deadly dull.

The Russians themselves were telling a story about the supposed penetration of the Congress by an American agent. When the leaders on the podium heard this report, they promptly summoned the head of the secret police and told him to get to work. He stood on the podium for a few minutes, carefully surveying the crowd in front of him. Then he calmly walked down to the middle of the hall, grabbed an individual by the coat collar, turned him over to the waiting police and returned to the podium. Impressed by his efficient performance, the leadership demanded: "But how did you do it?"

"Well," replied the head of the police, "Lenin taught me."

"What do you mean Lenin taught you?"

"Lenin taught us—that our enemy never sleeps," he replied.

The official statistics on attendance at the Congress support Herzen's prescient comment that "a Communist revolution in Russia would be the aristocracy turned upside down." There were 4,493 delegates. Of these only 1,266, or about a quarter of the total, were described as *workers*. Nearly as many (1,248) were listed as professional functionaries of the Communist Party, 621 as government bureaucrats and 352 as members of the Soviet armed forces. The remaining 1,006 were a miscellany of intellectuals, managers, employees and peasants.

The celebration of the Fiftieth Anniversary of the so-called October Revolution was comparable in tone and substance, although different in format. There were mass meetings in Leningrad and in Moscow and a big reception at the Kremlin. Brezhnev, now bearing the revived Stalinist title of "General Secretary" of the Party, took the lead and made the major speeches. There were no surprises, no bold, bright pronouncements. It was impossible to talk about the real history of the last fifty years, when the man who had dominated the Party and ruled the country for thirty of these years was now practically unmentionable and considered "a mad tyrant"—and his successor who had ruled for over ten years was now a complete unperson and thought of as "a bumbling fool." The most interesting feature of the celebration was a series of television programs, one for each of the fifty years. Stalin appeared only a few times, fleetingly, in old film strips; Khrushchev not once, even in the coverage of the Twentieth Party Congress in 1956, where he had made every major speech and had shaken not only Soviet society but the whole Communist world by his denunciation of Stalin.

As I noted earlier, the overwhelming burden of their external and internal problems seems to make the present top leadership in the Kremlin—particularly the troika of Brezhnev, Kosygin and Podgorny—a little more "collective" than was the case in previous succession crises. Since none of these problems—the conflict with China, the situation in industry and agriculture, the decline of ideology as a factor both inside the country and within the Communist world at large—seems likely to approach solution within any foreseeable future, it could well be that this "collective" will endure for some time, despite the system's impulsion toward the development of a single "boss." However, it is well to remember that it took Stalin himself nearly five years before he felt strong enough to exile Trotsky and another five years before he considered himself in a position to launch the great purges. Similarly, it took Khrushchev nearly five years before he could oust and discredit "the anti-Party group"; and, as we now know, he did not do this thoroughly enough to make himself really secure. For the time being, in any case, no one individual seems strong enough in character, ability and energy to dominate the others. Brezhnev is in the lead, but he has a bad health record already and is clearly taxing his physical capacity. Kosygin certainly wants to move ahead with his economic reform proposals, but he seems to have little taste for the Party infighting that such progress requires. Podgorny, not controlling any real sources of power, has been campaigning to enhance the status of the rather artificial "legislative" branch, the Supreme Soviet and the local Soviets throughout the country, but with no visible success.

In the circumstances, decisions tend to be adjustments to the lowest common denominator. Partly as a reaction to Khrushchev's pragmatism and "revisionism," partly because of the requirements of their conflict with China, and partly because of the enhanced influence of Politburo member and Party ideologist Mikhail Suslov, there has been a marked return to Communist orthodoxy. The many speeches and articles on the occasion of the Fiftieth Anniversary celebrations featured such themes as: the menace of imperialism to the world revolution; the necessity for united efforts in the anti-imperialist, i.e. anti-United States, struggle; the "indivisibility" of the Soviet Communist Party's national and international aims; and the acuteness of the ideological struggle and the danger of Western bourgeois influence in the Soviet Union. This general line was made even sharper and vigorously promoted internationally after the developments in Czechoslovakia and the launching of the ideological-revival campaign in 1968.

Soviet-American relations had a "tendency to freeze" after the fall of Khrushchev, to borrow the term first used by Communist Party General Secretary Brezhnev in September, 1965. This deterioration in our relationship reflected not just the general return to more militant Communist orthodoxy in the Kremlin, but, increasingly, differences in the international field, particularly with respect to Vietnam. In any case, beginning in 1965, the Soviet Government generally avoided either taking or accepting new initiatives in our relations, or engaging in any bilateral activities which might seem to give any semblance of justification to Chinese Communist charges of Soviet collaboration with the "imperialists." This posture was carried to absurd lengths when Kosygin refused an invitation to visit Washington during his stay at the United Nations in June, 1967, and hairsplitting diplomatic negotiation was required to arrange a meeting between him and the President at the "mid-point" of Glassboro, New Jersey. Some of the more spectacular features of the exchange programs, which were likely to get wide publicity, were suspended or canceled. In addition, relations were plagued by a number of more than usually serious individual incidents: the Soviet discovery and execution of the intelligence agent, Oleg Penkovsky, and the subsequent publication in the West in 1965 of his notes on the Soviet police and espionage apparatus; the arrest, detention and tragic death of the young American, Newcomb Mott, who had strayed across the Soviet border in

1966; and, of course, the defection of Svetlana Alliluyeva in 1967.

In the face of the hostile attitude of the post-Khrushchev leadership in the Kremlin, President Johnson, with considerable political courage, tried to maintain a forthcoming posture, stressing Soviet and American responsibilities as the major powers for continuing to try to make progress in solving our differences peacefully and in moving toward a measure of disarmament. For reasons I will go into further later, he endeavored to dissociate the Soviet Union as much as possible from the conflict in Vietnam. Consistent with this posture, the embassy in Moscow carried on a sort of holding action, trying to keep the benefits of the increased cooperation and exchanges of previous years from going down the drain during this period of political tension. Our watchwords were: firm, patient, persistent and polite.

However, it must be admitted that the freeze was not entirely on the Soviet side. The Congress was more than reluctant to go along with the President's position. It took more than two and a half years to get the Consular Convention ratified; and this was finally accomplished only after considerable controversy, in the spring of 1967, despite the manifest benefit of that convention for the United States. Similarly, the Congress consistently refused to take up President Johnson's proposal for legislation to improve East-West trade and thus give the executive a useful new instrument in the conduct of its relations with the Soviet Union and the Eastern European Communist countries. It even went so far in 1967 and 1968 as to veto any American participation in the construction of a passenger-automobile factory in the Soviet Union, an action best described by the old expression of "cutting off the nose to spite the face." Trade is not only profitable and beneficial to our own economy but can be used purposefully in political terms—in the case of the Soviet Union, to raise the pressure of consumer demand for the allocation of limited resources to the civilian sector of the economy. This obliges the leadership to consider where the funds can be found, and there are only two significant sources—military and science programs. In the instant case, just to produce 500 thousand automobiles, roughly a twentieth of our production, the Soviets are paying out $800 million abroad. For every one of these dollars, it costs them several dollars (in rubles, of course) at home just to build the plant and the Soviet components. This causes diversion of both foreign-exchange and domestic-budget resources. This program also leads to a whole set of new problems: building roads, gas stations and motels and, finally, having to deal with air pollution—all of which will force even further diversion of funds and effort.

The advent of a new administration in the United States did not change the fundamental factors affecting the American-Soviet relationship, but it did provide an opportunity for a fresh start toward some gradual improvement. President Nixon's posture in proclaiming that the "era of confrontation" is over and an "era of negotiation" is at hand was both right and timely in this respect. The situation has, in fact, been eased and the prospects improved by the opening of the Paris talks on Vietnam, by the heating up of the Sino-Soviet conflict and by Moscow's obvious desire to overcome the aggressive image left by its invasion of Czechoslovakia.

CHAPTER VIII

The Communist Monolith: How It Was
Achieved and How It Operated

Thus far I have focused on the Russian scene, trying to picture
the development of revolution in Russia, the formation of the
Communist Party organization inside the country, its seizure of
the Russian state and the establishment of the Soviet state
system. I have also outlined the rise of the Soviet Union as a
world power and considered in general terms its international
position. It is now time to turn back and look at the very
complicated picture of the world Communist organization and
its relationship to Moscow.

I have already noted that the original concept of Lenin and
his internationally minded colleagues was clearly that of Russia
as an instrument of world revolution; and that Stalin's concept

was just as clearly that of world revolution as an instrument of the Soviet national state. There are several reasons why Stalin was able to effect this subtle but all-important transformation without losing the allegiance of international Communism to Moscow. The first was the immediate and profound impact on international Communism of the Bolshevik Revolution in Russia, which gave a practical base and tangible power to what had previously been a purely theoretical movement. The second was the basic principle and practice of Communist organization—so-called "democratic centralism," which deprives the lay membership of any voice in or sometimes even knowledge of Party decisions while exacting unquestioning obedience to those decisions. Third was the stark fact that the national Communist parties were utterly dependent on Moscow for prestige, leadership and support, as well as for a secure base of operations. And, finally, there was the clever and effective development of the idea that the preservation of the U.S.S.R., as the flagship of world revolution, was the most vital concern of international Communism.

In the early days of the Revolution the Commissariat for Foreign Affairs—the Narkomindel—acted as the world revolutionary center, and the first Soviet Commissar for Foreign Affairs, Boris Chicherin, asserted in July, 1919, that assistance to outside proletarian movements was a recognized function of revolutionary diplomacy. It soon became clear to Lenin, however, that the requirements of state administration and of the world revolution made it necessary to develop separate operational machinery. To meet this requirement and to forestall the revival of the "opportunist-reformist"—in Russian terms—Social Democratic Second International, then being attempted in Bern, Switzerland, he and Trotsky issued the call for an international revolutionary gathering at Moscow. Delegates from a dozen countries responded, and in March, 1919, created the Third or Communist International, popularly called the Comintern, to promote "the violent overthrow of the bourgeois regime and the passing of power into the hands of the workers." Harmony prevailed at this first meeting, as the Soviet leaders displayed to their outside brothers the advantages of real over theoretical power. The delegates exchanged mutual felicitations and words of encouragement, issued calls for militancy to the workers of the world and received their directives and subsidies. Then they went back home to direct their own revolutions, at that time thought to be imminent throughout war-shattered Europe and its empires. In the first issue of the new organization's periodical, the *Communist International,* appearing in May, 1919, Lenin wrote: "The Third International has to a certain extent become identical with the U.S.S.R. . . . the International Union of Parties directing the movement of the proletariat to throw off the yoke of capitalism has the inestimable advantage of resting upon a basis of unprecedented solidity—on a number of 'Soviet' republics which are in a position to bring about on an international scale the dictatorship of the proletariat and its victory over capitalism."

The Second Congress of the Comintern, held at Moscow from July 19 to August 7, 1920, was the real organizational meeting. Considerably less harmony prevailed as Lenin and his Bolshevik colleagues proceeded to apply to the new organization the principle of "democratic centralism." One of the foreign participants was to write later: "There was considerable heated protest against the 'steam-roller' methods of the organization and some of the foreign delegates were indignant to discover that they had been invited to Moscow not to confer but to submit." But steam-roller tactics, backed by the fundamental reality of the comparative power position, easily won out. The Congress adopted an elaborate compendium of theses and statutes, which laid the foundations of the Comintern organization and defined the obligations and responsibilities of membership.

The structure of the organization, as laid down at this Congress, developed in practice and finally formalized in the constitution and rules adopted by the Sixth Congress in 1928, provided for:

1. A World Congress "to be convened once every two years," with votes "allocated in accordance with the membership of the given party and the political importance of the given country"—clearly a formula for the dominance of the Russian Communist Party.

2. An Executive Committee empowered to "give instructions to all sections of the Communist International and control their activities." It was specified that at least five out of fifteen members must be Russian since "the bulk of the work and responsibility of the Executive Committee lies within the party of the country where it finds its residence." The central committees of the separate national Communist parties, now called "sections" of the international organization, were made directly responsible to this Executive Committee. And the specific functions and powers assigned to this Executive Committee included the following:

· Take decisions mandatorily binding on all sections, that is, all national Communist parties.
· Annul decisions taken by any section.
· Expel entire sections, groups or individual members.
· Approve and authorize the programs of individual sections.
· Accept the affiliation of "organizations and parties sympathetic to socialism."
· Approve changes of officers of sections (it was explained that "the leading posts in the Party do not belong to the occupant of that post but to the Comintern as a whole").
· Approve transfers of individual members from one country to another.
· Fix the amount of and collect dues from the sections.
· Establish its own permanent bureaus for areas or individual countries, authorized to issue mandatory instructions to local sections.
· Assign to the sections its own representatives, "especially obliged to supervise the carrying out of the decisions of the world congresses and instructions of the Executive Committee."
· Publish the official organs of the Comintern.

3. The establishment of a Presidium of the Executive Committee as "the permanent body carrying out all the business of the Executive Committee in the interval between the meetings of the latter," that is, once every six months. This Pre-

sidium was, of course, the real residence of international Communist power. In addition to exercising the functions and powers nominally assigned to the Executive Committee, as we have just reviewed, the Presidium was exclusively charged with:

- Election of the political secretariat.
- Appointment of the editorial staffs of Comintern publications.
- Setting up permanent committees "for guiding the work of definite groups of sections of the Comintern and other departments as necessary for its work."

4. The setting up of an International Control Commission, empowered to "investigate matters concerning the unity of the sections and also the Communist conduct of individual members of the various sections." This was, of course, the secret police, or NKVD of the Comintern.

Twenty-one "conditions of admission" to the Comintern, approved by the Second Congress, were imposed on member parties, that is, "sections." The following were the principal requirements:

1. Complete acceptance and active propagation of real Communist ideology, in accordance with Comintern program and decisions.
2. Systematic and regular removal and replacement by Communists of all Social Democratic "reformists."
3. Creation and maintenance of "a parallel illegal apparatus" in countries where the Communist Party is legal.
4. Adoption of "cellular" organization, and especially the formation of Communist cells for propaganda and agitation "in every military organization" and in labor unions.
5. Renunciation of "social patriotism."
6. Active support of the liberation of colonies and suppressed nationalities, including those of each section's own country.
7. Organization of the Party on the "principle of democratic centralism," and the prevention of discussion of any questions after decisions have been taken with respect thereto by higher organs.

8. Rendering of "every possible assistance to the Soviet Republics in their struggle against all counterrevolutionary forces."
9. Submission of programs to the Comintern for approval.
10. Obedience to all decisions of congresses or of the Executive Committee or its Presidium.

The operation of this marvel of power centralization has been well described by the American Communist, Benjamin Gitlow, a repentant onetime member of the Executive Committee of the Comintern. In his book, published in 1939, he wrote:

> Decisions reached by the Politburo of the Communist Party of the Soviet Union were handed down to the Communist Party in question through the Comintern. The internationalism of the Communist International was thus never more than a reflection of Russian desires and Russian policy. Hence, the policy of every Communist Party became dependent on the exigencies of the foreign policy of the Soviet Union. That was not apparent in the early days . . . but with stabilization and crystallization under Stalin's personal dictatorship, it is clear that this characteristic of Communism was inherent from the start.

Subsequent Comintern congresses were held in Moscow in 1921, 1922, 1924, 1928 and 1935. They were for the most part occupied with: approval of the interim activities of the Executive Committee, usually by unanimous vote; reports of the various sections; establishment of subordinate international revolutionary agencies designed to broaden the base of the revolutionary movement by drawing in special groups and classes; and adoption of resolutions approving alterations in the "Party line" required by the Soviet Union's internal problems, such as industrialization and periodic purges, or by shifting values and changes in the international balance of power and by the flow and ebb of the revolutionary tide throughout the world. Typical of the subordinate organizations set up were: the Communist International of Youth, the Peasant International, the Red International of Trade Unions, the International of Educational Workers and the International Cooperative Alliance.

Work had also been going forward since the beginning on a basic "Program of the Communist International." This was

finally brought to finished form and adopted by the Sixth World
Congress on September 7, 1928. This long document was the
principal directive for all Communists for many years to come.
It continues to be cited in Communist writings and remains of
basic importance to students of international politics. For
present purposes, however, it may suffice to say, in broad outline,
that after reviewing Marxist-Leninist theses of the inevitability of
the revolutionary collapse of imperialist capitalism and reaffirm-
ing the Comintern aim to give the process a shove at the appropriate moment, the program proceeds to outline the strategy and
tactics necessary to assure the smooth establishment and functioning of the dictatorship of the proletariat along Soviet lines.

The struggle between Stalin and Trotsky, following Lenin's
death in 1924, shook international Communism to its depths.
For several years national leaders and aspirants jockeyed for
favor in accordance with their latest estimate of the battle
raging in the Soviet Union. In 1928, after his victory over and
exile of Trotsky, Stalin was in a position to move his henchmen
into the Presidium, the Executive Committee and the Central
Committee of the Comintern and through these agencies to
remake the Comintern in his own pattern. Mr. Gitlow again
describes the process: "In every party, the most tried and
trusted leaders fell under Stalin's ax precisely because of their
integrity, prestige and independence. And their places were
taken by sycophants beholden to Stalin. He put an end to
factionalism in the American party by directly appointing the
leader . . . and subjecting him completely to Russian pleni-
potentiaries with full powers." Stalin's methods were, in fact,
mainly the devices of character assassination and organizational terror which had served him so well in the internal
struggle, and the purge was soon accomplished. The process
destroyed whatever shreds of independence still remained to the
national sections, and they were henceforth purely satellites of
the Communist Party of the Soviet Union. Stalin had indeed
now made a reality of his concept of the world revolution as an
instrument of the Soviet national state.

In discussing Stalin's tactics in appealing to nationalism
and traditionalism during World War II, I mentioned the sur-

prising resolution of the Presidium of the Executive Committee of the Communist International, on May 22, 1943, dissolving the organization "as the directing center for the international working class movement." The text of the resolution explained that:

> The whole development of events in the last quarter-century and the experience accumulated by the Comintern convincingly showed that the organization . . . has been outgrown by the growth of the working class movement and by the complications of its problems in separate countries, and has even become a drag. . . .
>
> For example, in countries occupied by the Hitlerites, the basic task consists in promoting the armed struggle developing into a national war of liberation against Hitlerite Germany.
>
> The mobilization of the people can be best carried out by the vanguard of the working class movement working within the framework of its own country.
>
> Communists have never been supporters of the conservation of organizational forms that have outlived themselves. They have always subordinated forms and methods . . . to the fundamental political interests of the working class movement as a whole; to peculiarities of the concrete historical situation and problems immediately resulting therefrom.

In conclusion, the resolution said the decision was therefore taken "in consideration of the foregoing" and of the "growth and the political maturity of Communist parties and their leading cadres in separate countries."

If this resolution is carefully analyzed in the light of the prevailing circumstances, the conclusion is inescapable that the decision to "dissolve" the Comintern eliminated some of the disadvantages but practically none of the advantages of that organization, from the Russian point of view; and that the control of the world revolutionary movement by the Communist Party of the Soviet Union would not be essentially diminished. The "centralist" organization had, in fact, made the national Communist parties, through their ruling central committees, directly responsible to the very small Presidium of the Executive Committee of the Comintern, dominated by the Communist Party of the Soviet Union. This control was applied and assured by a political Secretariat, selected by the Presidium and operating in the directing center in Moscow and in regional and country offices throughout the world. During the years this international bureaucracy, predominantly Russian, had been trained and disciplined and developed to enormous proportions, and it was not liquidated by the passage of a resolution.

By the end of the 1920s the Comintern had served its basic purpose in bringing the world's revolutionary groups together and under Moscow's control. As the effectiveness of the real and invisible operating machinery developed, the public apparatus of the Comintern fell into progressive disuse. Gatherings of the world congresses and even the Plenum of the Executive Committee became increasingly rare, thus paralleling the experience in Russia itself as respects meetings of the Central Committee and of congresses of the Soviet Party. The visible organization which had antagonized and frightened the outside world had, in effect, become simply a mask for the real machinery of the dictatorship developing and functioning underneath.

Communist ideology and planning had foreseen and provided advance solutions for practically every conceivable world situation except that which actually developed in the 1930s, when an unprecedented degree of secrecy, deception and maneuver became vital to Soviet foreign policy. This situation was touched upon at the Seventh Comintern Congress in 1935 by the Italian Palmiro Ercoli. Declaring that the main task of world Communism was to ensure the victory of the Red Army, Ercoli added, evasively but significantly: "If anybody asks us what this position means and how we are going to act . . . we can give a single answer—in each given case we shall act as Marxists . . . we have a leader, Comrade Stalin, who has always found the line that led to victory." Here was a clear admission that henceforth Communist policy would not be openly discussed or declared; that unexpected and apparently incomprehensible actions might become inevitable; that complete power and authority would be placed in the hands of the leader; and that obedience, even to sometimes incomprehensible directions, was the chief duty of world Communism. The confusion of the Communists during the various gyrations of Soviet foreign policy after 1935 was obvious to all the world—but so was their loyal support of Soviet interests and policies. And during this critical seven-year period preceding Hitler's invasion of the Soviet Union, the public apparatus of the Comintern, though not yet officially "dissolved," was entirely inoperative.

The capitalist-Communist coalition in World War II clearly had made impossible the orthodox application of the Marxist-Leninist concept of "turning imperialist war into civil war." However, the development of the war brought other opportunities capable of maximum exploitation only outside the framework of the Comintern. Resistance movements in the German-occupied countries were seen by Moscow as a peculiar synthesis of a military anti-German organization with a popular underground revolutionary movement of the traditional type, with voluntary participation, rigid self-imposed discipline and secret and conspiratorial operating techniques. Here, then, were the organizations to be penetrated, captured and developed as the strong points in the immediate sphere of Soviet influence in Eastern Europe and as the nuclei of revolution in Western Europe.

Finally, it must be noted that the Comintern did not end in the internal strife that had marked the collapse of previous international political bodies, but as the result of a deliberate, agreed decision by the leading representatives of participating parties, with no apparent residue of intra-Party disagreement or antagonism. It was clear that nothing was further from Moscow's thoughts than to deprive itself of such a forceful weapon of world policy as the power to direct the activities of numerous parties in other countries, at a time when that power was becoming greater than ever before.

Thus the dissolution of the Comintern as a formal organization did not change the essential control. The key individuals remained. They continued to depend on Moscow, as did the national Communist parties. Indeed, the apparatus—the international bureaucracy—of the Comintern had produced a whole legion of Soviet-trained agents who could now serve Stalin's purposes, in many cases back in their own countries. I will mention just a few to illustrate: Klement Gottwald, who became

Prime Minister of Czechoslovakia; Georgi Dimitrov, who became Prime Minister of Bulgaria; Wilhelm Pieck, who became President of the so-called German Democratic Republic in Soviet-occupied East Germany, and his successor, Walter Ulbricht; and Maurice Thorez, who became a member of the postwar coalition government in France and built up the French Communist Party to a role of formidable strength in French domestic politics.

During the twenty-five years of its formal existence as an organization the Comintern did not bring about a Communist revolution in a single country. Many observers of the Soviet scene believe that Stalin actually feared a revolution in any major outside country which might rival that of the Soviet Union and remain out of the Kremlin's control, and that as a result he deliberately imposed a restraining influence. Indeed, Stalin's utter cynicism with respect to independent activity by other national Communist parties or sections was illustrated by his handling of potential revolutionary situations in Germany in 1923 and in China a few years later. In defeated Germany, after World War I, there developed wild inflation and a complete breakdown of the economic and social order. Not only Communists, but practically everyone else, thought the situation was ripe for a Bolshevik-type revolution and expected it to take place. In accordance with its Comintern obligations, the German Communist Party turned to Moscow for instructions. Stalin, with what one of his leftist opponents called "characteristic organic distrust in the proletarian revolution," said that the attempt would fail. Being master of the apparatus, his view prevailed and the spirit of the German Party was broken. It was only a few months later that Stalin made his famous and basic proclamation of "socialism in one country." He was similarly negative a few years later toward an appeal for advice and assistance from the Chinese Communists. Instead of backing them in the uprisings they launched in 1927, he continued to support Chiang Kai-shek and the Kuomintang.

However, the Comintern did provide the machinery which enabled the Kremlin to get an iron grip on practically every Communist Party throughout the world and to use the apparatus as an effective instrument of Soviet world policy, specializing in subversive activities and espionage for Moscow. It was the membership of these separate Communist parties which provided the raw material for the Moscow-trained Comintern professionals and functionaries. This was the dough, leavened by Marxist-Leninist-Stalinist ideology, which responded to the expert kneading of these Moscow-trained bakers.

One of the principal end products of this process was domestic "front" organizations in capitalist countries, supporting policies and interests of the Soviet Union, usually at the cost of jeopardizing the policies and interests of their own governments. The two principal methods employed were: first, the creation of organizations with innocuous or mass-appeal names, pursuing ostensibly "liberal" purposes and sponsored by a mixture of tested Stalinists and simple-minded citizens with vaguely "progressive" ideas; and, second, the infiltration or penetration, by the approved Party tactics of "boring from within," of labor unions or established and unimpeachable liberal or progressive organizations of every type. In either case the objective of the Comintern agent was the same: control of the key positions, especially the secretaryship and office staff, and of the publicity and publications of the organization. Stalin had laid out the essential rationale in a speech as far back as 1924, when he said: "The Party is the rallying point for the best elements of the working class, of those who are in touch with the non-Party proletarian organizations. The Party forms the best training school for leaders. The Party is the only organization competent . . . to transform all non-Party working class organizations into accessory organs and transmission belts linking up the Party with the working class as a whole."

These "front" organizations typically sprang up like mushrooms, to serve current Soviet purposes. A survey made shortly after World War II disclosed nearly a hundred of them, always with beguilingly democratic, progressive names, directed at practically every segment of the population: youth, women, consumers, minorities, professions, trade unions and religious, civic and progressive groups. A good example that sprang up in 1946, more or less on the heels of Stalin's famous speech of

February 9 of that year launching the Cold War, was called "The National Committee to Win the Peace." It was co-chaired by a retired Marine general and actor-singer Paul Robeson, and its list of sponsors included the publicity-fetching names of many famous American writers, actors and movie stars. These gullible people, still under the spell of wartime propaganda, were led to support Soviet positions practically across the board. It turned out that the executive director of this "National Committee" was one Abbot Simon, a member of the American section of the Young Communist League. Six years before, Simon had been a founder of another organization called the "American Peace Mobilization," which, during the period of Nazi-Soviet collaboration from 1939 to 1941, was calling President Roosevelt an imperialist warmonger and demanding that the United States stay out of the war.

Despite the disappearance of the overt organization, Moscow's own international Party apparatus continues to conduct this kind of activity incessantly throughout the world. New organizations appear or disappear according to shifts in the focus of Kremlin interest or in Soviet policies. They stage demonstrations, solicit signatures to declarations or petitions, arrange meetings, organize write-your-Congressman campaigns, seek television and press publicity and the like. While the groups and their labels change, the behind-the-scenes operating personnel tend to be the same professional agitators. For years the Department of Justice has maintained a current list of such "subversive organizations"; and if you ever happen to apply for federal government employment, you will find that list attached to the application and you will be required to state whether or not you have ever participated in any of these (currently about three hundred) organizations.

The overt successor to the Comintern was established in September, 1947, four years after the formal dissolution, under the name of the "Communist Information Bureau" or "Cominform."

We diplomats in Moscow had for some time detected an inclination on the part of the Kremlin to tighten the formal bonds between the various Communist parties. For this purpose,

Moscow had adopted the practice of organizing what were really big international Communist gatherings around important national Communist congresses. We noted, for example, that the British Party Conference, held in London early in 1946, seemed to be the occasion for a secret, large-scale Communist meeting. Visiting delegates of considerable importance in the Communist world were present from practically all countries of Europe and the Near East, together with a sprinkling of delegates from other parts of the world. We felt at the time that this kind of revived activity might well be a prelude to the overt re-establishment of an international Communist agency. Furthermore, the recapture of the initiative by the West through the Truman Doctrine and the European reconstruction program had provided the appropriate circumstances and put the Kremlin on the defensive. Consequently, while the actual time and place of the Cominform organizational meeting in Poland was a carefully guarded secret to which we were not privy, it was no surprise to us when *Pravda* on October 5, 1947, announced that the conference had taken place.

Now the actual public establishment of the Cominform probably added very little to the thoroughness or the effectiveness of the Kremlin's world-wide organization. This had continued to exist, stemming from the Secretariat of the Central Committee of the Communist Party of the Soviet Union, and other agencies in Moscow. But in the face of the new positive programs of the West, even the Communist faithful needed some kind of publicly declared program to which they could pledge allegiance. At the same time such a program served as a public commitment, making it impossible for the Communist leaders in the satellite countries and in France and in Italy to succumb to any temptation they might feel to secure American material aid for the reconstruction of their country's economy. It was thus a sort of multilateral ratification of Molotov's action in walking out of the Marshall Plan Conference in Paris.

Like all Communist documents of this nature, the Cominform declaration was filled with Communist double-talk and featured that particular Russian practice, often very revealing to us in the embassy, of accusing their opponents of doing what they themselves were doing or about to do. The title of the organization itself was deliberately misleading; while it was officially described as an information bureau, the declaration specifically described the tasks of the organization as including "an exchange of experience between parties, and, in case of necessity, coordination of their activities." The declaration also attempted to leave the impression that there had been little coordination of international Communist activities since the dissolution of the Comintern, by referring to the lack of bonds among the parties as "a great deficiency in the present situation." It described the Truman Doctrine and Marshall Plan "as only a farce, a European branch of the general world plan of political expansion being realized by the United States of America." Then it went on to describe American imperialist methods in this alleged "world plan of political expansion" in terms which, to my mind, are as good a short description as I have ever read of Russian Communist tactics: "The arsenal of tactical methods used by the imperialist camp is further very complex. It combines direct threats of force, blackmail and intimidation, all sorts of political tricks and economic pressure, bribery, the using for its own ends of conflicting interests and disagreements, with the aim of strengthening its position; and all that is camouflaged by a mask of liberalism and pacifism in order to deceive and befuddle people not too dexterous in politics."

The Cominform was to serve Moscow's purposes in various ways, notably in providing an instrument for organizing a common front against Tito's defection in 1948 and an organization from which Tito could be formally "excommunicated." However, the Cominform was never quite the cohesive and monolithic organization firmly controlled by Moscow that the Comintern had been. While Tito was the extreme example, the other Moscow-trained Communists who had come to power in other Eastern European countries were also subject to national pressures, and other cracks from time to time appeared in the Cominform structure. Deterioration increased rapidly after Stalin's iron hand was removed by his death in 1953. Khrushchev's pilgrimage to Belgrade in 1955 and half-apology to Tito seemed to set the Kremlin seal of approval on Yugoslavia's independent line and encouraged others in the same direction. Then, on April 17, 1956, two months after Khrushchev delivered his secret speech denouncing Stalin, the Cominform was in turn dissolved and its journal, *For a Lasting Peace, for a People's Democracy,* which had been propagating the Soviet line in multiple languages every week for about nine years, ceased publication. Soon afterward, popular uprisings took place in Poland and Hungary and Stalinist leadership was ousted from the ruling Communist parties in those countries. In Hungary the movement developed into a direct rebellion against Moscow, which was ruthlessly crushed by the Soviet armed forces.

By this time Communist China had also entered the picture and acquired status, further underlining the increasingly obvious diffusion of authority and the lack of central control. Differences began to arise within the Communist movement over substance and form, ideology and organization, strategy and tactics, autonomy and control. Unlike in Stalin's day, it was no longer possible to settle these differences by Kremlin dictate and there was no regular machinery for their resolution. Khrushchev tried hard to restore order and unity. In November, 1957, he got together all the ruling parties, except the Yugoslav, and hammered out with them a common "declaration," setting forth a basic anti-imperialist line for the world Communist parties and providing a loose definition for relations among them. This was a prelude to the convocation of a conference of eighty-one Communist and workers' parties in Moscow in November and December, 1960—twelve "ruling" parties, again minus Yugoslavia, and sixty-nine other, or "nonruling," parties. After a long series of meetings and discussions and obvious compromises, agreement was reached on a document of forty closely printed pages, described as "the militant standard and guide of action for the entire international Communist movement," which re-established at least a surface unity. This new "Communist Manifesto" declared that:

A new distinctive feature of our time is that the world's socialist system is being transformed into a decisive factor in the development of human society. The strength and invincibility of socialism have been shown in the past decades in the gigantic crisis between the new and the old world. The attempts by imperialism and its striking force, Fascism, to halt the course of historic development by military means have met with failure. . . . No efforts by imperialism can stop the progressive development of history. The firm prerequisites have been laid down for further and decisive victories for socialism. The complete victory of socialism is inevitable. . . . The decay of capitalism manifests itself chiefly in the principal country of contemporary imperialism—the United States. . . . American imperialism has become the biggest national exploiter. . . . American imperialism strives to dominate many states, using aid as its chief means.

The document then went on at some length to modify previous Communist doctrine to the effect that wars are inevitable as long as "imperialism" exists. The shift in the world balance of power, it claimed, now makes it possible for the Communist camp to prevent imperialist aggression and war. Since "time is working for socialism and against capitalism," the manifesto rejected what it called "the American doctrine of the Cold War" and proclaimed a policy of "peaceful coexistence." But it went on to define this "peaceful coexistence" in terms which I would consider, in fact, an accurate definition of "Cold War." Here is how the declaration put it:

Peaceful coexistence among states does not mean, as the revisionists assert, a rejection of the class war. Coexistence between states of differing social systems is a form of class struggle between socialism and capitalism. . . . Peaceful coexistence of states with different social systems does not mean reconciliation between the socialist and bourgeois ideologies. On the contrary, it implies an intensification of the struggle of the working class and of all Communist parties for the triumph of socialist ideas.

Even more militantly, the document declared:

The Communist parties are actively fighting for the consistent fulfillment of the anti-imperialist, anti-feudal democratic revolution. . . . They support the actions of national governments which lead to the consolidation of the gains they have won and which undermine the positions of imperialism. . . . The working class and its revolutionary vanguard will increasingly take the offensive against the rule of oppressors and exploiters in every aspect of political, economic and ideological life in every country.

However, despite the militant tone, the document itself revealed some fissures under the ostensibly monolithic façade of the Communist camp in its attacks on "dogmatists" (i.e., fundamentalists) on one side and "revisionists" (i.e., liberals) on the other, as well as in its warnings against the efforts of the imperialists "to divide and disrupt the solidarity of the working class" and its reference to the continued presence of "the vestiges of capitalism in the minds of the people" in the Communist-ruled countries.

The 1960 declaration was the last basic program of world Communism, subscribed to by all important "sections" of the movement except Yugoslavia. In practice, however, both Moscow and Peking would cite it frequently in ensuing years in support of their increasingly antagonistic positions.

I have discussed the serious differences that arose between the Western Allies and the Soviet Union during the war over Soviet treatment of the Eastern European countries and Stalin's determination to exclude the West from this region and establish his own dependent puppet regimes. And, in fact, a gradual process of remaking them in the image of the Soviet constituent republics took place in the postwar years. The process was slowed down by the pressures of world opinion, by the absolute necessity of a minimum of postwar reconstruction in some of the states and by internal resistance on both political and economic levels. It was also delayed by the initial draining off from these areas of every bit of their national wealth or production which could serve the immediate interest of Soviet postwar reconstruction. This not only was in accord with the natural priority which Moscow will always assign to the needs of Moscow, but also served the essential and inevitable purpose of reducing rapidly the living standards in the satellite countries to something more in keeping with the low standards of the Soviet Union itself.

In general, the first step in all the satellite countries was to secure control of the police. Once this was done, destruction of the power of the bourgeoisie could be undertaken in earnest. The land and the productive apparatus could be nationalized and recalcitrant owners liquidated as criminal elements. The taxing power could be used to destroy the merchants or at least reduce them to a status of absolute subjugation. Terror and espionage were introduced as major revolutionary weapons, on the Russian example. When these had served their purpose in consolidating Communist control on the governmental and economic levels, they were turned with full force against any institutions in a position to weaken or challenge the consolidation of complete Communist authority. If there were any deviations from the Soviet model or faltering in any of the satellite countries, we could expect to see an article in the Moscow press obliquely calling the local Communist rulers back into line, by citing the teachings of Lenin and Stalin. Presumably such an article would reflect more direct written or verbal instructions delivered through Soviet agents in the country involved. For in achieving the Sovietization of the satellite countries, it was clear that the channel used—as had been the case in the Soviet Union itself—was the Communist parties and Party agents stationed respectively in Moscow and in capitals of the countries concerned.

It was an amusing, if sometimes pitiful, sidelight to the relationship between the Soviet Union and the satellites to observe the Eastern European diplomats in Moscow in the postwar years. It was obvious that they were not the real channels of communication between the Soviet Government and the governments of their own countries. We would have specific indications from time to time that the satellite representatives did not even know what was going on between the two countries or in their own country. In fact, immediately after the Communist seizure of power in Eastern Europe, the new rulers were clearly embarrassed by their lack of trained personnel to handle diplomatic representation. They thoroughly distrusted and promptly liquidated their old bourgeois diplomatic services, but had no trained or experienced Communist personnel to replace them. Consequently, our satellite diplomatic colleagues in Moscow, during most of my first stay there, tended to be acquiescent leftist professors or writers. In many cases they were amiable and high-minded people. But nobody trusted them. They did not dare to associate with the non-Communist diplomatic corps, and they got no better reception from the Russians than any of the rest of us. In fact, I believe they were even more distrusted than we Westerners were. Any Russian official has been trained how to deal with a capitalist, but apparently he has not been trained how to deal with a hybrid. In those circumstances any Russian knows very well that his best bet is to do nothing and say nothing, but to remain on his guard. Occasionally, these unhappy diplomats would venture to invite to receptions colleagues whom they regarded as relatively neutral or safe, such as Swedes or Swiss or Indians, together with Russian officials or other satellite diplomats. I've heard many incredible stories about such occasions. No one said anything. If some good soul in an effort to be congenial happened to mention even the weather, the whole company froze, remembering that such information had recently been classified as an official state secret. Thus the whole evening would pass, through an infinite succession of courses, from vodka and caviar to gooey pastry, in an atmosphere of dead silence or conversation about utter trivia.

In the early stages of the game it was clear that the Kremlin preferred to digest its victims piecemeal. This enabled Moscow to extract the maximum possible contributions to the Soviet economy from each of the states. It also enabled the Kremlin to adapt its instructions and the timetable of the Soviet program to the state of development of the country in question, to the amount of resistance and to the effectiveness of its own control over the particular puppet leaders involved. Moreover, this tactic did not arouse so many embarrassing questions and suspicions in the minds of the West or provide concrete developments on which Western governments could hang accusations or base action in the United Nations. As the Sovietization program progressed and cooperation in the political, military, economic and cultural fields became desirable, even this was for a long time accomplished by means of a whole network of bilateral agreements of all kinds.

A study which we made at Moscow as early as 1946 disclosed a series of over twenty agreements in the economic field alone, between the Soviet Union and the satellites and among the satellites themselves, which had already accomplished the purpose of channeling the great bulk of satellite trade away from the West and toward the East. This was but a small first taste of the countless agreements which were to follow, the total effect of which was to tie all phases of satellite life to the Soviet system. In the economic field, in addition to the trade agreements, the bulk of the industrial and trading machinery, particularly in the ex-enemy satellite states, was taken under Soviet control through the establishment of joint companies, technically 50 percent Russian and 50 percent native, but dominated by the Russian element, which was given all kinds of extraterritorial privileges. Any American "capitalist-imperialist" must certainly dream about the Utopian kind of business arrangements that figured in some of these agreements. In many instances, the Russian partner had a guarantee of 50 percent of the profits and of his ability to take them out of the country, either in hard currency or in commodities. At the same time, he was protected from participation in any losses. The concrete investment was usually entirely native or in some instances expropriated foreign investments; the Soviet contribution was more usually just managerial and technical personnel. Thus Russians began to appear in the key positions in the larger industrial and business enterprises in the satellites, as well as throughout the entire state structure, particularly in the secret police apparatus and in the ministries of foreign affairs and in the Communist Party organization proper.

Moscow really went too far for its own good, especially in the economic field. In many cases, the Russians so drained the resources of the satellite states as to destroy their productive capacity. Satellite factories lay idle from lack of raw materials and machinery for which they had always depended on the West. In January, 1949, in order to provide better planning and coordination, while at the same time retaining its control, and in order to provide an Eastern response to the successful Marshall Plan organization in Western Europe, Moscow created a so-called Council for Economic Mutual Aid, often referred to by its initials, CEMA, or, more popularly, simply as COMECON. In fact, of course, COMECON capped the whole network of interdependent economic agreements between the Soviet Union and the satellites and provided a central economic management and planning organization, located in Moscow and of course run by the typical executive secretariat, with a dominant Russian element. Even so, COMECON has not been a startling sucess— and, indeed, is in no way comparable to the thriving Western European Economic Community or Common Market. By the time it was organized, Tito had already successfully rebelled against Soviet domination and control, and the other satellites had been increasingly encouraged to stand up for their own national interests, particularly in the economic field. And by the time I returned to the Soviet Union as Ambassador in 1962, Khrushchev was already saying to us, privately, with reference to Eastern Europe, "These children are getting too big to spank."

Tito had been Moscow-trained, but he was not one of the expatriate Communists who stayed in Moscow during the war, to be carried back to their own country on the shoulders of the Red Army. Tito spent the war in his native hills, taking an active and courageous part in the struggle against the common enemy. He was an independent and self-made man, who had not lost his national character. He could not stand what the Russians wanted to do to his country, and he could not stand a surrender to the Kremlin of the personal power which he had won mainly by his own efforts.

All the hypocritical wordage of the Cominform resolution which we found in our *Pravda* of June 29, 1948, did not obscure the obvious fact that here was a pure issue of power—of the indivisible power which, in the Russian mind, means 100 percent control from the top down. And this Cominform declaration was but a formal and ostensibly multilateral revelation of a decision already taken by the Kremlin with regard to a direct and bilateral dispute it had been carrying on with Tito for some months. Most of the accusations were farcical, in that Tito was condemned for doing most of the things which were established practice in the Soviet Union and which he had learned well during his Moscow training. The Kremlin certainly did not mind Tito's establishment of a secret police or of a strong military force. Indeed, they would have criticized him for doing anything else. But they did mind his refusal to let them operate these agencies through Russian "advisers." The Kremlin certainly could not criticize Tito for not having proceeded vigorously with the collectivization of agriculture. This step requires both a thoroughly established regime and a lot of material resources, such as tractors and other agricultural machinery. The Bolsheviks had themselves been obliged to postpone this step for nearly a dozen years after the Revolution, until they felt able to weather the destruction of millions of recalcitrant peasant farmers. But they vigorously resented Tito's making such a decision for himself.

It is clear from the correspondence made public by the Yugoslav Government, after the break, that the Soviet Communist Party Politburo had demanded the same authority over the satellite Communist parties that it exercised over subordinate organizations inside the Soviet Union. Even though those foreign Communist parties had achieved control of the governments of their own countries, they found that the Kremlin then expected not only to direct their activities as Communist parties and as governments, but also to establish its own control organization in the country—that is, intelligence agencies to gather information independently, to check on the activities of the Party and its members, and to develop a framework of Party officials whose first allegiance would be not to their own country but to the Soviet Union. Tito's refusal to submit posed a fundamental issue. Stalin undoubtedly recognized it as such, and would have dealt with Tito even more harshly than he did had it not been for the combination of Tito's own courage and popular support, the accessibility of Yugoslavia to the West and the promptness of Western support. I think one of the great and most courageous decisions in America foreign policy was President Truman's prompt support of the Yugoslav declaration of national independence by the provision of large-scale military and economic aid to support that declaration. In the ensuing years the Yugoslav example has been of the greatest importance in influencing developments inside the Communist world.

March, 1969, marked the fiftieth anniversary of the founding, in Moscow, of the Communist International. As the date of
the opening session, March 2, approached, a rash of articles
commemorating the event began to appear in the Communist
press. In article after article, the Comintern was hailed and
praised in such terms as these:

. . . fulfilled the historic mission of uniting Leninism with the
international workers movement . . .

. . . produced outstanding leaders, organizers and theoreticians
. . . many of whom later became leaders on a national scale . . .

. . . put forward the question of the national liberation movement,
expanded the struggle against colonialism . . .

. . . helped the young Communist parties in a practical manner to
master all forms of struggle—legal and illegal, peaceful and non-
peaceful, parliamentary and nonparliamentary . . .

. . . made Lenin's principle of organized party construction and
activity—the principle of democratic centralism—the property of
[all] Communist parties . . .

. . . made the education of the working people of all countries in the
spirit of proletarian solidarity with Soviet Russia the cornerstone of
its activities . . .

. . . created and transmitted to the world revolutionary movement a
single system of principles of the strategy and tactics of revolutionary struggle . . .

. . . delivered devastating repulses to all attempts to divert particular parties into . . . rejection of the coherent struggle for socialist
revolution and dictatorship of the proletariat . . .

Then, on March 25–26, the Soviet Party organized a so-
called "Scientific Conference" in Moscow to climax the celebrations. The keynote was struck by the Kremlin's top ideologist,
Party Secretary Mikhail Suslov. Speaking in the light of today's
"united front" tactics, he admitted that the Comintern had made
errors in branding the Social Democrats as the "greatest danger"
and "directing its main blow" against them, and in taking
national differences insufficiently into account. "Stalin's personality cult had also had an adverse effect." However, Suslov
continued, these errors "bear no comparison whatsoever to the

immense positive role it performed"; he then went on to hail the unshakable unity and binding discipline of the Comintern as a lesson for the international Communist movement today. A major address on the history of the Comintern was delivered by the senior graduate of the apparatus, Walter Ulbricht, the Kremlin's puppet ruler of East Germany. Another famous graduate, President Ho Chi Minh of North Vietnam, sent greetings to the assembly, together with regrets that the war prevented him from leaving Hanoi.

The articles in the Soviet press and the speeches at the meeting reflected a nostalgia for the good old days when Moscow's position as top dog in international Communism was unquestioned. By stressing the permanency of the principles and values of the Comintern experience, they revealed a certain longing to return to unity and orthodoxy. As a Yugoslav observer stressed, Suslov's theses about the Comintern "represent present Soviet policy views on the international workers movement in existing conditions . . . the attitude which sets solidarity with the Soviet Union as the criterion of everyone's Marxism."

The Soviet sentiments were not exactly shared, however, by commentators in the other Communist-ruled countries. Not only the Yugoslavs, but even the Czechoslovak and Rumanian Party organs had a very different view as to the lessons to be learned from the history of the Comintern. Prague's *Rude Pravo* put it this way:

One began to realize in the international Communist movement that the international application of the conclusions drawn from the proletarian revolution in Russia could not be based on a superficial analogy and a direct imitation of specific tactical approaches, but that in each country it had to be based on a broad fundamental analysis of the development of the national society . . . the system of internal relationships which extolled J. V. Stalin as the "Supreme Legislator" who was not to be criticized throughout the movement in the field of theory and practice greatly limited the scope necessary for developing theoretical thought, for a matter-of-fact and open confrontation of the findings and experiences of the Communist parties. The struggle of views which necessarily accompanies any creative search was debased to the campaign against "spies and

diversionists" and linked with a gross violation of socialist legality.
. . . The diversity of conditions under which the Communists conduct their struggle has assumed such breadth that the principles of democratic centralism that are in line with the needs of the internal setup of the Communist parties can no longer be applied to their mutual relations.

Bucharest's *Scinteia* was even more specific:

The negative features of the Comintern had its impact on our Party as well: establishment of the political line from the outside, the enforcement of theses which did not suit the conditions prevailing in this country, the practice of interference in the Party's affairs going so far as appointment of the leading cadres and even of the General Secretary from among people outside this country . . . principled discussions of problems of common interest should by no means be replaced by name-calling, by pronouncement of verdicts and excommunications . . . observance of the principles of each Party's independence, equal rights and noninterference in internal affairs . . . is a *sine qua non* of the remaking and strengthening of the unity of the Communist movement.

CHAPTER IX

The Fracturing of the Communist Monolith:
The Sino-Soviet Conflict and Its Consequences

Back in 1951, when I was Director of the Voice of America, I talked at the Russian Institute of Columbia University about Soviet-American relations and the world situation generally. I wound up by taking a glance into the future. In this connection I said:

> A basic feature of the great debate on United States policy toward China during these recent years has been discussion of the question whether the Communist ruler of China, Mao Tse-tung, is or is not purely a puppet of the Kremlin. I think it has been amply demonstrated that for all practical purposes we must consider Mao such a Kremlin puppet and that we must guide our policy accordingly for the presently foreseeable future. But if we take a really long

view, I believe we must conclude that it is unthinkable that the Chinese people, over any extended period of time, would be satisfied to remain slaves and victims of a foreign regime. Eventually that people will insist on coming into its own.

The Sino-Soviet rift is usually discussed or written about or documented in terms of modern Communist ideology. I believe this is quite insufficient. To me the differences between these two countries are fundamentally national in character, based on factors which have long existed and are likely long to endure and which have their roots deep in the history of the two countries. In my earlier brief review of Russian history, I discussed the invasion of the Russian lands by the Mongol Tatar hordes and their total destruction of the original Russian state and its capital at Kiev in the year 1240. I noted that these invaders, under various successors of Genghis Khan, continued their occupation, despoliation and oppression for nearly three centuries, reducing the Russian princes to a state of abject tributary vassalage. This long period of subjugation and oppression created a lasting antipathy among the Russian people toward the "yellow beaks" (*zheltorotiki*) from the east, a feeling reflected in Russian folklore and later incorporated in the literature, opera and ballet of the last century. Expression of this antipathy was somewhat muted after the Communists came to power in China, but even then, as we traveled around the Soviet Union—particularly in the area of the Sino-Soviet borders—we were constantly made aware of the fact that the feeling persisted.

In March, 1967, as the Sino-Soviet conflict heated up, these Russian attitudes were powerfully evoked in a work by the great young Soviet poet, Andrei Voznesensky, entitled *Prologue to a Poem*. In it Voznesensky denounced in ringing tones the threat to world culture posed by the Chinese regime and its "Red Guards" and, by clear implication, called Mao and his associates heirs of the barbaric Mongol and Tatar warlords of the past. He suggested that their victory would set world civilization back several centuries and described their creed as closer to Genghis Khanism than to Marxism. He concluded on a note of proud reaffirmation of Russia's ancient role as the shield for civilized Europe against the onslaughts of the Eastern barbarians. Poetry

is popular in Russia and the poets have traditionally given voice
to the deepest aspirations and emotions of the people. Consequently, while an English prose translation cannot capture
Voznesensky's ardor and power, I want to quote a few passages.
However, before I do so, I should explain that, besides Genghis
Khan, he invokes in particular the name of Kuchum, the last of
the Tatar Khans, who was defeated in Siberia by the Cossack
Yermak in 1582—a defeat bringing the power of the Tatars to a
final end and permitting the expansion of the Russian Empire to
the east. Kuchum has gone down in Russian history as a symbol
of primitive savagery, cruelty and perfidy. Now here is Voznesensky, as translated by an embassy colleague:

I sense Kuchum!
I sense the chain mail
   through the nonsense about "military communes,"
I sense Kuchum,
I sense the urine
   on the pearly statues of the Louvre—
I sense Kuchum,
The dust rises above the horde in a mushroom cloud . . .
I sense Kuchum! . . .
Is it possible that tomorrow the astronauts will fly off to Mars, and
   day after tomorrow
Return to the epoch of cattle-herding feudalism? . . .

Genghis Khanism is fermenting like dough in the kneading-trough,
   the lout,
Begone, evil vision, or is all this only a dream?
Vanish! . . .
Paris cannot be consumed in flame over the bonfires, like a moth!
To what end the centuries of history, if we now go back on all
   fours?
What's the point of "revisionism"
   and the sanctimonious buffoonery?
(I hear "Fresh caviar!" I hear "Surrender Lake Baikal!")
Can it be that once more we must bear the planet on our bent
   back?

The official line was not far behind the poet—less dramatic
of course, but certainly no less explicit. Here is a sample from a
Radio Moscow broadcast during the same period:

China is turning once again into that yellow dragon which, just as during the old Chinese dynasties, is ready to pounce on its weaker neighbors . . . the peoples and the governments of the states bordering China must be very vigilant so that they do not become prey to the wanton chauvinists who increasingly advance along the paths of adventure in the realm of foreign policy to overcome the isolation in which they find themselves.

The May, 1968, issue of the Soviet Party magazine, *Kommunist,* compared "the deification of Mao [to] the cult of the emperors in ancient China" and charged him with "fanning great-power, nationalistic passions." "The concept of the unconditional superiority of the Chinese nation over all other peoples and of its special historical mission is being resolutely instilled," *Kommunist* continued. "A hostile attitude toward the U.S.S.R. . . . is being fostered."

In private conversations Russians, including high Russian officials, went much further in expressing their views about the "yellow peril."

I certainly do not profess any expertise about the Chinese, my only direct experience with them having been short visits to Taiwan and Hong Kong some years ago and a few months' observation of some of the overseas Chinese communities in Southeast Asia at the same time. However, many who are experts have told me that, despite the servility the Chinese have shown toward a series of white conquerors over the years—or perhaps because of this—the Chinese do harbor a feeling of racial superiority. But whether or not this is an inherent Chinese attitude, it must be said that the Chinese in their turn were given some concrete reasons for developing a feeling of antipathy toward the white Russians. For, like the other imperialists, the Russians regarded the decaying Chinese Empire as suitable nourishment for their ambitions. It may well be that from a Chinese point of view the Russians were the worst of the lot. Generally speaking, Western European imperialism in China took the form of commercial exploitation, and when the time came, it was relatively easy for the Chinese to deprive these Westerners of their trading privileges and throw them out. However, Russian imperialism took the form of territorial expansion over the great Eurasian land mass and the detachment from China and annexation by Russia of very considerable slices of Chinese territory. And the Russians remained in these territories.

I referred earlier to this leapfrog process of Russian exploration and colonization across Siberia, from one great river system to another until the Russians finally reached the "great ocean"—through the border seas out into the Pacific. Since the resulting situation is not only a bone of contention between the Soviet Union and China but is likely to be a feature of world history for some time to come, it warrants some further examination. The real Russian pioneers were the peasants who resisted the imposition of serfdom in the last half of the sixteenth century, formed themselves into bands of Cossacks and took refuge in the Siberian fastness. In 1580 the outer or eastern limit of "Russian occupation" had been the town of Perm, west of the Urals. Two years later, the defeat of Kuchum by the Cossacks under Yermak opened the gate to the east and the rate of Russian expansion into Siberia accelerated amazingly. The site of the present city of Tobolsk was occupied and the original town was founded, there on the banks of the Irtysh River, in 1587. Then, as the eastward movement continued along the lowlands of the great Siberian rivers and their tributaries, Russian settlements were established at Tomsk on the Ob River in 1604; at Yeniseisk on the Yenisei River in 1619; at Yakutsk on the Lena River in 1632; and at Okhotsk on the Pacific shores in 1638. Thus in six decades Russia had expanded across Asia from the Urals to the Pacific.

The original line of Russian city-forts was well north of China or Chinese-controlled territory. Soon, however, while following the Lena to its source, Russian explorers came into the Amur River Valley and ran into tribes under the influence of the Chinese Manchu Empire. The Manchus, then close to the height of their power, forced the Russians to draw back and the Treaty of Nerchinsk, in 1689, fixed the first boundary between the Russian and Manchu empires to the north of the Amur River line. Although there were a few subsequent readjustments in Russia's favor, this delimitation was to remain valid, in the main, for over a century and a half. Then in the nineteenth century the Manchu dynasty declined and Russia again pressed forward. New treaties were concluded in 1858 (Treaties of Argun and Tientsin) and 1860 (Treaty of Peking), by which China ceded to Russia practically all the territories north of the Amur River and between the Ussuri River and the sea.

At the same time, the Russians had started to move southward into Central Asia from their Siberian outposts. By 1855 they had advanced to a line stretching east from the central Caspian to Lake Aral, then to a point south of Alma-Ata. This penetration of the Czarist forces southward again brought Russia into direct conflict with the Manchu administration in Turkestan. The Russian advance was slowed for a while, and various temporary and sketchy delimitations of the boundaries were arranged. Then in 1871 a revolt of the Moslem population in Turkestan further weakened Manchu control, and the Russian forces resumed their march. New local agreements repeatedly changed the boundaries between the Russian and Chinese zones of influence and control in Turkestan, and the Russian zone was steadily expanded to the south and east to the disadvantage of the Chinese. Indeed, the Russian expansion soon penetrated so far into Central Asia as to alarm the British rulers in India, and led to the conclusion of bilateral agreements between the Russians and the British defining their respective spheres of influence in the region. By the turn of the century the lines between Russia and China (and India) in Central Asia were drawn roughly along the boundaries existing today.

Two additional western provinces of China, Tannu Tuva and Mongolia, were growing restless and trying to break away from Manchu rule. In 1915 a Russo-Mongolian-Chinese agreement set up and delimited an "autonomous" Outer Mongolia under Chinese suzerainty. In 1917, after the Bolshevik Revolution, both provinces established Soviet regimes, declared themselves independent and, in fact, came under the protection of the Red Army. In 1944, while everyone was preoccupied with World War II, Tannu Tuva was quietly absorbed into the Soviet Union. Meanwhile, Outer Mongolia was being brought more and more into the Soviet orbit. It is today a so-called "People's

Democracy," dependent on Moscow and protected by a Treaty of Friendship, Alliance and Mutual Assistance with the Soviet Union. After the wartime summit meeting in Yalta and in accordance with decisions reached there, Chiang Kai-shek's government of the Republic of China accepted the ostensibly independent status of Outer Mongolia, but subsequently repudiated the agreement. In 1962 Communist China negotiated a border agreement directly with Outer Mongolia, but this did not inhibit Mao Tse-tung two years later from publicly bemoaning the fate of this piece of what he called "Chinese soil" which the Soviet Union had "put under its rule."

All in all, there were over twenty principal treaties and agreements between Czarist Russia and Manchu China ceding Chinese-controlled territories to the Russians and thus extending Russian boundaries steadily eastward; and the process continued after the Revolution with the detachment of Tannu Tuva and Outer Mongolia from China. Then, after the capitulation of Japan in World War II, the Soviet Union not only gained Japanese territory in the Far East, but also reclaimed certain privileged positions of Czarist Russia in Chinese territory, notably the occupation of the ports of Dairen and Port Arthur and control of the trans-Manchurian railway. After the Communists came to power in China, these latter privileged positions were returned to the new Chinese Communist Government. However, there was no Russian suggestion of going further.

As the Sino-Soviet dispute warmed up toward the end of the 1950s, the U.S. State Department began to receive reports from the embassy in Moscow about incidents along the borders between the two countries. Much later, we were to learn that during his official visit to Moscow in 1960 the Chinese Communist Chief of State, Liu Shao-chi, had first raised the question of a readjustment of the boundaries and had been rebuffed by Khrushchev. However, as the polemical correspondence between Moscow and Peking developed during the next couple of years, references to these border incidents began to appear publicly. On September 3, 1963, the Chinese Communist press accused the Soviet Union of enticing tens of thousands of the non-Chinese population of Sinkiang (i.e., Turkic-speaking Moslems) into the U.S.S.R. A Soviet Government paper, replying a couple of weeks later, in turn accused the Chinese Communists of a whole series of border violations. In November of 1963 an exasperated Khrushchev proposed that diplomatic talks be held about border questions, and arrangements were made for a Sino-Soviet Boundary Commission to meet in Peking the following February. There was no news about the meeting available at the time except for the fact that after a very few sessions it broke up. It has since been revealed that the Chinese sought Russian admission that the treaties relating to the boundaries were "unequal" ones imposed on China, and that they offered in return to accept those boundaries as a basis for negotiating minor realignments and readjustments designed to prevent recurrence of incursions across the frontiers by either side. The Soviet delegation rejected the Chinese proposals.

The meeting had barely adjourned when in March, 1964, Mao Tse-tung said publicly that the Amur River territory and Turkestan had been torn from China by the Czars and might someday be "peacefully reclaimed." In a talk with a group of Japanese newspapermen on July 10, he went even further, saying:

The Soviet Union occupies an area of 23 million square kilometers while its population is only 200 million. It is time to put an end to this allotment. Japan occupies an area of 370 thousand square kilometers and its population is 100 million. About one hundred years ago the area to the east of Lake Baikal became Russian territory, and since then Vladivostok, Khabarovsk, Kamchatka and other areas have been Soviet territory. We have not yet presented our account for this list.

At the same time, Mao also stated publicly that he considered all these territories had been gained by conquest and confirmed by the type of "unequal," colonialist treaty which Lenin had denounced way back in 1917.

The Chinese have so far not pressed their case, either diplomatically or militarily. It seems clear, however, that each side from time to time engages in probes which the other labels "provocations," and incidents continue to take place along the frontiers. At the beginning of March, 1969, Moscow chose to give widespread publicity to a series of small-scale but particularly serious armed clashes over possession of some of the islands in the Ussuri River, which marks the boundary between the Chinese province of Manchuria and the Soviet Maritime Provinces. Some thirty-odd casualties were incurred on each side. Angry charges of aggression, demands for retribution and threats of dire consequences were exchanged. Indignation meetings were organized in both countries, and massive demonstrations were staged against each other's embassies in Moscow and Peking. The Soviet Foreign Ministry held an unusual press conference and distributed pictures showing alleged Chinese atrocities; even more unusual, Soviet Ambassadors were instructed to tell Western governments about the Chinese menace. On its side, the Chinese Communist Foreign Ministry ominously suggested that Communist China "will have to reconsider its position as regards the Sino-Soviet boundary as a whole."

Some months later, in August, an even more sensitive sector of the border flared up—that in Central Asia, where Turkic-speaking minorities constitute a large element of the population on both sides. Again blood was drawn; casualties were undisclosed, but probably exceeded those in the Ussuri incident. Again there were reciprocal accusations, denials, warnings, demonstrations. The airwaves were filled with Russians telling their version in Chinese and Chinese telling their version in Russian.

On the heels of the Ussuri incident, another Soviet poet, the well-known Yevgeny Yevtushenko, gave voice to the Russian anger and apprehension. Accusing the Chinese of dreaming of the conquest of Russia and occupation of Siberia, he bewailed the fallen and shouted defiance. Here are some translated excerpts:

> The mother's mushrooms had been picked
>   for a long time awaiting his return
> But her son has fallen on the red snow of
>   the Ussuri.
> At first they shot him at point blank range
>   and then finished him with
>   bayonets. . . .

> *The old woman wanders, her grief*
> *unmeasured. . . .*
> *"My sons, my sons"*
> *She whispers (What does it mean to her*
> *—Mao—the Red Guards?)*
> *"Sons, were not enough of you killed in*
> *the last war?"*
> *Oh if Marx could see how pitifully played*
> *out is the tragic farce of the arrogant*
> *pseudo-Communist,*
> *What even a holy idea becomes in the*
> *hands of a monster. . . .*
> *You can see in the murky twilight*
> *The new Mongol Khans have bombs in*
> *their quivers.*
> *But if they attack the warning bells will*
> *peal*
> *And we shall have enough warriors*
> *For the new battle of Kulikovo.*

Soviet publicity on the border incidents has been voluminous, both at home and abroad. Two historic anniversaries were exploited to the full as warnings to the Chinese Communists: the lightning operations by Russian and Mongolian forces under the command of Marshal Zhukov in August, 1939, which sent the Japanese invaders of eastern Mongolia reeling back into mainland China, and the ten-day campaign of Soviet forces against the million-strong Japanese Kwantung Army in August, 1945, at the end of World War II. An elaborate ceremony was staged for the presentation of a Mongolian medal to the aging Marshal, in belated recognition of the first event, and Soviet media used both events to vaunt Soviet prowess against any would-be aggressors.

After the Ussuri River clashes, the Soviet Government in June, 1969, proposed a resumption of the 1964 negotiations "to define more precisely the borderline at some stretches." The Chinese finally accepted the proposal, and the dialogue resumed in Peking at the deputy foreign minister level in October, 1969. However, in their exchanges on the subject both Moscow and Peking specifically reserved their positions on the "unequal treaties." Consequently, while temporary arrangements may be worked out to lessen tensions along the borders, there is clearly little prospect of a definitive settlement. Thus the boundary between the Chinese People's Republic and the Soviet Union remains officially in dispute. It is the longest unsettled frontier in the whole world. Extending in an uninterrupted arc from the Pamir Plateau in Central Asia to the Pacific Ocean, it is 4,150 miles long, divided into two nearly equal sectors by the Soviet-protected Mongolian People's Republic, which itself has a border of two thousand-odd miles with China.

In addition to these two factors—the natural antipathy between the Russian and Chinese peoples and the conflict over the long-unsettled border which separates them—there are two other factors in the Sino-Soviet split which are, in my mind, decidedly national, as distinct from ideological, in character. These may be stated in the form of two succinct propositions. First, the Russians have no intention of sharing their wealth with the Chinese, either now or at any time in the future. Second, the Russians are not going to let themselves get involved in a conflict with the United States as a result of Chinese Communist actions or for Chinese Communist reasons; if the Russians are ever to be involved in a direct conflict with the United States, this will be for Russian reasons.

From the time Stalin turned down their appeal for advice and help in 1927 until their victory over Chiang Kai-shek in 1949, the Chinese Communists were on their own, without substantial aid or support from Moscow. However, after he had taken power in continental China, Mao Tse-tung made it clear that the Chinese People's Republic considered itself a member of the anti-imperialist camp headed by the Soviet Union. In February, 1950, the two regimes concluded, as the basis of their relationship, a thirty-year Treaty of Friendship, Alliance and Mutual Assistance, in which each pledged to come to the aid of the other in the event of an outside attack.

This basic agreement was accompanied or soon followed by a series of arrangements providing for economic and technical aid and trade, including the restitution to China of some of the industrial equipment which the Russians had removed from

Manchuria as war booty. These aid agreements were not exactly grants or "giveaways." They were rather in the form of Soviet credit for the purchase of Soviet machines, equipment and other industrial goods to be repaid in due course by the shipment to the Soviet Union of Chinese industrial and agricultural raw materials. Soviet shipments under these agreements in the 1950s were enormous, and Chinese expressions of gratitude to "the great Soviet people for its fraternal aid to the people of China" were frequent enough to evoke in these Soviet people the unwelcome specter of an unending responsibility for the maintenance of millions of hungry yellow dependents. According to Soviet statistics, Soviet exports to China rose from less than $400 million in value in 1950 to a high of $950 million in 1959, then rapidly declined to just over $200 million in 1963. On the other side, Chinese exports to the Soviet Union rose from less than $200 million in 1950 to a high of $1,100 million in 1959; then they, in turn, started to drop. By 1956 China had incurred a debit balance toward the Soviet Union of nearly $1 billion, but in that same year its deliveries to the Soviet Union exceeded its receipts from the Soviet Union, and it was reported that China had balanced the account—that is, paid for everything it had received from the Soviet Union—by 1963. Today trade between the two—at a level of $100-odd million each way annually—is not a significant factor in the economic picture in either country.

In a speech in Moscow on September 29, 1960, marking the eleventh anniversary of the "Chinese People's Republic," the designated Soviet spokesman, Vyacheslav Yelyutin, Minister of Higher Education, claimed: that the Soviet Union had aided or was aiding in the building and reconstruction of 291 large industrial projects in China, including metallurgical combines, automotive works, machine-building works and large electric power stations; that nearly 11,000 Soviet specialists had aided in economic and cultural building in China during these eleven years; that 8,000 Chinese had been trained in Soviet enterprises; that Soviet technical documentation had been provided to enable the Chinese to design hundreds of other large industrial enterprises; that Soviet scientists and experts had cooperated in setting up 340 departments of science and nearly 500 research laboratories in Chinese higher-educational institutions; and that nearly 5,300 students, 1,400 postgraduates and 280 lecturers from China had been admitted to Soviet higher-educational establishments and scientific research institutes.

From the documentation later made public by both sides in the Sino-Soviet controversy we know that, some months before Yelyutin spoke, Khrushchev had already ordered the return to the Soviet Union of all the Soviet specialists and technicians in China; and that, even as Yelyutin spoke, these specialists and technicians were coming back by the thousands. It is now clear that Communist China wanted, needed and expected a great deal more help than it got from the Soviet Union. Even before the precise documentation became available, the nature of the argument which was going on was apparent from the theoretical and ideological discussion that was published.

In Communist theory, as developed by Lenin and Stalin, the revolution brings about the "dictatorship of the proletariat," and the establishment of a "socialist" economic system, in which "he who does not work, does not eat"; and the state expects "from each in accordance with his ability, and to each in accordance with his work." Then follows a period of transition to the glorious promised land of Communism, when a superabundance of wealth and production supports the original Marxist motto: "From each in accordance with his ability, to each in accordance with his need." The theory is clear so far as one state is concerned. But when there are a number of states which have introduced the first stage of socialism, the question arises as to just when each state enters into the glorious epoch of Communism in relation to the others.

In an obvious effort to placate the Chinese Communists, Khrushchev, in a major speech to the Twenty-first Congress of the Communist Party of the Soviet Union on January 27, 1959, dealt with the subject this way:

How will the development of the socialist countries proceed toward Communism? Can a situation be imagined in which one socialist country attains Communism and carries out Communist principles of production and distribution, while other countries remain somewhere behind, in the first stages of building a Communist society? If one takes into account the laws of economic development of the socialist system of economy, such a prospect is hardly possible. It would be theoretically correct to assume that socialist countries, correctly using the opportunities inherent in the socialist order, will more or less simultaneously reach the highest phase of Communist society.

Now what does all this theoretical verbiage mean? If it were to be taken literally, it would mean that all the so-called socialist or Communist countries would have to share their wealth until the standard of living became roughly equal in all of them. I have already noted the Kremlin's efforts after the war in Eastern Europe to drain off the economies of the countries in that area and to bring about a reduction in the standard of living there to a level nearer that prevailing in the Soviet Union itself. In the case of China the shoe is on the other foot. As it has developed its economy, the Soviet Union has achieved a per capita Gross National Product of approximately $1,500 per annum. This is only 40 percent of the per capita GNP of the United States. But, while no reliable statistics are available for Communist China, a reasonable estimate is that the Soviet figure is about fifteen times the per capita GNP for China. Thus an effort to equalize the standard of living in the two countries would require a truly supercolossal grant aid program to Communist China by the Soviet Union. Indeed, since there is no foreseeable practical prospect that equalization could be accomplished by raising the Chinese per capita GNP to the Soviet level, actual reduction in the Soviet standard would inevitably be required to accomplish that purpose. Despite Khrushchev's politically motivated words at the Twenty-first Party Congress, it was quite clear to any objective observer that this kind of sharing of the wealth would never take place.

In fact, as the conflict between Moscow and Peking worsened, such pretense was dropped. At the Twenty-second Congress of the Communist Party of the Soviet Union in October, 1961, Khrushchev formally presented and the Congress adopted his twenty-year program for the building of a Communist society in the Soviet Union. The tune and the tone were quite different from the refrain at the Twenty-first Party Congress some two and a half years earlier. Here is how the question was now dealt with in the program itself:

> The Communist Party of the Soviet Union regards Communist construction in the Soviet Union as a component of the building of Communist society by the peoples of the entire world's socialist system.
> The fact that socialist revolutions took place at different times and that the economic and cultural levels of the countries concerned are dissimilar, predetermines the nonsimultaneous completion of socialist construction in those countries and their nonsimultaneous entry into the period of the full-scale construction of Communism. . . . The first country to advance to Communism facilitates and accelerates the advance of the entire world socialist system to Communism. In building Communism, the peoples of the Soviet Union are breaking new roads for mankind, testing their correctness by their own experience, bringing out difficulties, finding ways and means of overcoming them, and selecting the best forms and methods of Communist construction. . . .
> The construction of Communism in the Soviet Union promotes the interest of every country of the socialist community, for it increases the economic might and defense potential of the world's socialist camp and provides progressively favorable opportunities for the U.S.S.R. to expand its economic and cultural cooperation with the other socialist countries and increase the assistance and support it renders them.

The new document made a feeble gesture toward the previous simultaneity formula, by modifying it to say that there was a "prospect of effecting the transition to Communism . . . within one and the same historical epoch"—whatever that means! But the basic conclusion was stated in unusually explicit terms for a Communist document:

> The development and leveling of the economy of the socialist countries must be achieved primarily by every country using its internal resources to the full, by improving the forms and methods of economic leadership, steadily applying the Leninist principles and methods of socialist economic management and making use of the advantages of the world's socialist system.

All in all, the "Russia first" message came through loud and clear. The Soviet Union would go ahead to develop its own economy and improve the standard of living of its people as fast as possible. It would thus set an example for the others to follow if they could, relying primarily on their own resources.

I now turn to the fourth decisive factor of a national character—the proposition that the Russians do not intend to become entangled in any situation which might involve them in a nuclear confrontation with the United States for Chinese reasons. We should remember that the accession of China to the Communist camp was not without its great psychological advantages. It enabled Khrushchev to boast, as he frequently did, that "one-third of mankind [or one billion people] is building a new life under the banner of scientific Communism." It also enabled him to proclaim that there had been a shift in the world balance of power toward the socialist camp. Since the subtraction of 700-plus million Chinese from these formulations reduces them to absurdities, the Chinese Communists were not without some very real bargaining power.

While exact figures are not available, it is clear that during the 1950s the Soviet Union, in fact, delivered enormous quantities of conventional war equipment to China, as well as plans and know-how for the production of Soviet models of tanks, guns and aircraft, together with machine tools and plant equipment to enable the Chinese to build these items themselves. The Chinese Communists have revealed that in October, 1957, the Soviet Union actually went so far as to undertake to help them obtain atomic weapons. It should be noted that this was a critically vulnerable time for Khrushchev. The Chinese Communists had made no secret of their dissatisfaction with Khrushchev's denunciation of Stalin the previous year. Khrushchev was desperately trying to prevent an open break on this issue and was angling to get Mao Tse-tung to attend the upcoming 1957 conference of Communist parties in Moscow in the hope of establishing a united front and a common program for world Communism. How much help the Russians actually gave the Chinese in the atomic field we may never know. It is clear to me, however, that it was substantial and that the Chinese

Communists would not have been able to explode their first atomic bomb in October, 1964, without that help. Whatever the aid was, it was apparently not as much as Mao wanted, and he is reported to have increased his demands over the next year or so, even to the point of asking for actual atomic warheads and for thermonuclear weapons.

In any event, the enormous dangers of the game they were playing became apparent to the Russians, and in June, 1959, the Soviet promise of aid to the Chinese in the nuclear field was formally abrogated. On the heels of this Soviet action, Mao Tse-tung ousted his Minister of Defense and at a Plenum of his Party's Central Committee in the summer of 1959 cracked down on the pro-Soviet faction in that body. There is no doubt in my mind but that Khrushchev and other Soviet leaders rue the day they made the original decision to help the Chinese in the nuclear field; they were always completely silent—avoiding any response whatsoever—whenever we attacked them on the subject during the many long conversations on disarmament questions that have taken place between us over the years.

For a while in 1958 and 1959 the Soviets appeared not only to be supplying military equipment but even to be supporting Chinese Communist military initiatives. Shortly after a Khrushchev visit to Peking, in August, 1958, Chinese Communist forces launched a heavy and sustained bombardment of the offshore islands of Quemoy and Matsu, held by the Chinese Nationalists. Soviet media publicly supported Peking's actions. During the several weeks of the bombardment, the United States Seventh Fleet was convoying Nationalist supply ships. After Washington announced its intention of reinforcing the Seventh Fleet, Khrushchev on September 7 wrote to President Eisenhower on the subject. Defending Peking's right "to free its own territory," Khrushchev asserted that Soviet and Chinese Communist security interests were inseparable and warned that "an attack on the Chinese People's Republic . . . is an attack on the Soviet Union." It might be noted that Khrushchev himself was at this point in the most bellicose phase of his Sputnik diplomacy—about to launch an ultimatum on Berlin.

In any case, the strong-support posture did not last long.

Just a year later, when Chinese forces attacked Indian outposts on the frontier between the two countries, the Soviet reaction was unprecedented in world Communist affairs. On September 6, 1959, the official Soviet news agency, Tass, issued a communiqué which was in effect a declaration of neutrality. Tass led off with a typical "cover" charge that the Western press had started a noisy campaign about the incident "meant to drive a wedge between the two biggest countries of Asia—the People's Republic of China and the Republic of India—whose friendship is of great importance for safeguarding peace and international cooperation in Asia and throughout the world." But it then went on to say:

> The incident on the Chinese-Indian frontier is certainly deplorable. The Soviet Union maintains friendly relations both with the People's Republic of China and the Republic of India. . . . Soviet leading quarters . . . express confidence that the two governments will settle the misunderstanding that has arisen, taking into consideration the mutual interests of, and in the spirit of the traditional friendship between, the peoples of China and India.

This Tass statement was issued just before Khrushchev left for his visit to the United States, from September 15 to 27, 1959. Immediately after the conclusion of this visit Khrushchev proceeded to Peking, arriving there on September 30. In his discussions—or, perhaps more accurately, arguments—with Mao on this occasion, Khrushchev is reported to have warned him against "testing by force the stability of the capitalist system," and to have said that the Chinese course of action with respect to India was "fraught with negative consequences not only for Sino-Indian relations, but also for the entire international situation." The Chinese charged that on this occasion Khrushchev also tried to persuade the Chinese Communists to accept a "two-China policy," that is, to desist in their claim to Taiwan and to their right to reunite Taiwan with the mainland, by force if necessary. It is clear that Khrushchev's visit did more to accentuate the growing differences between the two countries than to reconcile them, and that the Chinese took little notice of Khrushchev's warnings.

While Peking has subsequently been relatively cautious with respect to the Formosa Strait, this was not to be the case with respect to India. In October, 1962, coincident with the Cuban missile crisis, the Chinese launched a major attack on the Indian frontier. They quickly overran the principal frontier posts in the Northwest Frontier area, and the great Indian province of Bengal lay open before them all the way to Calcutta. However, having accomplished their immediate purposes of humiliating the Indian armed forces, degrading the stature of Nehru and of India itself and evoking sentiments of fear and respect among all its small neighbors to the south, China stopped, and an uneasy truce has since prevailed on the Sino-Indian frontier. Once again, Moscow took an essentially neutral posture, weighting the Soviet position perhaps a bit on the Indian side by the provision of some military supplies and equipment to the Indians.

The United States and Britain had been negotiating with the Soviet Union for nearly five years before the partial Nuclear Test Ban Treaty was initialed in Moscow on July 25, 1963, and subsequently signed there on August 3. A shift in the Soviet position which led to the final conclusion of the treaty was evident only a few months before the event. There is no doubt in my mind but that the decisive new consideration from the Soviet point of view was the fact that they now saw in such a treaty an instrument which would put considerable pressure on the Chinese Communists and tend to isolate them in the world. And, in fact, the conclusion of the treaty was promptly followed by a furious exchange of polemical charges and countercharges between the two Communist capitals. In a Chinese Government statement dated July 13, 1963, Peking called the treaty "a dirty fraud" which "betrayed the interests of the Soviet people, the interests of the people of the countries in the socialist camp, including the people of China, and the interests of all peace-loving people of the world." When the Soviet Union promptly replied that the "powerful rocket-nuclear shield of the Soviet Union insures the security not only of the Soviet Union but of all the socialist countries, including the People's Republic of China," Peking made it clear that this was not enough. Peking's rebuttal said that "the Soviet Union's possession of nuclear weapons must in no way be made a justification for preventing other socialist countries from increasing their own defense capabilities." It was in this rebuttal, issued on August 15, 1963, that the Chinese revealed the previous nuclear arrangements between the two Communist countries and charged that "the Soviet Government tried to subdue China and curry favor with U.S. imperialism by discontinuing assistance to China." Subsequent correspondence became even more vitriolic. In a rerebuttal on August 21, the Soviet Government brought to the surface a private statement made by Mao some years before. This portion of the Soviet statement bears quoting:

Every Communist-Leninist will feel disgust at an attitude to thermonuclear war such as this: "Never mind if half of mankind perishes, if 300 million Chinese die, for on the other hand imperialism will be wiped from the face of the earth and those who survive will rapidly create on the ruins of imperialism a new civilization that will be a thousand times higher."

And it is precisely such an attitude to thermonuclear war that has been present on more than one occasion in the pronouncements of highly placed Chinese representatives. . . . By its latest statement against the Nuclear Test Ban Treaty, however, the Chinese leadership only confirms that today, too, it is being guided in its foreign policy by this anti-Marxist, anti-Leninist, inhuman conception. . . .

Though some people in Peking are ready to sacrifice half the population of their country, of mankind, the Central Committee of the Communist Party of the Soviet Union and the Soviet Government treasure the lives, not only of half the population of the Soviet Union, but also the life of every Soviet person, nor is it indifferent to the fate of the other peoples of the world. . . .

The Chinese leaders are trying to present matters as if they were also speaking on behalf of the oppressed peoples of Asia, Africa and Latin America, as if they were some kind of mouthpiece of theirs . . . the appeals of the Chinese leaders reek strongly of demagoguery and adventurism. They want to foist upon the peoples of Asia, Africa and Latin America the idea that the Nuclear Test Ban Treaty and other steps aimed at reducing international tensions interfere with the development of their national liberation struggle. Such rantings are a fraud. To stake the fate of the national liberation movement on a worsening of international tension, on pushing humanity to the brink of a thermonuclear world war, as the Chinese leaders are doing, is tantamount to promising the people freedom after death.

This first phase of the public polemics culminated in an important article, published in the Soviet Government newspaper *Izvestiya* on June 29, 1964, discussing the Sino-Soviet Treaty of Friendship, Alliance and Mutual Assistance of February 15, 1950. Its authoritative author was Valerian Zorin, then Deputy Minister of Foreign Affairs, a member of the Central Committee of the Party and a diplomatic and legal expert who has long faithfully served the Kremlin's interests. In this long article Zorin came to the conclusion that the Chinese People's Republic had special interests "which cannot be supported by the military forces of the Soviet camp." He thus made it clear that the Soviet Union does not want a situation to arise in which it might legitimately be called upon to honor its obligations under that treaty with Communist China, and that the Soviet Government was already seeking an escape hatch.

After the ouster of Khrushchev the new Soviet leadership refrained from public attacks for over a year, but resumed with a major editorial in *Pravda* on November 28, 1965, and gradually developed a sustained new campaign as the so-called "cultural revolution" raged in China. In one of a series of editorial articles in the authoritative Party journal *Kommunist,* in May, 1968, Moscow reverted to the subject of the military dangers involved in Chinese Communist policies. "As early as at the 1957 Moscow Conference of Communist and Workers Parties," *Kommunist* charged, "Mao Tse-tung defended the anti-Marxist thesis that world imperialism can be defeated only through war with the use of nuclear missile weapons and alleged that the resulting countless losses, deprivations and sufferings of people are without significance." *Kommunist* then goes on to reveal the Kremlin's basic concern in terms close to those once voiced to me privately by a high Soviet official, saying:

Mao Tse-tung's group does everything within its power to exacerbate international tension wherever it considers this advantageous, and to pour oil on the fire of emerging conflicts. . . . The ruling clique in China strives to bring the U.S.S.R. and the United States into nuclear conflict and thus benefit by establishing its domination on the international arena through—in the words of a Chinese proverb—"sitting on the fence and watching two tigers fight." Essentially, this is all there is to the secret meaning of the whole Maoist "strategy of world revolution."

Now I turn to the ideological front in the Sino-Soviet conflict. You will note that I put it in fifth place. Indeed, I would almost go so far as to say that I regard the ideological controversy more as a result of the rift than as its cause. As was apparent with respect to the question of sharing the wealth inside the Communist camp, the real reasons for decisions reached are partially concealed and camouflaged by the ideological argumentation in which they are discussed. The ideological documentation is, in fact, overwhelming, and by now would probably fill a set of books about the size of the *Encyclopaedia Britannica*. This documentation takes the form of correspondence exchanged between the two parties and with other parties, speeches of the principal protagonists, Party statements and government statements, authoritative articles in the official press, communiqués, accounts of private conversations later revealed to the public, diplomatic notes and the like. There have already been four volumes of selected documentation published in English translation, covering the dispute from its beginnings through 1965 in some two thousand pages of print. The record continues to build up rapidly, particularly as polemics have reached a new crescendo on both sides during recent years. All this voluminous verbiage is, of course, a gold mine for the Kremlinologists or the Sinologists. It is also fascinating and sometimes very pungent and earthy reading, but well beyond the scope of our present interest.

There are, however, two aspects of the ideological struggle of which I would take note—one is the personal rivalry between Khrushchev and Mao Tse-tung, and the other the rivalry of the two Communist capitals for influence within the Communist world and with the lesser-developed nations of Asia, Africa and Latin America.

There was really no authoritative and accepted leader of world Communism to replace Stalin when he died in 1953. The potential successors in the highest Party offices in the Soviet Union were men whose talents were in the field of practical politics or administration, rather than of abstract thought and ideological controversy. Khrushchev was a pragmatist who made his moves mainly out of political and power considerations. Whatever his personal reasons for his denunciation of Stalin, this could not but lower the prestige of Moscow as a source of inspiration and direction for Communist comrades either inside or outside the Soviet frontiers. Likewise, his reconciliation with Yugoslavia and acceptance of "an independent and separate road to Communism" confounded loyal supporters throughout the world and promoted the spread of independent-mindedness throughout Eastern Europe and the whole world movement. In practice, then, Khrushchev was indeed a "revisionist," as Mao has repeatedly charged. In a sense, it might be said that with Stalin's disappearance Mao Tse-tung was, in fact, the outstanding old-line Communist in the world, with a whole library of ideological works already to his credit, now combined with his newly founded prestige as ruler of China. At the Ninth Congress of the Chinese Communist Party in April, 1969, it was officially proclaimed that the "thought of Mao Tse-tung" is the only authentic continuation of the work of Marx and Lenin and represents the "general line" for world Communism in the modern era. Mao's disdain for Khrushchev as a Marxist "illiterate" was quite apparent, and he has since made it clear that he regards Khrushchev's successors as even lesser men simply following in Khrushchev's "revisionist" footsteps.

The public polemics, according to the Soviet view, started in April, 1960, with the publication of a Chinese Communist article entitled "Long Live Leninism," which was only thinly veiled in its attacks on Soviet policies. Then for a while, particularly after Khrushchev's denunciation of Peking's European satellite, Albania, at the Twenty-second Communist Party Congress in Moscow in November, 1961, the public exchanges took the form mainly of Soviet attacks on Albania and Chinese Communist attacks on Yugoslavia, with both sides and most of the rest of the world knowing that the two Communist "big brothers" were talking not about these smaller countries but about each other. But by the end of 1962 the attacks were becoming more and more direct, and by the time Khrushchev was ousted—an ouster that the Chinese Communists had called for many months before—the public exchanges had degenerated into really vituperative name-calling involving Mao and Khrushchev personally.

Meanwhile, the struggle for influence within the Communist movement and in the third world was going on apace, with the Chinese making considerable gains. A majority of the world's Communist parties remained nominally loyal to Moscow —in the case of the ruling parties in Eastern Europe and the big Western European parties mainly because of physical proximity, traditional ties and relative satisfaction with their own power positions; in the case of lesser parties mainly because of their dependence on Moscow for support. However, the major parties became increasingly reluctant to support Khrushchev's call for a world Party conference to excommunicate the Chinese. The conflict between the two giants meant that there was no longer any one control center. The individual parties thus had much more room for maneuver and for the development of their own national policies. A formal split would end this happy situation and subject them again to the line and discipline of the contender with whom they sided, be it Moscow or Peking.

These views were frankly set forth in a reply to the Soviet leadership written in August, 1964, by the long-time head of the Italian Communist Party, the late Palmiro Togliatti; and published shortly afterward—to Moscow's discomfiture—in the Italian Communist press. In his memorandum, Togliatti stressed the national differences between the world's parties, openly opposed "every proposal to reinstitute any international centralized organization," counseled a muting of Sino-Soviet polemics combined with quiet negotiations and expressed the hope that it might be "possible to give up the idea of holding an international conference," in order to "avoid a formal split." Such a split, he added, would lead to "founding an international Chinese center which would create its 'sections' in all countries." In fact, many of the Communist parties in the Far East had already sided with the Chinese, notably the Japanese, the

Indonesians, the New Zealanders and the Australians; and elsewhere the Chinese were already busy setting up splinter groups of their own left-wing supporters in the countries where they could not win over the old-line Party apparatus. In doing this, they were following the example of Lenin and the Comintern in their struggle after the October Revolution to set up Communist parties throughout the world which would take over Marxism from the Social Democrats.

A critical phase of the struggle focused on the third world, as the Chinese attempted to take over control of the various Afro-Asian solidarity organizations, to promote Latin-American membership in those organizations, and thus to extract the national liberation struggle from Soviet influence. Initially the Chinese played their hands well. At the third Asian-African Solidarity Conference in February, 1963, in Moshi, Tanganyika, the Chinese rather than the Russians succeeded in playing the major role, the first time that this had ever occurred in such a gathering, and there were indications that the more revolutionary Chinese line was gaining increasingly wide support among radical anticolonialists. The Chinese topped this performance at Moshi at a conference of Afro-Asian journalists in Djakarta, Indonesia, the following April. A resolution to admit the Russians as delegates, proposed and strongly pushed by Outer Mongolia, was crushingly defeated by a vote of 41 to 8. The Chinese had thus gone a long way toward having Moscow's representatives treated as "second-class members" of Afro-Asian front organizations.

The next major battle in this contest was related to the question of Soviet participation in the big high-level second Bandung Conference planned to be held in Algiers in November, 1965. A preparatory meeting of the Asian-African Solidarity Conference in Algiers in April, 1964, degenerated into a bitter clash between Chinese and Soviet representatives. Subsequently, on May 4, the Soviet Government published a statement protesting Chinese efforts to exclude the Soviet Union from the new conference. But to no avail. The struggle continued, and the Communist Party newspaper *Pravda,* in an editorial on August 14, 1964, in effect threw in the towel and withdrew the Soviet Union's application to participate in Bandung II.

The tide was about to turn, however. After the ouster of Khrushchev the new Soviet leadership dropped the polemics against China. At about the same time, Mao Tse-tung launched his "cultural revolution" and stepped up still another notch the shrillness of his attacks on Moscow. Within a year it was clear that the Afro-Asians were tired of the bombast between the two Communist centers and had shifted to regard Moscow as reasonable and restrained in the face of Chinese Communist extremism. Thus by the fall of 1965 it was so clear that the Soviets would be voted into membership in the Bandung Conference that the Chinese Communists themselves took steps to wreck the meeting. It was indefinitely postponed and remains postponed.

Now why was this such an important question to the Soviet Union, and why did the Chinese Communists try so hard to keep the Soviets out of these Afro-Asian conferences? The answer is that the Chinese are, in fact, out to prove that the "white" Russian has no more right to be a participant in such a conference than do other "white" imperialists; and that the Soviet claim of admissibility is based solely on Russian conquest of Asian lands and Asian peoples in Central Asia and eastern Siberia and the subjugation of those peoples to the "white man's rule" out of Moscow. And indeed there is a very solid basis for the Chinese effort. Except for the Portuguese colonies in Africa, Soviet Central Asia and the island of Sakhalin are probably the only remaining areas of the world where colonial settlement and exploitation are actively at work today. Behind a thin façade of local government in such famed and storied cities as Bukhara, Samarkand and Tashkent, the Russian rules. He controls the ruling Communist Party; he controls the industries; he controls the great collectivized farms. He is the administrator and the teacher. He is a superior person; he lives in the best houses, usually in a segregated part of town. My own impression, when I first visited these areas in the 1960s, was that I was back in French-ruled North Africa, in the Algeria and Morocco of the 1930s. It is either a great feat of Soviet propaganda or eloquent testimony to the ignorance of the Afro-Asian leaders that Moscow has so far been able with its professions of revolutionary ideology and boasts of economic progress to mask or hide these social and political realities from them.

But, in the longer term, the Russians are vulnerable to charges of colonialism, and they know that the Chinese Communists are not likely to overlook this vulnerability. Indeed, they have shown particular concern about the doctrinal development of Mao Tse-tung's so-called "Theory of People's War"—of the revolution of the countryside against the cities. This theory was put forward in a famous article, published in the *People's Daily* of September 3, 1965, and written by Marshal Lin Piao, Vice Chairman of the Chinese Communist Party, Minister of Defense of the Chinese People's Republic and now the designated successor of Mao as Chinese Communist leader. Lin Piao put it this way:

Comrade Mao Tse-tung's theory of the establishment of rural revolutionary base areas and the encirclement of the cities by the countryside is of outstanding and universal practical importance for the present revolutionary struggles of all the oppressed nations and peoples, and particularly for the revolutionary struggles of the oppressed nations and peoples in Asia, Africa and Latin America against imperialism and its lackeys. . . .

Taking the entire globe, if North America and Western Europe can be called "the cities of the world," then Asia, Africa and Latin America constitute "the rural areas of the world." Since World War II, the proletarian revolutionary movement has for various reasons been temporarily held back in the North American and West European capitalist countries, while the people's revolutionary movement in Asia, Africa and Latin America has been growing vigorously. In a sense, the contemporary world revolution also presents a picture of the encirclement of cities by the rural areas. In the final analysis, the whole cause of world revolution hinges on the revolutionary struggles of the Asian, African and Latin American peoples who make up the overwhelming majority of the world's population.

While Russia was not specifically named, Moscow has assumed it was included in the definition of the city area (Western Europe). Indeed, Lin Piao went on to clarify things a bit, saying, "Khrushchev is finished. And the successors to Khrushchev revisionism will fare no better. The imperialists, the reactionaries and the Khrushchev revisionists, who have all set themselves against people's wars, will be swept like dust from the stage of history by the mighty broom of the revolutionary people."

I might add a couple of American footnotes to the Sino-Soviet conflict. For some years the Kremlin had used the device of organized mass demonstrations against the American Embassy in Moscow to publicize its differences with the United States on various foreign policy questions, ranging from the Lebanon landings in 1958, to the Congo crisis, to Cuba, to Vietnam. There were a half-dozen of them while I was there as Ambassador. They were unpleasant affairs, usually resulting in the breaking of all the windows in our chancery building and in splotching its façade with varicolored inks. And they were not without danger—we were always worried that some of the window-breaking missiles would injure members of the staff or some of the children living in the building's apartments. However, despite a pretense of spontaneity, they were on the whole well organized and well controlled, and the Soviet Government promptly paid for the damages after the necessary propaganda photographs had been taken for distribution to the world press. However, on March 4, 1965, the Soviet authorities made the great mistake of allowing Asian students, particularly Chinese, in Moscow to participate. They turned out to be a very different kettle of fish from the docile, disciplined Russian workers. The first thing we knew, the Russian police really had to exert themselves to protect the embassy from invasion by the Asian students and even had to summon the army to help. The result was that we became the spectators of a great battle between Russians and Chinese taking place in the snowy streets in front of us, with many injuries on both sides.

This clash became a *cause célèbre* in Sino-Soviet relations. Chinese fury was redoubled when the world press reported that, in making my usual protest to Foreign Minister Gromyko, I had added my appreciation for the really valiant efforts of the Soviet militia to protect us from the mob. The Russians learned from this episode that such demonstrations are not really a useful instrument of diplomacy, and there have been no more against Western embassies since that date. However, the belated Soviet restraint has not stopped the Chinese Communists from taking a page out of the Russian book. The demonstrations against the Soviet Embassy in Peking in 1967 and again after the border clashes in 1969 have made those against our embassy look like small affairs—and have provoked the Kremlin to retaliation in kind against the Chinese Embassy in Moscow.

On the occasion of the November 7, 1964, celebration of the anniversary of the Bolshevik Revolution, the new Soviet leadership organized the usual festivities, including the great Kremlin reception attended by all the Party and government leaders, visiting representatives from foreign Communist parties and governments and the foreign ambassadors in Moscow, as well as most of the elite of the Soviet capital. Peking had sent Chinese Prime Minister Chou En-lai, apparently to probe for any change in Soviet policies following the ouster of Khrushchev. Members of the Politburo made the usual toasts, most of which were reasonably restrained—at least to the point where I did not feel it necessary to walk out. Deputy Prime Minister Mikoyan even made a toast to "peaceful coexistence"—to the obvious irritation of Chou En-lai—and a few minutes later the two were observed in heated argument. Some time after we thought the talking was all over, General Secretary of the Party Brezhnev, who was acting as master of ceremonies, unexpectedly invited the Minister of Defense, Marshal Malinovsky, to give a toast. The Marshal had obviously had too much to drink and pronounced a toast which included a violent attack on the United States. Now it was my turn to be irritated, and I think I showed my feelings very plainly. I was contemplating departure when Prime Minister Kosygin walked over to me to make a peaceful gesture. So, after speaking my mind to him, I stayed until the end of the affair. While Kosygin and I were talking, Chou En-lai was pointing toward us and calling the attention of the Afro-Asians to this outrageous spectacle of Soviet collusion with the imperialists. Not long after Chou's return to Peking, presumably to give a negative report on his probings, the incident at the

Kremlin reception on November 7, 1964, became grist for the Chinese propaganda mill.

In trying to understand Soviet motivations and moves in the foreseeable future, it will be essential to weigh in our own calculations the Kremlin's primary concern about China.

As tensions have mounted, Moscow has strengthened its government and Party cadres in Siberia and the Far East and redoubled its armed forces there (from fifteen to thirty divisions). The Soviet military presence in Outer Mongolia has been correspondingly reinforced. But Moscow has found no way comparably to increase the thin Siberian population to help counterbalance the teeming masses south of the border. The Soviet Government has upped the allocation of investment funds to the area and raised pay differentials and other benefits to entice settlers. But it is up against a difficult problem in this respect, because of both the socialist system and the stigma traditionally attached to Siberia as a prison. Despite strenuous efforts over the years it has been difficult just to maintain the population level in Siberia, since workers have tended to take the higher income for a few years, then return with their savings to a more comfortable life in European Russia.

I had an interesting discussion a few years ago with a Deputy Mayor of Khabarovsk, the key Siberian city at the confluence of the Amur and Ussuri rivers. We compared the settlement of our American "Wild West" with the settlement of the Russian "Wild East." The Mayor readily agreed our problem had been made easy by the possibility of enrichment by gold strikes, or the knowledge that at worst free land would be available for settlement and cultivation. In the Soviet Union he could offer no private gain other than higher pay. But higher income was a limited incentive, unless something worthwhile was available to spend it on. This meant that, in advance of migration and settlement, he had to try to provide better and more adequate housing than was available elsewhere, convenient transportation, educational facilities, good markets with equipment and food and such amenities of life as radio, TV, opera, ballet, theater and sports. With limited funds available, this was an almost impossible task.

Speculation has been recurrent as to the possibilities of a war between the Communist Goliaths. I think there will not be such a conflict in the presently foreseeable future. It is true that both sides keep making bellicose sounds and whipping up dangerous popular passions within their own countries. But China is no match for the Soviet Union in modern military terms, despite its almost unlimited manpower. The real threat which worries the Kremlin is a longer-range one—Peking's proven ability and apparent determination to develop a significant nuclear-missile capability. Individual Russians have been quoted as suggesting that the time has come to mount a lightning deterrent blow like that Marshal Zhukov delivered against the Japanese forces in Mongolia in 1939. One can be sure that there are in Moscow, especially among the military, advocates of a preventive strike to destroy the Chinese nuclear and missile installations. They are not likely to prevail over the more cautious Kremlin leaders, who must ponder the reaction to such an initiative within the Communist camp and in the world generally, as well as the imponderable consequences in China itself. Only a serious false step on the part of Peking—such as an accidental missile launch or a massive incursion into Soviet territory which could be portrayed as justifying Russian retaliation—would seem likely to trigger major Soviet military action.

I might add that a war involving a third of mankind would not be to anyone's interest—and certainly not to that of the United States. In the long term, our security and welfare lie in a pluralistic world, with a reasonable balance of diverse elements of power, rather than in one in which rival forces eliminate one another successively up to the point of a final East-West showdown.

To look at the other side of the medal, it is not inconceivable that, after the disappearance of Mao from the scene, there could be a kind of reconciliation—prompted mainly by Chinese needs for Soviet help and equipment—which the Western press would probably portray as a recreation of the monolithic Communist bloc. In my view, this would be no more real than the Sino-Soviet "alliance" of 1950 has proven to be. Basic conflicts of character and national interests will continue to predominate over any ideological ties. The Chinese are already accusing the Russians of collaborating with the American imperialists—they probably suspect that there either is or eventually could be some truth in this charge. On their part, the Russians are uneasy about the possibility of an eventual rapprochement between China and the United States. At this point, I can see no good reason for us to disabuse either side.

CHAPTER X

The Fractured Monolith: Picking Up the Pieces

It might be said that in their battle for influence in the Communist world Moscow and Peking have been vying for a rapidly diminishing prize. The smaller countries and the lesser Communist parties have taken advantage of the opportunities offered to develop and assert national policies. Historically experienced in dealing with a succession of overlords and inspired by the Yugoslav example, the Rumanians took the lead in self-assertion. In the early 1960s they successfully resisted Khrushchev's attempts through COMECON to dictate their line of economic development and took a neutral attitude toward the Sino-Soviet conflict. Indeed, they even had the effrontery to offer to mediate between the two giants. They also called for changes in the structure of the Warsaw Pact alliance which would lessen

Russian military domination of that group. Poland and Hungary likewise sought their own "national roads to Communism," leaving their agriculture largely in private hands and experimenting with various "free market" economic reforms. With the exception of the artificial creation called the German Democratic Republic, only Czechoslovakia retained its old-line, unpurged Stalinist leadership in the person of President and Party Secretary Antonin Novotný.

As the tide of battle turned against the Chinese Communists, the men in the Kremlin not only resumed polemical attacks against what they now called the "Maoist clique" but began to look for ways to restore order amidst the growing chaos in world Communism. Typically enough, they reverted to Khrushchev's original line. In December, 1966, a Plenum of the Central Committee of the Communist Party of the Soviet Union issued a new appeal for a "well-prepared" world Communist conference, stressing the need for unity of the Communist forces against "American imperialist aggression in Vietnam" and against the "revival of militarism, revanchism and Nazism" in West Germany. A *Pravda* editorial promptly sought to reassure the reluctant Communist brethren that the purpose of such a new conference would not be the excommunication of Communist China or other opposition parties. The theme of the Central Committee appeal was thereafter developed in speeches by the Kremlin leadership and in bilateral and multilateral meetings with other Communist parties. Finally, in December, 1967, the Soviet Party got seventeen other key parties to join it in issuing a call for a new preparatory, consultative meeting to be held in Budapest the following February.

All was not harmony among the sixty-seven middle-level delegations meeting in Budapest, and the Rumanians went home after the head Syrian delegate, an old-line Comintern agent, had accused them of nationalistic deviations. However, after ten days of discussion, the sixty-six remaining delegations on March 6 issued a call for a new world Communist conference to take place in Moscow in November. They agreed on a single theme for the conference, designed to forestall discussion or action with respect to the Sino-Soviet conflict: "The Tasks of the

Struggle Against Imperialism at the Present Stage and the Unity of Action of Communist and Workers Parties and All Anti-imperialist Forces." A continuing working group was set up to develop more detailed plans and documents. At the end of April the working group fixed the conference date as November 25. In a fiery speech at a Kremlin reception on July 2, General Secretary of the Soviet Party Brezhnev hailed the coming conference as a great step forward for world Communism.

Then came the explosion in Czechoslovakia.

The political ferment which had been churning up in Eastern Europe since Khrushchev's secret speech denouncing Stalin in 1956 was late in reaching Czechoslovakia. It finally hit the country in mid-1967 in the form of a rebellion in the Writers Union. After violent arguments and much maneuvering by various factions, the rebels took over the Union and demanded an easing of the Stalinist repressions in the country. When Novotný moved to crack down on the rebellious writers in the fall of 1967, political figures began to take sides and the conflict moved from the Writers Union into the Central Committee of the Party. Here it was aggravated by the national antagonism between the Czechs and the Slovaks and the Slovak feeling that Novotný had imposed a Czech dictatorship on their relatively poor section of the country. In December, Novotný called Brezhnev to his aid, but to no avail. A Central Committee Plenum on January 5, 1968, ousted him as First Secretary of the Party and elected in his place the Slovak Communist Alexander Dubcek.

From Czechs and others who knew him I take it that Dubcek was a sort of compromise candidate, a run-of-the-mill Party functionary who had kept out of trouble—all in all a rather unlikely candidate for the role of national hero which events were later to thrust upon him. Then, in March, Novotný was also forced out as President and replaced by General Ludvik Svoboda. Svoboda, a lieutenant colonel at the time of Hitler's invasion of Czechoslovakia, had fled to the U.S.S.R. and been picked up by the Russians in the 1940s to head the Czech forces being formed in the Soviet Union. For a while after the war he was Defense Minister in the democratic government of Czechoslovakia. After the Communist takeover he was one of the many victims of the Stalinist-type purges but was rehabilitated in the 1950s, after Khrushchev had inquired about him, and made head of the Czechoslovak Military Academy. He was to turn out to be the strong man.

Fear disappeared with Novotný, and events moved rapidly. In April the Party adopted an "action program," liberal in nature, providing for political and economic reforms and for the rehabilitation of the victims of Novotný's purges. Censorship was abandoned. The press was free. Political factions were organized, some of them in the guise of clubs. Suggestions were even made that outright political opposition be permitted. The pent-up feelings of twenty years of Stalinist oppression and terror overflowed on all sides in this "Czechoslovak spring." Like May wine, the effervescence of the new freedoms went to everyone's head. Communism, which was going to be given "a human face," must win the voluntary and willing confidence and support of the people.

In a speech on the 150th anniversary of the birth of Karl Marx, Party Secretary Cestmir Cisar declared that both Leninism and Stalinism were "monopolistic interpretations of Marxism. Each Marxist party," he went on, "must have its own policy which takes into consideration national conditions and peculiarities." He saw the events in Czechoslovakia bringing about "an unprecedented upsurge of Czechoslovak Marxist thought." Journalists began to dig into the cases of the hundreds of victims of the Novotný purges and to imply Soviet involvement in many of the most flagrant injustices. The first great democratic President, Thomas G. Masaryk, was hailed again as the "father of the country" and pertinent—to the Russians, impertinent—questions were asked about the circumstances of the death of his son, Jan, the popular Foreign Minister at the time of the Communist takeover in 1948. Liberal ideas found their most extreme expression in an eloquent manifesto called "Two Thousand Words," signed by a long list of outstanding intellectuals, including many members of the Party and even some members of the Central Committee. Addressed to "workers, farmers, civil servants, scientists, artists and everyone," it called for true political freedom and real democracy in Czechoslovakia.

While the document was promptly rejected by the Party and the National Assembly, it had a wide impact and its authors and signers were not disciplined.

The Soviet press took up the cudgels. It attacked Thomas Masaryk, charging him with plotting to murder Lenin back in the 1920s, and denied any Soviet involvement in Jan Masaryk's death. It attacked the Cisar speech. It attacked the "Two Thousand Words"—in many, many more than two thousand words. Articles began to refer to "right revisionists," to "bourgeois nationalists," to "politically immature elements" in Czechoslovakia, then to "subversive bridgebuilding" efforts of the West and other sinister "foreign influences." Radio Moscow stepped up its broadcasting in Czech and Slovak.

The Kremlin became increasingly alarmed. Brezhnev lectured the Czech leadership at a conference of Eastern European Communist parties at Dresden in March, then hailed them to Moscow for another lecture in May—meanwhile having convoked the Central Committee of the Soviet Communist Party to launch a major ideological revival designed to stem any infection in the Soviet Union itself. The Russian Commander in Chief of the Warsaw Pact forces was dispatched to Prague, where he extracted agreement to hold joint maneuvers on Czechoslovak territory, to begin in late June. Soviet Prime Minister Kosygin took an unprecedented "holiday and cure" at the Czech resort of Karlovy Vary, a nine-day sojourn which coincided with the visit of a Soviet military delegation headed by Defense Minister Marshal Grechko. In May the Party leaders of Bulgaria, Hungary, Poland and East Germany met with the Soviets in Moscow. The Rumanians were not invited; they had already expressed their full support of Czechoslovakia's new course, and Ceaucescu was preparing to pay an official visit to Prague. Early in July the "hard-core" five, continuing to work together under Kremlin direction, addressed separate letters to the Presidium of the Czechoslovak Party proposing an immediate meeting to discuss the situation. Prague hesitated and debated, then proposed holding individual consultations with the other parties, including the Rumanians and Yugoslavs. A flurry of indecisive exchanges took place, and as the Czechoslovaks continued to balk, the others went ahead and convened in Warsaw without them. As the meeting went on, the Czechoslovak Party Presidium, on July 15, requested it "not to adopt any conclusions on the situation in Czechoslovakia."

On the morning of July 18, back in Moscow for a visit, I was having breakfast in the American Embassy and listening to the Russian news broadcast. My ears pricked up as the announcer read the text of a long, tough and threatening letter which had been sent to the Czech leadership by the top leaders of the five parties assembled in Warsaw. In unprecedented language the document referred to "counterrevolutionary forces" at work in Czechoslovakia, which, it charged, were not only a matter of concern to the Czechs but a threat to the security of the whole Communist camp—there is no harsher language in the Communist lexicon.

After some further exchanges of argumentative correspondence and political maneuvering, including Czech rejection of a summons to Kiev, the Czech leaders agreed to meet bilaterally with the Soviets on Czechoslovak territory on July 29, then with the leaders of the five Warsaw Pact letter-writers on August 3. At these meetings in Cierna and Bratislava, the Czechoslovaks subscribed publicly to rather general commitments to Communist unity and principles and to the re-establishment of firm Party control in the country: "unbending loyalty to Marxism-Leninism . . . education of the masses . . . irreconcilable struggle against bourgeois ideology and all antisocialist forces . . . fraternal mutual assistance and solidarity." Privately they probably accepted more specific demands from the Soviet side, including a clamp-down on the press and non-Communist political activity and suppression of attacks on the Soviet Union, in return for an understanding that the Soviet and other troops then maneuvering on Czechoslovak soil would be withdrawn. However, on their return to Prague the Czech leaders managed to leave the public impression that nothing had really been changed and that liberalization and democratization would continue. Privately, there were hints that Brezhnev and his Eastern European associates had been obliged to back away from the tough and threatening terms of the Warsaw Pact letter.

At the beginning of August the Czech Defense Minister announced that the maneuvers on Czechoslovak soil had ended and that outside forces had departed. On the same day it was announced in Moscow that new Warsaw Pact exercises were beginning in East Germany, southern Poland and the western Ukraine, i.e., around the borders of Czechoslovakia. As the Czech leadership moved slowly toward tightening things up, mainly by exhortation and with little apparent result, Soviet propaganda attacks resumed and intensified. On August 17 the Politburo of the Soviet Party addressed what amounted to an ultimatum to the Presidium of the Czechoslovak Party. The communication noted "the fact that in the press, on the radio and on television the results of the meetings in Cierna and Bratislava are being depicted as a victory of the Czechoslovak Communist Party over the Communist Party of the Soviet Union and other fraternal parties." It then went on in some detail to charge not only failures to fulfill the commitments the Czechs had undertaken in these meetings but specific violations of those commitments and concluded by warning that "delays in this matter are most dangerous."

The members of the Presidium of the Czechoslovak Party were heatedly debating a response to this letter on the evening of August 20 when they were informed that the invasion had started. The Czechoslovak armed forces were promptly ordered not to resist, but by one o'clock in the morning of August 21 the Presidium had issued a proclamation to the people declaring that the invasion "took place without the knowledge of the President of the Republic, the Presidium of the National Assembly, the Presidium of the government, and the First Secretary of the Communist Party's Central Committee." The proclamation further declared that "the Presidium considers this action to be contrary to the fundamental principles of relations between socialist states and a denial of the basic norms of international law." Despite the confusion, other Party and governmental bodies managed to meet and put on the record similar condemnations of the invasion. The Czechoslovak delegate to the United Nations delivered an impassioned protest at a meeting of the Security Council; the Soviet delegate exercised his 105th veto to defeat a resolution condemning the invasion.

With no armed opposition, the military plans for the invasion worked well, and the half-million-strong invading forces —almost entirely Soviet forces with only token contingents from the four other Warsaw Pact countries—were soon in position all over the small country. Dubcek, Prime Minister Oldrich Cernik, Presidium member Cisar (who had delivered the objectionable speech on Marx's anniversary) and a few other liberal leaders were seized like criminals and flown off to the Soviet Union.

Political preparations for the invasion, however, were a complete flop. Except for some members of the secret police forces and for the head of the Czech News Agency, there were no active collaborators. When the latter tried to have an appeal for Soviet help and other documentation justifying the invasion published, the subordinate personnel of the radio, press and television organizations sabotaged the attempt. The invaders thus stood naked before the whole world. Indeed, the Czechs had made better political preparations than the Soviets. Foresighted officials in the information media had made plans for just such a contingency, so that, as soon as the Soviet forces belatedly took over the principal broadcast and press centers, clandestine radios and presses started operating. These underground activities, backed by a practically unanimous public opinion, frustrated Soviet efforts to find a justifying political cover. Pro-Soviet Czechoslovak conservatives were assembled at the Soviet Embassy on August 22, but President Svoboda rejected their proposals for a new Moscow-line Party Presidium and government; and none of the participants dared, individually or collectively, to admit publicly that he had made any appeal for Soviet intervention or that he considered the invasion either necessary or justified. In the circumstances, Moscow was obliged to temporize. On August 23, Svoboda was invited to Moscow, accompanied by Deputy Prime Minister Gustav Husak and a few of the conservatives. On Svoboda's insistence, Dubcek and his associates were released and restored to office, though only after accepting onerous conditions as to their future policies.

In a speech to the Seventh Congress of the Soviet Communist Party on March 8, 1918, Lenin had told the comrades that
"periods of retreat, retirement and temporary defeat" were to be
expected and counseled that "in order not to get lost in these
zigzags and twists of history . . . the important and only theoretically correct thing is not to cast out the basic program."
Thus, while the Kremlin obviously continued to smart under its
setback in Czechoslovakia itself and in the world at large because of the ineptness and failure of its political preparation for
the invasion, it clearly regarded this situation as temporary.
Dubcek and his progressive associates continued to be sniped at
by the Soviet press, and the Czech economy, already in bad
straits and in desperate need of Soviet and other outside credit
and supplies, was allowed to continue to deteriorate. While
Moscow had been unable to install Soviet hard-liners in the
positions of Party and government leadership in Czechoslovakia,
it was able to protect them and gradually to strengthen their
positions. The Soviet First Deputy Foreign Minister was sent to
Prague repeatedly and for long periods. Judging from the accounts in the Czech press regarding his activities, he was
keeping the pressure on the reinstated progressive leadership
and at the same time meeting frequently with known pro-Soviet
elements. He also noticeably cultivated Gustav Husak, who had
emerged as the strong man in the now separate Slovak state and
Party.

Underneath, however, the country continued to smolder,
ready to burst into flames with the slightest breeze. On March
28, 1969, a Czechoslovak victory over a Soviet hockey team was
enough to provoke widespread mass demonstrations, resulting
in the destruction of the Soviet airline offices in Prague and
attacks on other Soviet establishments in the country. The
Soviet Defense Minister and Deputy Foreign Minister rushed to
Prague and again tightened the screws on the Czech leadership,
demanding a strengthening of the security police, purging of the
information media and redoubling of Party discipline and controls. At the critical period several days of Warsaw Pact military
maneuvers were arranged to take place on Czechoslovak territory. All of this immediately preceded a scheduled meeting of
the Central Committee of the Czechoslovak Communist Party.

On the eve of the meeting the Executive Committee of the Presidium of the Party issued a statement, saying that rumors and accusations of treachery and collaboration on the part of some ten high Party members, which had been circulating since the August invasion, were unfounded and unfair. These conservative, pro-Soviet elements were thus strengthened by clear evidence of Soviet protection, and it seems likely that many members of the 163-man Central Committee of the Party were intimidated. Also on the eve of the plenary meeting, the Slovak leader, Gustav Husak, had made an outspoken, public attack on the "so-called reformers" as responsible for "inconsistency, high-handedness and disunity in leadership." He declared that the time had come when it was "necessary to defeat and remove from public life hostile, antisocialist forces."

It was thus not surprising, when the Central Committee met on April 17, that Dubcek was ousted as First Secretary of the Party and replaced by Husak. Dubcek was given the lesser post of President of the National Assembly and remained in the Presidium of the Party, but that body was reduced from twenty-one to eleven members and its composition altered to ensure a Moscow-line conservative majority. In a TV address Husak promptly made it clear that he intended to follow the hard line he had advocated on the eve of the Central Committee meeting. A series of repressive measures followed, and purges of journalists and other reformers gradually began to bring the internal situation under tighter Party and police control. Attempts at anti-Soviet demonstrations on the first anniversary of the invasion brought about hundreds of arrests, but were effectively contained. The conservatives used the occasion—and their restored control of the information media—to launch a new campaign against Dubcek and other progressives remaining in even nominal positions in public life, and to call on Party organizations to expunge from the record, as "politically incorrect," the anti-Soviet resolutions they had passed a year earlier. Their efforts were successful. In September, 1969, a Central Committee Plenum ousted Dubcek from the ruling Presidium and from the presidency of the National Assembly—he was probably spared worse by Husak's moderating influence—and dropped about thirty of his supporters from the full Central Committee. At the same time, in an act of abject self-abasement before Moscow, the Central Committee adopted a formal resolution declaring that the invasion "was in no way an act of aggression . . . in no way an occupation of Czechoslovak territory," since it "was motivated by the interests of defending socialism in Czechoslovakia from right-wing, antisocialist and counterrevolutionary forces, by the common interests of the security of the socialist camp."

Fear and tight censorship in the country and the ousting of many foreign correspondents have brought a drastic reduction in reports reaching the outside world about dissidence in Czechoslovakia. For the time being, the country has become a tomb of lost hope. On the other hand, the long-range outlook is far from clear. Popular hatred of the Russians is certainly at an historic high point and is not likely to diminish. While Husak is obviously a hard-line Communist as compared with Dubcek, he also appears to be an able and intelligent administrator. Moreover, his record indicates that he is basically a strong nationalist and not exactly a Stalinist. He proved this in 1954 by his opposition to the Novotný regime. He was at that time sentenced to life imprisonment for "bourgeois diversionism, nationalism and chauvinism" and served nearly nine years of this sentence before being released and rehabilitated. If his national feelings should come to the fore again and conflict with Soviet purposes, then he will inevitably follow his predecessor into limbo.

The machinery of Soviet retribution, patiently, relentlessly grinding down its victims, bit by bit, is an awesome and dreadful thing to see in action. As one rueful Czech put it: "The Russians have applied pressure to the helpless victim slowly enough so that no one would hear the bones crack."

When it took the decision to invade, the Kremlin clearly expected to have no difficulty in finding "quislings" to support and justify its action. This expectation had been clear even in the threatening letter sent to Prague by the five "hard-core" Warsaw Pact members on July 18, 1968. "We know," the message declared, "that forces exist in Czechoslovakia capable of defending the socialist regime and defeating antisocialist elements. . . . Let us mobilize and lead them into battle." Indeed, as the invading forces crossed the Czechoslovak borders, the Soviet news agency Tass issued an "authorized statement" in Moscow alleging that "Party and state leaders of the Czechoslovak Socialist Republic have requested the Soviet Union and other allied states to give the fraternal Czechoslovak people immediate assistance, including assistance with armed forces."

When the Prague end of the cover operation fizzled and the Tass claim was revealed as false, Moscow was obliged *post facto* to try to produce another justification for its action. For some weeks there was a flurry of inconsistent Soviet explanations and rationalizations. Then the Kremlin finally came forth with a line that has sometimes been referred to in the press as "The Brezhnev Doctrine," but which the Yugoslav and many other Communist parties refer to and categorically reject as "The Doctrine of Limited Sovereignty" of the Communist countries. This doctrine was first enunciated at some length in an article in *Pravda* on September 26, 1968. The following are the doctrinal excerpts extracted from a long post-mortem on the developments in Czechoslovakia:

. . . Communist Parties have and must have freedom to determine their country's path of development. However, any decision of theirs must damage neither socialism in their own country nor the fundamental movement, which is waging a struggle for socialism. This means that every Communist Party is responsible not only to its own people but also to all the socialist countries and to the entire Communist movement. . . .

A socialist state that is in a system of other states constituting a socialist commonwealth cannot be free of the common interests of that commonwealth. The sovereignty of individual socialist countries cannot be counterposed to the interests of world socialism and the world revolutionary movement. . . .

Each Communist Party is free in applying the principles of Marxism-Leninism and socialism in its own country, but it cannot deviate from these principles. . . .

The weakening of any link in the world socialist system has a direct effect on all the socialist countries, which cannot be indifferent to this. . . .

World socialism as a social system is the common achievement of the working people of all countries, it is indivisible, and its defense is the common cause of all Communists. . . .

Those who speak of the "illegality" of the allied socialist countries' actions in Czechoslovakia forget that in a class society there is and can be no such thing as nonclass law. Laws and the norms of law are subordinated to the laws of the class struggle and the laws of social development.

Soviet Party General Secretary Brezhnev took up the refrain in a speech to a Polish Party Congress in Warsaw on November 12, supplementing *Pravda*'s rationale with these words:

. . . when the internal and external forces hostile to socialism seek to turn the development of any socialist country toward the restoration of the capitalist order, when a threat arises to the cause of socialism in that country, a threat to the security of the socialist community as a whole, this is no longer merely a problem of the people of that country but also a common problem, the concern of all socialist states. It goes without saying that such an action as military aid to a fraternal country to cut short the threat to the socialist order is an extraordinary enforced step, it can be sparked off only by direct actions of the enemies of socialism inside the country and beyond its boundaries, actions creating a threat to the common interests of the camp of socialism.

Meanwhile, Soviet Foreign Minister Gromyko had had to deal with the question when he addressed the United Nations General Assembly on October 3. While the presentation of the doctrine was modified for this audience, it was no less firm and defiant:

. . . The countries of the socialist commonwealth have their own vital interests, their own obligations, including those of safeguarding their mutual security and their own socialist principles of mutual relations based on fraternal assistance, solidarity and internationalism. This commonwealth constitutes an inseparable entity cemented by unbreakable ties such as history has never known. . . .

The Soviet Union and other socialist countries have on many occasions warned those who are tempted to try to roll back the socialist commonwealth, to snatch at least one link from it, that we will neither tolerate nor allow this to happen. . . .

The Soviet Union deems it necessary to proclaim from this rostrum, too, that the socialist states cannot and will not allow a situation where the vital interests of socialism are infringed upon and encroachments are made on the inviolability of the boundaries of the socialist commonwealth and, therefore, on the foundations of international peace.

The General Assembly listened but did not applaud. The United Nations is, after all, the principal custodian of what man knows as international law, and the fulcrum of man's hope for the improvement of that legal system and the creation of a world of universal justice.

Almost since its founding, the United Nations has had a Special Committee on the Question of Defining Aggression. The Soviets, seeking to hamstring what they regard as the inevitable "imperialist's" tendency to intervene in the affairs of other states, have traditionally taken a lead in the committee and as long ago as 1956 tabled a very elaborate and detailed draft definition of aggression. On February 26, 1969, a somewhat embarrassed Soviet delegate tabled a new draft, considerably revised to cover the Soviet dilemma in Czechoslovakia and to accommodate the doctrine of limited sovereignty. A new provision in the preamble now states that "the use of force by a State to encroach on the social and political achievements of the peoples of other States is incompatible with the principle of peaceful coexistence of States with different social systems." Since Moscow claimed it was acting to protect rather than encroach on such "achievements" in Czechoslovakia, "use of force" was presumably permissible; by logical extension, so would be use of force by a stronger power to protect the *status quo* anywhere within its own socialist or capitalist camp.

But the new draft is even more remarkable for its omissions than for its additions. Article 6 of the 1956 draft included among the pretexts that could *not* be used to justify aggression "any revolutionary or counterrevolutionary movement, civil war, disorders or strikes," or "the establishment or maintenance in any State of any political, economic or social system." Article 7 condemned the concentration of troops near frontiers (such as the Warsaw Pact maneuvers along the Czechoslovak borders in

August, 1968). These provisions are absent in the new document. This is a typical Moscow attempt to have it both ways—to live in the real world and in a world of its own, to benefit from traditional international law when this is to Soviet advantage, to reject that "bourgeois" law when it is not.

Underlying the rationale of the so-called "Brezhnev Doctrine" was the charge, sometimes implicit but more often explicit, that the developments in Czechoslovakia were promoted primarily by propaganda and other subversive efforts on the part of outside imperialist powers, notably West Germany and the United States. These charges fell very flat in the world at large in view of the obvious efforts of the Western powers, as events unfolded in Czechoslovakia, to avoid any actions which might by any stretch of the imagination be considered provocative and of their restraint after the invasion and occupation of the country.

The Soviet doctrine of "limited sovereignty" for its associates is not really new. The essential concept was already there when the Bolshevik regime, at the turn of the 1920s, used the Red Army to crush the independence movements in the Ukraine, in Georgia and Armenia and in Central Asia. Stalin used every method short of force to try to topple Marshal Tito and bring Yugoslavia to heel in 1948. As I noted earlier, he refrained from using force, not because of moral scruples or respect for legal concepts, but because of the adverse military circumstances then prevailing. The uprising in East Germany in 1953 was crushed by Soviet tanks, as was the Hungarian rebellion in 1956. In both these cases the forces used were already "legally" stationed inside the country, and the intervention was "invited" by elements which could be portrayed as legally constituted authority.

What *was* new in the case of Czechoslovakia was that the invasion took place from outside the borders of the country and that Moscow was caught with its cover story down. The Soviet leaders were thus forced to be embarrassingly explicit in public in trying to justify a naked aggression which had taken place in plain view of the whole world. After some hesitation, they concluded that a bold, defiant stand was necessary, even unavoidable. At the same time, they sought to deflect world attention by blocking the sources of public information inside Czechoslovakia and by making gestures and pronouncements in the international arena calculated to restore a peaceful image to the Soviet Union. In his speech to the United Nations General Assembly on September 19, 1969, Soviet Foreign Minister Gromyko skipped the subject of Czechoslovakia entirely. In the Soviet press and in Communist literature generally, the long and painful definitions of the doctrine have been dropped; they have been reduced, in typical fashion, to such simple terms as "socialist (or proletarian) internationalism" and "mutual support." Thus Chapter IV of the basic document of the International Conference of Communist Parties, adopted at Moscow on June 17, 1969, declares that "relations between the fraternal parties are based on proletarian internationalism, solidarity and mutual support, respect for independence and equality, and noninterference in each other's internal affairs." A number of participants refused to accept this part of the document, but everyone knew that the last two principles were subordinated to the first two, which were euphemisms for the doctrine of limited sovereignty of the Communist countries.

In the West, the invasion of Czechoslovakia in 1968 had an impact comparable to the Soviet-directed Communist takeover of that country twenty years earlier. I served as *rapporteur général* of the Fourteenth General Assembly of the Atlantic Treaty Association, held in Lisbon in October, 1968, under the presidency of the distinguished international statesman Paul Henri Spaak, former Prime Minister of Belgium, Secretary General of NATO and President of the United Nations General Assembly. The discussion focused on the Czech events. All agreed that this demonstration of Soviet readiness to use military force for the attainment of its political objectives had destroyed the hopes which had built up in Europe for a period of effective East-West détente. There was no longer any expectation that France would withdraw from the Alliance or that NATO was in danger of breaking up. Instead, the Assembly called on NATO to "give priority attention to the strengthening of its defenses to avert any possibility of surprise movements or encroachments from the other side." And, indeed, the NATO foreign and defense ministers, meeting in Brussels the following month, did just that, at the same time issuing a warning to the Soviet Union "to refrain from using force and interfering in the affairs of other states."

Within the Communist world the Rumanian and Yugoslav leadership condemned both the invasion of Czechoslovakia and the justifying doctrine, as did most of the major Western Communist parties, the Cubans being a noteworthy exception. The Chinese Communist reaction was aptly epitomized in the title of an article in the Party organ, *People's Daily*, which read: "'International Dictatorship' and 'Limited Sovereignty' Are the Gangster Theories of Soviet Revisionist Social-Imperialism." This widespread disapproval of other parties threw a new roadblock in the way of Moscow's efforts to restore some order in the world Communist movement. Promptly after the invasion the preparatory working group in Budapest voted to postpone indefinitely the meeting it had previously scheduled for Moscow on November 25.

On October 16, nearly two months after the invasion, Moscow induced the Czechoslovak leadership to accept an arrangement under which the bulk of the outside forces would be removed from Czechoslovakia in return for a treaty between the two Communist countries permitting the retention of a Soviet garrison—estimated at about seventy thousand men—on Czechoslovak territory. A week later the Budapest group decided that the Moscow conference could take place the following spring and agreed to move to Moscow to continue the preparation of documents for submission to the conference. Meeting in the Soviet capital on March 10, 1969, the group definitely rescheduled the long-delayed "International Conference of Communist and Workers Parties" for June 5.

Delegates of seventy-five Communist parties—as against eighty-one attending the 1960 conference—foregathered on the appointed date in the magnificently ornate St. George's Hall of the great Kremlin Palace, the pride of the Czars and of the old Russian nobility and the scene of countless imperial balls and ceremonies. Here, until June 17, they discussed, debated and differed, postured and pronounced. Unlike the 1960 conference, which had been meeting for nearly a month before there was any announcement that it was even going on, the speeches were made available to the press and the separate delegations even held press conferences. This was itself a measure of the evolution which had taken place within the Communist movement in the intervening nine years, and a recognition by the Kremlin of its inability any longer to prevent the public release of the differing views of individual parties. Thus even Russian citizens could for the first time, through their own press and radio, learn of the multiplicity of views expressed by the conference participants and hear Communist voices highly critical of Soviet policies.

There had been a prior agreement in the preparatory group that China would not be discussed, and an effort was made to get the same kind of understanding with respect to Czechoslovakia. Despite this, and despite a strong Rumanian protest, Soviet Party Chief Brezhnev devoted a large section of his speech to condemning Mao Tse-tung. "Frankly speaking," he explained, "until just recently we had no intention at all of touching on this question at the meeting. However, the events of the recent period, particularly the nature of the decisions taken by the Ninth Congress of the Chinese Communist Party, have forced us to deal with it. . . . It is doubly important to speak about it, because a section of progressive world opinion still believes that the present Chinese leadership has revolutionary aspirations, believes its assertions that it is fighting imperialism." Brezhnev then went on at length to reiterate all the main Soviet accusations against "Maoism": splitting and seeking hegemony in the Communist movement; fighting, not the imperialists, but the "Marxist-Leninist parties"; labeling the Soviet and other parties "traitors, social strikebreakers, social-imperialists"; trying "to equate the Soviet Union with U.S. imperialism"; harboring "great-power aspirations, with its claims to the territory of other countries"; engaging in "feverish military preparations" and regarding war "as a positive phenomenon in historical development"; continuing "provocations by Chinese military personnel on the Soviet border"; and "exhorting the So-

viet people "to accomplish a revolution.'" He concluded that
"China's foreign policy has, in effect, departed from proletarian
internationalism and shed its socialist class content."

Brezhnev did not refer to Czechoslovakia by name. He did
so indirectly, however, by referring to "the notorious theory of
'limited sovereignty' . . . which imperialist propagandists have
fabricated and put into circulation." In this connection, he
asserted:

As for us Soviet Communists, we hold that the present world
situation again forcefully bears out the validity and viability of
Lenin's concept of proletarian internationalism. In our time, the time
of a global confrontation of two worlds—capitalism and socialism—
Lenin's principles about the internationalist class approach to national problems remains in full force. As valid as ever, for example,
is Lenin's definition that to be an internationalist is to do "the utmost
possible in one country for the development, support and awakening
of the revolution in all countries."

Two score or more of the delegates followed Brezhnev's suit
in attacking the Chinese Communists. Others, notably the Italians, expressed their strong disapproval of the invasion and
occupation of Czechoslovakia.

The "Principal Document"—and it was called just that, not
a declaration or manifesto—carried as its title the agreed single
theme of the conference: "Tasks at the Present Stage of the
Struggle Against Imperialism and United Action of the Communist and Workers Parties and All Anti-imperialist Forces."
Adopted on June 17, 1969, it was a thirty-page compendium of
vague or contradictory formulations, obvious compromises and
general exhortation to revolutionary action, divided into four
sections.

Section I contained a Communist analysis of the situation
in the capitalist-imperialist camp, featuring the charge that "the
United States of America, the chief imperialist power, has
grown more aggressive." However, exploitable weaknesses were
seen in the form of rivalry and contradictions between the
United States and other imperialist powers, and of widespread
dissent, antiwar and social protest in the capitalist countries.

Section II examined the allegedly growing strength and

influence of "the world socialist system, comprising fourteen states," of the Communist parties in the capitalist countries and of the allied forces in the "national liberation" struggle, which "receives indispensable aid from the world socialist system, from the Soviet Union first and foremost." Modifying the original Comintern line, the document called for cooperation with Social Democrats willing "to break with the policy of class collaboration with the bourgeoisie," as well as with "progressive" labor, farm, intellectual, professional, women, youth and religious organizations, in order to unite them all in "an anti-monopoly and anti-imperialist alliance."

Section III, in the words of *Pravda*, "defines the aims of the anti-imperialist struggle on an international scale." Briefly headlined, these were, notably: "all-out support" to Vietnam; "struggle against the menace of thermonuclear war and mass extermination"; "compelling the imperialists to accept peaceful coexistence" (with a long explanation of how this principle helps rather than hampers class and liberation struggles); "preventing the spread and prohibiting the use of nuclear weapons"; "struggle against the military-industrial complex of the United States of America and other imperialist states"; "dissolution of NATO" and other blocs; "dismantling of all military bases on foreign soil"; "curbing of revanchist forces in West Germany"; solidarity with those "constant targets of aggressive imperialist encroachments," East Germany, North Korea, Cuba, the Arabs; solidarity with the peoples of Asia, Africa and Latin America "to rid our planet of the curse of colonialism and prevent its revival in new, camouflaged forms"; struggle against "racialism" and "all forms of oppression of nations and national minorities."

Section IV dealt with relations among the parties, and contained the contradictory formula which I quoted above in connection with Czechoslovakia. Proclaiming that "all parties have equal rights," it stressed that "At this time, when there is no leading center of the international Communist movement, voluntary coordination of the actions of parties . . . acquires increased importance." Bowing to the wishes of many parties maintaining relations with China and other absentees, this section also provided that "the absence of certain Communist parties should not hinder fraternal ties and cooperation among all Communist parties without exception."

China and Czechoslovakia, representing the most important developments in world Communism in many years, were not mentioned in the document. Moscow was unable to get into the document the extreme language used in Soviet propaganda with regard to the "ideological aggressiveness of imperialism" and "ideological subversion within the socialist camp." And it is interesting to note the step-down from the 1957 conference, which described the Soviet Union as the "head" of the Communist camp, and from the conference of 1960, which made Moscow the "vanguard," to the 1969 formula that "there is no leading center."

Four smaller parties refused to sign the "Principal Document" at all. The Italians accepted only Section III; indeed, the increasingly wide divergence between the Soviet Party and this largest Party in the non-Communist world was one of the features of the conference. The French signed, but made it clear they remained opposed to the invasion of Czechoslovakia. The Rumanians signed but only after Party Chief Ceaucescu criticized "insufficiently precise formulations," deplored the "accusations" made against "certain" absent parties and stressed the importance of the provision approving continued relations with parties not present at the conference.

In addition to the "Principal Document," the conference adopted without debates or differences: a call for "Independence, Freedom and Peace to Vietnam!"; an "Appeal in Defense of Peace"; and a summons to celebrate "On Vladimir Ilyich Lenin's Birth Centenary." The Soviet delegation submitted the latter proposal, and the Kremlin appeared to consider it a particularly important supplement to the "Principal Document." Calling on "all Communists, all fighters for the socialist transformation of society, all champions of progress and peace, for a worthy celebration of the great Lenin's birth," the document proclaimed that

All the experience of world socialism, the working class and national liberation movements have confirmed the world significance of

Marxist-Leninist teachings [providing] proof that Leninism is historically correct and expresses the fundamental needs of the modern
age. . . . Lenin's teaching is omnipotent because it is true. . . .
Communists regard it as their task to firmly uphold the revolutionary
principles of Marxism-Leninism and proletarian internationalism.
. . . Communists will always be true to the creative spirit of
Leninism.

It seems clear that the Soviet intent was, in this indirect
way, to associate the participants with the "Leninist" ideological
revival already under way in the Soviet Union and, in effect, to
commit them against the development of independent, national,
and thus non-Leninist (i.e., non-Russian) versions of the Marxist gospel.

Mustering seventy-five of the world's eighty-eight Communist parties, with a fall-out of only six from the 1960 meeting,
was ostensibly a success for Moscow, at least numerically. But
this over-all figure requires some analysis. Five of the fourteen
ruling parties were absent—China and its European satellite
Albania, Yugoslavia, and two Asian parties which dared not
offend China, North Korea and North Vietnam. These fourteen
ruling parties contained nearly 92 percent of the world's 45
million Communists, and the five absentees had nearly as many
Party members as the participants—20.5 versus 21.3 million. In
terms of population, the absentees ruled over 800 million
people, the participants only 340 million, or less than half as
many. Outside the Party-ruled countries, the important Japanese Party and the broken Indonesian Party abstained, so that
Asia was practically unrepresented, only India and East Pakistan being present. The bulk of the participants in the Moscow
conference came from Europe and Latin America (fifty-one of
sixty-one nonruling parties), with a sprinkling from the Near
East and Africa. Except for the big Italian and French parties
(1.5 million and 275 thousand members respectively), both of
which expressed dissent, the nonruling participants were
mainly unrepresentative, small to minuscule groups, dependent
for their survival and the livelihood of their leaders on Soviet
funds.

No such analysis as the foregoing has emanated, or will

emanate, from Soviet sources. On the contrary, a postconfer-
ence article in the world Marxist review *Problems of Peace and
Socialism* by the Soviet Party's General Secretary, Leonid Brezhnev, was entitled "The Communist Movement Is in a Period of
Further Uplift" and referred to the meeting as "an important
milestone . . . in cementing the ranks of Communist and
workers parties." Naturally, this is the refrain which has been
echoed by all Soviet spokesmen and media, both at home and
abroad. Indeed, the Soviet Party promptly proceeded to establish
its own interpretation of the vague and sometimes contradictory
results of the conference. A resolution adopted at a Plenum of
the Central Committee on June 26, 1969, ratified the proceedings and documents, then went on:

The conference confirmed again that the main trend in the
cohesion of the socialist system is persistent implementation of the
principles of socialist internationalism, correct combining of national and international tasks of socialist states, the development of
fraternal mutual assistance and mutual support. The conference
declared with great force that defense of socialism is an internationalist duty of Communists.

The call "On the centenary of V. I. Lenin's birth" . . . reaffirms
unfailing loyalty of Communists to Leninism and stresses its universal international importance. The appeal in a condensed form
outlines the ideological basis for unity of the international Communist movement. . . .

. . . both the documents of the conference and the speeches of
its participants expressed the widest support for the policy of the
CPSU . . . CPSU Central Committee attaches great importance to
the conclusion of the conference that the consistent struggle for
purity of Marxism-Leninism, against revisionism, dogmatism, and
nationalism is a necessary condition for consolidation of the ranks of
Communist parties, for rallying of Communists throughout the
world, for enhancing their vanguard role in the entire revolutionary
movement.

The CPSU Central Committee points out that the exchange of
opinions that took place at the conference has shown convincingly
that the foreign political course of the present leadership of the
Communist Party of China and its splitting policy are resolutely
rebuffed by the overwhelming majority of the fraternal parties. . . .

The CPSU will conduct an uncompromising struggle against the anti-Leninist ideological lines of the present leaders of China, against their splitting policy and great-power foreign political course. The CPSU will do its utmost to protect from any encroachments the interests of the Soviet people who are building Communism.

The themes of the Central Committee resolution have been, and continue to be, developed, elaborated and disseminated in all Soviet publications and by all the vast propaganda machinery at the Kremlin's disposal. Moscow thus portrays the 1969 Conference of Communist and Workers Parties as having: restored the unity of the world movement in support of Soviet policies; given approval to the "doctrine of limited sovereignty" (otherwise described, of course); recognized that the Soviet version is the only valid interpretation of Marxism; and condemned the Chinese Communists.

The Sino-Soviet negotiations following Chairman Kosygin's brief meeting with Chinese Prime Minister Chou En-lai on September 11, 1969, have been conducted at what the Communists call the "state level." The Chinese announcement of October 7 regarding the talks in Peking stressed that "the struggle of principle between them will continue for a long period of time [but that] this should not prevent China and the Soviet Union from maintaining normal state relations on the basis of the five principles of peaceful coexistence." The negotiations have accordingly envisaged an easing of tensions and reduction of incidents along the border and restoration of diplomatic and some related intercourse between the *governments* of the two countries. Both sides have, however, carefully avoided any suggestion of a re-establishment of relations at the "Party level," that is to say, between the Soviet and Chinese *Communist parties.*

CHAPTER XI

Foundations and Instruments of Soviet Policy

Soviet leaders over the years have not been reticent in talking about their world outlook and aims. Back in 1918, Lenin himself laid down the basic proposition: "We are living not merely in a state, but in a system of states, and it is inconceivable that the Soviet Republic should continue to exist for a long period side by side with imperialist states. Ultimately, one or the other must conquer."

Shortly after Lenin's death in 1924, Stalin expanded on the theme, saying:

Lenin never regarded the Republic of the Soviets as an end in itself. To him, it was always a link needed to strengthen the chain of the revolutionary movement in the countries of the West and East, a link needed to facilitate the victory of the working people of the whole world over capitalism. Lenin knew that this was the only right conception, both from the international standpoint and the standpoint of preserving the Soviet Republic itself. Lenin knew that this alone could fire the working people of the world to fight the decisive battles for their emancipation.

Khrushchev picked up the refrain in his speech to the Supreme Soviet in December, 1957, when he said:

We have retained a great revolutionary spirit, and we assure the comrades in the struggle for the cause of the working class that we shall always be true to the principles of Marxism-Leninism, to the principles of proletarian internationalism, and that we shall, in the future as in the past, consider ourselves as a vanguard which raised high the Leninist banner and led by Lenin was the first to fight capitalism and has successfully carried this banner for the past forty years. We give assurances that we shall firmly hold in our hands the Leninist banner, shall confidently march toward the victory of Communism, and shall persistently struggle for peace throughout the whole world.

I should perhaps interpolate, in connection with Khrushchev's reference to the "struggle for peace," a brief explanation to the uninitiated of the double meaning involved. The source of the explanation is unimpeachably Communist. The April, 1948, issue of the official journal of the French Communist Party, *Les Cahiers du Communisme* (*The Notebooks of Communism*), published a speech of Soviet Politburo member and Foreign Minister Molotov, in which he at one point referred to "the victory of peace." Since many members of the huge Communist Party in France are not too well up on Marxist double-talk, the journal made the meaning clear by inserting in brackets after the phrase "the victory of peace," this interpretation: "that is to say, the victory of Communism."

Speaking in the Kremlin ten years after Khrushchev, on the Fiftieth Anniversary of the October Revolution in November, 1967, General Secretary of the Communist Party of the Soviet Union Brezhnev made it clear that nothing had changed. He was perhaps even more explicit than his predecessors:

We must never forget that the mission that falls to the Communists is the grandiose and complex mission of the revolutionary transformation of the entire society. The process of changing humanity from capitalism to socialism is a complex and varied process. On its path are hidden certain failures, temporary retreats, and even defeats for individual parts of the struggle. The Communist movement draws its lesson from this.

Experience shows that it is possible to defeat such a strong and perfidious opponent as imperialism only by confronting it with sober political calculation, cold-bloodedness, and tenacity, as well as decisiveness and selfless preparation for struggle. The Communists are confronting this opponent with a strategy that is supported by a scientific analysis of the correlation of forces, both within countries and in the international arena.

. . . The struggle for peace remains for us even today a task filled with profound class-revolutionary content, since to fight for peace means to isolate the most militant and aggressive circles of the imperialist bourgeoisie, to turn public opinion against them, and to wreck their antipeople plans.

These quotations are only fragmentary indications of the general philosophy and objectives of the Soviet Government in the field of foreign affairs, but a library of Russian Communist literature would disclose no significant departure from the established line.

Like other governments, especially of the major powers, the Soviet regime seeks power, prestige, wealth and security for itself and for the people and territory it rules. The main difference arises out of the fact that Communist ideology teaches the Soviet leaders that this security cannot be assured in a world divided between Communism and capitalism and that, accordingly, they must eventually achieve world domination. Another difference arises out of the unlimited extent to which the doctrine teaches that the end justifies the means. In 1920 Lenin himself declared that "It is necessary . . . to use any ruse, cunning, unlawful method, evasion, concealment of truth. . . ."

It must be added that in the last fifty years the Soviet dictatorship has gone far toward substituting its own scale of values for those previously prevailing in international intercourse among modern nations. The Soviet statesman chooses his weapons from the arsenal solely on the basis of their utility in any given circumstance. He does not have to be influenced by considerations of established international practice and usage, except insofar as they affect the utility of the weapon in question. He regards the established international rules as suspicious devices of an antagonistic world. Thus the dividing line between the "legitimate" and "concealed" instruments of Soviet foreign policy becomes blurred and shifting.

Moreover, to a degree not often characteristic of Western statesmen or even cold-blooded professional diplomats, the Soviet leaders have a keen appreciation of the relativity of national power "in a system of states." They accordingly seek maximum present security and the attainment of their final goals not only through an absolute increase in the power potential of the U.S.S.R. but also through reduction of the strength of other nations. This is why the Soviet Union is constantly engaged in divisive maneuvers both between and within capitalist societies, why it has always conducted the world's most extensive propaganda campaign and why it continues wishfully to predict new economic crises in the capitalist world.

The foundation of national power is, of course, the total human and material resources of a given country. In terms of the conduct of foreign policy, this power is reflected primarily in terms of the basic strength of the national economy, including mastery of science and technology, and of armed-forces-in-being. From the beginning these items have had the highest priority within the Soviet system.

In a preceding chapter, I discussed the inadequacy of the Soviet system to solve the economic problems of a modern society and the difficulties facing the present Soviet leadership in connection with industrial management and agricultural production. This is all true, but it should not blind one to the fact that the Soviet Union has, nevertheless, developed over the years into the second greatest economic power in the world. The Soviets did not start the process. The basic resources were already there, and the Industrial Revolution came to Czarist Russia in the latter part of the nineteenth century. By 1914 Russia was producing something like 5 million tons of pig iron, 4 million tons of steel, 40 million tons of coal, 10 million tons of oil and a food-grain export surplus of about 10 million tons. The

Revolution and the Civil War brought a setback and these levels of production were not reattained until about 1928. Then the sustained Soviet drive for the development of the basic economic strength of the country, under the first three Five-Year Plans, tripled and in some cases quadrupled these figures by the time of the Nazi invasion in 1941. The prompt postwar resumption of that drive, in the face of the wartime devastation of the country and the needs of the long-suffering Russian population, was a remarkable manifestation of will, determination and totalitarian control. Today the Soviet Union is producing about 90 million tons of pig iron, 110 million tons of steel, 325 million tons of crude oil and nearly 600 million tons of coal. In addition, it has developed vast resources of natural gas and of hydroelectric power. Only agriculture has lagged behind.

It should be noted that totalitarian economies contain elements and possibilities of concealment and maneuver not available to capitalist democracies where industrial development is guided by the laws of supply and demand and governmental appropriations for special projects of national importance are matters of public knowledge and debate. With complete control of the national economy, the Soviet Government can arbitrarily organize its economic relations with outside countries on the basis of political as well as economic considerations and thus exploit those relations for the attainment of political or power objectives.

It should also be noted that the Soviet Union has concentrated on basic heavy and extractive industries of high war potential and allowed production of consumer goods to fall far behind international standards. While Soviet output of industrial products is more than half that of the United States, output for personal consumption is less than a third. Indeed, there is reason to believe that the Soviet leadership consider that our economic system involves a great waste of resources. I remember how appalled Khrushchev was, during his visit, by the number of passenger automobiles in the United States. He commented on the fact that most of these machines, weighing three thousand pounds or more, were carrying only one or two persons, weighing 150 to 300 pounds. This, he said, he would

never allow to happen in the Soviet Union. I confess I thought
he had a point. But all mankind is addicted to certain follies,
one of which seems to be the yearning to possess a private
automobile. The Russians are no exception, and the post-
Khrushchev leadership has already had to make a first concession toward meeting this demand by committing several
billion rubles to the construction of an automobile plant designed to produce about 500,000 passenger cars a year, or twice
as many as present total production. On balance, however, it
must be said that the Soviet economy is much leaner and more
muscular than our own.

Ever since the Revolution and the Civil War, it has been
Soviet policy to maintain large conventional military forces-in-
being, enough to deter any attack either from the West or from
the East. Since his death, Stalin has been accused of not having
anticipated the inevitable attack by the Nazi forces and not
having prepared the country for that attack. It may well be that
if Stalin had not undertaken the purge of the Officer Corps of
the armed forces in 1937, and had he not been so anxious to
appease Hitler and give him no cause for attack during the
period of Nazi-Soviet nonaggression pact from 1939 to 1941, the
Soviet Union would have been in a better defensive posture. On
the other hand, it is difficult to see how Stalin could have in-
vested much more of the country's limited resources in actual
military production and still have accomplished his basic purpose of building up heavy industry. In any case, it was Stalin
who expressed more pithily than anyone else the basic Soviet
attitude toward military power. During one of their wartime
meetings and arguments about Soviet behavior in the countries
of Eastern Europe, Churchill cited the importance of the views
and influence of the Vatican. Stalin responded by asking a
question: "How many divisions has the Pope?"

Khrushchev, confronted by this perennial problem of how
to use the limited resources available, became a missile man,
and accorded much lower priority than his predecessors to
conventional forces, particularly naval forces. In fact, he would,
from time to time, describe naval vessels as nothing more than
incinerators or crematoriums in the nuclear age. He told me

once with a note of irritation that he had been trying to reduce his regular military budget in order to get more money for investment in agriculture. He said that he had been unable to prevail over the marshals and admirals, but at least he intended to hold their budget at its present level so that he could use the annual budgetary increment of about two and a half billion rubles for agricultural and other purposes. Even after the Cuban crisis had confirmed that the "missile gap" was now on the Soviet side, he was capable of declaring, rather testily: "Your McNamara says he can destroy us four times over; well, we can destroy you once and that's enough."

In fact, Khrushchev did hold the Soviet overt military budget at a fairly stable level of around thirteen billion rubles. I think his successor as Chairman of the Council of Ministers, Kosygin, would have liked to follow suit. In the fall of 1964 we had informed Kosygin of our intention of making some reduction in the American military budget for the following fiscal year. On the basis of this information, Chairman Kosygin actually cut the Soviet budget 500 million rubles for the calendar year 1965 and in his budget address to the Supreme Soviet, in December, 1964, referred to this as a case of reduction in military budgets by "mutual example" between the Soviet Union and the United States. Later, when the mounting costs of the Vietnam hostilities obliged the President to go in for a supplemental budget early in 1965, Kosygin charged that we had let him down. It seems likely, however, that Kosygin's colleagues in the Politburo disagreed with him in wanting to hold back military expenditures. As I noted earlier, Party Secretary Brezhnev was long closely associated with the military forces, and the new Soviet leaders were beholden to the military establishment for its cooperation in the conspiracy to oust Khrushchev. Some members undoubtedly also considered it important that the Soviet Union show increased military expenditures in the face of the escalation of hostilities in Vietnam. In actual practice, the Soviet overt military budget was increased to 13.4 billions in 1966; to 14.5 billions in 1967; to 16.7 billions in 1968; and to 17.7 billions in 1969. You will note that I have referred to the "overt" military budget in connection with these figures. A factor to be borne in mind is that in the Soviet budget many military expenses are concealed under other headings, such as research and space programs, which we estimate amount to something like an addition of one-third to the published military budget. Another factor to remember is that military pay in the Soviet Union is little more than "cigarette money," so personnel costs are small as compared with the U.S. military budget.

Military service is compulsory and universal in the Soviet Union, beginning at age eighteen. The period of service used to be a uniform three years, but a new law promulgated in October, 1967, reduces it to two for the army and air force, while retaining three years for the navy. The change apparently reflects the fact that the postwar "baby boom" has produced a bulge in the conscript-age population sufficient to maintain the armed forces at their present level of about two and a half million men with a shorter period of service in the branches which consume the bulk of the personnel. However, in lieu of the third year of active service, compulsory preservice military training is now required for all male teen-agers during the last two years of secondary schooling, i.e., from sixteen to eighteen years of age. Comparable training is required for all youth not in school at special training centers established at all "enterprises, institutions and collective and state farms."

The Soviet ground forces are organized into about 140 divisions. Forty-six of these divisions are "combat-ready," and of these, 22 are stationed in East Germany. About 55 divisions are of reduced strength—4 of these are in Hungary—but can be brought to full strength within two weeks. The remaining 39 are cadre, or "skeleton" divisions, which can be filled out in about six weeks. The air force maintains nearly 4,000 combat-ready aircraft, mainly MIG-21s and SU-7s. The surface navy is still small by American standards, but is no longer neglected. Priority has been given to the submarine fleet, which numbers 380 craft, many of which are nuclear-powered and missile-firing. Only 10 of these, each carrying 16 missiles capable of being launched from submerged positions, are comparable to our Polaris craft, but more are being built.

Soviet first priority, however, has gone to catching up with the United States in the field of intercontinental ballistic missiles, or ICBMs. By the end of 1969 the Soviet strategic forces had slightly surpassed us in numbers of ICBMs (over 1,200 versus 1,054) placed in underground, "hardened" sites. In addition, the Soviet Union has more than 700 medium- and intermediate-range ballistic missiles, MRBMs and IRBMs, targeted against our NATO allies in Europe. Moscow used to count on this threat alone as the major component of its deterrent toward us. The principal counter to these Soviet MRBMs is considered to be the American Polaris missiles, or SLMs, carried by and launched from our 41 nuclear-powered submarines. The United States also still maintains a long-range nuclear-bombing fleet numbering nearly 700 aircraft as against a Soviet counter-capability of probably less than a third this number.

However, the missile debate is not simply a numbers game, and one can get into great arguments on the subject of relative American and Soviet strengths. The Soviets have tended to build bigger and more powerful missiles and to fit them with much more powerful nuclear warheads. Many argue the case in terms of total megatonnage of explosive power, in which the Soviet side tops us. However, there are many other factors which complicate the question, such as accuracy of the weapons and the interaction of weapons systems against each other. On balance, I would say that there is a kind of stalemate today, based on the capability of each side to do unacceptable second-strike damage to the other. But the situation is not static. The United States is already initiating a program of increasing its total number of separately targeted warheads, by making one missile carry several different warheads (MIRVs). The Soviet Union has also started experimenting in this field. In addition, Moscow has introduced two unsettling new elements. The Soviets have been experimenting with what is called a "fractional orbit ballistic system," or FOBS, which would permit them to orbit their missiles around the South Pole and thus avoid our Early Warning System in the North Pole region. Even more unsettling is the fact that the Soviet side has deployed a light antiballistic missile (ABM) system in the Moscow area of the Soviet Union.

When the Soviet ABM deployment was confirmed at the end of 1966, I was back in the Department of State as a Deputy Under Secretary, and it fell to me to propose to the Soviet Ambassador that the two governments initiate discussions with a view to curtailing the strategic arms race. The proposal was promptly accepted "in principle," provided such talks would cover both offensive- and defensive-missile systems, a proviso acceptable to us. However, despite this acceptance "in principle" and despite considerable prodding on our part, it was more than a year and a half before Moscow even reconfirmed its original decision. It is clear that a considerable debate took place within the Kremlin leadership and probably with the military during this period and that a corollary decision was taken to speed up the deployment of "hardened" ICBM or "offensive" missiles. Meanwhile, in September, 1967, Defense Secretary McNamara had announced our decision to go ahead with a light ABM system in the United States.

Moscow's reconfirmation of its readiness to negotiate on strategic weapons came on the eve of the Soviet invasion and occupation of Czechoslovakia, and I would suppose the timing was calculated to help cover up the Kremlin's embarrassment about that action. It also came at a point when the United States was in the midst of Presidential elections. There was consequently some delay on our side also. However, after his assumption of office, President Nixon reconfirmed our readiness to talk, as well as the decision to go ahead with the deployment of an altered but still light ABM system designed primarily to "safeguard" our Minuteman missile strike force. He also cleared the way by realistically redefining our nuclear-weapons objective, not as "superiority" but as "sufficiency," and assigned the negotiating role to the Arms Control and Disarmament Agency of the Department of State. Strategic arms limitation talks— SALT, as they have come to be called—will be complicated and lengthy. Moreover, the results will inevitably be limited, because of the categorical refusal of the Soviet side, in accordance with traditional Russian concealment and secrecy, to accept any kind of inspection and verification on their own territory.

Since the end of World War II the Soviet Union has

concentrated heavy human, technical and material resources on the development of advanced rocket propulsion and of space vehicles. Unlike the United States, where our major space programs are operated by a civilian agency, the National Aeronautics and Space Administration (NASA), Soviet space programs from the beginning have been and continue to be administered by the Soviet military, under conditions of the utmost secrecy. The Soviet reasons for making this great space effort are probably multiple, but I believe that, at least initially, their principal motivations were both military—i.e., probing for possible military uses and advantages and at the same time insuring themselves against being caught by some technological military surprise—and psychological—i.e., the desire to establish an image of the Soviet Union as the world's leader in science. Whatever the exact mix of reasons, the result of the Soviet space effort was a series of spectacular and impressive firsts; the first earth satellite in October, 1957; the first solar orbit in January, 1959; the first moon shot in September, 1959, followed by the first lunar satellite photographs a month later; the first man in space in April, 1961; and the first walk in space in March, 1965—to mention only the main events. We dramatically restored damaged American prestige and achieved some of our own "firsts" with the Apollo moon-landing program. We are also ahead in terms of practical applications, such as telephonic and television communications, weather reporting, earth resource surveys and navigation. However, with their initiation of multimanned experiments in the creation of permanent space stations or platforms in October, 1969, the Soviets have outdistanced us by two years or more in what must be the next great step toward man's mastery of space.

I have already noted (and will examine further in a following chapter) how Khrushchev tried to exploit the prestige and power potential of the Soviet space program by launching an era of Sputnik diplomacy, and how he finally overplayed his hand in Berlin and Cuba. There is reason to believe that Khrushchev's successors blamed him not for his attempt to cash in but for his failure to do so. They have given top priority to regaining the image—and hopefully the reality—of scientific-technical superiority achieved with the orbiting of Sputnik I and Lunik I. Quite apart from their nearly completed crash program to overtake the United States in nuclear missiles, the Kremlin leadership has continued a space effort somewhat different in content but comparable in size with our own. This represents an annual investment in space programs estimated at about 2 percent of Soviet GNP, or a relative burden on their national economy more than double our own space effort. Soviet allocations for related scientific and technological programs have mounted rapidly in recent years, and Kremlin leaders have called for continued increases. A Party-government decree in October, 1968, reorganized the Soviet structure for administering scientific and technological affairs and introduced material incentives for scientific workers. While the boastful bombast of the Khrushchev era has been muted, Soviet media continue to proclaim that only Communism is capable of reaping the full benefits of the scientific and technological revolution of our times and that this factor will be decisive in the conflict between the two systems.

In the conduct of their day-to-day intercourse with other governments, the Soviet Government ostentatiously follows the established and traditional forms. After the initial Bolshevik confusion of revolutionary and state purposes, Moscow built up for itself all the elaborate apparatus of Western diplomatic practice: a foreign office, world-wide diplomatic and consular services, capable of great attention to protocol and of lavish representational display, and an array of treaties. The Soviet Foreign Service is of very high caliber—different in training and outlook, of course, but otherwise comparable to our American Foreign Service in professional competence. Since 1957 the Soviet Ministry of Foreign Affairs has been headed by one of the most remarkable—and certainly the most durable—of the world's diplomats, Andrei Andreyevich Gromyko. Educated as an economist, with a doctor's degree, he was at an early age a senior associate in the Soviet Academy of Sciences and executive secretary of the editorial board of the weighty journal *Problems of Economics*. Transferring to foreign affairs on the eve of

World War II, he headed the Ministry's Department of American Affairs, then went to Washington as Counselor of the Soviet Embassy. In 1943, only thirty-four years old, he was named Ambassador to the United States and followed this up as Soviet Ambassador (Permanent Representative) to the United Nations. He was recalled to Moscow as Deputy Minister of Foreign Affairs in 1948 and, except for a three-year tour as Soviet Ambassador to Great Britain, served in that No. 2 position until his elevation to the post of minister. He has participated in practically every important international meeting since the Dumbarton Oaks Conference in 1944 (which produced the original draft Charter of the United Nations) and hasn't forgotten a word that was said at any of them—or, indeed, in any of the thousands of diplomatic conversations he has had as Ambassador and Foreign Minister. This phenomenal memory, vast experience and native ability give him a real advantage over most of those with whom he deals. Gromyko is indeed a worthy interlocutor and a formidable opponent.

It is of course true that basic Soviet policies are developed in the Kremlin, starting with the Secretariat of the Party's Central Committee and ending in the Politburo, and that the Ministry is considered only an operating agency. Khrushchev was quite capable of treating "his" Foreign Minister like a servant, in a manner embarrassing not only to Gromyko but to others, sometimes including me, who might be present. Gromyko has, however, been a member of the Central Committee since 1956. The post-Khrushchev leadership visibly depends on his experienced advice, and I am sure he has played an increasing role in basic policy decisions. This would seem to be confirmed by the unusual honors bestowed on him on the occasion of his sixtieth birthday, in July, 1969, when he was given both of the highest state awards: the Order of Lenin and the insignia of Hero of Socialist Labor.

After many years of denouncing Western foreign aid as an ill-disguised instrument of imperialism, the Soviet Union in the mid-1950s suddenly decided to undertake an aid program of its own. Since then economic and military aid to the less-developed countries of the non-Communist world has become a key instrument in Soviet efforts to project its presence and expand its influence. From a small beginning in 1954, the program has grown dramatically, has broadened in scope and content. In 1954 the Soviet Union and its Communist associates extended about $6 million in foreign aid. By the end of 1967 the cumulative total of Communist economic assistance had grown to nearly $9 billion and its military aid program to about $5.5 billion. During 1967 nearly fifteen thousand academic students and about two thousand technicians were being trained in the Soviet Union and the Eastern European countries. In addition, an estimated twenty thousand economic technicians from the European Communist countries were engaged in aid activities abroad. Figures for later years are not available but would presumably be comparable.

Generally speaking, Soviet aid programs have been more selective and more clearly politically motivated than those of the Western countries. Their motivation has been not only to establish Soviet presence and influence in key emerging countries but to reduce or eliminate Western influence. For these ends, Moscow has been ready to accept and deal with nationalist governments of the ex-colonial countries even to the point of restraining local Communist parties subservient to its directives from overt revolutionary activity that would offend those nationalist governments. India and the United Arab Republic, for example, countries in which Communist parties have either been banned or sharply attacked by the ruling political parties, have received more economic assistance than any other beneficiaries of Soviet aid. Moscow has overlooked such attacks in the expectation that "revolutionaries" like Nasser can do more damage to Western influence in the Near East and Africa in the name of anticolonialism and Arab nationalism than the Soviet Union could possibly hope to achieve alone or through weak local Communist parties. Similarly, Moscow has counted on India's influence among the Afro-Asian nations and has sought to bolster India's strategic position as a counterweight to China in Asia. However, the Soviets have usually insisted that their aid go into the so-called "public sector" of the economy of the aided nations, thereby moving them toward "socialism" or at least "state capitalism," that is to say, toward more Communist-oriented forms of economic and social organization.

During its relatively short history, the Soviet aid program has had a number of spectacular setbacks, particularly in Africa; and at home the aid program has been perhaps even less popular with the underprivileged Soviet citizen than it has been in the countries of the West. Consequently, the new leadership in the Soviet Union has shown itself inclined to be even more selective than Khrushchev was, and to take a hard look at the longer-range implications and potential benefits to Soviet interests of its investments in assistance programs abroad.

Theoretically, any international organization not directly or indirectly under Moscow's control is repugnant to Soviet practice and ideology. Gromyko once said to me that if we had not set up the United Nations under the stresses and pressures of the wartime alliance, it would never have been possible to set it up later. And indeed, even in 1945, the Soviet Union agreed to participate only on the basis of such safeguards as the application of the great-power veto in the Security Council and limitations on the initiative and authority of the General Assembly. Shielded by these protective devices, the Soviet Union has tried to use the UN forum as a sounding board for its propaganda, frequently as a means of distracting world attention in one direction while it pursued objectives in another. The Soviet representatives in the UN have also consistently blocked the development of an international security organization inside the UN with sufficient strength and authority to exercise a collective will against the U.S.S.R. or any of its associates or protégés. They are not likely to repeat their historic error of 1950 when the Soviet delegate walked out of a Security Council session on Korea, instead of staying and exercising his veto, and thus enabled the Security Council to set up collective action to defend South Korea against the aggression from the North.

An interesting feature of Soviet participation in the United Nations has been the extent to which it has used its own Ukrainian or Belorussian delegations or Eastern European associates to take advanced positions or lead the attack in cases where the Soviet Union considered its own interests best served by remaining aloof or in which it did not want to be in the position of assuming a direct commitment or obligation. While the Soviet Union has gradually extended its representation to some of the specialized agencies of the UN, particularly those which serve the purpose of expanding Soviet contacts with the underdeveloped countries, Moscow has consistently refused to participate in any of the postwar arrangements such as the World Bank or the International Monetary Fund, designed to stabilize and strengthen the (prevailingly capitalistic) world financially and economically.

These, then—its Foreign Service, its official aid program and its membership in the United Nations—are the principal "overt" or official instruments for the conduct of Soviet foreign policies. At the next level, Moscow has an assortment of semi-official, sometimes semiconcealed instruments of policy. To begin with, the Soviet Union has what is undoubtedly the world's largest propaganda organization, starting with a world-wide broadcasting service of unmatched power and number of transmitters, mostly shortwave. In some advanced countries, such as the United States, where almost all radio broadcasting is on the standard wave bands and shortwave listening is not common, Radio Moscow probably doesn't have many listeners, but it undoubtedly has a big audience throughout Asia and Africa. And even in the developed countries you may be sure that the local Communists listen carefully and take their cue from Moscow, then give a considerable secondary circulation to Moscow's views and positions in their own publications and other media of information. Another important component of this propaganda apparatus is the relatively new press agency, Novosti. It distributes propaganda articles, photographs and recorded radio and television programs to local media through-out the world. It also acts as host and helper to foreign journalists and publicists coming to the Soviet Union who, without Novosti's help, find little material available. Still another component is the Soviet publishing and book distributing agency, International Books, which has developed outlets throughout the world. Finally, there is the official Soviet press agency, Tass, which is steadily expanding its news distribution services and makes a specialty of providing news files to publications in the lesser-developed countries either gratis or at a low charge which cannot be matched by Western commercial news agencies.

An organization following a somewhat different approach is the Union of Societies of Friendship with Peoples of Foreign Countries. This organization, which has existed since World War II, specializes in promoting and sponsoring the formation of Societies for Cultural Relations between the Soviet Union and a given country or Societies of Soviet-[Given Country] Friendship. Its activities have expanded considerably over the years. Its chairman told me that they now have more than a hundred such Friendship Societies in the Soviet Union, matched by their corresponding partners abroad. This, to my knowledge, includes some very large and influential organizations, even in such a country as France, where their fellow-traveling proclivities are a considerable nuisance to the government and an obstacle to the development of soundly based and really representative official exchange programs. The Union of Societies of Friendship has not had much success in the United States. There is a small Soviet-American Friendship Society of the fellow-traveling variety established here, but it is not regarded even by Moscow as a suitable counterpart organization. Consequently, the American section of the Union is simply called the Institute of Soviet-American Relations. Apart from maintaining correspondence and exchanging delegations with the corresponding organizations abroad, the national sections in Moscow sponsor foreign visitors, arrange foreign participation in Soviet meetings and the like.

One of the most far-flung and successful of the "front" organizations is a postwar creation, the so-called World Peace Council. Formed in 1949, on the heels of the signature of the North Atlantic Treaty, it was for many years headed by the late eminent French scientist (and Communist) Frédéric Joliot-Curie. The WPC first attracted world-wide attention with its meeting in Stockholm in 1950, which issued a much-publicized appeal for the outlawing of nuclear weapons. Since that time its meetings have consistently featured resolutions supporting Soviet positions on such issues as Korea, the Geneva Conference on Indochina and disarmament. In this period it claims to have built up over one hundred affiliated sections throughout the world.

In June, 1969, the WPC celebrated its twentieth anniversary with a gala "Peace Assembly" in East Berlin which reportedly drew 56 international and 320 national organizations, and 1,102 people from 101 countries. The delegates represented a wide spectrum of organizations, from Quaker and Red Cross observers to groups of academics, parliamentarians, trade-union officials, students, journalists, women and the usual collection of "peace" bureaucrats. Among the delegates were such individuals as former Indian Defense Minister Krishna Menon, American Communist intellectual Herbert Aptheker and Negro comedian Dick Gregory, the North Vietnamese Minister of Culture and the Sudanese Minister of the Interior. Moscow—whose Soviet Peace Council is nominally only one of the hundred national sections—sent a typical delegation of writers and academicians, plus one cosmonaut. The agenda might have been the basic outline for a Brezhnev speech: (1) Vietnam and Southeast Asia; (2) European security; (3) the Middle East; (4) colonialism and neocolonialism; and (5) disarmament. The Kremlin might also have prepared the final appeals of the assembly, calling for an end to American and Israeli aggression, recognition of the German Democratic Republic, struggle against colonialism; and disarmament on Soviet terms. After the meeting concluded WPC Secretary General Romesh Chandra proceeded to Moscow, where he was received by Soviet Party ideologist and Politburo member Mikhail Suslov and Party Secretary Boris Ponomarev. Tass reported that these gentlemen "wished the WPC further successes in its lofty activities."

In the international labor field, the Soviet Union had a great but rather short-lived success after World War II. Before the war there were two principal international labor organizations. The first was the International Federation of Trade Unions (IFTU), powered mainly by the British Trade Union's Congress (BTUC) and the American Federation of Labor (AFL), from which Soviet labor was excluded by a rule barring labor movements which were not "free"—that is, were con-

trolled by their national governments. The second was the
International Labor Office, ILO, an organization of representatives of labor, employers and government, affiliated with the
League of Nations, to which the U.S.S.R. was ineligible on the
grounds that the Soviet Government should not represent all
three elements. The Soviets tried to set up their own revolutionary Red International of Trade Unions or Profintern, as an
appendix to the Comintern, but the Red International never
really got off the ground.

The big break for the Soviets finally came through the
Anglo-Soviet Trade Union Committee, one of the products of
Allied good will and fraternity during World War II. Beginning
in June, 1943, by as clever a bit of diplomatic finesse as was
ever perpetrated, the Russian delegates jockeyed the BTUC into
agreeing to call an International Labor Meeting, which would of
course have to include the Soviet Union. The British stalled and
evaded as long as possible, but finally felt obliged to act. After a
preliminary conference in London, a plenary assembly at Paris,
in October, 1945, set up the new World Federation of Trade
Unions (WFTU), representing, it was claimed, "65 nations and
70 million workers." Under Soviet influence, the WFTU organization followed standard Communist lines, with the federation's
main responsibilities delegated to an executive committee of
twenty-six members and then, in turn, to a small steering
bureau of seven members. Since the voting was to be based on
claimed membership, the Soviet delegation came out with over
two hundred votes against about a hundred for the British,
American, French and Italian organizations.

The Congress of Industrial Organizations (CIO) and the
Latin American Federation of Labor (CTAL) enthusiastically
supported the Soviet WFTU initiative from the start. The CIO
had been excluded from IFTU by a rule prohibiting membership
of more than one national organization; and the CTAL, as a
regional organization, had no direct international affiliation at
the time. The AFL refused to take part in the WFTU, and a
resolution adopted by its convention in 1946 charged that the
organization "was conceived by the Russian dictatorship . . .
and has clearly and unmistakably proved itself as an agency to
foster Russia's expansionist foreign policy."

While the AFL resolution may have been a bit premature, the Russian delegates soon made it come true, by trying to force the WFTU to take a stand against the Marshall Plan. This action led the British and the CIO to withdraw and to join hands with AFL and some smaller European trade unions to found a rival international federation in 1949 called the International Confederation of Free Trade Unions (ICFTU). For many years the ICFTU provided an effective counter to the WFTU, but the leadership deteriorated and differences arose, particularly about the establishment of contacts with the Eastern European unions. The AFL-CIO withdrew in 1969, and, while the ICFTU continues in being, it has been greatly enfeebled. The WFTU has also gone on and has been able to retain as members the main Communist-dominated trade unions in France and Italy. But the WFTU, too, has been disrupted by conflict between its Soviet and Chinese Communist members and by differences respecting the Soviet invasion of Czechoslovakia. The WFTU remains an instrument of Soviet policy, dutifully passing resolutions supporting Moscow's positions and trying to extend its activities and influence to the underdeveloped countries of Asia, Africa and Latin America, but it has not nearly the power once envisaged.

I previously noted how Stalin permitted the Russian Orthodox Church to restore the Patriarchate and utilized the Church both for internal and external support of the Soviet war effort. Since the war the Church has, in fact, continued to serve, under close government control, as an instrument of Soviet foreign policy. In the aftermath of the war the Russian Church emerged from its isolation and re-established relations with many world religious organizations, including the World Council of Churches. The Moscow Patriarchate also undertook a vigorous offensive, and a successful one, to gain control or hegemony over the Slavic Orthodox churches in Eastern Europe and over Russian émigré churches in many countries throughout the world; and after a long campaign and with the active support of Soviet diplomacy, it obtained control over the Czarist-established Russian churches in Jerusalem and the Holy Land. Alexei, Patriarch of Moscow and All Russia, and Nikodim, Metropolitan of Leningrad and Novgorod, who acts as a kind of foreign secretary of the Church, have both traveled widely abroad and received many foreign religious visitors. In July, 1969, the Patriarchate organized a World Religious Conference in the old monastery center of Zagorsk, the aim of which, according to Nikodim, was "to help awaken and strengthen all the believers' responsibility for the destinies of world peace, to bring together the peace-making forces of the many parts of the world, to work out authoritative recommendations and fraternal appeals." The agenda of the conference was almost precisely the same as that of the World Peace Assembly in Berlin and the resolutions were similar. The meeting was participated in by "representatives of all denominations of the U.S.S.R.—Christians of different beliefs, Moslems, Buddhists and Judaists," plus guests from forty-four foreign countries. It received scant mention in domestic Soviet news media, but was elaborately publicized abroad. Two days after the conference closed, *Pravda* of July 6, 1969, carried a long article on methods of improving antireligious and atheistic work in the Soviet Union.

In recent years, as it has sought to woo to the Communist cause the scores of new nations emerging from colonialism, the Soviet Union has increasingly sought to organize or gain control of a whole series of institutions and activities which would increase its contact with, and influence on, important segments of the elite of those emerging countries. I discussed earlier the rivalry between the Russian and the Chinese Communists in this respect, particularly as it related to the question of Soviet participation in the projected Bandung Conference, scheduled to take place in Algiers in 1965. Perhaps the most interesting story about Soviet efforts—and consequent problems—in this connection is that of the so-called Tricontinental Conference which took place in Havana, Cuba, in January, 1966. At the Twentieth Session of the United Nations General Assembly in 1965, the Soviet delegation submitted a proposed resolution on "the inadmissibility of intervention in the domestic affairs of states and the protection of their independence and sovereignty." On December 21 the Soviet proposal became UN Resolution 2131, by a practically unanimous vote of 109 to 0, including the affirmative votes of the Soviet Union and Cuba. The resolution stated, in part: "No state shall organize, assist, foment, finance, incite, or tolerate subversive, terrorist, or armed activities, directed towards the violent overthrow of the regime of another state, or interfere in civil strife in another state."

Within two weeks after the passage of this UN resolution, the Soviet Union and Cuba were the central figures at the Tricontinental Conference in Havana. While the conference was sponsored by the Afro-Asian People's Solidarity Organization, the Soviet Union and Cuba were, in fact, the principal organizers and financers. Soviet airplanes transported many African, Asian and Latin-American delegates to Havana. The Soviets supplied prepaid airline tickets to other delegates and assisted Cuba in paying conference expenses. The Soviet delegation was headed by Sharaf Rashidov, a candidate member of the Politburo of the Central Committee of the Soviet Communist Party and a frequently elected deputy to both the Supreme Soviet of the Uzbek Republic and the All-Union Supreme Soviet. The delegation included also a number of Soviet Government and Party officials, among them the Soviet Ambassador in Havana. The decisions of the Havana conference could not more directly have defied the Soviet-sponsored UN resolution. Here are a couple of typical passages from the conference document:

All the revolutionary forces represented at this conference should intensify their efforts to supply all types of economic, financial and material assistance, including arms and munitions, to the authentic representatives of those countries engaged in armed struggle in order to liberate their countries. . . .

The conference solemnly proclaims that all progressive countries as well as all revolutionary movements will extend a consistent and unconditional aid to all peoples engaged in a struggle for national liberation.

In his speech to the meeting, Soviet delegate Rashidov was even more specific, saying: "We express our fraternal solidarity with the armed struggle being waged by the Venezuelan, Peruvian, Colombian and Guatemalan patriots for freedom against the stooges of imperialism."

A few weeks later the Organization of American States (OAS), by a vote of 18–0, condemned the decisions of the

Havana conference as a violation of the principles of nonintervention and of the self-determination of peoples. The OAS
resolution declared that the action of the conference in setting
up a permanent committee of twelve members, consisting of
representatives of Communist countries and of Communist
groups in other countries of those three continents, as well as a
special organization for the promotion of subversion, terrorism
and civil war in Latin America, constituted a danger to the peace
and security of the Western Hemisphere. On the heels of this
action, the Latin-American ambassadors in Moscow demanded
an accounting from the Soviet Foreign Ministry. A Deputy
Foreign Minister played to them the old record to the effect that
it was not the Soviet Government which was represented at
Havana, but only "Soviet public organizations and private citizens." I hardly need to say that my Latin-American colleagues
were far from satisfied with this lame explanation. And, indeed, as the world learns more about Soviet organizational and
operational methods, it is becoming harder and harder for the
Soviet Union to operate at the three levels of state, Party and so-
called "social organizations," and then successfully maintain the
fiction that they are separate and independent.

In discussing the operation of international Communism, I
pointed out that Moscow's control depended less on the overt
organizational structure, such as the Comintern or the Cominform, than on the direct relationship of the Secretariat of the
Central Committee of the Communist Party of the Soviet Union
with the leaders and functionaries of the other Communist
parties, most of whom were Moscow-trained. Much of this basic
relationship remains, despite the disappearance of the formal
organizational framework. The relationships have undoubtedly
been disturbed and in many cases weakened by the disarray in
the Communist camp, particularly by the conflict between Moscow and Peking and by the invasion of Czechoslovakia. But
most of the national Communist parties around the world are
still dependent on Moscow for aid and support. General Secretary Brezhnev in a public speech said that, during the first year
of the new post-Khrushchev leadership, the Soviet Party had
received delegations from over sixty other parties and held

satisfactory consultations with them. In March, 1966, guests from eighty-odd Communist parties attended the Twenty-third Congress of the Soviet Communist Party. Only four parties turned down the Soviet invitation, and a few others either were not invited—as in the case of the Chinese and the Albanians—or simply did not respond. Attendance at the celebration of the Fiftieth Anniversary of the Bolshevik Revolution in November, 1967, was comparable. And delegates from seventy-five parties were mustered for the Moscow conference in June, 1969. Thus, while the international apparatus is certainly not as effective today as it was in Stalin's time, it is still a unique instrument in the hands of the Kremlin—the like of which is not at the disposition of its opponents—capable of reaching into the very heart of hostile societies.

This brings me, finally, to a consideration of one of the more fearsome, concealed instruments of Soviet policy—espionage. The Soviets did not exactly invent espionage, which is one of the oldest professions in the world. It was a characteristic of Czarist Russia, too, and I noted earlier how the Czars used the secret police internally and secret agents and double agents abroad to try to control the rising tide of revolution. The Soviets have done much better than their predecessors, developing the espionage function to an unparalleled degree of sophistication and effectiveness.

The most startling and by all odds best-documented description of the system we owe to the tortured conscience of a young cipher clerk named Igor Guzenko, working in the Soviet Embassy in Ottawa just after World War II. In September, 1945, Guzenko went to the Canadian police with documentary evidence of the existence of several parallel undercover networks of Soviet espionage, based upon a combination of Soviet diplomatic establishments, professional Comintern agents and facilities, and the apparatus of local Communist parties. The Canadian Government set up a special Royal Commission to investigate, and its six-hundred-page report makes for reading more fascinating than most "whodunits." The commission was able to trace in detail only the military espionage network in Canada, but it disclosed beyond question the existence and general functions of parallel NKVD and Comintern (also referred to as political or Party) systems in Canada, linked to similar espionage networks in other countries, notably Great Britain and the United States. The three systems in Canada were supervised, respectively, by the military attaché of the embassy, by a second secretary who was a NKVD functionary and by a second secretary who was a Party functionary. Each separately reported to and received instructions from his respective headquarters in Moscow.

The NKVD system, which, the commission found, had been operating in Canada "at least as early as 1924," was responsible for keeping tab on Russian members of the embassy staff and checking and reporting on members of the Communist Party of Canada, as well as for general espionage.

The Comintern system had the task of obtaining and submitting biographical and other material on Canadian Communists and other Communist sympathizers, and transmitting Moscow's political directives to Canadian Communist leaders, not only regarding general lines of political propaganda but also on specific techniques and operations. Examples of the latter were instructions to create or to get control of functional organizations such as the Canadian Association of Scientific Workers; to occupy important positions in labor unions; when necessary for special purposes, to direct certain Canadian secret Communists to take up temporarily an anti-Communist line; to get members into controlling positions in the executive organs of youth movements, international friendship councils and the like, which would be important from a propaganda point of view.

The principal operators of the military system in Canada were two professional Communist agents, Sam Carr and Fred Rose, naturalized Canadian citizens, officials of the Communist Party of Canada, both with Moscow training and experience. They were able, in the words of the Royal Commission, "to draw into the net" dozens of strategically placed Canadian citizens— scientists, officials, military officers and government employees —holding positions of public responsibility and trust. Through this network they obtained and sent to Moscow, notably: actual samples of uranium 235 enriched and of uranium 233; authentic reports on the development of atomic research; detailed information on radar, antisubmarine devices, improved explosives and propellants; and Canadian citizenship documents for use in facilitating the movement of Soviet agents.

The main end product of the Comintern process was individual Communists dedicated to serving Moscow. Here, too, we have a graphic description from the work of the Canadian Royal Commission: "The most startling single aspect of the entire fifth column network is the uncanny success with which the Soviet agents were able to find Canadians who were willing to betray their country and to supply to agents of a foreign power secret information to which they had access in the course of their work, despite oaths of allegiance, of office, and of secrecy which they had taken."

Examining this astonishing phenomenon in some detail, the commission concluded that "the original and principal motivation was supplied by the psychological development courses in communist 'cells'; and that 'financial incentive' (in the form of expense money for which receipts were given) was only gradually and tactfully introduced to supplement and perhaps eventually supplant the original motivation," or to provide possibilities of "blackmail, if the agent's enthusiasm for the cause should later wane."

Unfortunately, space does not permit me to explore the tortuous paths to subversion uncovered by the commission, despite the fact that its revelations regarding the techniques of—to quote a chapter heading in the commission's report— "The Development of Ideological Motivation" are literally hair-raising. It might be useful, however, to summarize the commission's description of the principal steps in the developmental process:

1. The initial contact in an ostensibly nonpolitical "front organization" of the "reformist" or "improvement" type.
2. The invitation to join a secret "cell" or study group.
3. Study of a curriculum of political and philosophical works, supplemented by reading of current Communist literature and discussion of current affairs, designed progressively to develop:

- Initially a critical attitude toward Western democracy and its ideals.
- Then a sense of loyalty to what appears to be an international ideal.
- Then a blending of that ideal with the current doctrines and policies of Communist parties throughout the world and the current conception of the national interest of the Soviet Union.

4. Indoctrination designed gradually to replace the original loyalty to principles professed by the Communist Party with overriding loyalty to the Party as such.
5. Exploitation of individual social or psychological maladjustments due to racial prejudice or discrimination and the like.
6. Progressive absorption in the multiple Party activities and resulting isolation from the rest of society.
7. Gradual habituation to an atmosphere of secrecy and conspiracy, calculated to develop the psychology of a double life and double standards.
8. The invitation to subversion or treachery.
9. Finally, the act.

I have already recounted how Stalin set out to obtain the secret of the atomic bomb and how he succeeded in doing so by penetrating the inner recesses of the laboratories at Los Alamos. During the war American citizens acting as Soviet agents succeeded in reaching high policy levels of the U.S. Government. In the early 1960s the KGB succeeded in penetrating perhaps the most sensitive of American agencies, the National Security Agency.

The British services proved to be even easier to penetrate, and this, in turn, has been very costly to the United States. Only recently have we learned the full details about the cases of Donald Maclean, Guy Burgess and Harold Philby, in the form of revelations by Philby himself, who was finally obliged to flee to the Soviet Union in 1963, where he took Soviet citizenship and now resides. Philby revealed that the three associates became Soviet agents in 1933, when they were students at Cambridge University. Burgess and Maclean entered the British diplomatic service and rose to high levels before fleeing to Moscow in 1951 to avoid detection. Both specialized in American affairs and became privy to highly classified information which they regularly passed to the Soviets. Philby himself acted as a double agent while rising to top levels in the British Secret Service; then, after the defection of his associates, as a respected Middle East correspondent of the London *Observer*. Then there was George Blake, a younger British diplomatic and intelligence officer, who was caught and tried in 1961 and condemned to forty-two years' imprisonment. He was in jail only a few years when Soviet agents engineered his escape and smuggled him out to Moscow.

In France, a few years ago, it was discovered that one of the Assistant Secretaries General of NATO, a French citizen, had been acting as a Soviet agent, and passing to Moscow top-secret information about NATO defense plans, including the military plans for dealing with the Berlin crisis.

I could go on and on citing individual cases, but these examples will perhaps suffice. One of the characteristics of the Soviet espionage apparatus is its ability to take many years to develop what is called "deep" cover for its agents. A case in point is that of the Russian Colonel Rudolf Abel, who lived as an American citizen and a professional photographer in Brooklyn for many years before he was detected by the Federal Bureau of Investigation in 1957. In his quarters were found all kinds of copying equipment and a direct radio communications link with Moscow. Abel's thirty-year prison sentence was cut short in 1962 when *sub rosa* arrangements were made to release him to the Soviets in return for Francis Gary Powers, the U-2 pilot downed over the Soviet Union on May 1, 1960.

Over the past twenty years the FBI has turned up incriminating evidence with respect to some forty persons attached to the Soviet diplomatic establishments in Washington and New York or employed by the United Nations, all of whom were as a result asked to leave the United States. Unfortunately, the Soviets have usually retaliated by ousting wholly unincriminated members of the American Embassy staff in Moscow —on the "old Russian principle," as one top Russian official once put it to me, mixing his sources, of "an eye for an eye and a tooth for a tooth."

Of course, the embassies in Moscow are constant targets for penetration by the Soviet secret police. Among the more publicized examples is the story of the famous hand-carved replica of the great seal of the United States presented to Ambassador Harriman in 1945 by Russian "friends" and mounted on the wall of his study in the embassy residence. There it hung until 1952, when someone belatedly had it taken apart and found the electronic bug inside which had been dutifully recording ambassadorial conversations all those years. In the years I resided there I found it best simply to assume that everything in the residence was recorded, if not also photographed, and conducted myself accordingly. However, we did do a major sweep of the embassy office building during my stay and in 1964 dug more than fifty microphones out of the walls.

There is reason to believe that the troubles of the Central Intelligence Agency (CIA) in 1967 and 1968 resulted primarily from the adept placement by Soviet agents in the hands of unwitting Americans of some of the classified information about CIA activities they had been able to obtain through espionage. With all respect to the CIA, it must be said that the United States is quite new to the international intelligence game. Before World War II there was nothing except the feeble efforts of the separate military services. Then, during the war, we tried to develop the Office of Strategic Services, and our first permanent intelligence service, the CIA, was organized only after the war. It is true that we have had intelligence successes, the most notable example being that of CIA's Soviet agent Oleg Penkovsky. However, it would be an accurate generalization to say that these have more often than not been voluntary offerings of individuals who have come to their own conclusions about the nature of the regimes under which they live.

In fact, underlying all Moscow's activities in the international field is what has sometimes been called the Soviet "strategy of deception." To beguile and mislead the outer world, Moscow has adopted and corrupted our own Western vocabulary and relies on it almost exclusively. Its propaganda is loaded, in its upside-down way, with such borrowed terms as "democracy" and "peace." There is little overt appeal for Marxist revolution. Inside the Soviet Union elaborate hoaxes are contrived in an attempt to cover the nakedness of totalitarianism with the mantle of democratic procedures. A constitution, with civil rights provisions adapted from Western models, is promulgated and publicized, but not observed; it is rarely referred to in the legal process. Stupendous elections are organized, with great fanfare and reference to such Western devices as "election speeches" and the "secret ballot"; but that ballot is a single Party-dictated list which gives the so-called voter no choice.

About the only thing the Soviets have really taken from Marx is his long-since disproven prediction about the inevitability of proletarian revolution. And this mistaken prediction would long since have become only a passing phenomenon of intellectual history had it not been embodied in the official ideology of a world power, which has converted Marxism into a kind of mystical doctrine, to justify the rule of a political minority. Bertram Wolfe points out that Marx's basic theory actually went down the drain the minute Lenin decided in 1917 that Russia could "bypass" the capitalist stage of development. This was the first clear-cut decision by a Communist leader that leadership and state power could circumvent or transcend what Marx considered to be immutable laws of history beyond man's control. Economic determinism was thus abandoned in favor of human intelligence, will and power. It is not exactly a tribute to the level of intelligence of mankind that so many people in the world have so long been so deceived.

CHAPTER XII

U.S.–Soviet Confrontations after World War II
and the Development of U.S. Policy

There is, of course, a great deal of arbitrariness and artificiality involved in trying to put into book form a review of the Russian scene and of Soviet-American relations over the years. This seems to be unavoidable in order to fit attitudes and events into suitable categories, chronologies and chapters. The real world is not like this; it is unruly and disorderly.

If you are concerned with Soviet-American relations in the Department of State in Washington, you find that these relations are global in scope and continuous in nature. On any given day you are likely to find yourself considering and dealing with situations in the Soviet Union itself and in Indonesia and in Germany and in Iran and in Cuba. You will be trying to weigh

them all at once and to see what they add up to, and you will try
to consider them not only from the American point of view but
also with that part of your mind that you have tried to train to
think Russian style.

If you go to see a high Soviet official in Moscow, you are
likely to have a long and miscellaneous agenda which may well
include such things as: a protest about the arrest of an American citizen; a reminder that you await a reply to your proposal
for strategic weapons talks; a proposal for an exchange of
embassy sites in Washington and Moscow; a reference to the
dangers involved in renewed North Korean harassment of South
Korea; an argument about Vietnam; a pointed inquiry about
Soviet activities in the United Arab Republic; a complaint about
some outrageous assertion of Soviet propaganda; a review of the
status of the implementation of the official exchanges agreement. And all this is only your half of the agenda; the Soviet
official will probably have his own as well. However, I now
return to my compartments.

In Chapter V I talked about the origins and build-up of the
so-called Cold War. In doing so, I unavoidably trod upon a considerable part of the ground I now want to explore more
thoroughly—U.S.–Soviet confrontations of the postwar period. I
noted earlier how differences had begun to emerge between the
wartime allies, even before the end of hostilities and the delivery of Stalin's famous speech of February 9, 1946, which in
effect amounted to a declaration of the end of the alliance. I
pointed out that Roosevelt's and Churchill's efforts, particularly
at the Yalta Conference, to bind Stalin to respect the freedom
and right to self-determination of the liberated peoples of Europe came to nought, partly because the political terminology
meant one thing to them and another thing to Stalin, but mainly
because the course of military operations left the Red Army in
physical control of the entire Eastern half of Europe. I observed
how the Kremlin set out to exclude the Western powers from
these countries, to establish puppet regimes in them and in
general to remake them in the image of the Soviet Republics. I
noted that the West, and the United States in particular, paid an
unnecessarily high price for Russian entry into the war against

Japan and thus facilitated Stalin's extension of the Soviet empire in the East and into the Pacific at the expense of both China and Japan.

In another context, I also examined the situation after the war to the south of the Soviet Union—Western support to Turkey in resisting Soviet demands for the cession of two Turkish provinces and control of the Turkish Straits; the American assumption of the protective burden in Greece which an exhausted Britain had been compelled to offload; and President Truman's first and basic application of the "containment" policy by his proclamation of the so-called Truman Doctrine. While the immediate objective of the Truman Doctrine was the extension of economic and military assistance to Greece and Turkey, its terms went well beyond this immediate purpose to proclaim that the United States would take action to stop any aggression, direct or indirect, which threatened the peace and security of the United States. And this Doctrine has, in fact, continued to be a basic tenet of American policy since March 12, 1947.

To fill out this picture to the south, I must now back up a bit. The general area "in the direction of the Persian Gulf," was described by Soviet Foreign Minister Molotov as of special interest to the Soviet Union in his negotiations with Nazi Foreign Minister von Ribbentrop in 1939. In August, 1941, Soviet and British armed forces were sent, respectively, into the north and south of Iran, in order to forestall pro-German activities and the threat of a German invasion of the country from the positions Hitler's armies held in the Soviet Union itself. In January, 1942, Britain, the Soviet Union and Iran concluded a treaty of alliance, under which the occupying powers undertook to respect Iran's territorial integrity and sovereignty, and to evacuate their forces within six months after the conclusion of hostilities with the Axis powers. The United States also sent into Iran logistic forces to set up the main line of supply for the delivery of American wartime aid to the Soviet Union. At the Teheran Conference, in December, 1943, the pledge to maintain the independence, sovereignty and territorial integrity of Iran was reconfirmed in a declaration signed by all three Allied leaders: Roosevelt, Churchill and Stalin.

Despite these pledges, the Soviet Union proceeded to develop its influence in the north, supporting the left-wing Tudeh Party and fostering the separatist tendencies of minority elements. The northern Iranian province adjoining the Caspian Sea is Azerbaijan, inhabited mainly by a Turkic-speaking people close kin to the inhabitants of the adjoining Soviet Republic of Azerbaijan, a territory originally conquered by Czarist Russia and then, after a brief try at independence, reconquered by the Red Army in 1921. In September, 1944, the Soviet Government suddenly demanded an exclusive oil concession covering the northern provinces of Iran and applied such pressures that the Iranian Prime Minister was forced to resign. The demand was blocked by the Iranian Parliament, which passed a law prohibiting the granting of oil concessions to anyone during the war.

As soon as hostilities terminated in 1945, Great Britain and the United States promptly withdrew their forces from Iran. The Soviet Union at first refused to do the same, but was finally forced to evacuate the northern provinces some months later under the pressure of world opinion mobilized in the new UN Organization. However, Soviet agents were left behind to start a movement for Azerbaijan's secession from Iran and adherence to the Soviet Union. A puppet regime was, in fact, set up there and remained in power until December, 1946, when, despite Soviet protests and threats but with strong Western backing, the Iranian Government sent its forces in to oust the regime and restore Iranian authority.

American policies during the war were influenced mainly by President Roosevelt, with his arrogant confidence that he could solve all international problems simply by the exercise of his own personality, and his corollary tendency to act as his own foreign minister, sometimes without even consulting his Secretary of State; and to a lesser extent by Secretary Cordell Hull, with his dedication to the principles of law and free trade, and his corollary conviction that an international organization was "the central and decisive problem of the postwar future." Secretary Hull thought he had laid the basis for such postwar organization in the declaration issued by the Moscow foreign ministers meeting in October, 1943, signed by himself for the

United States, by Foreign Secretary Anthony Eden for Britain and by Foreign Affairs Commissar Molotov for the Soviet Union. In a public statement on March 21, 1944, Secretary Hull said that the Moscow declaration had laid the foundation for a "cooperative effort in the postwar world toward enabling all peace-loving nations, great and small, to live in peace and security, to preserve the liberties and rights of civilized existence, and to enjoy expanded opportunities and facilities for economic, social, and spiritual progress." Then, he continued, "there would no longer be need for spheres of influence, for alliances, for balance of power, or any other of the special arrangements through which, in the unhappy past, the nations strove to safeguard their security or to promote their interests."

For somewhat different reasons, therefore, President Roosevelt and Secretary Hull agreed in opposing Churchill's proposals for an Allied invasion of Europe through the Balkans and his efforts to make a deal with Stalin to divide the Balkans into agreed Western and Soviet spheres of influence. As the Germans retreated, the Red Army followed in their wake, and it was clear that the Soviet Union would, in fact, be in control throughout Eastern Europe. Then, in July, 1944, the Soviets startled their Western Allies by an act seeming to extend Stalin's expansionist ambitions right into the Mediterranean. A Soviet military mission was surreptitiously dropped into the headquarters of the Greek Communist-influenced resistance movement and self-designated "provisional government" in the mountains of Thessaly. A month later the resistance organization, about-facing from its previous position, presumably under Russian influence, agreed to send six representatives to join the legitimate Greek Government-in-Exile in Cairo and then to disband the rival provisional government it had set up. On the heels of these events, Churchill obtained President Roosevelt's approval for sending a British force into Greece as soon as the Germans evacuated the country; and, in fact, the British troops arrived there in October. Churchill visited Moscow in that same month, and had his famous session with Stalin in which, on "a half sheet of paper," the two sketched out an abortive scheme for a percentage division of authority in the Balkan countries.

In November, 1944, Greek Prime Minister George Papan-dreou re-established his coalition government in Athens and set about disbanding the private resistance forces and creating a new national Greek Army. The Communist members thereupon withdrew from the coalition and attempted to stage a coup, which was finally put down in February, 1945, after bitter fighting, mainly by the British forces. The truce then reached provided for the establishment of a new Greek Government under a new Premier, with the Archbishop of Athens, the head of the Greek Orthodox Church, acting as Regent. This "Regency" government invited the principal Allied powers to supervise elections in Greece in March, 1946, an invitation rejected by the Soviets, to the tune of articles in the Soviet press declaring that internationally observed elections were "farcical" and "could only result in a falsification of the people's will." Indeed, in January, 1946, the Soviet delegate to the United Nations put "the Greek case" on the Security Council agenda, charging that the presence of British troops in Greece constituted interference with that country's internal affairs and contributed to interna-tional tension. The debate was inconclusive. The British Foreign Secretary pointed out that British forces were in Greece at the express invitation of that country's legitimate government, and no action resulted. In the supervised March elections the Royal-ist-Conservatives won 231 out of a total of 354 seats, with the Liberal-Republicans getting most of the rest. The Communists and their allies called for a boycott, but total abstentions amounted to only 15 percent of all the eligible voters registered. A subsequent plebiscite in September recalled the King to Greece by a vote of 71 percent of the electorate.

For the next round on Greece in the UN, Moscow used its Ukrainian arm. On August 24, 1946, the delegate of the Ukrain-ian Republic lodged a complaint about internal conditions in Greece, and about incidents along the Greek western and north-ern frontiers, allegedly provoked by Greek armed forces. It is of passing interest to note that the Ukrainian delegation was headed by Dmitri Manuilsky, long-time Chairman of the Execu-tive Committee of the now dissolved Comintern. After long and frequently vitriolic debate, the U.S. representative proposed that the Security Council establish a commission to investigate the facts, with authority to call on Albania, Bulgaria, Greece and Yugoslavia to provide information. The Soviet side submitted an opposing resolution calling upon the Greek Government "to take measures for the immediate cessation of provocative activities by the aggressive monarchist elements"; to "put an end to the agitation regarding the state of war said to exist between Greece and Albania"; and to "terminate the persecution of national minorities in Greece." The Soviet resolution was voted down on September 20 by a 9–2 vote. The U.S. resolution then received 8 affirmative votes, 1 negative—the veto of the Soviet Union.

Meanwhile, guerrilla activities had resumed in Greece and were rapidly intensifying. This time the Greek Government itself was the complainant in the UN Security Council. Appearing personally before this body on December 12, 1946, the Greek Prime Minister charged that Greece's northern neighbors were engaged in an intensive propaganda campaign to promote the incorporation of Greek Macedonia into the Yugoslav Federal Republic and were giving active assistance to the revolutionary bands, which were using Yugoslav, Bulgarian and Albanian territory as a privileged sanctuary and base for their operations in Greece. The United States resubmitted its resolution for an Investigatory Commission.

To everyone's astonishment, Soviet representative Gromyko, after making some negative noises, this time announced that he would support the resolution; and indeed, on December 19, he did so with an affirmative vote. Secretary of State James Byrnes had argued the matter vigorously with Soviet Foreign Minister Molotov, then in New York for a Council of Foreign Ministers. However, the underlying reasons for the Soviet turnabout are still not really clear. Some believe that Molotov had become convinced that another Soviet veto would provoke the United States into undertaking a more active role in support of the Greek Government. Others think that Tito had, in fact, gone further in supporting guerrilla activities in Greece than the Kremlin considered safe. In any case, the Investigating Commission was set up and in a report to the Security Council in May, 1947, stated that the evidence examined brought it to the "conclusion that Yugoslavia, and to a lesser extent Albania

and Bulgaria, have supported the guerrilla warfare in Greece."
More bitter debate ensued, and on July 29 the Soviet delegate
vetoed a Security Council resolution which took note of the
commission's report, found that a serious dispute existed and in
effect called on Yugoslavia, Albania and Bulgaria to cease and
desist. At the following session of the United Nations General
Assembly in October, that body—in which no veto exists—did
vote to set up a Special Committee on the Balkans, to reside in
the city of Salonika in northern Greece and keep its eye on the
situation.

This, then, was the atmosphere in which on March 12,
1947, the Truman Doctrine was launched. Under it, the United
States rapidly supplied substantial military and economic aid to
Greece, along with military advisers, but no combat forces. The
Greek armed forces' strength and effectiveness rapidly increased. Then, in 1948, came Tito's break with the Kremlin,
after which Yugoslavia was fully occupied in assuring its own
independence and security. By September, 1949, Secretary of
State Dean Acheson could declare publicly: "With respect to the
Greek question, the Balkan Commission has concluded that
Yugoslavia has decreased, and may well have ceased, its aid to
the Greeek guerrillas, and that guerrilla activities in general are
declining." Guerrilla activities did drag on for some time, with
minor aid to the Greek guerrillas supplied through Albania and
Bulgaria. Essentially, however, the victory in this first Com-
munist-backed civil war had been won. (The political troubles in
Greece in recent years—involving the seizure of political power
by a group of young military officers, a new crackdown on
Communists and anyone accused of supporting them, an attempted countercoup by the King of Greece and the King's flight
from the country—point up the fact that victories rarely stay
won, and the *status quo* rarely remains static.)

Throughout our history, thanks to our relative inexperience, Americans have had a traditional if extremely naïve
concept that war should be left to the soldiers and peace to the
diplomats. The armed forces are supposed to bring the hostilities to complete victory, or "unconditional surrender," or some

other kind of absolute conclusion. The forces are then abruptly withdrawn and disbanded, and the diplomats, thus deprived of tools and power, are supposed to pick up the pieces and clean up the mess. We are gradually learning that this is the best way to win the battle but lose the war. However, we had not yet learned this lesson at the end of World War II. The call immediately arose to "get the boys home," and we fell all over ourselves in our haste to do so, leaving behind only minimal occupation forces for Germany. The Russians, of course, did not make the same mistake. Their forces remained in place. It is true that we then had a monopoly of the atomic bomb. However, those who really knew the cataclysmic nature of this new weapon already realized the limitations and inhibitions inherent in its use. Moreover, as we knew later, the Soviets were already well on their way toward acquiring this same weapon.

Reflecting a similar attitude, we were probably entirely too hasty and abrupt in terminating our massive wartime Lend-Lease programs. We soon came to realize that our relief contributions through the United Nations Relief and Rehabilitation Agency were barely enough to prevent mass starvation and physical suffering, and that much greater efforts would be required if the shattered economies of our wartime allies in Europe were to be really revived and restored to operation. Thus the stage was set for Secretary of State Marshall's famous speech of June 5, 1947, at Harvard University, offering American assistance "in the return of normal economic health in the world." He declared that this policy was "directed not against any country or doctrine but against hunger, poverty, desperation and chaos . . . and that our assistance should provide a cure rather than a mere palliative. Any government that is willing to assist in the task of recovery," he said, "will find full cooperation on the part of the United States Government. Any government which maneuvers to block the recovery of other countries cannot expect help from us." Stating that "it would neither be fitting nor efficacious for this government to undertake to draw up unilaterally a program designed to place Europe on its feet economically," he invited the Europeans to take the initiative.

The Western Europeans, under the leadership of the British and French Foreign Secretaries, promptly responded, summoning a conference of all European nations, including the Soviet Union, to meet in Paris on June 27. All showed up at the appointed time. Then, two days later, with discussions at the conference barely getting under way, Moscow issued a critical public statement. After summarizing the Marshall speech, the statement said that the Soviet Government had received the proposal for a conference "favorably, despite the fact that the system of planning on which the socialist national economy in the U.S.S.R. is based precludes the possibility of the various crises and economic shake-ups" mentioned in that speech. Then it went on to say:

Naturally, the present conference will achieve its objective only if it correctly formulates its tasks and methods of work . . . it is one thing to ascertain the economic needs of the European countries for American aid in the form of credits and deliveries of goods by means of estimates drawn up by the European countries themselves. This is acceptable and may prove useful. . . . It will be an entirely different matter if the conference engages in drawing up an all-embracing economic program for the European countries as envisaged by the French. . . .

Attempts to compel the conference to engage in drawing up an all-embracing economic program, which will inevitably entail intervention on the part of some states in the affairs of other states, cannot be accepted as a basis for cooperation among the European countries. Certain powers at present are making such attempts, which are doomed to failure.

A few days later, on July 2, Soviet Foreign Minister Molotov and his delegation withdrew from the conference and returned to Moscow. The Eastern European governments were in a quandary; and as late as July 8 the Czech delegation indicated its willingness to continue participation. However, the Prime Minister of Czechoslovakia, Klement Gottwald, then in Moscow for trade negotiations, received direct instructions from Stalin to order the withdrawal of the Czech delegation, and of course did so. As I mentioned earlier, Gottwald was another of the former Comintern functionaries who returned to their native countries after the war; and it is also worth noting that the withdrawal of the Eastern European governments from the Paris conference was first announced not by them but by Moscow.

The Soviet decision to reject participation in the Marshall Plan for itself and its satellites was second in importance only to Stalin's speech of February 9, 1946, in developing the Kremlin's postwar theses of the revival of the capitalist-imperialist menace and of the enduring irreconcilable antagonism between the capitalist and Communist systems. Even those of us then serving in Western embassies in Moscow, however, were puzzled and confused by this decisive second step. We remembered Stalin's earlier bid for a $2 billion reconstruction loan from the United States to the Soviet Union itself, and we saw the desperate needs all around us. We thought that by joining in the Soviet Union could, in fact, have considerably modified the cooperative international concepts of the Western Europeans and left a good measure of autonomy to the individual country recipients of aid. Even at worst—assuming that Soviet participation and attitudes reduced the whole scheme to a point where Congress would not have appropriated money for it—Moscow would at least have been able to block the rapid recovery of the capitalist states of the West with Marshall Plan aid.

On second thought, however, we realized that the return to Communist orthodoxy was an ideological imperative to continue to justify Communist minority rule in the Soviet Union—a consideration as applicable now as it was when Stalin made his speech. The idea of participating in the Marshall Plan with the intent of modifying or wrecking it probably seemed like a risky long shot, particularly in view of some of the practical considerations the Kremlin undoubtedly saw. Moscow had already made a good start in Sovietizing Eastern Europe and integrating the region into the Soviet-controlled economic and political system. An all-European recovery scheme would certainly hamper this process, if not even threaten to reverse it, by strengthening the attraction of trade and other economic relationships between the Eastern European countries and Western Europe. Moreover, the very political and economic instability prevailing in Europe held out real hope of Communist takeovers, since the Communist parties, particularly in France and Italy, had enhanced their status by active participation in the wartime resistance and gained a broad base of popularity and voter support. In addition, participation would have involved the revelation of vital statistical data about the state of the economies of these countries and indeed of the Soviet Union itself—the kind of data which, as I mentioned earlier, had been decreed to be state secrets.

Finally, Stalin certainly continued to believe that a severe economic crisis was impending for the United States itself. Only two months earlier, in May, 1947, the leading Soviet economist, Eugene Varga, had been denounced for asserting that a capitalist crisis was not imminent and that capitalism was entering an era of stabilization and expansion. Believing just the contrary, the Kremlin clearly felt the Marshall Plan was designed not only to revitalize the capitalist economies of Western Europe but to stave off economic disaster in the United States itself—a scheme in which a good Communist could hardly take part. This was, in fact, one of the themes advanced by the Soviet delegate to the United Nations in a speech on September 18 when he said: "The United States counted on uniting all these countries directly dependent on the interests of American monopolies, which are striving to avert the approaching depression by an accelerated export of commodities and capital to Europe." He then went on to say, in bland disregard of the all-European nature of the original proposals: "This plan is an attempt to split Europe into two camps and, with the help of the United Kingdom and France, to complete the formation of a bloc of several European countries hostile to the interests of the democratic countries of Eastern Europe and most particularly to the interests of the Soviet Union."

After the Marshall Plan episode, Soviet attitudes and actions became increasingly intransigent, hostile, even aggressive. After the establishment of the Cominform in September, 1947, the next blow fell in Czechoslovakia. Thanks to the partial occupation of Czechoslovakia by Western, and particularly by United States, troops, the Czech Government-in-Exile, headed by a great liberal-democrat, Eduard Beneš, had been able to return to Prague after the end of hostilities. However, the capital itself and the eastern part of the country were occupied by the Red

Army. Consequently, the price of the return was agreement to the establishment of a coalition government, with Beneš as President, long-time Comintern functionary Gottwald as Prime Minister, and another liberal-democrat, son of the first President of Czechoslovakia, Jan Masaryk, as Foreign Minister. In February, 1948, the Czech Communists under the watchful eyes of a special Soviet envoy—Valerian Zorin, whose article on China I mentioned earlier—engineered a sudden takeover, and Czechoslovakia disappeared behind the Iron Curtain.

More than any other single Soviet-inspired move, this *coup d'état* destroyed any remaining Western illusions about Soviet intentions and stimulated Western rearmament. Democratic Czechoslovakia had represented the only remaining link between the Soviet Union and its former allies, and to many had been a symbol that compromise and cooperation were still not wholly impossible. Shortly after the coup, Foreign Minister Masaryk, widely known, respected and liked in the West, fell to his death from a fourth-floor window in his office—whether he jumped or was pushed is still not known. In Czechoslovakia non-Communist parties were immediately liquidated, and abroad the Czech diplomatic service was promptly purged. The affair was discussed vehemently but ineffectively in the Security Council.

Meanwhile, on the Western side, Marshall Plan arrangements had been going ahead vigorously. A series of consultations between the three principal Western Allies, Britain, France and the United States, and the Benelux countries—Belgium, Netherlands and Luxembourg—had been taking place in London to consider the role of West Germany in these arrangements. On March 6, 1948, it was announced:

> Since it has not proved possible to achieve economic unity in Germany, and since the eastern zone has been prevented from playing its part in the European Recovery Program, the three western powers have agreed that close cooperation should be established among themselves and among the occupation authorities in Western Germany in all matters arising out of the European Recovery Program in relation to Western Germany. Such cooperation is essential if Western Germany is to make its full and proper contribution to European recovery.

A further announcement, published on June 7, said that the three Western occupation powers "have reached the conclusion that it would be desirable that the German people in the different states should now be free to establish for themselves the political organization and institutions which will enable them to assume those governmental responsibilities which are compatible with the minimum requirements of occupation and control and which ultimately will enable them to assume full governmental responsibility."

At the same time, the conferees announced their recommendation that the elected political heads (minister-presidents) of the separate West German states be authorized to convene a Constituent Assembly to prepare a constitution providing for the establishment of an "all-German" government. The three powers also agreed that there should be no general withdrawal of their forces of occupation from Germany, without prior consultation, "until the peace of Europe is secured."

In that same month, on June 18, the three Western powers introduced a new separate currency in the Western zones of occupation. This is a rather complicated subject, but I might explain, briefly and perhaps too simply, that previously all four occupying powers had issued a single interchangeable currency for all of Germany. The Soviet authorities had used their unlimited supply of this currency to buy up everything possible on the German market, a factor contributing to the prevailing economic chaos. The new currency would bring an end to this practice and create a stable monetary base for economic recovery in the Western zones.

While all this was going on, the Soviet representative on March 20, 1948, had walked out of the Allied Control Council meeting in Berlin. Ten days later the Soviet authorities started gradually to introduce new requirements and restrictions on the movement of Western Allied personnel and supplies between West Germany and West Berlin. In the week following the introduction of the Western currency reform, the Soviet authorities effected a complete blockade of the Western sectors of Berlin by road, rail or barge, and suspended delivery of supplies or electric power into the Western sectors of the city. After a couple of weeks of unavailing exchanges between the military governors in Berlin the three Western powers protested to the Soviet Government, and negotiations were undertaken in Moscow. My Ambassador, General Bedell Smith, was, of course, our representative, along with his British and French colleagues, and I was the Ambassador's man Friday. The negotiations lasted for over a month, involving two meetings of the ambassadors with Stalin and repeated larger meetings with Foreign Minister Molotov and aides, but in the end came to nothing. At one point we almost reached an agreement by which we would, I thought, have lost our shirts (a new currency arrangement), but happily the Soviets did not seem to realize this.

I never worked so hard in my life for no result. Stalin's practice, which he imposed throughout the whole Soviet apparatus, was to work at night. Consequently, meetings would usually be scheduled for eleven o'clock or midnight or even later, after which we spent most of the rest of the night preparing reports and recommendations to our respective capitals. In a final sign-off note which we delivered to the Soviet Government on September 26, the Secretary of State reviewed the course of developments and negotiations and concluded:

The issue between the Soviet Government and the Western occupying powers is therefore not that of technical difficulties in communications nor that of reaching agreement upon the conditions for the regulation of the currency for Berlin. The issue is that the Soviet Government has clearly shown by its actions that it is attempting by illegal and coercive measures, in disregard of its obligations, to secure political objectives to which it is not entitled and which it could not achieve by peaceful means. It has resorted to blockade measures; it has threatened the Berlin population with starvation, disease and economic ruin; it has tolerated disorders and attempted to overthrow the duly elected municipal government of Berlin. This attitude and conduct of the Soviet Government reveal sharply its purpose to continue its illegal and coercive blockade and its unlawful actions designed to reduce the status of the United States, France and the United Kingdom as occupying powers in Berlin to one of complete subordination to Soviet rule, and thus to obtain absolute authority over the economic, political and social life of the people of Berlin, and to incorporate the city in the Soviet zone.

The Soviet Government has thereby taken upon itself sole responsibility for creating a situation, in which further recourse to the means of settlement prescribed in Article 33 of the Charter of the United Nations [i.e., peaceful negotiations between the parties involved] is not, in existing circumstances, possible, and which constitutes a threat to international peace and security. In order that international peace and security may not be further endangered the Governments of the United States, France and the United Kingdom, therefore, while reserving to themselves full rights to take such measures as may be necessary to maintain in these circumstances their position in Berlin, find themselves obliged to refer the action of the Soviet Government to the Security Council of the United Nations.

Blocked on the surface, the Western Allies had undertaken a gigantic airlift of coal, food and all manner of supplies for the two million-plus inhabitants of West Berlin. The Germans called it an air bridge; this is perhaps a more accurate description because for nearly a year, day and night, the air to Berlin was filled with an incessant stream of lifesaving aircraft. The U.S. Air Force bore the brunt of the burden, and its performance was characterized by gallantry and dogged heroism. It was a striking demonstration of Western determination. In the end, Allied willingness to pay the price of the airlift convinced Stalin of the futility of the attempted blockade. When he had reached this conclusion, a few exchanges between our representatives at the United Nations sufficed to bring about agreement, on May 5, 1949, to restore the situation to that prevailing prior to March 1, 1948. A meeting of the Council of the four Foreign Ministers later the same month confirmed the agreement but did not otherwise make progress on German questions.

The ending of the blockade was generally considered an Allied victory—the more important because it marked the first postwar setback of the Kremlin in Europe. My friend and colleague, Ambassador Robert Murphy, who was at the time political counselor to our Military Governor in Berlin, General Lucius Clay, thought that the airlift decision was a mistake. He counseled, instead, action to reopen the surface routes, using whatever force might be required. He believed this would have succeeded in shorter time and at less cost and would have been a more decisive demonstration of our will and determination. We did not make a recommendation from the embassy in Moscow, though we did submit an assessment which would have supported more decisive action, since we concluded that the Soviet Union was not in a position to go to war with us at that time.

I agree that stronger action at that time might have spared us troubles later. However, the one thing you really learn in the diplomatic business is that you can't go back and remake events. You have to deal with the situation as you find it on any given day. So perhaps it is best to be philosophical and say that maybe the decision to resort to an airlift instead of forcing a showdown on the surface had its own real virtues. We certainly gained valuable experience in the construction and operation of various kinds of cargo- and passenger-carrying aircraft. We also made ourselves seem reasonable and restrained, in the face of an extreme challenge. And in the end the blockade not only did not succeed in driving the Western Allies out of Berlin but did not prevent us from going ahead with our plans for the establishment of the Federal Republic of Germany. This step was taken on May 23, 1949. As a counter to this move, Stalin, in October, 1949, set up in the Soviet Zone of occupation a so-called German Democratic Republic, headed since that time by a Stalin-trained Russified Comintern agent, first Wilhelm Pieck and, after his death, Walter Ulbricht. The formalized partition of Germany which took place in this fateful year of 1949 remains as the symbol and focus of the incompatibility of Eastern and Western objectives in Europe.

As one hostile Soviet move followed another in Europe— the Sovietization of Eastern Europe, the rejection of the Marshall Plan and Moscow's mobilization of the Communist parties in Western Europe in opposition to that plan, the establishment of the Cominform, the takeover in Czechoslovakia, the blockade of Berlin—a real "war scare" arose, particularly in Western Europe and North America. Concern mounted about the defense of Western Europe. On March 17, 1948, Britain, France and the Benelux nations signed a collective defense agreement known as the Treaty of Brussels. They did so in consultation with and with the encouragement of the United States, but stressed to us, as reported by Secretary of State Acheson, "that despite their determination to do their utmost in self-defense, their collective strength might be inadequate to preserve peace or insure their national survival unless the great power and influence of the United States and other free nations were also brought into association with them."

Ensuing consultations between the executive and legislative branches in Washington led to the passage of a "Sense of the Senate" resolution by a vote of 64–4, on June 11, 1948, calling for "development of . . . and association of the United States, by constitutional process, with such regional and other collective arrangements as are based on continuous and effective self-help and mutual aid . . . thus . . . contributing to the maintenance of peace by making clear its determination to exercise the right of individual or collective self-defense under article 51" of the United Nations Charter. On the basis of this resolution, negotiations went forward vigorously for the conclusion of the North Atlantic Treaty, which was signed in Washington on April 4, 1949, by twelve North American and Western European nations—the United States, Canada, Belgium, Denmark, France, Iceland, Italy, Luxembourg, Netherlands, Norway, Portugal and Great Britain. The treaty was to be of indefinite duration, but provision was made for any member to elect to withdraw, following one year's notice, after twenty years.

The participating governments set forth their common purpose in the preamble of the treaty, which I quote:

The parties to this Treaty reaffirm their faith in the purposes and principles of the Charter of the United Nations and their desire to live in peace with all peoples and all governments. They are determined to safeguard the freedom, common heritage and civilization of their peoples, founded on the principles of democracy, individual liberty and the rule of law.

They seek to promote stability and well-being in the North Atlantic area.

They are resolved to unite their efforts for collective defense and for the preservation of peace and security.

While the treaty provided for cooperation in "strengthening their free institutions" and for the encouragement of economic collaboration, its essential purpose was mutual defense. The operative part of Article 5 reads as follows:

> The parties agree that an armed attack against one or more of them in Europe or in North America shall be considered an attack against them all; and consequently they agree that, if such an armed attack occurs, each of them, in exercise of the right of individual or collective self-defense recognized by article 51 of the Charter of the United Nations, will assist the party or parties so attacked by taking forthwith, individually and in concert with the other parties, such action as it deems necessary, including the use of armed force, to restore and maintain the security of the North Atlantic area.

This rather complicated language does not in itself constitute an automatic commitment to military action by the member countries. In practice, however, this apparent permissiveness has been largely removed by the development of the organizational structure of NATO. The North Atlantic Council is a permanent and continuous political body. The Military Committee is the same on the military side. Defense plans are coordinated and provide for automatic responses in certain contingencies, under the direction of a Supreme Allied Commander, now permanently headquartered in Belgium, to whose command specific Allied forces are committed.

These moves found their expression in a series of monumental legislative enactments, sharply breaking with American isolationist and neutralist traditions and fundamentally altering the posture of the United States in world affairs. The first of these was the Economic Cooperation Act of April 3, 1948, providing backstopping for the Marshall Plan and setting up the so-called Economic Cooperation Administration or ECA. This was supplemented about a year later by the passage of the so-called Point Four program providing for the extension of technical assistance to underdeveloped areas. In later years these two programs were to be combined as the International Cooperation Administration or ICA, now renamed the Agency for International Development or AID. Then, in support of NATO collective defense, came the Mutual Defense Assistance Act of October 6, 1949, setting up the military aid programs.

Meanwhile, in other but related fields, Congress in 1947 passed the National Security Act, providing for the establishment of the National Security Council and of the Central Intelligence Agency, and in 1948 the Information and Educational Exchange Act, under which the United States Information Agency, USIA, operates. It was the latter act which led to my assignment in 1949 as Director of the Voice of America, charged with building up a world-wide radio broadcasting system. The legislative record during those years when the United States veered from isolationism to internationalism was a remarkably bipartisan one. An outstanding role was played by a senior Republican Senator from Michigan, Arthur Vandenberg, a former isolationist who had learned the lessons of history. He made a good counterpart for that other Midwesterner who was President of the United States and a Democrat, Harry S Truman. I might add that we used to say the most influential lobbyist on Capitol Hill in those days was Joseph Stalin. He had a genius for making some aggressive move or issuing some outrageous statement whenever there seemed to be some doubt or hesitation in the Congress.

Soviet reaction to the creation of NATO was predictably hostile, and was set forth at great length in an official memorandum published on March 31, 1949, after the treaty had been announced but before it was formally signed. The memorandum contended that the Soviet Union's many treaties with its Eastern European satellites were bilateral in nature, and directed solely against a possible repetition of German aggression. The North Atlantic Treaty, on the contrary, was described as a multilateral agreement creating a "closed grouping of states." Since of the great powers in the wartime alliance only the Soviet Union was not a member, the memorandum stated, the treaty "must be regarded as a treaty directed against one of the chief allies of the United States, Great Britain and France in the late war, against the U.S.S.R." The treaty could not be justified under the self-defense provisions of the UN Charter, it argued, since "as is known to all, neither the United States of America, Britain, France, nor the other parties to the pact are threatened by any armed attack." Verging on insult, the memorandum charged that "The North Atlantic Pact is designed to intimidate the states which do not agree to obey the dictate of the Anglo-American grouping of powers that lay claim to world domination, though the bankruptcy of such claims was once again affirmed by the Second World War, which ended in the debacle of Fascist Germany which also had laid claim to world domination." On the basis of all this, the Soviet Government arrived at the following conclusions:

1. The North Atlantic Treaty has nothing in common with the aims of the self-defense of the states who are party to the Treaty, who are threatened by no one, whom no one intends to attack. On the contrary, this Treaty has an obviously aggressive character and is aimed against the U.S.S.R. . . .
2. . . . runs directly counter to the principles and aims of the United Nations Charter.
3. . . . runs counter to the treaty between Great Britain and the Soviet Union signed in 1942, under which both states assumed the obligation to cooperate in the maintenance of peace and international security and not to conclude any alliances and not to participate in any coalitions directed against the other high-contracting party.
4. . . . runs counter to the Treaty between France and the Soviet Union signed in 1944 [for the same reasons]. . . .
5. . . . runs counter to the agreements between the Soviet Union, the United States of America and Great Britain, concluded at the Yalta and Potsdam conferences, as well as at other conferences of the representatives of these powers held both during and after the Second World War.

Some years later, after NATO had been expanded to include, first Greece and Turkey and then the Federal Republic of Germany, Moscow did, in fact, denounce these wartime treaties with Great Britain and France. Then, in May, 1955, the Soviets set up the Warsaw Pact as an Eastern counterpart to NATO. Its membership included—besides the Soviet Union—Poland, Hungary, Rumania, Bulgaria, East Germany and, initially but since withdrawn, Albania. Unlike NATO, however, which is a basic multilateral alliance, the Warsaw Pact actually was more a supplement to, or a superstructure over, a network of bilateral mutual defense treaties the Soviet Union had already concluded with the other Eastern European Communist states.

The basic Soviet line toward NATO has not changed from that taken in the initial memorandum. Soviet statements and Soviet propaganda never speak of NATO without attaching the term "aggressive," and a fixed objective of Soviet foreign policy has been to weaken NATO by dividing its membership and by inducing the United States to remove its forces from the European continent. Repeated calls have emanated from Moscow and from Warsaw Pact meetings for "the simultaneous liquidation of both military alliances," a move which would, in fact, end NATO while leaving the Soviet Union's network of bilateral treaties unaffected. A highlight in Moscow's campaign was an unprecedented regional meeting of European Communist parties convoked in Karlovy Vary, Czechoslovakia, in April, 1967, to consider "European security" questions. The conference heard a tough speech from the General Secretary of the Soviet Party, Leonid Brezhnev, condemning NATO in general, and the U.S. military presence on the European continent and in the Mediterranean in particular, referring to us as "forces beyond the ocean which are alien to Europe." (The Russians, as the occasion or their interests require, describe themselves as Europeans to the Europeans and Asians to the Asians.) After more oratory, the Karlovy Vary conference adopted a long resolution which, in brief:

· Called for a campaign by the European parties to induce the Western European governments to withdraw from NATO after the initial twenty-year period.

· Seconded the moves of the Warsaw Pact states for the liquidation of both military alliances.

· Supported the organization of "a conference of all European states on the question of security and peaceful cooperation in Europe."

For a while these Soviet efforts seemed to be making some headway in Western Europe and stimulated hopes for a relaxation of tensions, for a détente. Such hopes were abruptly dashed by the invasion of Czechoslovakia in August, 1968. The Soviet campaign in Europe was thus stalled, at least for a time, by its own actions, and, instead of breaking up, NATO tended to close ranks again. On April 9, 1969, on the eve of a special session of the NATO Council in Washington commemorating the organization's twentieth anniversary, the Soviet Government again issued a long official statement, repeating and reconfirming most of the allegations in its original 1949 memorandum and adding some new ones, including—with obvious reference to Czechoslovakia—the charge that NATO had become "an organizer of subversion, espionage and ideological subversion; and an inspirer of counterrevolutionary coup attempts in socialist countries."

But the least that must be said for the Kremlin leadership is that it is persistent. A meeting of the Party chiefs of the Warsaw Pact countries in Budapest renewed the appeal for the calling of a "pan-European conference" on security and the President of Finland was persuaded to offer Helsinki as a site for such a gathering. In his speech to the United Nations General Assembly on September 19, 1969, Soviet Foreign Minister Gromyko discussed the proposal, expressing "satisfaction" with what he claimed was "the fact that in recent months there has been a definite growing interest in Europe in the collective efforts of the countries of this region with a view to easing tension and strengthening peace." This project, subtly oriented toward diminishing American influence in Europe, will be with us for a long time to come.

After the surrender of Japan in the summer of 1945, the Chinese Communists, under the leadership of Mao Tse-tung, began making rapid strides against the disorganized and weakening Kuomintang government of Chiang Kai-shek. The United States made almost continuous efforts to mediate between the two warring sides, arranging truces in the hostilities, calling conferences of representatives of both elements, even trying to set up a coalition government. In addition to our regular diplomatic establishment, we sent two of our eminent World War II soldier-statesmen, Generals George C. Marshall and Albert C. Wedemeyer, as Special Presidential Emissaries. We passed a special China Aid Act in 1948 and, under this and through disposal of war surplus, provided enormous quantities of mili-

tary equipment and other assistance to the Nationalist Government. A large proportion of these supplies fell into the hands of
the Chinese Communists, as Nationalist leaders surrendered or
defected or simply abandoned the field of battle to the advancing Communists. On July 30, 1949, the State Department, at the
request of the President, issued a "White Paper," reviewing
events since 1944 and concluding, in part:

It must be admitted frankly that the American policy of assist-
ing the Chinese people in resisting domination by any foreign power
or powers is now confronted with the gravest difficulties. The heart
of China is in Communist hands. The Communist leaders have
forsworn their Chinese heritage and have publicly announced their
subservience to a foreign power, Russia, which during the last fifty
years, under Czars and Communists alike, has been most assiduous
in its efforts to extend its control in the Far East. . . . The unfortu-
nate but inescapable fact is that the ominous result of the Civil War
in China was beyond the control of the government of the United
States.

By December all continental China was in the hands of the
Communists and the remnants of the Nationalist Government
and their supporters had fled to Formosa. In the same month
Mao Tse-tung went to Moscow, where, during the next two
months, he negotiated the alliance and territorial and aid agreements which I discussed earlier. Since the days of Secretary of
State Hay's declaration of the "open door" policy, and owing
largely not only to extensive trade but to the activities of several
generations and many thousands of American missionaries, the
United States had long had a sentimental attachment for China.
Thus the reaction to the Communist takeover in that country
was bitter. The search for a scapegoat focused mainly on Secretary of State Acheson and the specialized "China hands" in the
Foreign Service and led to Senator Joseph McCarthy's vicious
witch-hunts in the early 1950s, until he himself was finally
halted in December, 1954, by the censure of his senatorial
colleagues. The whole process further poisoned our relations,
not so much with Communist China—we had none—as with
the Soviet Union itself.

The real confrontation with the Soviet Union in the Far East, however, came in Korea. The wartime allies had agreed that Korea, after the defeat of the Japanese, should become free and independent; and in Moscow, in December, 1945, the United States and the Soviet Union agreed to set up a "joint commission" to make the necessary arrangements. After repeated meetings and fruitless negotiations in that body, the United States took the question to the United Nations General Assembly. Addressing the Assembly on September 17, 1947, Secretary of State Marshall declared:

> For about two years the United States Government has been trying to reach agreement with the Soviet Government, through the joint commission and otherwise, on methods of implementing the Moscow agreement and thus bringing about the independence of Korea. . . . Today the independence of Korea is no further advanced than it was two years ago. Korea remains divided at the 38th parallel with Soviet forces in the industrial North and the United States forces in the agricultural South. . . . We believe that this is a matter which now requires the impartial judgment of the other members of the United Nations.

In response to this appeal, the United Nations on November 14 passed a resolution calling for free elections throughout Korea, and setting up a UN commission to supervise such elections. The resolution also recommended that as soon as a national Korean Government could be established, after the elections, it should organize its own security forces and the occupation forces should withdraw within ninety days.

The Soviet Union refused to cooperate in any way or even to admit members of the UN commission into North Korea. However, elections were held in South Korea under UN supervision; and on January 1, 1949, the United States recognized the resulting government of the Republic of Korea headed by President Syngman Rhee. About six months later American occupation forces were withdrawn, and this withdrawal was also observed and certified by the UN commission.

While these activities were going on in the South, the Soviet Union proceeded unilaterally to set up its own satellite government in North Korea and to withdraw its occupation forces, also by July, 1949. To understand the situation in North Korea, however, requires some background. Korea has a short common border with the Soviet Union, and a considerable number of Koreans constitute a minority element in the population of the Soviet Union's Far Eastern provinces. Like the rest of the Soviet population, they are required to serve in the Red Army. It is now clear that from the early years of World War II many of these Soviet Koreans had been organized in separate formations and trained to return to Korea as a "liberation force." Other Koreans had been imported to join this force. The North Korean Prime Minister, Kim Il Sung, is an example. He had been born in North Korea, but after the Japanese annexation of the country was taken by his family to Manchuria, where he grew up. He had joined and fought with the Chinese Communist guerrillas after the Japanese occupation of Manchuria in the 1930s. Then in 1941 Kim and a number of other Manchurian Koreans went to the Soviet Union for training. By the time the Soviet forces entered Korea in August, 1945, Kim Il Sung was a Soviet Army major; and he and a body of Soviet-Korean Communists, estimated variously between ten and thirty thousand men, accompanied those forces. Since there were only about six thousand indigenous North Korean Communists, it was easy for the Soviet Koreans to take over, and by the time of the Soviet withdrawal they held all the major positions of power in both the Party and government in North Korea.

In the circumstances, it can hardly be doubted that Stalin ordered, or at least approved, the decision to launch the invasion of South Korea on June 25, 1950, and thus to settle the reunification issue by force on Communist terms—though competent observers have suggested that Stalin's hand may have been forced by the Korean exiles who had come back expecting to rule the whole country and not just the least populous half of it. It is almost certain that Moscow did not expect American intervention, particularly in view of a speech made by Secretary Acheson on January 12, 1950, which seemed to leave both Korea and Formosa outside his definition of the American defense perimeter. Consequently, the Soviets obviously expected a quick victory for the Northerners.

Moscow was also, as it happened, the victim of another miscalculation. In January, 1950, after the Communist takeover of mainland China and while Mao Tse-tung was still in Moscow, the Soviet delegate to the Security Council had demanded the immediate seating of Red China's representative in the place of the Nationalist Chinese delegate. When this was rejected, the Soviet delegation walked out and for some months thereafter boycotted the Security Council. Thus, when the Council met on the very day of the invasion, no Soviet representative was present; and within two days the Council passed an unvetoed resolution authorizing the United Nations to "furnish such assistance to the Republic of Korea as may be necessary to repel the armed attack and to restore international peace and security in the area." Large American forces and smaller contingents from a dozen other nations were provided under this resolution and fought in Korea under the UN flag. On the day the Security Council resolution was passed, the United States Ambassador in Moscow saw a Soviet Deputy Foreign Minister and stated: "In view of the universally known fact of the close relations between the U.S.S.R. and the North Korean regime, the United States Government asks assurances of the U.S.S.R. that the U.S.S.R. disavows responsibility for this unprovoked and unwarranted attack, and that it will use its influence with the North Korean authorities to withdraw their invading forces immediately."

Two days later the Soviets replied that "the events taking place in Korea were provoked by an attack by forces of the South Korean authorities"; that "the Soviet Government adheres to the principle of impermissibility of interference by foreign powers in the internal affairs of Korea"; and that the Soviet Government was willing to attend Security Council meetings but could not do so because the absence of China had "made it impossible for the Security Council to take decisions having legal force."

This statement was the starting point for a vast and scurrilous campaign utilizing the world-wide resources of Soviet propaganda in support of the North Koreans. The United States was attacked for intervening in a civil war, for committing aggression and for practicing bacteriological warfare and committing all manner of atrocities. When the Soviet Government attempted to put their charges on a bilateral official level, the American Ambassador in Moscow rejected their representations, saying that these should be addressed not to the United States but to the United Nations, which was in charge of operations in Korea by resolution of the Security Council. It is, of course, true that the United Nations commander in chief was the American General, Douglas MacArthur, but this designation, too, was at the specific request of the Security Council.

Initially, aided by surprise and the lack of effective opposition, the North Koreans easily overran the whole country, and the situation seemed desperate. But the United Nations military operations were brilliantly conducted, and by November 6, 1950, General MacArthur could issue a communiqué stating, in part:

The Korean war was brought to a practical end with the closing of the trap on enemy elements north of Pyongyang and seizure of the east coastal area, resulting in raising the number of enemy prisoners of war in our hands to well over 135,000, which, with other losses amounting to over 200,000, brought casualties to 335,000, representing a fair estimate of North Korean total military strength. The defeat of the North Koreans and destruction of their armies was thereby decisive.

Soon, however, General MacArthur was compelled to note an ominous new development: intervention by Chinese Communist forces. In a subsequent communiqué, on November 28, he added:

Enemy reactions developed in the course of our assault operations of the past four days disclosed that a major segment of the Chinese continental armed forces in army, corps and divisional organization of an aggregate strength of over 200,000 men is now arrayed against the United Nations forces in North Korea. There exist the obvious intent and preparation for support of these forces by heavy reinforcements now concentrated within the privileged sanctuary north of the international boundary and constantly moving forward. Consequently, we face an entirely new war.

A resolution had been promptly presented in the Security Council calling for an end to this Chinese intervention, but the Soviet representatives had now returned to this body and the resolution was vetoed. However, the United Nations General Assembly had just passed, on November 3, the so-called "Uniting for Peace" resolution authorizing the Assembly to act when "because of lack of unanimity of the permanent members, the Security Council has failed to exercise its primary responsibility for the maintenance of international peace and security." Consequently, on February 1, 1951, the Assembly itself passed a resolution finding that "the People's Republic of China, by giving direct aid and assistance to those who were already committing aggression in Korea and by engaging in hostilities against United Nations forces there, had itself engaged in aggression in Korea"; it called upon Communist China to withdraw and upon "all states and authorities to refrain from giving any assistance to the aggressors."

Bitter fighting followed the Chinese intervention, and led to violent reactions in the United States. Much of this focused on President Truman's action in dismissing General MacArthur in April, 1951, after the General had threatened to attack Communist China itself with air and naval forces, in disregard of a warning that all his policy statements should be cleared through Washington. In subsequent Congressional hearings, General MacArthur continued to advocate extending the war to China. He had a considerable amount of Congressional and public support. The administration resisted, and in a statement to the Congressional committees on June 1, Secretary Acheson pointed out that "Against the dubious advantage of spreading the war in an initially limited manner to the mainland of China, there must be measured the risk of a general war with China, the risk of Soviet intervention and of World War III, as well as the probable effects upon the solidarity of the free-world coalition." However, the administration did encourage rapid build-up of the military strength of the United States and a speed-up in the development and arming of the NATO alliance.

By the middle of 1951 a military stalemate had developed in Korea, roughly along the 38th parallel, where it had all begun. The situation could not have been very pleasant from Moscow's point of view. The Chinese were in North Korea and the country was devastated. Victory was impossible locally, and the unwelcome prospect of a much wider war had been opened up by important elements on the American side. The rapid Western military build-up was disturbing. Consequently, Stalin pressed the Chinese and the North Koreans to negotiate, and on June 25 his representative at the UN dropped a hint that truce talks would be possible. It is clear that the North Koreans felt betrayed, but they yielded to the pressure and joined the armistice talks which began on July 10, 1951. These negotiations were to drag on for over two years, frequently bogged down or interrupted by arguments over exact lines of demarcation and over Communist demands for forcible repatriation of North Korean and Chinese prisoners, thousands of whom had made it clear that they did not wish to return to their Communist-ruled homelands. Meanwhile, hostilities continued until the armistice agreement was finally concluded in July, 1953, several months after Stalin's death.

After the Communist takeover in Czechoslovakia and the Berlin blockade, the Korean War had a decisive influence in hardening Cold War attitudes and sharpening the lines of conflict. Aside from the military build-up, during this period Congressional legislation and administrative action not only established a complete embargo on trade and other transactions with Communist China and North Korea, but placed many restrictions on our relations with the Soviet Union in such fields as shipping and trade, many of which still remain on the books as obstacles to improvement in Soviet-American relations.

The Korean conflict also gave a new impetus to the development of our network of bilateral and multilateral agreements for collective defense. This process had started in 1947 with the conclusion of the Inter-American Treaty of Reciprocal Assistance, commonly referred to as the Rio Treaty, involving twenty-one American republics. The North Atlantic Treaty, or NATO, with eleven (eventually fourteen) other governments followed in 1949. Then during and following the Korean War came:

In 1951:   Treaty of Mutual Cooperation and Security between the United States and Japan—this was related to the peace treaty concluded with Japan in the same year by all the wartime Allies except the Soviet Union, which refused to sign.

Security treaty between Australia, New Zealand and the United States, commonly referred to as the Anzus Alliance.

Mutual defense treaty between the United States and the Republic of the Philippines.

In 1953:   Mutual defense treaty between the United States and the Republic of Korea.

In 1954:   Southeast Asia collective defense treaty, between the United States and seven governments, commonly referred to as SEATO—the protocol to this treaty provided certain guarantees to Cambodia, Laos and South Vietnam.

Mutual defense treaty between the United States and the Republic of China.

All of these are formal alliances, involving forty-two other countries in total, ratified by the United States with the advice and consent of the U.S. Senate. In addition, the United States has been associated since 1955 with the Baghdad Pact, now known as the Central Treaty Organization or CENTO and involving Great Britain and Turkey (also members of NATO), together with Iran and Pakistan. Other less formal acts have publicly expressed special United States interest in the security of many other countries, ranging from Canada and Panama in this hemisphere to Greenland, to Spain, to Israel, to Saudi Arabia. Finally, I should note that in a broad sense the United States is committed under the provisions of the United Nations Charter to come to the assistance of any nation in the world that may become the victim of aggression.

In the quarter-century since World War II the United States has thus become deeply committed to a policy of global collective security. Today, largely because of our unhappy experience in Vietnam, many are questioning the policies which led to this involvement, are yearning for the days when we could rely on others for our basic security rather than being relied on by others. It is natural to our system that these questions should be debated, but I would hope that the debaters will not lose sight of the fundamental realities. Not only are we not alone on this shrinking planet, but we are by all odds the richest and most powerful element, which affects all the other elements by its inaction as much as by its action. If we were ever to revert to isolationism, there would be many threads to be unraveled. It is impossible to say what such an unraveling process would do to the fabric of world security and peace into which these threads have been woven.

CHAPTER XIII

Germany and Berlin: A Problem
in Crisis Management

One could almost say that Germany has been the central issue
in world politics since the time when, over a century ago, the
German state, belatedly unified and fired with national ambition, set out to find its place in the international sun. Twice in
this century, first under Kaiser Wilhelm, then under Hitler,
Germany has provoked great world conflicts in which it could be
defeated only by grand coalitions of opposing powers, which, in
both cases, included not only the Western European democracies but Russia and the United States. Since the end of World
War II defeated Germany has been the main bone of contention
between the Western and Eastern members of the strange
wartime alliance. It is in Germany that the vital security inter-

ests of the major powers, and particularly those of the Soviet Union and the United States, are most directly engaged. Thus the division of Germany has meant the division of Europe—and in a broad sense the division of the world.

The problem of Germany is not only vitally important, but it is also exceedingly complex. I have already touched on many of the developments leading up to the present situation. When the Nazis invaded the Soviet Union, Britain and the United States immediately and unreservedly pledged their support to Moscow; their policies were somewhat naïvely based on the expectation of continued collaboration between the Allied powers after the defeat of Germany to establish a new world order of harmony, prosperity and peace. To this end, the Soviet Government was induced to subscribe to the principles of the Atlantic Charter of 1941 and of the Declaration of Moscow of 1943 and to join in the creation of the United Nations organization in 1945.

The three powers had set up a so-called European Advisory Commission in London in 1943 to study and recommend policies on postwar arrangements. By September, 1944, this tripartite Commission had worked out and signed a protocol allocating zones of occupation to the forces of the three powers. The allocation of these zones was ostensibly just a matter of temporary military convenience, pending the conclusion of a peace treaty with a reunited Germany, but the Russians—with their greater appreciation of psychological warfare—saw to it that the historic capital of Germany, Berlin, was within their zone of military operations and occupation. While the city was itself divided into occupational sectors, the trusting Western Allies at that point took for granted their right of access through the Soviet Zone to their sectors in Berlin. At the Yalta Conference in February, 1945, France was admitted to the Great Power club and was also given a zone of occupation in Germany and a sector in Berlin; these were carved out of the areas allocated to Britain and the United States, with nothing ceded by the Soviet Union. General agreement was also reached at Yalta on other occupational arrangements, and these were subsequently spelled out in the "Instruments of the Initial Occupation and

Control of Germany" signed by the four powers on June 5, 1945. Aside from confirming the zones and sectors of occupation, these documents proclaimed the assumption of supreme authority in Germany by the principal Allied powers and established two agencies to administer this authority:

• The Allied Control Council, with the four supreme military commanders as members and with subordinate divisions to supervise various aspects of the administration of Germany, such as reparations, finance, transport, and legal. The Control Council, acting unanimously, was to make decisions for Germany as a whole, with each Allied commander being responsible for the application of these decisions in his own zone of occupation.

• The Allied Kommandatura to govern Berlin, likewise acting on the basis of unanimity.

Meanwhile, in April, the Red Army took Berlin and was to remain in exclusive occupation of the city for the better part of two months. Meanwhile, also, President Truman had repaired the omission of the European Advisory Commission by an exchange of letters with Stalin to obtain specific assurances with respect to Western rights of access to Berlin. In accordance with this exchange of letters, the American and Soviet commanders in Germany, General Clay and Marshal Zhukov, on June 29, 1945, worked out arrangements for use by the Western powers of specific road, rail and air lines between their zones of occupation and Berlin. American forces then withdrew from their advanced military positions in Saxony and Thuringia, in the Soviet Zone of occupation, and on July 1, 1945, moved into their sector of Berlin. The British and French entered the city at the same time. All three found that the industries remaining in their sectors had been completely dismantled by the Russians and, together with most other movable property, taken into the Soviet Zone or to the Soviet Union. They also found, as I noted earlier, that the Red Army had brought with it into East Germany practically the whole German section of the Comintern—including the present President of the so-called German Democratic Republic—together with a large group of former German prisoners of war who had been selected for and subjected to extensive Communist political indoctrination.

At the final Allied summit conference in the Berlin suburb of Potsdam an elaborate set of principles with respect to Germany was worked out and incorporated in the "Potsdam Protocol," signed on August 1, 1945. This document included both negative features of Allied purposes, such as demilitarization, denazification, reparations and punishment of war criminals, and positive provisions intended to show the Allied nations and Germany that there could be a future for the German people. These positive features provided, notably, for:

· Reorganization of the judicial system "in accordance with the principles of democracy, of justice under law, and of equal rights for all citizens without distinction of race, nationality or religion."

· Restoration of local self-government throughout Germany on "democratic principles," and in particular through elective councils, as rapidly as consistent with military security.

· Encouragement of "all democratic political parties with rights of assembly and of public discussion."

· Freedom of speech, press and religion, and formation of free trade unions, subject only to "the necessity for maintaining military security."

While no central German Government was to be established "for the time being," the protocol specified that during the period of occupation Germany should be "treated as a single economic unit" and that "certain essential Central German Administrative Departments, headed by State Secretaries, should be established, particularly in the fields of finance, transport, communications, foreign trade and industry." These German departments were to act under the direction of the Allied Control Council, which was charged with establishing common policies in these fields. Controls were to be imposed upon the German economy only to the extent necessary to insure the purposes of disarmament and demilitarization and payment of reparations and to prevent Germany from again developing a war potential.

The Potsdam Conference also accepted the Oder-Neisse line as the German eastern border (provisionally, pending the conclusion of a peace treaty); approved the transfer of the German population from Eastern Europe to Germany proper; and charged the Council of Foreign Ministers with the preparation of a peace settlement.

Five meetings of the Council of Foreign Ministers between September, 1945, and December, 1947, failed to produce any agreement on a peace settlement for Germany. The main stumbling blocks were disagreements on reparations, on getting a start toward reunification by the establishment of the Central German Administrative Departments foreseen in the Potsdam Protocol and on the treatment of Germany as an economic whole. The United States insisted on the development of a viable German economy, so that we would not, in fact, be paying reparations to the Soviet Union through our aid programs, and so that German production, particularly of coal, would contribute to general European recovery. The Soviet Union, on the other hand, demanded vast reparations and stressed the punitive aspects of the Potsdam Protocol.

Continued Soviet refusal to implement the economic provisions of the Potsdam Protocol had the effect of placing an unbearable burden on the Western powers for the support of their zones of occupation, and had economic repercussions in Western Europe which threatened to make it impossible to carry out any meaningful program of economic recovery. Both of these results may, in fact, have been calculated by the Soviets to serve their own purposes. In any event, the situation led to the fusion of the three Western zones and to economic negotiations between the three powers and the Benelux countries, then to the currency reform and the blockade of Berlin.

The Soviet walkout from the Allied Control Council for Germany on March 20, and from the Allied Kommandatura for Berlin on June 16, 1948, brought to an end the quadripartite machinery for Germany set up by the Potsdam agreements.

All of this had its political consequences in Berlin. Even before the Western Allies arrived in July, 1945, the Soviets had appointed provisional governments of the city and of its subdivisions. After the Allied arrival, they did reluctantly agree to elections, to take place on October 20, 1946. Then, during 1946, in the hope that by this maneuver they could "legitimize" Communist rule in Berlin and in East Germany, the Soviets forced the merger in their East Zone of the Social Democratic Party (SPD) with the Communist Party (KPD) into a so-called Socialist Unity Party (SED). The merger took place in April, 1946, and the obvious intention was to "capture" the socialist voters of Berlin and the East Zone. However, the SPD of Greater Berlin resisted Soviet pressures and insisted on running under its own name as a separate party in the elections. The Social Democrats won 48.7 percent of the votes, the Christian Democratic Union (CDU) 22.2 percent and the Liberal Democratic Party (LPD) 9.3 percent. The Communist-dominated Socialist Unity Party received only 19.8 percent. When the new city Parliament elected the SPD leader, Ernst Reuter, as Governing Mayor of Berlin, the Soviets vetoed the election. Since the Parliament refused to elect another, the city's affairs were conducted by a Deputy Mayor, Louise Schroeder.

From the beginning the Soviet occupation authorities had refused to allow the police in their sector to take direct orders from the city government. Then, after the blockade was imposed in the spring of 1948, the Soviets tried to intimidate, and hoped to overthrow, the elected city government by organizing mass riots and demonstrations around the City Hall, located in their sector. When these efforts were unsuccessful, the German Communists on November 30 formally split the city government, establishing a new "rump" government in East Berlin. They promised to legalize this government's existence by free elections, but never did so. After this, most of the legal deputies to the city Parliament withdrew to West Berlin and reconstituted the legal government there. They then re-elected Ernst Reuter as Governing Mayor of the entire city, but of course their authority could not in practice be exercised in the Soviet sector.

This, then, is the story of the division of Berlin. At the Paris meeting of the Council of Foreign Ministers in June, 1949, which confirmed the lifting of the blockade, there was no agreement on restoration of quadripartite controls; but Soviet Foreign

Minister Molotov did agree to "facilitation of the movement of persons and goods and the exchange of information between the Western zones and the Eastern zone and between Berlin and the zones."

Meanwhile, progress was being made in Western Germany toward the drawing up of a "basic law" or constitution, and in the spring of 1949 the United States, Britain and France replaced the military occupation of Western Germany with an Allied High Commission operating under an occupation statute. Following free elections and the adoption of the basic law, the Federal Republic of Germany was formally proclaimed on September 12, 1949. Berlin was not included as an integral part of the Federal Republic, though it was allowed to elect representatives, with advisory status only, to the German Bundestag (Parliament). Formally, the quadripartite status of Berlin was reaffirmed and maintained by the three Western Allies, but in practice the Soviet seat in the Allied Kommandatura remains vacant. On October 21 the Soviet Union and the German Communists responded to these Western moves by promulgating in the Soviet Zone of occupation the so-called German Democratic Republic. Neither free elections nor public discussions preceded the formation of this government. The first "elections" were not held until 1950, and these were single-list "elections" conducted under the auspices of the SED "bloc party" system and the National Front, a Communist cover organization created to coordinate the activities of social and mass organizations.

The question of German disarmament and rearmament was complex and difficult. Promptly after the occupation, the German armed forces in the American Zone were disbanded. All known war material was collected and inventoried, then either destroyed or, when possible, converted to peacetime uses. By the end of 1948 the United States had destroyed or dismantled and delivered as reparations all industrial plants especially adapted for the production of tanks, general armament, aircraft, war explosives and poisonous war substances, and all underground plants of every kind. The same process was carried out in the British and French zones and presumably also in the Soviet Zone.

Recognizing Soviet apprehensions about Germany and possibly even about Allied attitudes, Secretary of State Byrnes had taken the intitiative in 1945 in proposing to both Foreign Minister Molotov and Stalin the conclusion of a quadripartite twenty-five-year treaty which would contain guarantees against any resurgence of German militarism. Encouraged by their reaction, the United States submitted a draft treaty for comment and possible amendment in February, 1946. The proposal was discussed at meetings of the Council of Foreign Ministers in 1946 and in 1947, and the United States agreed to a forty-year term for the treaty when Molotov objected that the proposed twenty-five-year period was not long enough. However, the negotiations finally came to nought because the Soviet side kept trying to tie numerous extraneous and controversial issues into the proposal.

When the NATO agreement was concluded early in 1949, there was of course no question of including occupied Germany. However, it is interesting to note that the unanimous report of the Senate Committee on Foreign Relations of June 6, 1949, which recommended ratification of the treaty, did deal briefly with the German problem in the following terms:

> While Germany is not a party to the North Atlantic Treaty, the impact of the treaty upon Germany's future will be highly important. The Committee believes it may make possible a solution of the German problem and a constructive integration of Germany into Western Europe.
>
> It should be kept in mind that all the signatories of the pact, and particularly France and the other European countries, have suffered deeply from German aggression. All these signatory states are determined that Germany shall never again be permitted to threaten them. On the other hand, it is entirely possible that the German people may turn to the Soviet Union unless adequate and sincere efforts are made to provide them wtih a decent and hopeful future as an integral part of free Europe. Our European partners might be reluctant to accept Germany if it were not for the additional unity and security which the pact will afford.

And, indeed, both attitudes and events were to evolve in the direction foreseen in the Senate report. The first move toward putting arms once again into the hands of German forces, however, was made by the Soviet side. On May 23, 1950, the United States, Britain and France protested to the Soviet Government against the "remilitarization" of the Soviet Zone, calling attention to the fact that some fifty thousand men in the so-called Police Alert Units in the Soviet Zone were receiving basic infantry, artillery and armored training and were equipped with standard Soviet military weapons. This Soviet move broke the ice, and the movement was stimulated further by the uneasiness and apprehensions aroused by the Communist invasion of South Korea in June of that year.

Following a meeting in Washington in September, 1950, the Foreign Ministers of Britain, France and the United States stated that they had "given serious consideration to the problem of the security of the Federal Republic," in both its external and its internal aspects. They recognized "the fact that outright military units had been created in the Soviet zone of occupation and that this fact together with recent events in Germany and elsewhere had given rise to a situation of great concern." They said that "the allied governments consider that their forces in Germany have, in addition to their occupation duties, also the important role of acting as security forces for the protection and defense of the free world, including the German Federal Republic and the Western sectors of Berlin." Announcing that they would increase and reinforce their forces in Germany, they then declared, in the language of the NATO pact, that "They will treat any attack against the Federal Republic or Berlin from any quarter as an attack upon themselves."

A month later the French Government put forward publicly a plan for the creation of a European Defense Community, with an integrated European army which would include West Germans. This revolutionary plan provoked much public discussion and intense diplomatic activity among the Western European countries and with the United States, including a series of high-level meetings. The result was a package of diplomatic documents signed at Bonn, Germany, in May, 1952. Under these interrelated agreements the Federal Republic would enter the European Defense Community. The occupation would come to an end, being replaced by a series of contractual arrangements under which the Western Allies retained responsibility for questions affecting all of Germany and for Berlin. Most of the signatories, including the United States, promptly ratified the Bonn Agreements. However, in the end the concept of submerging the French military forces in a European Defense Community proved to be too much for French nationalism to take, and on August 30, 1954, the agreements were voted down by the French Chamber of Deputies.

On the political side, Moscow had become alarmed by the rapidity of European economic recovery, including the establishment of the European Coal and Steel Community, which married the iron and coal resources of France and Germany and brought to an end this perennial source of conflict between these two countries. When the proposals for the creation of a European Defense Community were added to this, Moscow launched a series of diplomatic initiatives in the hope of stemming the tide. On March 10, 1952, the Soviets submitted to the other principal powers a draft peace treaty with Germany, using most of the disputed language of the Potsdam Protocol and providing for the withdrawal of all foreign forces from Germany within one year. This was, of course, not acceptable to the Western powers, who by now found the concept of integration of Germany into Western European life preferable to the reestablishment of an independent Germany subject to the kind of threats and pressures the Soviets had already shown their readiness to use in the Eastern Zone.

Meanwhile, the government of the Federal Republic, under Chancellor Konrad Adenauer, was pressing for free elections throughout all Germany. In December, 1951, the Western powers had proposed and had passed through the United Nations General Assembly a resolution to set up a UN commission to "investigate conditions for free elections" in Germany. This UN commission did, in fact, proceed to Germany in the spring of 1952; it made favorable reports on conditions in the Federal Republic but was refused admission to the Soviet Zone. A few months after Stalin's death, in June, 1953, a wave of riots swept East Berlin and other cities in Soviet-occupied Germany. The

West cautiously refrained from intervening, and the Soviet armed forces quickly and brutally suppressed the outbreaks. There was a profound emotional reaction in West Germany, and in the ensuing national elections in September the Communist Party received only 2.2 percent of the total votes. All this activity on both sides did culminate in another meeting of the quadripartite—that is, United States, Britain, France and the Soviet Union—Council of Foreign Ministers in Berlin in January–February, 1954. Foreign Minister Molotov again presented his draft peace treaty, together with a "proposal for a general European Treaty on Collective Security." On the other side, the Western powers supported the so-called Eden plan for reunification of Germany by free elections. There were long debates, but no results.

After the rejection by the French Parliament of the European Defense Community agreements, the Western powers moved fast to limit the damage by finding a new formula. An instrument was at hand in the form of the Brussels Treaty of Economic, Social and Cultural Collaboration and Collective Self-Defense, which had been signed in March, 1948, on the heels of the Communist takeover in Czechoslovakia, by Britain, France and the Benelux countries—Belgium, the Netherlands and Luxembourg. These five Western European powers now invited West Germany and Italy to join them. The treaty was revised and modified to create what was now called the Western European Union. The agreements contained provisions regulating the levels of, and establishing control machinery for, armaments and armed forces of the members. In related voluntary acts, the Federal Republic of Germany renounced the production in Germany of atomic, biological or chemical weapons, as well as strategic bombers, large warships and missiles; and Chancellor Adenauer declared that Germany would "refrain from any action inconsistent with the defensive character" of the NATO and Western European Union treaties and would never "have recourse to force to achieve . . . reunification of Germany or . . . modification of her present boundaries."

The ratifications of the new agreements and of Germany's adherence to NATO were completed by May 5, 1955, on which date the Federal Republic recovered its sovereignty and entered the NATO alliance. The Allied High Commissions in Bonn were dissolved and replaced by embassies. However, the United States, Britain and France retained their prerogatives with respect to Berlin and to all-German questions, that is, reunification and the conclusion of a peace treaty. Moscow responded on May 14, 1955, by concluding a multilateral Treaty of Friendship, Cooperation and Mutual Assistance with its Eastern European satellites and establishing under its terms the so-called Warsaw Pact organization.

Notwithstanding the continued impasse on Germany, the United States and its Western Allies had been probing for changes in Soviet foreign policy after the death of Stalin, and had been encouraged by such developments as the conclusion of the armistice in Korea, some easing of Moscow's pressures on the Eastern European countries, the achievement of the Indo-china settlements at Geneva in 1954 and the Soviet turnabout on Austria which had led to the signing of the Austrian State Treaty on May 15, 1955—strangely enough, on the day following the conclusion of the Warsaw Pact. On May 10, even before these latter two events, the Western Allies, having agreed that it was desirable to have a new try with the new top-level leadership in Moscow, had proposed the holding of a new summit conference. I have already discussed this meeting in other contexts. For present purposes I should, however, note the terms of the directive of the heads of government of the four powers, issued on July 23, 1955, at the conclusion of that summit meeting in Geneva. The portion relating to Germany reads as follows:

The heads of government, recognizing their common responsibility for the settlement of the German question and the reunification of Germany, have agreed that the settlement of the German question and the reunification of Germany by means of free elections shall be carried out in conformity with the national interests of the German people and the interests of European security.

This statement was the furthest point to which the Western Allies were able to bring the Soviets after the war toward a public acknowledgment of their responsibilities for all Germany.

It is a rather guarded commitment to free elections and thus to self-determination for the German people. While nothing concrete emerged from the discussions of this "directive" at the subsequent foreign ministers meeting or later, this particular statement remained a point of frequent and useful reference for the Western Allies and a source of embarrassment to Moscow in the maneuvers and negotiations of subsequent years. The Geneva Conference did break the ice in Europe enough, however, to lead to a visit to Moscow by Chancellor Adenauer in September, 1955, during which the Soviet Union and the Federal Republic of Germany agreed to re-establish diplomatic relations. A week later, in order to reassure the East German Communists, Moscow concluded an agreement with the regime it had set up in the Soviet Zone, ostensibly granting the German Democratic Republic greater sovereignty and control of its internal and external affairs and placing the relationship between the two on a par with the relationship between the Western powers and the Federal Republic.

The European scene was relatively quiet during the next couple of years, so far as the East-West conflict was concerned. On the Soviet side, Khrushchev was preoccupied with his denunciation of Stalin at the Twentieth Party Congress, and with his struggle for power internally against the so-called "anti-Party" group; then with trying to contain the ferment stirred up in Eastern Europe by the "de-Stalinization" campaign, including the upheaval in Poland and the Soviet suppression of the revolt in Hungary. On the Western side, Nasser's nationalization of the Suez Canal led to the ill-considered and ill-fated decision of Britain, France and Israel, in November, 1956, to invade Egypt. American opposition to this move helped bring an end to the hostilities. However, it also disrupted the machinery of inter-Allied cooperation, and some months of repair work were required before Western collaboration could be restored to its previous basis of mutual understanding and trust. Despite the Suez interruption, however, the Western Europeans—now including the Federal Republic of Germany as a full partner—continued to move ahead, with strong American encouragement and support, toward strengthening their continental system. On

March 25, 1957, they concluded the Treaties of Rome, which created the European Economic Community, commonly called the Common Market, and the European Community of Atomic Energy, commonly called Euratom.

Then the launching of the first man-made earth satellites— Sputnik I on October 4 and Sputnik II on November 3, 1957— astounded the world and opened an era of Soviet Sputnik diplomacy. I was at the time in Bolivia, inspecting our aid programs and activities in that country. However, I was shortly afterward reassigned to the Department of State as Deputy Assistant Secretary for European Affairs, handling Soviet and Eastern European Affairs. When I arrived and called on Secretary Dulles in mid-February, 1958, he asked me what I thought of Khrushchev as compared with Stalin. I replied that I thought Khrushchev was probably the more dangerous of the two, that I considered him to be a "true believer," while Stalin clearly had been a cynical and cautious realist. The Secretary replied that that was precisely how he felt. We agreed that Khrushchev's "de-Stalinization" campaign and other maneuvers in getting to the top had probably released some promising evolutionary forces inside the Soviet Union and the Communist camp, but that in foreign policy Khrushchev would be erratically and dangerously aggressive and generally hard to deal with.

As I talked with the Secretary that day, the first salvos had already been exchanged in what was to be a long political-propaganda war. Khrushchev had initiated his effort to exploit the world's awe and unease by a boastful speech on the occasion of the Soviet Revolutionary Anniversary on November 6, in which he demanded a new summit meeting of leaders of socialist and capitalist countries to agree on "measures for reducing international tensions." On December 10, on the eve of a NATO Council meeting—to be attended by chiefs of state of the member countries, a decision providing in itself a measure of the impact of the Sputnik launchings—this proposal had been put forward officially in a long bombastic note, signed by Soviet Prime Minister Bulganin and addressed to President Eisenhower and the heads of most other governments in the world. On January 8, 1958, another Bulganin letter of the world-circular variety put forward an agenda of loaded Soviet "proposals" to be considered at the proposed summit meeting. These were mostly declaratory in nature and without provisions for inspection or enforcement. They ranged from a declaration of nonintervention in the Middle East, to public renunciation of the use of nuclear weapons, to the conclusion of a nonaggression pact between NATO and the Warsaw Pact, to a proclamation of intention to develop relations of friendship and peaceful cooperation, to an unpoliced agreement to make Central Europe "a nuclear-free area," to acceptance of the division of Germany.

Meanwhile, the December NATO meeting had dealt in a preliminary way with the first communication, and the position worked out there had been incorporated and amplified in replies sent to Chairman Bulganin by President Eisenhower on January 12 and February 15, 1968. The President pointed out that both the United States and the Soviet Union, as signers of the United Nations Charter, were already committed to nonintervention in the Middle East, to nonaggression and the nonuse of force and to the development of friendship and peaceful cooperation in international relations. On disarmament matters, Bulganin was reminded of the Soviet rejection of the far-reaching Western proposals put forward at the recent disarmament talks in London and of the Soviet declaration of its intention to boycott the United Nations Disarmament Commission. As for Germany, the President referred to the terms Bulganin had agreed to in Geneva in 1955 for the reunification of the country by free elections. The letter then went on to propose that both countries refrain from abusing the veto in the United Nations Security Council, that the Soviet Government honor the provisions of the Yalta agreement in Eastern Europe and that we move forward toward concrete and controllable measures of disarmament and toward an agreement that "outer space should be used only for peaceful purposes." (I might note that Khrushchev's Sputnik mood was evident in a speech he made in Minsk a week later, in which he sneeringly dismissed this space proposal by saying the United States "wants to ban what it hasn't got.")

The President continued, saying that he was prepared to meet to discuss any proposals to ease the international situation.

However, he pointed out: "High-level meetings, in which we both participate, create great expectations and for that reason involve a danger of disillusionment, dejection and increased distrust if in fact the meetings are ill-prepared, if they evade the root causes of danger, if they are used primarily for propaganda, or if agreements arrived at are not fulfilled." Therefore, the President concluded: "It would be essential that prior to such a meeting these complex matters should be worked out in advance through diplomatic channels . . . so that it can be ascertained that such a top-level meeting would, in fact, hold good hope of advancing the cause of peace and justice in the world."

The exchange of argumentative, publicized communications between Washington and Moscow was to continue with little letup far beyond Mr. Dulles' days in the State Department, though I should note that the nominal addressee changed in March, 1958, when Khrushchev ousted Bulganin and himself took over as Prime Minister, or, in Russian terminology, Chairman of the Council of Ministers of the U.S.S.R. Within the next year and a half there were to be well over two hundred major notes, press statements and speeches related to these exchanges with the Soviet Union. In general, these communications continued along the lines of the original salvos, developing and embellishing the themes summarized above. They might be said to have fallen into three phases. The first half of 1958 was featured by the Soviet drive for an unprepared propagandistic summit conference, designed to exploit the Sputnik launchings and equate the Soviet Union with the United States and the Warsaw Pact with NATO, combined with a major effort in the United Nations Security Council to brand our Strategic Air Force flights over the Arctic as a war danger. In the summer the Soviet drive merged into the Near Eastern crisis, following the revolution in Iraq and the appeals of Lebanon and Jordan which led to the landing of United States troops on the shores of the eastern Mediterranean. In the fall the Soviet drive focused more and more on Germany and Berlin. This was the most serious phase, characterized by increasingly open threats of the use of force against the Western Allies in Berlin.

During this period, the Bureau of European Affairs of the

State Department had the primary drafting responsibility. In practice this meant me, as Deputy Assistant Secretary in charge of Soviet and Eastern European Affairs, and the Office of Soviet Affairs in the Bureau. As soon as a new Soviet missive hit us, we would start drafting a response, frequently on the basis of a personal suggestion from the Secretary or Under Secretary. Since the subjects of the communications were varied, however, including various aspects of disarmament and of United Nations activities, as well as European questions and Soviet-American relations in general, a departmental working group developed, some members of which might join in the initial drafting process and most of whom usually participated in the meetings in the Secretary's office to discuss the final product. The principal members included the Department's expert on atomic and disarmament matters, officers of the Policy Planning staff and of the Bureau of United Nations Affairs and the Department's legal adviser. I acted as a sort of executive secretary of the group, at that stage, and often as chairman.

Early in the Sputnik campaign, the Soviet side developed the practice of launching its missives in time to catch the Sunday papers in the United States and most of the Western countries. This usually meant a quick Saturday statement to be issued by the Department's spokesman, designed to take the Sunday headline play away from the Soviet blast. It also frequently meant the convocation of Sunday afternoon sessions at Secretary Dulles' house to work on a substantive reply.

In the early stages, President Eisenhower and the Secretary of State were annoyed by the fact that the Soviets were on the offensive, magnifying and attempting to exploit the tremendous impression made by their space successes. They resented being put on the defensive and were irritated by the Soviet debasement of the diplomatic process for propagandistic purposes. They became more relaxed, however, and at times even seemed to relish the contest, as it became clear that we were coming out at least even in the purely propagandistic aspects of these frenetic exchanges; that our quick responses and firmness had forestalled any panicky reaction on the part of our allies and third countries; and that we had been able to force the Soviet hand toward concrete and specific steps in the field of international diplomacy. Two such concrete "spin-offs" from these exchanges, for example, were the agreements to hold conferences of experts at Geneva in 1958: one on measures to prevent surprise attack and the other on nuclear-test-detection methods. Moscow sent a political rather than expert delegation to the Surprise Attack Conference, and their insistence on discussing political rather than technical aspects of this question not only brought the meeting to an abrupt end but made clear the political-propagandistic character of the Soviet objectives. However, Moscow did send eminent Soviet scientists to the Nuclear Test Conference, and their agreement to the technical report on the difficulties of test detection cut the ground out from under Soviet hopes for a hasty, uninspected ban on nuclear tests. Gradually, the grandiose Soviet proposals for a world-wide summit meeting were reduced to acceptance of the need for preliminary preparatory work by the foreign ministers, and finally to abortive prepreliminary discussions by the American, British and French Ambassadors in Moscow with the Soviet Foreign Minister.

As 1958 wore on, Khrushchev increasingly focused on his real target of Germany. In a threatening speech in Moscow on November 10 and in corollary notes to the United States, Great Britain and France on November 27, his immediate goal was revealed to be the ouster of the Western Allies from Berlin and the consolidation of the Soviet hold on East Germany. In the notes the Soviet Union proposed to end the "occupation regime" in West Berlin and to make West Berlin what they described as "a demilitarized, free city." The Soviets declared they would turn over control of Allied access to Berlin to the authorities of the German Democratic Republic within six months. This Soviet move opened up a "Berlin crisis" which was to last over four years. The move was not wholly unanticipated, however, in view of the increasingly clear revelation of Soviet purposes and the increasingly threatening tone of their communications and statements. Thus, even before Khrushchev spoke on November 10, Secretary Dulles in his press conference of November 7 had already stressed the firmness of our commitments in Germany and our determination to "hold West Berlin, if need be by military force." After the Khrushchev speech, the Secretary dealt with the subject again, in the same firm tone but at even greater length. We were able to get out a press statement on the Soviet note on the very day of its delivery and publication, despite the fact that the Soviets had, with typical delicacy, chosen to hand it over on our Thanksgiving Holiday. This statement held the situation through the December meeting of the NATO foreign ministers, where a solid alliance stand was achieved. Fully coordinated replies to the Soviet note were then delivered in Moscow by the three Allied embassies—just to reciprocate the Soviet courtesy—on New Year's Eve. In their notes the Western powers rejected the Soviet ultimatum, but indicated their willingness to discuss Berlin as a part of the general problem of Germany and of European security.

We gathered together in pamphlet form the Soviet note and our reply, along with pertinent commentary; and the resulting State Department publication, *The Soviet Note on Berlin: An Analysis*, received world-wide circulation and a sympathetic reaction. Meanwhile, we were also working up practical measures to counter this direct Soviet threat to our really vital interests. We had set up an interdepartmental working group in Washington which addressed itself to the task of contingency planning for the defense of Western interests in Berlin and of Western access to the city. This organization had as its nucleus the State Department group which I have described, plus the Assistant Secretary of Defense for International Security Affairs and comparable representatives of the United States Information Service (USIA) and the Central Intelligence Agency (CIA). This interdepartmental group was also having working sessions several times a week, and meetings with the Secretary of State and other principals from time to time, to report and to get their suggestions for our further work. In many discussions, we had all agreed that a second airlift was not sufficient and that the substitution of East German for Soviet controls on the autobahn and railways would be a major political setback, not acceptable to the West. We therefore planned to send armed convoys on the surface into Berlin, in case the Soviets should carry out their threats, and devised plans calculated to prevent the other side from reducing our positions by "salami" tactics.

All this planning also had to be coordinated with our Allies. For this purpose we had set up in Washington a corresponding inter-Allied working group consisting of key members of our own American groups and experts attached to the Allied embassies in the capital. All our contingency planning thus represented agreed positions of the three principal powers, Britain, France and ourselves. During this period we also kept the German Embassy fully aware of everything that was going on and likewise made a point of reporting from time to time to the North Atlantic Council.

The death of Secretary Dulles and his replacement by Secretary Herter in the spring of 1959 did not slow down the pace of contingency planning, inter-Allied consultation or diplomatic exchanges. Neither did it diminish Soviet pressure for Allied withdrawal from Berlin or the Soviet threat to act unilaterally. Public apprehension mounted as Khrushchev visited East Germany in March and made more bellicose speeches. President Eisenhower commented, in a report to the people on television on March 16:

The Soviet Government has announced its intention to enter into a peace treaty with the East German puppet regime . . . [which] the Soviets assert will deny our occupation rights and our rights of access. . . . Their proposals have included a vague offer to make the Western part of Berlin—though not the Eastern part, which the Soviets control—a so-called "Free City." It is by no means clear what West Berlin would be free from, except perhaps from freedom itself . . . no one, certainly not the two million West Berliners, can ignore the cold fact that Berlin is surrounded by many divisions of Soviet and East German troops and by territory governed by authorities dedicated to eliminating freedom from the area. . . .

We cannot try to purchase peace by forsaking two million free people of Berlin.

We cannot agree to any permanent and compulsory division of the German nation. . . .

We cannot recognize the asserted right of any nation to dishonor its international agreements whenever it chooses. . . .

We must not, by weakness or irresolution, increase the risk of war. . . .

The President declared "we would never negotiate under a dictated time limit or agenda, or on other unreasonable terms." However, he concluded, we were considering with our allies a reply to the latest Soviet note (March 2), which "appears to be a move toward negotiation on an improved basis."

Following the President's speech, the Allied governments did agree to propose to Moscow a meeting of the foreign ministers. The Soviets grudgingly accepted, temporarily dropping their pressures for a summit conference. The meeting convened in Geneva on May 11, 1959, and was to drag on, with a short recess, until August 5. The Western side presented a new "Western Peace Plan," which had been worked out through the machinery of the interdepartmental and inter-Allied working groups. It provided for gradual steps toward German reunification, knit together with proposals for European security measures, leading finally to a peace settlement in Europe. The Soviets rejected this new plan, despite its provisions designed to protect legitimate Soviet security interests. Instead, they pulled out again their old peace treaty proposals and new variants which called for direct negotiations on a basis of equality between the Federal Government of Germany and the East German regime. As time went on, it became increasingly clear that the Geneva meeting would result in an impasse, at best, or a break, at worst. Khrushchev had not formally withdrawn his ultimatum, despite the Soviet acceptance of the foreign ministers meeting, and indeed was continuing to go around making threatening noises in his public declarations.

In the circumstances, we were frankly looking for maneuvers which would make it possible to continue the dialogue and prevent open conflict—it must be admitted that we were seeking a means to get Khrushchev off the hook of his public commitment to act unilaterally. We found the means in a somewhat tangential context. The 1958 U.S.-U.S.S.R. exchanges agreement had provided for the holding of national exhibitions by both countries in 1959, and for the opening of these exhibits by the No. 2 man in the Soviet Union, First Deputy Chairman of the Soviet Council of Ministers, Frol Kozlov, and by Vice President Richard M. Nixon. On the eve of Kozlov's departure from

New York in June to return to Moscow, President Eisenhower authorized Under Secretary Robert Murphy and me to visit him and to convey a personal invitation for Khrushchev to pay a visit to the United States later in the year. We were able to do so, quietly and without attracting press attention, at the headquarters of the Soviet United Nations delegation in New York. The invitation was accepted with alacrity and announced on August 3, two days before the end of the Geneva Foreign Ministers Conference. The President explained to our allies and to the American people:

> The reasons for my invitation to him are simply: first, to give him the opportunity to see what America and Americans are really like—to let him see a great and thriving nation living in real freedom; second, to give him face to face the basic convictions of our people on the major issues of the day, including West Berlin, and to hear from him directly his own views on those issues.

The visit, which took place in September, did take the heat out of the immediate situation. Khrushchev was visibly impressed by what he saw and by the President personally. At Camp David he agreed that (1) all outstanding international questions should be settled not by the application of force but by peaceful means through negotiation; and (2) negotiations on Berlin would be reopened and, while they were not to be prolonged indefinitely, no time limit would be placed upon this process. Moreover, he invited the President to pay a return visit to the Soviet Union the following year. In December the Western heads of government met in Paris and decided to invite Khrushchev to a quadripartite summit meeting; the invitation was accepted and the meeting fixed for May 16, 1960, in Paris.

But a spectacular event was to intervene and the summit itself was to be one of the great fantasies of all diplomatic history. On May 1, 1960, Soviet missiles brought down a U-2 photographic reconnaissance aircraft flying over Soviet territory. Secretary Herter and a delegation which included me were attending a NATO meeting in Turkey and were scheduled to pay an official visit to Greece on the way home. We had our first inkling that something had gone wrong, en route to Athens, in the form of a report that an American "weather research plane" flying out of Adana, Turkey, was overdue. We recognized this report as a previously planned statement to cover failure of a U-2 plane to complete its mission on schedule, but there was nothing that we could do in our peripatetic situation.

In Moscow, Khrushchev began playing a game of cat and mouse. There was a meeting of the Central Committee on May 4. It later became clear that the U-2 had been discussed there, but nothing was said publicly. Then, in a dramatic speech to the Supreme Soviet on May 5, Khrushchev announced that an American plane had been downed over Soviet territory and added some sly comment. If the craft proved to be a military plane, he opined, this could be a matter of "special concern." He carefully avoided mentioning that the pilot and a reasonably intact plane had been captured. Back in Washington, the Acting Secretary, believing that the plane would have been destroyed and the pilot killed, authorized the issuance of a further development of the cover story, to the effect that the pilot of the "weather research plane" had probably lost consciousness as a result of an oxygen failure and strayed over Soviet territory.

In a second speech Khrushchev then delightedly revealed that the flier and evidence regarding the plane's mission were in Soviet hands; he speculated mischievously on the responsibilities and uncontrollable acts of the Pentagon and American intelligence. By the time the Secretary's party got back to Washington late Friday night, May 6, the cover story had been torn to shreds and Khruschchev had already indicated that the line he would take would be to blame the military and the CIA, thus in effect charging that President Eisenhower did not control his own government.

Long meetings ensued on Saturday in Secretary Herter's office. The orthodox and traditional (and, in this case, plurality) view was that no government, and certainly no chief of state, ever publicly admits responsibility for "spying." CIA Director Allen Dulles was, of course, prepared to resign and assume full responsibility personally. In the discussion, I was one of the few nontraditionalists. It seemed to me essential to issue an honest statement. Not only were the reporters besieging the Department's press office, ready to punch holes in any further attempt to cover up, but the prime witness was in Soviet hands. Placing the blame on subordinate executives would simply support Khrushchev's thesis and put the President in an impossible situation in any negotiations with him. Besides, I argued, the U-2—which had been photographing the Soviet Union regularly for over four years, to Khrushchev's full knowledge and frustration—had introduced a new dimension into intelligence activities and had to be dealt with in a new dimension, too. This was not just a case of sacrificing an agent. My proposed line of action might be unprecedented, but so was the situation.

No final conclusion was reached that day, since the President was in Gettysburg, and a temporizing statement was given to the clamoring press. However, after a talk between them on the following day, the President authorized the Secretary of State to issue a statement on Monday, May 9, assuming full governmental responsibility for these flights as a duty to the American people and free peoples everywhere to take measures to lessen and overcome the dangers of surprise attack, and asserting that "the United States has not and does not shirk this responsibility." At a news conference two days later, the President reaffirmed the Secretary's statement. He referred to such activities as a "distasteful but vital necessity" and said "we must not be distracted from the real issues of the day by what is an incident or a symptom of the world situation today." Khrushchev, on the other hand, had exploded both publicly and privately with violent attacks on Secretary Herter and hostile remarks toward the President.

Despite all this, preparations for the summit went ahead on the Western side. Preliminary consultations took place in Paris on the fourteenth and fifteenth between the three Western foreign ministers and chiefs of state. Khrushchev showed up on schedule, too, but his purpose in coming soon became clear. When the four heads of government came together at the Élysée Palace on the morning of the sixteenth, he insisted that the gathering should not be considered a formal session, but a "preliminary meeting." As de Gaulle, presiding, called on President Eisenhower to speak, Khrushchev seized the floor and unleashed a violent tirade against the President. He said his government could not negotiate under the threat that American aircraft would continue to fly over the Soviet Union and demanded condemnation of the flight, a cessation of such activities and punishment of the guilty, together with an expression of regret. In addition, he revoked the invitation to the President to visit the Soviet Union and postponed any Soviet participation in a summit conference from six to eight months—that is, of course, until after the upcoming American elections.

President Eisenhower replied in restrained and conciliatory terms. He made no apologies for the overflight and justified it under the circumstances. However, he said such flights had been discontinued and would not be renewed under his administration, adding that he could not speak for the succeeding one. He reminded Khrushchev of his, the President's, "open skies" proposal at Geneva in 1955 and said he favored United Nations aerial surveillance to detect preparations for surprise attacks. He made clear that he did not accept Khrushchev's ultimatum and said the latter had apparently come to Paris with the sole intention of sabotaging the meeting. The British in particular made strenuous efforts to salvage the conference, but they were unavailing. On the evening of the sixteenth, after a public press conference in Paris as vitriolic as his more private appearance had been in the Élysée Palace, Khrushchev left for home.

There was much violent controversy about the whole affair in the United States, including elaborate Senate hearings. I personally think that, on balance, the whole episode came out for the best. There was no prospect of any meaningful agreement at the summit conference, and it was preferable that the break come on this rather extraneous issue of the U-2 incident than on Berlin. Indeed, while I could not prove it and for obvious reasons never sought to discuss the matter with him, I think Khrushchev's behavior throughout indicated that he had come to pretty much the same conclusion himself. He was the man who was publicly committed to act if he didn't have his way about Berlin, and I think he didn't relish the prospect. As matters turned out, the West gained a fairly long breathing spell before it had to face the next round of Soviet threats. Finally, I think the Soviets were impressed by our determination to do everything we could to deny them the advantages of making secret military preparations, and that, in the long term, this realization on their part will be an essential condition for any meaningful progress in the disarmament field.

Most new administrations, especially when they involve a change of party, come into office with a certain distrust of the professional bureaucrats and a desire to introduce at least new faces—if not new policies—on the Washington scene. However, for reasons still not wholly clear to me, President Kennedy and Secretary Rusk asked me to stay on as Assistant Secretary of State for European Affairs, thus making me the senior Assistant Secretary in any government department in the new administration. Maybe it was partly because of the job I had done in building up the Voice of America, as some of the President's entourage suggested to me; more likely, it was because the President himself, even before the elections, had predicted that the next President would face a Berlin crisis and wanted continuity of experience available to him. In any case, he was, in fact, faced with this problem immediately.

Even before the inauguration, Khrushchev on January 6 had made a saber-rattling speech, devoted mainly to Soviet support of "wars of national liberation" in general, but also declaring again that the time had about arrived to conclude a peace treaty with Germany and settle the Berlin question. One of the President's first acts after the inauguration, therefore, was to call in former Secretary of State Dean Acheson—to the delight of those of us who had worked with him before—to review exactly where the United States stood on European problems. This intensive review led to a few changes, but mainly to a confirmation of the contingency planning that had taken place already with respect to possible developments in Germany or in Berlin or on the access routes.

Those of us concerned with Soviet relations were anxious that President Kennedy meet with Khrushchev personally, before the latter might unilaterally provoke a new crisis, and we found the President in full agreement. We also agreed, however, that this encounter would have to be combined with appropriate meetings with the Allies. Arrangements had already been made for British Prime Minister Harold Macmillan and Chancellor Adenauer to visit the United States. Consequently, we worked out a program combining a visit to President de Gaulle in Paris with a meeting with Khrushchev in Vienna and then a brief stop in England on the way back, all to take place during the first week of June, 1961.

Vienna was a grim experience for the President—and for all of us who accompanied him as his principal advisers. It was clear that Khrushchev was out to cow "this young man," and his presentation was brutal. He made it clear from the outset that he still wanted the Allies out of Berlin. The first step would be the signature of a peace treaty with both German states. If the West balked, the Soviets would sign a separate treaty with the East German regime and West Berlin would then become a "demilitarized free city." Token Allied troops could remain, but would have to be joined by Soviet contingents. Alternatively, neutral troops, including some friendly to the Soviets, could take over under United Nations aegis. In other words, as the President noted, Khrushchev was saying: "What's mine is mine. What's yours is negotiable." The young President stood up to this provocation with dignity, frankness and determination but yet with admirable restraint. He stressed to Khrushchev that Moscow was challenging a vital Western interest and that he could not possibly give way even at the risk of war. Khrushchev did not budge and even confirmed his demands in a written memorandum at the conclusion of the meetings. As they parted, the President, shaken but uncowed, remarked: "It will be a cold winter." Now he knew what he was up against.

Following our return to Washington, the President directed a redoubled effort to get all our ducks in a row with respect to German planning and the operations that clearly lay ahead. He and Secretary Rusk decided that I should leave the day-to-day operation of the Bureau of European Affairs to my Deputy and concentrate on the German task. It was not a simple organizational problem. On the political side, the British, French and ourselves had primary responsibilities, but the Federal German

Government and the government of Berlin were also vitally involved—and, behind these, all our NATO Allies. On the military side, we had the British, French and American commanders in Germany, the German forces and the NATO Commander in Chief. Just on the American side, half a dozen principal elements of the State Department itself were involved, as well as, in varying degrees, a dozen other government departments. A sort of skeleton existed in the form of the United States and Allied groups I have already mentioned. However, they had to be strengthened, expanded and restructured.

The first step was to set up, inside the U.S. Government, a "Berlin Task Force," on a full-time basis. The Defense Department assigned Paul Nitze, then Assistant Secretary, later Secretary of the Navy and Deputy Secretary of Defense. The Joint Chiefs of Staff designated Major General David Gray. The Treasury was represented by Henry (Joe) Fowler, then Under Secretary and later Secretary of the Treasury. The USIA and CIA and, as necessary, other agencies sent comparable senior-level officials. We set up a permanent supporting staff, operating twenty-four hours a day, seven days a week, in the State Department's Operation Center.

On the Allied side, we organized a so-called Quadripartite Ambassadorial Group, which I also chaired and which included the British, French and German Ambassadors in Washington. This group also met daily during the critical periods, and set up expert subgroups to deal with specific questions. Similar quadripartite bodies were organized in Berlin and Bonn and, for military matters, at NATO headquarters in Paris. In due course, we were able to tie all these elements together with a sophisticated communications system enabling us to have immediate exchanges of views and to reach rapid decisions.

On the American side, the President was kept continuously informed of the activities of the Berlin Task Force, sometimes by the Secretary of State or through his Assistant for National Security Affairs, McGeorge Bundy, and his military adviser, General Maxwell Taylor, sometimes by direct consultation with me. When important proposals were to be considered, the President would call together Secretaries Rusk and McNamara and other principals concerned, together with his White House aides and key members of the Berlin Task Force.

So much for the machinery—it was a sort of pioneering experiment and experience.

On June 15, 1961, following his return to Moscow from the meeting in Vienna, Khrushchev made a speech inferentially renewing his ultimatum, by declaring that the German problem "must be settled this year." On July 17 the United States replied to this and to Khrushchev's Vienna memorandum, in a note reflecting the firm stand President Kennedy had taken at that meeting. A less direct but more substantial reply was made by the President on July 25, in the form of a radio-television address to people at home. Reviewing his Vienna talks and the threat to Berlin, he declared: "We are clear about what must be done—and we intend to do it. I want to talk to you frankly tonight about the first steps that we shall take." He first reported on actions already taken to increase the size of the Marine Corps, expand air- and sealift capabilities, speed up arms procurement and put our bombers on ground alert. Then he announced new measures, including: a supplementary military budget of over $3 billion, increases of over 200,000 men in the authorized strength of the armed forces, together with a temporary call-up of reserves to fill these new quotas, and the retention or reactivation of ships and planes scheduled for retirement.

Vienna and its aftermath were having serious repercussions throughout the world, but nowhere as serious as in East Germany. Since the postwar Communist takeover, something over three and a half million people, or a fifth of the total population of the Soviet Zone, had fled to the West. The East German regime had closed its borders with West Germany, but as long as the Allied presence kept West Berlin open, the city continued to provide an escape hatch. After Vienna the East Germans panicked and began to flow into West Berlin in such numbers that a major civilian airlift had to be organized to fly them out to West Germany. In July there were over thirty thousand such escapees, and the world was watching East Germany bleed to death. It was clear that if East Germany were not to expire, there would have to be some drastic action to stop the hemorrhage, and we were asking ourselves what it would be. Before we could answer our own question, we were caught by surprise—through a failure of specific local intelligence—when, on the night of August 12–13, the East Germans, with Soviet backing, started erecting a formidable wall through the heart of the great city of Berlin. We promptly got out statements and notes to the Soviet Government and to the Soviet commander in East Germany, protesting this violation of the quadripartite status of Berlin and warning against any interference with Allied access. This may seem—and did seem to many at the time—to have been too little in such dramatic circumstances. But it had never been considered by any of the Western Allies that East Berlin—the sector of the city allocated to Soviet occupation—was in itself a *casus belli.* However much we deplored the partitioning of Germany and of Berlin, once it took place, we did not contemplate changing the lines of demarcation by force, or allowing anyone else to change them by force. Indeed, the United States and its Western Allies were even then in the process of preparing to go to war, if necessary, to prevent Soviet encroachment on our own rights and positions in West Berlin and in West Germany.

I think it must be said frankly, though, that we did not initially fully anticipate the traumatic reaction of the West Berliners, in particular, and of Germans, in general, to the sudden building of the wall through their beloved capital. It was immediate and overwhelming; and the first and essential problem was clearly one of how to reassure and calm the Germans. The problem was discussed not only in the task force but also in the White House, particularly in the light of an appeal from Berlin Mayor Willy Brandt for help in restoring morale. The President made two decisions. The first was to send Vice President Lyndon B. Johnson to Bonn and Berlin, accompanied by General Lucius Clay, former Commandant in Berlin during the airlift days. Arriving in Berlin on Saturday, August 19, Vice President Johnson pulled out all the stops and made some of his more inspired speeches. The Berliners went wild with enthusiasm. Their beleaguered city had not been forgotten. The second Presidential decision was to reinforce the U.S. garrison by an additional battalion which would proceed there in convoy across the autobahn. The battalion set out immediately and reached Berlin without serious Soviet interference on Sunday afternoon, to be met by Mayor Brandt together with Vice President Johnson and General Clay. Again there was great joy, and scenes reminiscent of the liberation of Paris.

A few weeks later the President asked General Clay to return to Berlin as his personal representative, with the rank of Ambassador, in order to provide continuing reassurance to the population of the city and of West Germany. This was an unorthodox appointment, which presented its difficulties for the Berlin Task Force, for the Ambassador in Bonn and for our regular military commandant in Berlin. It also caused some occasional uneasiness to the President himself, since General Clay had a tendency toward taking rather violent initiatives, while the President's basic purpose had been to build up a position of strength from which we could negotiate. One of these initiatives, arising out of East German interference with the movement of American officials into and through East Berlin, brought American and Soviet tanks into direct confrontation at the Berlin wall.

Meanwhile, Khrushchev continued to boast and threaten. One of his many speeches contained an implied threat to air access. President Kennedy warned him publicly that "Any interference with free access to Berlin would be an act of aggression." Khrushchev's next move was to resume nuclear testing, thus implying a risk of nuclear confrontation. Kennedy responded in early September by announcing that he had authorized resumption of underground testing, and the Secretary of Defense announced a few days later that we were deploying forty thousand more troops to Europe. These moves and countermoves provided the basis for a quick diplomatic exchange with Moscow and an announcement by the President on September 13 that Secretary Rusk was prepared to discuss the Berlin situation with Soviet Foreign Minister Gromyko at the forthcoming session of the United Nations General Assembly in New York. On the following day the Soviet Foreign Ministry confirmed the arrangement. These were bilateral talks, since we had at this stage developed some difficulties within the Western alliance. President de Gaulle had flatly refused to participate in any discussions, and the Germans were showing both public and private uneasiness about possible concessions to the Soviets. The talks between the American and Soviet delegations in New York, in fact, solved nothing; neither did Gromyko's subsequent conversation with President Kennedy. However, Khrushchev did publicly lift his December 31 deadline after these exchanges.

Anxious to find means to keep the dialogue going, President Kennedy seized upon one of the many ideas produced in the Berlin Task Force which had caught his fancy. It was a project to place the communications between West Germany and West Berlin, both on the surface and in the air, under an International Access Authority. He tried this out first on Alexei Adzhubei, Khrushchev's son-in-law, toward the end of November, 1961, when Adzhubei came to Washington and interviewed the President, acting ostensibly in his capacity as editor of the Soviet government newspaper Izvestiya. Despite negative public reactions from Khrushchev and his East German puppet, Walter Ulbricht, and despite continuing difficulties with our French and German allies, the President directed us to have Ambassador Llewellyn Thompson follow up on the proposal in discussions with Soviet Foreign Minister Gromyko in Moscow early in 1962. Thompson did so with the usual lack of result.

The fact that the International Access Authority idea appeared so reasonable and attractive to an uneasy world public opinion seemed to annoy Khrushchev, and he decided to provide a practical demonstration of the fragility of the Allied position on access to Berlin, even through the air corridors. So in February, 1962, the Soviet authorities in East Germany informed us that the Soviet Air Force intended on given dates to use the air space over East Germany for maneuvers and warned that Allied aircraft should keep out of the way. Since the air lanes were the really vital life lines to Berlin, as had been demonstrated during the blockade in 1948, we were not about to comply. A real game of "chicken" ensued. We requested our civilian airlines, mostly manned by Air Force Reserve pilots, to continue flying normal schedules, and we put Allied military aircraft through the corridors. The Soviet Air Force harassed the flights but were at some pains to avoid collisions or other serious incidents.

While all of this was going on, I accompanied Secretary Rusk, in March, 1962, to a disarmament conference in Geneva. There, on the side, we were able to have many talks on Germany and Berlin with Foreign Minister Gromyko and the principal Soviet expert on German affairs, Deputy Foreign Minister Vladimir Semenov. We of course protested the Soviet actions in the air corridors and rehashed the standard positions on both sides. However, we had worked out new proposals, which had been dubbed a *modus vivendi*—"a means of living." These proposals included several items in which Khrushchev had expressed an interest, including an agreement which would ensure against acquisition of nuclear weapons by Germany, an exchange of nonaggression declarations between NATO and the Warsaw Pact, and the formation of East-West German Committees. All of this would operate under the umbrella of a permanent conference of deputy foreign ministers of the United States, France, Britain and the Soviet Union. Gromyko did not accept this plan; neither did he reject it. He came back with a few variants, and the meetings ended inconclusively.

After our return to Washington, Secretary Rusk and I resumed the talks with Soviet Ambassador Anatoly Dobrynin and continued them through the end of May. By now we were simply repeating the same old phonograph records to each other. The Soviet objective remained just one thing—the elimination of the Allied presence and protection from West Berlin. By the end of April the Secretary felt obliged to say publicly, as he had been saying privately, that the Allied garrisons were simply not negotiable. The Soviet Party newspaper *Pravda* asked: "Then what is there to be negotiated?"

Tensions mounted in Berlin as the anniversary of the "wall" approached. Emotions were aroused as the East German police shot and killed one refugee after another trying to escape across the wall. Soviet fighters buzzed Allied civil aircraft in the air corridors. The West Berliners stoned buses carrying Soviet troops.

While the pot was boiling on this burner—Berlin—another pot was starting to boil on another burner—Cuba. Following President Kennedy's call-up of 150,000 reservists and a visit to Moscow by Cuban Defense Minister Che Guevara, Tass, on September 12, 1962, distributed an "authorized" Soviet Government statement devoted mainly to Cuba. It was an almost hysterical diatribe against alleged American provocations throughout the world, but particularly toward Cuba and Cuban-Soviet relations. After boasting of the Soviet Union's overwhelming nuclear-missile prowess "from its own territory," the statement admitted that the Soviet Union was sending military aid and technicians to Cuba, but said these were "exclusively for defensive purposes." Rather surprisingly, the long document ended with a reference to Germany and suggested that negotiations on this subject could be put on ice until after the upcoming American mid-term elections. Could this be Soviet recognition that our firm stand had paid off and that Moscow did not want to push matters to a showdown? I did not know at this point that our intelligence had uncovered the Soviet effort to alter the strategic balance by secretly implanting missiles in Cuba. However, that is another story as well as being the final act in the Berlin crisis, and I will go into it in the next chapter.

There were further flare-ups and adjustments over the next couple of years, but it is clear in retrospect that with the withdrawal of the Soviet missiles from Cuba the battle for West Berlin had essentially been won. President Kennedy paid an official visit to the Federal Republic in June, 1963, and I went out from Moscow to confer with him there. It was on this occasion that he flew into Berlin and further bolstered the West Berliners' morale with his famous statement: "Ich bin ein Berliner!—I am a Berliner!" In October of that year a series of holdups of American convoys on the autobahn brought me racing back to Moscow from a vacation in southern England. While these were serious incidents, the final result was that an improved understanding on rules and procedures for traffic on the autobahn was worked out between the Western and Soviet authorities in Berlin. The finis was written on June 12, 1964, when the Soviet Union and the German Democratic Republic signed a Treaty of Friendship, Mutual Assistance and Cooperation in Moscow. Thus Khrushchev finally had a "treaty" of sorts, but it was in a form that clearly indicated Soviet acceptance of the *status quo*. The only reference to Berlin was a brief passage which declared that "The high contracting parties will regard West Berlin as an independent political entity."

One can feel relieved about the restoration and maintenance of the *status quo*—it is certainly better than war. But even the maintenance of the *status quo* requires vigilance and continued effort. West Berlin remains a beleaguered city, subjected to constant threats and pressures, hard to maintain economically, with fragile communications with the West on which it depends for life. Western statesmen must regularly demonstrate our tenacity of purpose in defending this vulnerable but vital interest. President Nixon did so during his first official journey to Europe early in 1969. Visiting West Berlin on February 27, he hailed the steadfast "determination of the free people of Berlin to remain free" as a vital force in itself, and again pledged "that we, the people of the United States, stand with you in the defense of freedom."

But the problem of Germany is not solved, nor is a permanent solution presently foreseeable. The Communist regime in East Germany has greatly strengthened its political control and its economy in the years since the economic hemorrhage was stemmed by the building of the wall through Berlin in 1961. Though still far behind the Federal Republic, the G.D.R. has become the world's tenth industrial power. Its production and pool of scientific talent and labor skills have become an important adjunct to the Soviet economy. Even more than Czechoslovakia, the German Democratic Republic is the keystone to the arch of Soviet control in Eastern Europe. At a gathering of the Communist clan in East Berlin on October 6, 1969, the twentieth anniversary of the G.D.R.'s creation, Soviet Party Secretary Brezhnev declared that "Socialism has triumphed irrevocably in your land. . . . Those who might contemplate testing the . . . inviolability of the frontiers of our states . . . will meet a crushing rebuff from the entire might of the Soviet Union, of the entire socialist community." In recent years the Soviet Union and the G.D.R. itself have tried by every possible device to secure legitimacy, legal acceptance of "the fact of the existence of two German states." This is the not-so-hidden factor, for example, in such Soviet projects as its campaign for a European Security Conference; as G.D.R. President and Party Chief Ulbricht revealed at the same anniversary celebrations: "The G.D.R. will participate with equal rights and with the same status as all other European states, in every way."

The aspiration of the German people on both sides of the present dividing line for reunification of the country remains strong. However, with the death of former Chancellor Adenauer, and simply with the passage of time, German leaders have shown an increased willingness to live with the division, and even to accept increased contacts with East Germany. This is particularly true of the Social Democratic Party, headed by former Berlin Mayor and present Federal Chancellor Willy Brandt. I believe we Americans can rely on our German allies to take a sensible lead in this direction. Their efforts may help to bring about some relaxation of tensions and to promote a peaceful evolution of the situation in Europe.

CHAPTER XIV

Cuba and the Soviet Problem in Latin America

Distances are rapidly shrinking in the modern world. A century ago a voyage to Russia consumed months. When my wife and I returned to the United States in 1966, by a combination of plane and ship, it took us seven days. Since the direct air link has been established under the terms of the Civil Air Agreement between the U.S. and U.S.S.R., we have gone back to visit Moscow in about ten hours. A missile can make the journey in about thirty minutes.

My fellow Floridians, who see the Cuban menace looming on the very edge of the horizon, are surprised when I say I was even closer to the problem in Moscow than in Miami. The Russians are fond of diplomatic formations, such as arrival and departure ceremonies for official visitors, Kremlin receptions and big National Holiday parties—all largely outmoded in the West—where diplomats are lined up in strict protocol order. As the Lord willed it, one Carlos Olivares Sánchez had arrived and presented his credentials as Ambassador of Cuba shortly before I presented mine as Ambassador of the United States. So for over four years this big, swarthy, nearsighted Cuban and I repeatedly stood side by side at such functions, each acutely aware of the other's presence but studiously avoiding conversation or even a direct exchange of glances. As he came along the line to greet the diplomats, Khrushchev loved to pause before this ill-assorted pair and quip: "Aha! Cuba and America! Why don't you two get together?" I usually responded with something to the effect that "We might if you would change your policy." My Cuban neighbor would crack a weak smile. He had the disadvantage of not knowing Russian.

The Cuban issue had the most profound—and in the end even contradictory—effect on United States relations with the Soviet Union. As I mentioned in the German context, Khrushchev had started to heat up the Cuban situation in 1962 as a kind of counterthreat to the United States in connection with the Berlin crisis. When as Ambassador I paid my first call on him early in October, Khrushchev had confirmed to me that he was suspending any action on Berlin until after the U.S. elections, and had then been at some pains to assure me that a fishing port the Soviets were building in Havana was just that and not something else. The real import of Khrushchev's tactics in that conversation became clear to me a few days later, on Sunday, October 21, when the embassy received an advance text of the speech which the President would deliver at 7 P.M. the following evening over American television, revealing the Soviet attempt to smuggle missiles into Cuba and demanding their withdrawal.

This was the opening of a tense and hectically busy week for us in the embassy, delivering and receiving, translating, encoding and dispatching a dozen major communications between the two capitals. We did not even have time to think about the fact—of which Secretary Rusk reminded me later—

that we were sitting in the middle of United States target No. 1. The whole process was complicated by the seven-hour time differential between Moscow and Washington. We were instructed to deliver the text of the President's forthcoming speech, together with a covering letter from him to Khrushchev, exactly one hour before the broadcast—but 6 P.M. October 22, Washington time, was 1 A.M. October 23, Moscow time. Some subtle advance negotiation was required to make sure that a responsible official would be on hand to receive the communication at that hour. Later exchanges were easier, as the Soviet Foreign Ministry geared itself up to deal with the crisis. Even so, the pace of events in the end outdistanced them.

The Soviet note of Friday, October 26, agreeing to withdraw the missiles, was brought to the embassy by an officer of the American section of the Foreign Ministry—an unprecedented procedure as we were usually called to the Ministry to receive such communications. He arrived somewhat breathless in the embassy's chancery at precisely 5 P.M. As he delivered the note, he apologized for the absence of the official seal on its final page, saying that he had not had time to go by the Ministry to have the seal affixed. It was this note which, in contrast to the usual meticulous typing of Soviet diplomatic notes, contained corrections of typographical errors in the same violet ink and same handwriting as its signature: N. Khrushchev.

We had three demonstrations against the embassy during that week—or, more correctly perhaps, two and one-half demonstrations. The third one, organized for that fateful Friday, October 26, was called off just as it was about to start, and the crowd quickly dissipated so the Khrushchev note could be delivered to us precisely at 5 P.M.

I had previously made appointments to pay my first calls on a number of Soviet ministers during the week of the crisis. I decided that I would keep these appointments, if the other side didn't cancel, but that, as the aggrieved party in the missile crisis, I would open up and express my regret that our conversation had to take place under such unhappy circumstances. Somewhat to my surprise, they all agreed about the difficulties of the situation, but said this was a matter between me and their political leaders which they hoped would be satisfactorily settled; they were then ready to talk about the special interest of their own departments.

When the Kremlin's decision to withdraw missiles and bombers became known, the sense of relief in Moscow was unmistakable. It was strikingly demonstrated over the weekend in the tumultuous applause given to the performances of the New York City Ballet—then playing in Moscow under the exchanges agreement—and at a reception given for the ballet on Monday, October 29, by the Soviet Minister of Culture, Mme. Yekaterina Furtseva. At the latter occasion she and I both received ovations from the assembled elite of Moscow with our little speeches about "wisdom prevailing" in Soviet-American relations.

I shall not go into detail about the long exchanges which took place during this crisis week. Most of the documents have been published and are readily available. At first Moscow inferentially denied that Soviet missiles had been sent to Cuba and angrily protested the United States blockade of the island and surveillance of Soviet shipping. After a long and rambling review of Soviet-American relations, including the Vienna summit conversations, the Friday letter finally admitted the fact. Khrushchev then went on to offer to cease shipments of offensive weapons to Cuba and to withdraw or destroy those already there, in return for the lifting of the blockade and a United States pledge not to invade Cuba. Before Washington could reply, on Saturday, October 27, a more formal communication from the Soviet Government added the further condition that American missiles should be simultaneously removed from Turkey. This new note was deliberately overlooked in the President's reply, which essentially accepted the offer in Khrushchev's letter of the twenty-sixth but carefully specified that our assurances against an invasion of Cuba would be given "upon the establishment of adequate arrangements through the United Nations to ensure the carrying out and continuation of these [Soviet] commitments." On the following day, October 28, Khrushchev confirmed that "the Soviet Government has given a new order to dismantle the arms . . . described as offensive, and to crate and return them to the Soviet Union."

Subsequently, Deputy Foreign Minister Vasili Kuznetsov was sent to New York to negotiate with American and United Nations representatives a more formal settlement, confirming the withdrawal and providing for on-the-site inspection in Cuba. At the same time no less a figure than Deputy Prime Minister and Politburo member Anastas Mikoyan was sent to Havana to deal with Fidel Castro. Mikoyan met a hostile reception and was unable to do anything with Castro, despite the fact that his devotion to duty was such that he remained there trying for over a month while his wife died and was buried in Moscow. Without Castro's cooperation, the New York negotiations petered out. We continued, and have since maintained, our own intelligence surveillance.

It was clear that Khrushchev had arranged to smuggle the missiles into Cuba as a means of altering the balance of power sufficiently to force the United States to accept a settlement of the German issue, that he had not consulted Castro when he felt obliged to withdraw them and that the episode had thus been extremely humiliating to Castro. There was also reason to believe that there had been something less than full consultation with Khrushchev's colleagues in the Soviet leadership and that there was some resentment in those quarters.

All in all, it seemed wise for the United States to play along with—or at least not publicly to challenge—Khrushchev's face-saving version of the confrontation, to the effect that his action had "protected Cuba" and "saved the peace." Indeed, the reaction to these momentous events produced the most significant and far-reaching thaw in U.S.-Soviet relations since the Cold War began—a thaw which was to last about two years and to be marked by the successful negotiation of the Nuclear Test Ban Treaty, the "hot line" agreement and the Consular Convention, as well as general expansion of technical and cultural exchanges and cooperation. I approach the subject of Cuba, therefore, with a sense of personal involvement.

It is now more than a decade since the triumph of Castro's revolution in Cuba. For the greater part of that time Cuba has been a member of the Communist camp. In terms of any ordinary balance sheet, those years and the expenditure they represent in Soviet treasure show up as a pretty bad investment. Cuba's limping economy is almost totally dependent on Soviet aid. Her military establishment, the largest in Latin America, is completely supplied from Soviet sources. Cuba's needs for oil and refined petroleum products must be supplied by tanker from the Black Sea.

This assistance has been costly for the Soviet Union. Even before the United States broke relations with Cuba on January 3, 1961, Castro had already completed arrangements with Moscow for considerable military and economic aid. By the end of 1965 the Soviet Union and other Communist countries had supplied Cuba with assistance in these two fields estimated at over $2 billion in value. Of this, nearly three-quarters were supplied by the Soviet Union. Since the spring of 1966 the U.S.S.R.'s role has become even stronger as a result of Castro's falling out with the Chinese Communists.

Despite his dependence on assistance from other Communist countries, Castro has picked quarrels not only with Communist China but with the Soviet Union itself. He has taken an extremist line on Vietnam by vociferously advocating intervention on the side of the North Vietnamese. He has promulgated a personal theory of revolution which is even more activist than that of the Communist Chinese, and which, not surprisingly, is wholly unacceptable to Moscow. He has carried on endless battles with the traditional parties and front organizations of Latin America which Moscow has so carefully nurtured over the years.

Under these circumstances, one might well ask: "Why, if Cuba has cost so much and Castro has been so ungrateful, does the Soviet Union put up with them—why doesn't it just cut its losses and get out?"

The answer to this question is not simple. It involves the complicated interplay between the Soviet Union's aspirations as a great power and its desire to preserve—or salvage—its credentials as leader of the world Communist movement. Contradictions between these two factors in the Soviet world outlook could be, and were successfully, avoided by Moscow as long as it enjoyed undisputed control over the ideology and doctrine of Communism. The solution then was an uncomplicated one— ideology was simply twisted as necessary to justify Soviet national interests. But the monolithic world Communist movement dominated by Moscow no longer exists, and Cuba, in its way, has contributed to the process of fragmentation.

The problem is that revolutions which succeed on their own without being primarily dependent on Soviet support also have a dynamism of their own. And Moscow, despite intensive efforts, has not been able to work out a satisfactory method of disciplining these movements and making them responsive to Moscow's will. The result has been to lessen the utility of ideology and to strengthen the inclination within the Kremlin to turn to more pragmatic approaches and solutions—approaches which in any event were more in line with the greater flexibility Moscow discovered it needed as it sought to adjust its policies to the postwar world.

Moscow has therefore found the Cuban relationship very uncomfortable. Irrespective of Castro's professed Communism, the Soviet Union would have leaped at the opportunity of establishing a foothold in Cuba, in line with its purely national interest in challenging United States influence in Latin America and undermining United States security. But Castro's Communism cannot be ignored, and the effect is to limit Soviet flexibility in an area where Soviet power must compete with the United States under difficult and trying circumstances. Moscow simply cannot afford to abandon a country like Cuba unless at the same time it is prepared to forgo its pretensions to leadership of the Communist camp. As was demonstrated in the case of Czechoslovakia, it is deeply ingrained in the Kremlin mentality that no extension of the Communist world must ever be lost. This is perhaps particularly true in the case of Cuba, which represents the only extension of Communism in a country not directly contiguous to that world or not achieved under the shadow of the Red Army. In a sense, it is the only development in fifty-odd years that has given any substance to claims that world revolution is inevitable.

It is thus not surprising that the Soviet-Cuban relationship has had many ups and downs over the years and has seriously interfered with the pursuit of Soviet objectives throughout Latin America. The Soviet Union has sought to expand the Soviet presence in the area by attempting to project an image of international respectability, an image of the Soviet Union as a great power possessing a well-developed industrial machine with advanced technology capable of accomplishing great feats in space, and willing—through the development of normal trade and cultural relations—to share these accomplishments with other nations. It seeks to prove the effectiveness of Communism as a political and economic formula in the eyes of the developing nations, or, as Khrushchev liked to say, "to demonstrate before the world the superiority of Communism over capitalism."

Yet initial Soviet success in Cuba came not as a result of any practical application of the Communist theory of revolution to the situation prevailing in Batista's Cuba, nor from the attraction of Soviet technology. The Communists who traveled to Havana in the train of Fidel Castro in January, 1959, had thrown in with the Twenty-sixth of July Movement at the last possible moment before its triumph. The leaders of the Cuban Communist Party probably hoped to profit, as did Khrushchev, from Castro's later profession of the faith, but they were hardly anticipating this development in January, 1959. If, in fact, Castro had been a Communist all along, the fact that this was kept secret was, in large measure, the reason for his success.

Nevertheless, in Cuba with its newly professed Communist faith the opportunistic Khrushchev saw a golden opportunity to plant a model "socialist" state at the very doorstep of the United States. He moved in hard. The Soviet press hailed Castro's revolution as the beginning of the end of Yankee imperialism in Latin America. Within a few months, in July, 1960, Tass was issuing an "authoritative" statement, proclaiming the unacceptability of the Monroe Doctrine and warning against United States intervention in Cuba. On its heels, Khrushchev wrote Castro pledging Soviet aid if Cuba was attacked. Later that year, on the occasion of the famous shoe-pounding session of the

United Nations General Assembly, the two men met. I was attending the session and shall never forget the spectacle of Khrushchev and Castro bear-hugging in public. Even then, contrary to established myth, Castro looked more like the bear than did the Russian.

Then, in January, 1961, came the change of administrations in Washington and, shortly afterward, the ill-fated Bay of Pigs invasion. I think it quite likely that Khrushchev had developed some serious illusions arising from President Kennedy's failure to use our armed strength in Cuba at that time and that these contributed to his decision to take a harsh line and try to browbeat this young man at Vienna when they met there in June. And Khrushchev did not seem to learn his lesson, even after he had been faced down by our forces on the autobahn, in the air lanes to Berlin and in the city itself. In trying to change the balance of power by surreptitiously introducing missiles into Cuba, he made another grave miscalculation of United States determination and fortitude. Happily we calculated correctly in that week of crisis, and the men in the Kremlin did not like what they saw over the brink of the nuclear abyss they had approached.

As a result of the missile crisis, the Soviets came to recognize that we were prepared to defend our vital interests, by nuclear means if necessary. With this came also some appreciation of the limits on Soviet ability to direct, or profit from, political change abroad. The Kremlin has apparently become increasingly doubtful that the readily foreseeable future will bring either Communist revolutions or upheavals in Latin America in which the Communists would be permitted to seize control.

This attitude was reinforced by the Dominican crisis, which made it clear that the United States would not sit back and risk a Communist takeover, even when the Communist element was relatively well disguised. Consequently, the Soviets have geared their policies toward the more limited goal of encouraging anti–United States sentiments and "independent" foreign policies on the part of Latin-American governments or serious contenders for power. They have therefore concentrated on state-to-state relations aimed primarily at establishing a Soviet "presence" in as many countries as possible. They see in this certain gains in international prestige, a chance to reason with likely antagonists in the United Nations, limited trade profits and a visible Soviet "availability" to ultranationalists seeking alternatives to close ties with the United States.

After the missile crisis Moscow made a strenuous effort to appease Castro and gain his support for the Moscow line in the raging Sino-Soviet conflict. He was brought to the Soviet Union for two long visits, in the spring of 1963 and again at the beginning of 1964, when Khrushchev gave his undivided attention for days on end to his tropical guest. The Soviets upped their aid and committed themselves to a long-term agreement to buy Cuban sugar. During the January, 1964, visit Khrushchev even persuaded Castro to condemn "splitters"—that is, the Chinese—in the world Communist movement.

In fact, however, Castro's original and consistent line was closer to that of Mao Tse-tung than to that of the Kremlin. As early as February, 1962, in the so-called Declaration of Havana, Castro had proclaimed that "the duty of every revolutionary is to make revolution." While he wavered somewhat under Soviet blandishments, this wavering was obviously tactical and due mainly to his preoccupation with his own crushing economic and political problems. His propaganda continued to criticize those leftists who did nothing to precipitate revolutionary upheaval—namely, the traditional Communist Party leaders of the Western Hemisphere. The Soviet Union sought to moderate the differences between Castro and the other Latin-American Communists, and its efforts seemed to bear fruit in the Havana Conference of Latin American Communist Parties in November, 1964. The main stress of the final communiqué of the conference was on the right of each party individually to determine its own correct line and to implement it without competition from externally supported splinter groups, in which Castro found his chief supporters, and an injunction in the communiqué against factional activity was designed to restrain Castro from creating or supporting other splinter groups.

During 1965 the Soviets pushed hard for the creation of

"broad united fronts." They argued that Castro had a better chance of breaking out of his Latin-American isolation by making common cause with non-Communists against Yankee imperialism than by scaring the reformist elements with insurgency and Castroite slogans. Castro was unresponsive, and the united fronts, in fact, made little headway, with the one exception of Chile, where an historical tradition of such activities actually predated World War II. Moreover, American intervention in the Dominican crisis prevented a possible takeover by the Castro-supported Communists from the democratic front led by Juan Bosch; and military coups in Argentina and Brazil terminated, at least temporarily, opportunities for action.

Despite these setbacks, the Soviet leadership apparently approached the January, 1966, Tricontinental Solidarity Conference in Havana with the expectation that their popular-front doctrine would remain intact. Judging from the enthusiasm for a tricontinental meeting demonstrated by the Soviets at the Afro-Asian People's Solidarity Conference held in Ghana in May, 1965, there seems little doubt that they felt assured Castro would invite only Moscow-line Communists from Latin America to the Havana Conference. The Chinese, at the same time, by their coldness to Castro's proposal for the conference, made it clear that they also anticipated Soviet domination of the Latin-American delegations and a repetition of the anti-Chinese performance of the 1964 conference.

Moscow, however, underestimated the wiliness of the Cuban leader. Whether by plan or as a result of repeated Chinese accusations that he was selling out to Soviet "revisionism," the Latin-American delegations Castro invited to the conference were far from a homogeneous group. Mixed in with the old time Moscow-liners were assorted Trotskyites, Castroites and even representatives of such pro-Chinese groups as the Dominican Popular Movement. To avoid any Moscow charges of disloyalty, Castro went out of his way to denounce Trotskyites and others who had criticized Cuban and Russian inaction during the Dominican crisis. But he also had caustic words for revolutionary groups which spend their time theorizing instead of acting. While the conference did not commit Moscow's followers in Latin America to an explicitly adventurous course, the extremist nature of the resolutions adopted there did place new obstacles in the way of alliances between Communists and non-Communists against United States imperialism. The Tricontinental Conference thus marked a new and ultramilitant tack on Castro's part. With the conference's blessing, he proceeded to establish in Havana the headquarters of the Latin-American Solidarity Organization and the Afro–Asian–Latin-American People's Solidarity Organization. Then, in defiance of Moscow and the existing Communist parties of Latin America, Castro sought to assume the leading ideological and political role of the Communist movements in the Afro–Asian–Latin-American arena by capturing this ideological machinery created for penetration of the uncommitted world.

As I have already noted in another context, the conference and Castro's subsequent activities so alarmed the Latin-American governments that they called on Moscow to explain, and Soviet ambassadors and other spokesmen were forced to fall back on the lame story that the Soviet representation at the conference did not speak for the Soviet Government.

It appeared, in fact, that the Soviets and their more trustworthy Latin-American followers wanted to forget the Tricontinental meeting as rapidly as possible. Soviet media gave the proceedings minimal attention and dropped the subject as soon as they ended. Then in March–April, 1966, at the Twenty-third Congress of the Soviet Communist Party in Moscow, the Soviet and Latin-American Communist leaders, with the exception of the Cubans, ignored the Tricontinental Conference and its themes.

The public stance of the Soviets, plus their efforts to repair their fences through the private diplomatic disclaimers, produced a major explosion from Castro. In a statement denouncing the Latin-American signatories of a letter addressed to U Thant protesting the conference, he restated his conviction of "the right of the peoples to sweep out those governments, which are traitors and serve foreign interests." Castro followed up at the Soviet Party Congress through his delegate, Armando Hart, with demands for much more effective joint action against

American aggression in Vietnam. Hart also denounced popular-front tactics in Latin America as "ideas, tactics and methods arising from the situations of twenty years ago [which] have become obsolete." Although none of this was very pleasing to the Soviets, they apparently did not dare to try to pull Castro back into line by restricting economic aid during Cuba's severe economic crisis of 1966.

Moscow bided its time for well over a year, preoccupied with domestic problems and developments in its conflict with Peking. On March 9, 1967, however, an extensive statement on the Latin-American revolutionary situation appeared in *Pravda*, which took a line in direct opposition to what Castro had been saying since the Tricontinental Conference. The article cited as examples of those parties taking the correct path the very parties furthest removed from guerrilla tactics, the Argentinean and the Chilean, and noted with approval their inclusion of all patriotic and anti-imperialist forces—including even portions of the bourgeoisie—in a broad democratic and anti-imperialist front. Castro replied to this article on March 13 in a speech which contained pointed criticism of Moscow's interest in developing better state-to-state relations in Latin America. Subsequently, on April 17, the Cuban press reproduced a tract on guerrilla warfare, allegedly written by Che Guevara, which was followed two days later by a Castro speech eulogizing the absent guerrilla leader. Thus Castro was back in the "action" camp of Guevara and firmly opposed to the ideological position of the Soviet Union in Latin America.

The dispute between Castro and the Soviet Union has also been carried on at the theoretical level. Castro, and his French-born theoretician Régis Debray, sought to undermine the theoretical foundations of the present Communist movement in Latin America by preaching a doctrine of revolutionary voluntarism. This doctrine gives primacy to an action-oriented program of revolutionary struggle and holds that true Marxist parties will grow out of the development of the guerrilla movement. In Castro's words: "Revolutionaries who have revolutionary spirit will end up Marxists," and "Practice often comes first, and then theory." This doctrine obviously rejects the credentials of those Communist parties which are not prepared to engage in revolutionary activity.

A Soviet response to this theoretical challenge came in the form of a major article in the April, 1967, issue of the *World Marxist Review* entitled "The World-Historical Significance of Lenin's April Theses." The major inference which the article sought to draw from the "April Theses" was that Lenin placed great emphasis on the organization of political institutions as a means of bringing about a successful revolution. It explained that Lenin opposed "playing at seizing power" before conditions are ripe for such a move. Today, it continued, it is necessary "for the working people to hold strong positions in the political life of their nations, formalized in political institutions." While there was no name-calling, the article was clearly intended to assert the primacy of the existing Communist parties in Latin America and to lecture Castroites on the necessity for long, arduous political and organizational work to precede revolutionary activity. Such activity, moreover, must be undertaken by Communist parties which have a solid understanding of the Marxist-Leninist dialectic, and not by groups which hope to acquire their theory as they fight. It also emphasized the achievement of power through electoral alliances and other forms of united-front activity in direct contradiction to Castro's program. The article did, however, make a gesture toward bridging the tactical gap between Moscow and Havana by stating that "in some of the Latin American countries . . . both the need and the possibility to find a revolutionary way out of those crises can be sensed."

Having set out that theoretical position, the Soviets then muted the polemics on their side and seemed anxious to find whether it would be possible to ease their dispute with Castro. When Cuban subversives were seized on the Venezuelan coast on May 8, 1967, Soviet media downplayed direct references to Cuba and, instead, launched a campaign charging that the United States, with the aid of Venezuela and other Latin-American countries, was organizing a new provocation against Cuba.

Moscow's overtures to ease the situation did not receive a corresponding response from Castro. When Soviet Prime Minister Kosygin visited Havana at the end of June, following his participation in the United Nations session on the Mideast and his talks with President Johnson at Glassboro, he was given a markedly cool reception. A month later, on the July 26 anniversary, Castro warned his followers not to count on outside help in the event of a clash with the United States, an indication that Kosygin may have done a little plain speaking himself. Differences were further aggravated during the August meeting in Havana of the Organization of Latin-American Solidarity (OLAS). A full split developed between the Soviet-oriented Latin-American Communists and the Castro-style revolutionaries, with the latter predominating. In the main, the resolutions followed the Castro-Debray line. One commission of the conference actually passed a resolution condemning the Soviet Union for dealing with dictatorships and reactionary governments in Latin America. It seems clear that only some quick work on the Soviet side prevented its adoption by the plenum of the conference.

Then, in October, 1967, came the Castroite debacle in Bolivia. Not only was Régis Debray arrested, but Che Guevara and several other Cubans, along with a number of Bolivian guerrillas, were killed. Moscow did not publicly gloat or say "We told you so," though the Kremlin leaders probably felt that way. Soviet press coverage was minimal, and Soviet expressions of regret at the loss of Che Guevara and his comrades were decidedly perfunctory. But Castro was being much less restrained toward the Soviets than they were toward him. At about this time he was receiving a friendly interviewer, Herbert Matthews, the former *New York Times* correspondent who had written favorably about him a decade before. In their talk Castro presumptuously charged the Kremlin with heresy. "True Marxism-Leninism," he said, "is not Communism as it is practiced in Russia, Eastern Europe or China." In this context, he talked with disdain about the forthcoming International Preparatory Conference which Moscow was organizing at Budapest in its efforts to restore Communist unity under its leadership. He went on to complain to Matthews against Soviet diplomatic and trade relations with Latin America's "oligarchic regimes," saying that the Kremlin "should not be helping governments that are trying to destroy us."

A few weeks later, on November 6, the Cuban Ambassador to the Soviet Union failed to show up at a Kremlin reception given for the heads of all diplomatic missions in Moscow as part of the Soviet celebration of the Fiftieth Anniversary of the Bolshevik Revolution. He thus associated himself with the Communist Chinese representative, who was the only other foreign diplomat—Communist or capitalist—to boycott the reception. Cuban publicity on the anniversary focused on the Bolshevik takeover in 1917 and on the figure of Lenin, with practically no mention of the present Soviet leadership or of the celebrations in Moscow. In turn, the Soviet leadership's telegram of greetings on the ninth anniversary of Castro's seizure of power in Cuba on January 2, 1968, reflected the atmosphere of the conflict and contained an ominous note. Whereas past messages had attributed Cuban "achievements" to the leadership of Castro and the Cuban Communist Party, and had noted "with great satisfaction" the development of Soviet-Cuban relations, the latest telegram did not refer to Castro and the Cuban Party, except in the address, and was very reserved on the question of bilateral relations. Even more interesting was the telegram's failure to reaffirm the Soviet Union's policy of giving "all kinds of assistance" to the Cuban economy, which past messages had consistently done.

Castro's own speech on this ninth anniversary was free of polemics and said nothing of Cuban-Soviet differences. He was even careful to absolve Moscow from responsibility for the recent imposition of gasoline rationing and for the shortage of other commodities in the Cuban economy. Two days later, however, on January 4, while speaking to the huge Cultural Congress of five hundred delegates and observers from some seventy countries, which he had organized in Havana, Castro showed that he continued to be rebellious. In a transparent thrust at the Soviet Union he declared that "At times we have observed alleged vanguards ending up far in the rear in the struggle against imperialism"—meaning, of course, against the United States.

We now know that for over a year Castro's undercover agents had been building up a case against the old-line Moscow puppet Aníbal Escalante and thirty-odd other leading pro-Moscow Communists as "traitors" to the Cuban revolution. They were accused of spreading pro-Soviet and anti-Castro propaganda and literature, of passing secret and tendentious information to Moscow and of trying to organize pressures against Castro to make him toe the Moscow Party line. Members of the Soviet Embassy staff in Havana were charged with having been co-conspirators. After a secret trial at the beginning of February, 1968, Escalante was given a fifteen-year prison sentence, while sixteen of his collaborators received sentences of eight to ten years each. Raúl Castro's report on the trials in effect said that it was treason for Cuban Communist Party members to hold pro-Soviet views. Yet Moscow remained almost completely silent in the face of this defiant affront—reporting briefly only the fact of the sentences without revealing the substance of the charges.

While all this was going on around the turn of the year, unusually protracted negotiations were taking place in Moscow for the annual renewal of the trade and aid agreement between the two countries. Many observers expected that Moscow would try to use the leverage of its trade and aid programs with Cuba to bring Castro to heel. Indeed, the protracted nature of the negotiations may indicate that there was a certain amount of plain talk, possibly some threats and certainly some deliberate delay on the Soviet side. In the end, however, despite all the difficulties in the relationship, the new agreement came out—at least on paper—at about the level of previous years. Announcing the conclusion of the negotiations on March 22, 1968, Tass said that the new trade agreement, concluded within a framework of the Six-Year Soviet-Cuban Trade Agreement covering 1965 through 1970, provided for trade between the two countries in 1968 valued at 875 million rubles, or 10 percent above the levels of trade in 1967. At the same time, according to the Tass announcement, the Soviet side extended a new credit to Cuba of 295 million rubles. This is the equivalent of $335 million, corresponding roughly to our estimates of previous credits over the years running at a rate of about $1 million a day.

Cuban-Soviet economic relations are not only a substantial burden for Moscow, but have given the Soviet leaders some specific headaches. I remember a few years ago, when some members of our embassy staff were traveling deep in Siberia, they went to a local tobacco kiosk and asked for cigars. The kiosk operator leaped at them, pulled out a dozen boxes of the finest Havana cigars and begged them to buy the whole lot. This was his assigned quota, he explained, but he had not been able to sell them. His Russian customers smoked only cigarettes. The Soviet position in the world sugar market has also been affected. At the end of April, 1968, the United Nations organized a conference in Geneva to renew the International Sugar Agreement. Unexpectedly, the Soviet delegate proposed that in the new international agreement the U.S.S.R. should be regarded as an importer of sugar. He pointed out that the Soviet Union, traditionally an exporter of the commodity, had become a major importer during the past seven years, in some years importing nearly four million tons. He explained that the Soviet Union buys great quantities of sugar on the world market and thus helps to ensure the stability of the world sugar market.

As the mounting tensions in Soviet-Cuban relations approached a critical point, there was a change in the ambassadorial guard in both Moscow and Havana. The new Cuban Ambassador to the Soviet Union, appointed in September, 1967, is Raúl García Peláez, a lawyer. He was an original July 26-er and is a member of the Central Committee of the Cuban Communist Party. This represented an upgrading of the Moscow post, particularly on the Party side. The Soviets also upgraded their representation in Havana, but on the professional side. Their new Ambassador, Alexander Alexeyevich Soldatov, appointed early in 1968, is one of Moscow's top career diplomats. After some years of service as Deputy Soviet Representative to the United Nations, he was for six years Soviet Ambassador to Great Britain and for the previous two years a Deputy Minister of Foreign Affairs. His appointment to Cuba at this difficult stage indicated that the Soviet side, at least, intended to emphasize state-to-state relationships, rather than Party ties, and to assure a tighter administration of Soviet trade and aid programs.

The change of ambassadors may have been a contributing factor, but other considerations are probably more important in explaining the greater restraint on both sides and the distinct easing of the tension in Soviet-Cuban relations since early 1968. Castro was obviously disheartened by the failure of the subversive effort in Bolivia—with the imprisonment of Régis Debray and the death of Che Guevara in that country—and by other setbacks to Cuban-supported subversion elsewhere in Latin America. The complete lack of local popular support for these subversive expeditions could not fail to give him some sobering second thoughts. He must have been impressed, too, by the increasing effectiveness of the armed forces in such countries as Bolivia, Guatemala, Venezuela and Colombia in dealing with guerrilla warfare, a capability acquired in substantial measure through training in counterinsurgency schools conducted by United States military personnel with experience in Vietnam. Castro has tried to establish a cult of the dead Che Guevara as an inspiration to revolutionary activism. He also presumably continues to operate his subversive training centers for Latin Americans on the island, though these are probably today receiving relatively little technical or financial support from the Soviet Union or other Communist countries. However, there have been no new major Cuban efforts to spark revolutionary activity in the other Latin-American countries, and we hear less reference to Che Guevara's call for the creation of "two, three, many Vietnams" in this hemisphere.

Perhaps even more important than his reversals in trying to promote revolution abroad has been Castro's failure to solve his mounting economic and social problems at home. He has been obliged to abandon many of his grandiose schemes for industrial development and to turn back to Cuba's basic natural resource—agriculture and particularly sugar. In 1967 and 1968 sugar production was barely half of Castro's proclaimed and boasted target of ten million tons per annum. In his speech on the tenth anniversary of his takeover in Havana on January 2, 1969, Castro admitted this, as well as a drop in labor productivity generally, criticized the "total inexperience and ignorance" of his government officials and called for a year of "decisive effort" in agriculture. And as an anniversary present to the Cuban people, he followed his previous year's announcement of the rationing of gas and oil with an announcement of sugar rationing in Cuba itself. In a speech on March 13, at the University of Havana, he went even further in discussing his domestic problems, which he admitted included juvenile delinquency, increasing crime and truancy and persistent and apparently growing illiteracy.

In the circumstances, Castro's dependency on Moscow is enhanced. Castro showed his awareness of this in his tenth-anniversary speech, in which he hailed Cuba's "solidarity with the Soviet Union." After admitting that "at times we have had differences of opinion with the Soviet Union and have said so promptly and honestly," Castro went on: "but they have continued their aid during past bad years with gifts of armament and food and continued remittances even when we had poor sugar harvests and were unable to deliver as promised."

However, Castro's really handsome gift to Moscow had been delivered earlier in the form of a speech by the Cuban Premier on August 23, 1968, supporting the Soviet invasion and occupation of Czechoslovakia. While Moscow undoubtedly expected that the smaller and dependent Communist parties in Latin America would stay in line, this endorsement of the action by Castro must have been a hoped-for but not really expected dividend. And they must have welcomed it doubly—not only because they wanted all the support they could get for their brutal action in Czechoslovakia but because Castro's acceptance of "the necessity" of great-power intervention in a smaller country could not fail to spread disillusionment and discredit the Cuban leader among his extremist followers in Latin America and thus make easier the pursuance of Moscow's own softer line in this hemisphere. The only real reason that Castro gave for his statement of support was the assertion that he was "convinced that the Czechoslovak regime was heading toward capitalism."

If the word "Communism" were substituted for "capitalism," then Castro's sentence would read like justification for United States interventions in Guatemala in 1954, in Cuba, his own country, in 1961 and in the Dominican Republic in 1965—though I would suppose that Castro did not have such an interpretation in mind. What he did have in mind was more likely his domestic economic and social problems and the possibility that his failures might generate opposition inside Cuba itself, for he went on in his long speech to make it clear that there would be no political or economic liberalization in Cuba, as there had been in Czechoslovakia, and that sympathy for the Czechoslovaks reflected an "inadmissible romantic and idealistic attitude." But Castro also seemed to have an even broader purpose in view. He quoted the Tass statement issued at the time of the invasion of Czechoslovakia, declaring that the Communist countries "will never permit anyone to tear away even one link of the community of socialist states." He then asked rhetorically whether that statement included Cuba and went on more specifically: "Will they send the divisions of the Warsaw Pact to Cuba if the Yankee imperialists attack our country, or even in the case of the threat of the Yankee imperialist attack on our country, if our country requested?" Continuing, he declared: "We, as revolutionaries . . . do have the right to demand that they adopt a consistent position with regard to all the other questions that affect the world revolutionary movement."

Whatever the mix of reasons, Cuban attacks on Soviet policies of state-to-state relations in Latin America and of nonviolent tactics at this stage have been muted. Castro has also noticeably failed to assert the leadership he so boldly assumed at the Tricontinental Conference in Havana in January, 1966, in taking over the Afro–Asian–Latin-American People's Solidarity Organization and the Latin-American Solidarity Organization and establishing a headquarters for both of them in Havana. Relatively little has been heard of the activities of either of these Havana-based organizations for some time. In a speech to Cuban workers on July 14, 1969, Castro even seemed to be saying that he had shelved his program of active subversion and the promotion of violent revolution in other Latin-American countries. "We are not impatient, we are not in a hurry," he said. "We will wait while, one by one, they break with the past, while, one by one, they develop their revolutions. . . . How long will we wait?" Castro asked—then answered: "For as long as is necessary—ten, twenty, thirty years if necessary— though nobody thinks even remotely it will take that long."

On its side, Moscow has shown a substantial measure of reciprocity. The negotiations for the trade and aid agreement for 1969 took about half the time of those during the tense year of 1968. The accord was signed on February 7, 1969, and appears to provide for levels of trade and aid at least equal to previous years. The Soviet leaders' telegram of congratulations on the tenth anniversary, while not really effusive about Castro personally, was considerably warmer than in 1968. A large mass meeting was organized in Moscow to celebrate the occasion, and separate governmental, Party and "social" delegations—all headed by senior Soviet officials—were sent to Havana to participate in the celebrations there. During his stay in the Cuban capital, the head of the government delegation, Deputy Prime Minister V. N. Novikov, signed an additional technical aid agreement under which Moscow undertook to provide assistance to Cuba in the fields of television, land irrigation and reclamation and also in the operation of a nuclear reactor provided to the Cuban Academy of Arts and Sciences. In July, 1969, a seven-ship task force of the Soviet Northern Fleet sailed ostentatiously down the Atlantic Coast of the United States to pay a week's "friendship" visit to Cuba—"an historic event in the relations of the two countries," in the words of Havana Radio.

It is not clear whether Castro will, in fact, modify his violent revolutionary line or whether his recent quiescence has been merely tactical in nature. Despite his previous expression of contempt for the preparatory meetings in Budapest, he sent an "observer" delegation to the International Conference of Communist Parties in Moscow in June, 1969. Moscow was obviously pleased, though the Cuban delegates played no significant role and did not sign the "Principal Document."

It is clear that Moscow has not altered its line. The Soviet conception of the proper revolutionary tactics for the Western Hemisphere was reaffirmed in a major article in *Pravda* on March 19, 1968, by Dr. Viktor Volsky, Director of the Latin

American Institute of the Soviet Academy of Sciences, entitled "Latin America: A New Stage in the People's Struggle." Then the May issue of the authoritative Party magazine *Kommunist* reminded Castro in passing that he had been able to choose the Communist course "only because of the existence of the Soviet Union." Even after Castro's support of the invasion of Czechoslovakia, *Pravda* on November 20, 1968, carried an over-all review of the Communist movement in the Western Hemisphere stressing the correctness of the course of the old-line Moscow-oriented Communist parties, again praising in particular the very parties which Castro had earlier so vehemently condemned. The article specifically attacked "the ultraleftist concepts . . . [which] ignore the leading role of the working class in the national liberation struggle, reject the worker-peasant alliance, deny the Party's role as the revolutionary vanguard and . . . insist on the violent armed road to winning power."

Pravda noted that the defeat of the Venezuelan partisan movement after five years of armed struggle had compelled the Venezuelan Party to follow new tactics and decide to participate in the elections in December, 1968, with the result that the Party's "prestige is growing in the trade unions and among the peasantry and students." It also noted that the Bolivian Communist Party had had to reconsider its course after "analyzing the events that occurred in that country between March and October, 1967." At the time of the national elections in Chile in March, 1969, the entire Soviet press praised the conservative Chilean Communist Party as "a major, influential political force in the country," with great influence in the trade-union movement and in the student and youth movements. The Party's gains in the elections (from eighteen to twenty-four deputies) were hailed, and its tactics of calling for "unity of popular forces" were approved. These Soviet pronouncements were slightly less polemical in tone, but they were certainly no softer in substance than the comparable articles in *Pravda* and *Kommunist* in 1967 which had provoked Castro into sharp rebuttals. But this time he remained quiet.

Meanwhile, Moscow has continued to move ahead on the state-to-state or governmental-relations level, adding two Latin-

American countries, Colombia and Peru, to those with which it maintains diplomatic relations and concluding trade agreements with a half-dozen others. The opportunism of Soviet policies and tactics toward Latin America was strikingly illustrated by the case of Peru. When the Peruvian armed forces overthrew constitutionally elected President Fernando Belaúnde Terry in October, 1968, the Soviet press and propaganda media called it "a dirty affair." They linked the coup in Peru with other military takeovers in Latin America, which they represented as parts of a plan encouraged, if not actually engineered, in the Pentagon to establish dictatorships of military "gorillas" which would suppress "popular" movements in the hemisphere.

However, after the new military government confiscated the American-owned International Petroleum Company on October 26 and in general took an anti-Yankee stance, the Soviet press fell silent while the Kremlin reconsidered. Then the diplomats and the trade people were put to work. At the beginning of February, 1969, diplomatic relations were established between Moscow and Lima, and by the end of the month a trade agreement had been signed. The Soviet press and propaganda media were now back in business. They cited Peru's actions in seizing the IPC as an example for all Latin America. They praised the "socialist" aspects of the military government's new five-year plan of development. They hailed the establishment of diplomatic and economic relations. These same themes were elaborated in speeches by the Soviet and other Communist delegations at a previously scheduled meeting of the United Nations Economic Commission for Latin America which took place in Lima in April.

When a military coup ousted Bolivia's President Siles Zuazo, on September 26, 1969, Moscow did not repeat the mistake it had made with Peru. The event was reported factually. Then, as the head of the junta, General Ovando Candia, made nationalistic pronouncements and declared his readiness to establish good relations with the Communist countries, Soviet comment took on an increasingly warm tone and Soviet media began to draw analogies between events in Peru and Bolivia.

These Soviet actions lead me to suspect that the Kremlin

analysis of these military takeovers foresees some possibilities of the development of a Nasser-type anti-imperialist socialist revolution in those countries which is well worth exploring and, if the analysis proves correct, exploiting. They pose an intriguing question as to whether the Kremlin expects eventually to be presented with the alternative of supporting more Egypts in Latin America rather than the Castro-Guevara concept of more Vietnams. However, this is a question for the future.

For the present the Soviet Union is in Cuba. Moscow has been able to ease its relationships with Castro somewhat and to reduce his importance as an obstacle to the conduct of Soviet Government and Party policies in the other countries of Latin America. The Kremlin leadership is certainly not now thinking of reducing or withdrawing the Soviet presence in Cuba. The initiative for such withdrawal, it seems to me, would almost inevitably have to come from the Cuban side, and the conditions necessary for such a shift seem remote at the moment. In Albania we witnessed a radical shift in posture when Peking stepped in to replace Soviet support. But Communist China is still in disarray, and it is likely that Castro's previous experiences with the Mao regime have convinced him of the problems involved in becoming dependent on the Chinese Communists for support. The other conceivable alternative for Castro would be an attempt to make it up with the United States. Since the U.S. starting price for any negotiations includes elimination of any Soviet military presence in Cuba and Castro's renunciation of subversive activity in Latin America, I see little prospect of this in the foreseeable future. From Moscow's point of view, a reconciliation on such terms would be considered as a loss of Cuba to world Communism and a major blow to the Soviet world-power image. The very possibility is surely another factor limiting Soviet flexibility in this situation.

Finally, a few words should be added about the likely Soviet reaction to the possible overthrow of Castro. This would depend in large measure, of course, on the attendant circumstances. Moscow does not have a formal treaty commitment to come to Cuba's aid in the event of external attack, but there is no doubt in my mind that a renewed effort to upset the Castro regime through armed intervention, whether from the United States or some other Western Hemisphere country, would produce a grave crisis.

Should Castro fall as the result of internal forces, much would depend on the likely composition and orientation of the new regime. The Soviets would have no great difficulty in adjusting to new Cuban leadership provided that it retained its Communist orientation. They might, in fact, see certain advantages in having a more stable and responsible figure in control of Cuba's policies. But political upheavals are filled with uncertainties, and I suspect that Moscow would see its interests best served by using its influence on behalf of internal stability in Cuba. The Soviets have a limited military presence in Cuba, and this provides them with some leverage, but they would certainly be most hesitant to commit it in a domestic power struggle. Any large-scale Soviet intervention can be ruled out, since the Kremlin leaders are undoubtedly aware that the United States could not remain disinterested under such circumstances.

CHAPTER XV

Vietnam: A War of National Liberation?

After the ouster of Khrushchev, I found myself obliged to spend an increasing amount of time debating with Soviet leaders and officials about Vietnam. Fortunately, I had not only kept up with my homework, but had had occasion to work directly on Vietnamese problems back in 1957 and to spend some months in South Vietnam. During that time I visited all parts of the country and the adjoining countries of Cambodia and Laos. Even then I found that an understanding of the situation required a knowledge of the background, and that this background runs deep in Southeast Asia.

South Vietnam is an elongated strip of territory lying along the eastern coast of Southeast Asia, slightly over 100 miles in breadth at its widest point and approximately 750 miles long from north to south. Its population is estimated at about seventeen million, largely concentrated along the coastal plain, with over two million people in the Saigon-Cholon metropolitan area. The interior portions of the country from the central to northern regions are mountainous, sparsely populated and generally untouched by modern communications. Temperatures on the coastal plain are tropical and are accompanied by the usual high humidities. Rainfall is generally concentrated in a four-to-five-month period, although these periods vary somewhat from north to south. Two crops are possible in most of the coastal area if water is available, either through rainfall or irrigation. Rice production has been the chief activity throughout the flat southern Mekong River Delta area and northward along the coast. Rubber plantations are found in the areas north and west of Saigon, and limited amounts of tea and coffee are raised in the higher inland area.

The people now known as Vietnamese have a high, though not accurately measurable, Chinese component, ethnic as well as cultural. They are traceable to tribes resident in southern China, below what is now Shanghai, as far back as 1200 B.C. These tribes appear gradually to have moved south and settled in the Tonkin Gulf area, apparently mixing with the indigenous population, of Polynesian origin, they found there. Their own dynastic leadership having been overthrown by other Chinese warlords in 257 B.C., the so-called Nam (South)–Viet (State) tribes lived under a succession of rulers from China proper until 968 A.D. despite an unsuccessful Jeanne d'Arc–type revolt in A.D. 43 under the Trung sisters, still celebrated as national heroines. After A.D. 968 the Nam-Viet gained independence under native dynasties and resumed their southward march. They now called their state An-Nam (South Peace), presumably to mark their relative freedom from reconquest by further Chinese warlords, including Kublai Khan, whom they successfully resisted around A.D. 1260 (i.e., shortly after another heir of Genghis Khan, Batu Khan, had conquered and despoiled the Russian state at Kiev). The Annamese destroyed and annexed the indigenous Cham kingdom by 1471 and by the early eighteenth century had swept down into the area of today's South Vietnam. In 1789 the capital was moved from Hanoi to Hué.

The Vietnamese language, while of mixed origin, is said even today to draw one-third of its vocabulary directly from the Chinese and was traditionally written in modified Chinese characters. The Latin characters used today were introduced by Portuguese and French missionaries in the mid-seventeenth century.

Over the centuries the Vietnamese people have developed distinctive ethnic and cultural characteristics and a strong national consciousness, but the population still counts about 10 percent in minority groups. Originally the region was populated by Polynesians and Khmers, the latter being part of the early Khmer Empire centered in what is now Cambodia, with its great temples at Angkor Wat, the ruins of which are a world-famous tourist attraction. A residue of these peoples still occupy the Cochin China area or extreme southwestern portion of Vietnam. The extremely primitive Moi or mountaineers, still living in the inland plateau regions, are the remnants of the Polynesian coastal dwellers, through the years driven into the hills by the successive pressures of the Annamese or Vietnamese as they moved down from the north. The principal minority is, of course, the so-called overseas Chinese, emigrating in later years directly from the mainland, and numbering nearly 800,000.

Among this predominantly agricultural people, the village has traditionally been the center of communal life, a form of existence which has retained, in common with other similarly situated regions of the globe, an almost unchanged pattern of living from generation to generation. The French made little effort to change this social environment following their advent during the 1860s. Not until World War II, the Japanese occupation and, more important, the postwar struggle for independence was the even tenor of village life disturbed.

Under the French colonial administration illiteracy was the rule in rural areas. Only in a few urban areas was there limited opportunity for education and exposure to Western—that is, French—institutions. Here the mandarin families, whose wealth and prestige were based almost entirely on land ownership, sent their sons to local French elementary and secondary schools and then to universities in metropolitan France. In these institutions they obtained an education heavily oriented toward classical and liberal arts, with little attention to the more mundane requirements of the local political or economic scene. Unlike the British administration in India, the French colonial administration in Indochina deliberately refrained from training local personnel in the methods of public and private administration. Governmental and limited industrial and banking functions were performed, from top to bottom, by the French, while trade and commercial activities were largely in the hands of the overseas Chinese.

As the French extended their sway in Southeast Asia in the last half of the nineteenth and the first half of the twentieth centuries, they established a central administration in Saigon for what they called French Indochina. This term covered what we now know as the Kingdom of Laos (then called the Kingdom of Luang-Prabang), the Kingdom of Cambodia and the three states we now think of as constituting Vietnam: Tonkin, with its capital at Hanoi; Annam, under a so-called emperor residing in Hué; and Cochin China, with its capital at Saigon.

During World War II, Indochina remained nominally under French control. After the fall of France, in June, 1940, the Vichy regime in occupied France appointed the French officials in the territory. The Japanese, then dominant in Southeast Asia, tolerated this French administration but secured the use of naval bases and gained a monopoly of the rich exports of rice, rubber and other valuable commodities from the Indochinese states. However, in March, 1945, the Japanese ousted the French administration and tried to set up nationalist governments headed by their own puppets. This was a short-lived experiment, for in August, 1945, after the bombing of Hiroshima, the Japanese withdrew. In Hanoi, the Vietminh seized power. Vietminh was the short name for "Vietnam League for Independence," a resistance and political organization led by the Communist leader, Ho Chi Minh. Soon the Vietminh set up administrative committees throughout the states constituting Vietnam—Tonkin, Annam and Cochin China—liquidating the administration of the mandarins who had conducted the local governments under the French. The Vietminh then declared all Vietnam to be an independent republic.

Meanwhile, the principal wartime Allies had decided that Northern Vietnam should be occupied by the Chinese and Southern Vietnam by the British. The British and Chinese soon yielded to French demands, however, and French troops landed at Haiphong on March 6, 1946, then occupied Hanoi. The French opened negotiations with Ho Chi Minh, declaring that they recognized the Republic of Vietnam as a "Free State forming part of the Indochinese Federation and of the French Union." Only weeks later, however, the French authorities in the South set up a separate Republic of Cochin China, thus taking away the southern half of the country. Despite this, Ho Chi Minh went to France for negotiations, possibly counting on receiving effective support from the French Communists. But such support was not forthcoming, and in September he returned to Hanoi, after signing a meaningless agreement with France at Fontainebleau. Soon afterward, as the French tried to reassert their authority in the North, the Vietminh forces rose against them. The French tried to find a way out by using the former Annamese Emperor, Bao Dai, who was living in France. In March, 1949, they concluded a series of agreements with him purporting to establish the independence of all Vietnam under his rule but within the French Union.

In a very real sense the tragedy of Vietnam goes back to the fall of France in 1940 and the feeling of humiliation that was thereby engendered in the French leadership, in particular General de Gaulle. After the liberation, this was translated into a determination to regain France's position as a world power, a process which unavoidably meant the recapture of France's empire throughout the world, and notably the restoration of its position in Indochina. President Roosevelt had opposed the return of the French colonial administration to Indochina, and his attitude was responsible for the original decision to exclude them from occupying the country after the Japanese withdrawal. Indeed, for a short time during this period we gave some modest assistance to Ho Chi Minh to support Vietminh activities against the Japanese and hasten their exodus. Consequently, when the French did return, we stood aside.

After reneging on their initial promises of independence and substituting for this their deal with the absent and powerless Bao Dai, the French had little alternative but to try to reestablish their position by force. This they attempted to do in a bloody struggle which was to last for nearly eight years and end in the humiliating defeat at Dienbienphu. American aloofness disappeared, however, after the Communist takeover on mainland China, and particularly after the North Korean attack on South Korea. During the period 1950–54 the United States, in fact, largely underwrote the cost of the ever-increasing French military effort. An official U.S. source estimated that American military assistance to France in Indochina during this period reached a figure of $1.2 billion. An unofficial estimate, which tried to include diversion to Indochinese purposes of the massive American aid to France under the Marshall Plan, concluded that the total American subsidies of the French effort in Indochina during these years, in fact, totaled the better part of $5 billion. While the ranks of the French forces were filled with local "mercenaries," hired at excessively high rates by Asian standards, the officers were French from top to bottom; and during these years of bitter strife the losses in the French officer corps were enormous, including the bulk of the current graduates from the French military academy, Saint-Cyr. In the end, the effort was in vain.

Not long after Stalin's death, a meeting of the quadripartite Council of Foreign Ministers in Berlin, early in 1954, paved the way for a settlement in Indochina. In accordance with a decision taken there, a conference was organized in Geneva in July, 1954, under the co-chairmanship of Great Britain and the Soviet Union. After long negotiations, agreements were reached for the cessation of hostilities in Vietnam, Cambodia and Laos. Vietnam was partitioned at the 17th parallel, with a demilitarized buffer zone set up along the line of demarcation to a depth of five kilometers on either side. The Vietminh forces—now called the People's Army of Vietnam—were to withdraw to the northern zone and the French forces to the south. An International

Control Commission was set up to supervise the operation, consisting of India, as chairman, Canada and Poland. A prohibition was established against the creation of new military bases or the introduction of weapons or munitions into either part of Vietnam. The military demarcation line was described as "provisional," with a declaration that this "should not in any way be interpreted as constituting a political or territorial boundary." The agreement provided that general elections should be held in July, 1956, under the supervision of the states-members of the International Control Commission.

The United States was represented at the Geneva Conference by Under Secretary of State Bedell Smith, former Ambassador in Moscow in the early postwar years. However, the United States refused to participate fully in the negotiations and in the end, along with the representatives of South Vietnam, did not sign the agreements themselves. Our aloofness, with its implicit hint of possible military intervention, is generally believed to have played a crucial part in inducing the Soviets and the Communist Chinese alike to urge Hanoi to settle for a temporary division of Vietnam at the 17th parallel and for independent status for Cambodia and Laos.

In lieu of his signature, Under Secretary Smith made a unilateral declaration in which he:

1. Took note of the conference declaration and of the armistice agreements concluded there, including that between the Franco-Vietnamese command and the command of the so-called People's Army of Vietnam.
2. Undertook to "refrain from threat or the use of force to disturb them."
3. Expressed the "grave concern" with which the United States would view any renewal of the aggression as a serious threat to international peace and security.
4. Pledged, as regards the proposed all-Vietnam elections, and with specific reference to the Vietnamese Government's reservations of May 10 with respect thereto, "not to join in an arrangement which would hinder" the right of the people of Vietnam to determine their own future.

On the heels of the agreement, some thirty thousand members of the Vietminh forces left South Vietnam for the North and nearly a million Vietnamese civilians left the North as refugees to settle in the South.

Also following the agreement, the Eisenhower administration moved forward toward the conclusion of the Southeast Asia Collective Defense Treaty (SEATO), which had been under consideration for some time, as part of the effort to convince Communist China that it would not have a free hand in Southeast Asia. The agreement was concluded late in 1954 and entered into force on February 19, 1955. The signatories included, from outside the area, the United States, Great Britain and France; and, from inside, Thailand, the Philippines, Pakistan, New Zealand and Australia. In addition to the direct bilateral and multilateral mutual-defense obligations undertaken by the parties, they agreed in a separate protocol that these obligations would also apply to "the states of Cambodia and Laos and the free territory under the jurisdiction of the state of Vietnam." This proffered assistance has been rejected by Cambodia, held in reserve by Laos and eagerly sought by successive governments in South Vietnam.

In the United States the SEATO Treaty received overwhelming support. At this time the United States had just been through the traumatic experience of Korea and of the Korean settlement, and the great debate over responsibility for the "loss of China" was still going on. There was a real belief that unless the United States participated in a major way in preserving the independence and security of these new nations they would be subject to progressive pressures by the parallel or combined efforts of North Vietnam and Communist China, and that the spread of Communist control by subversion and aggression would create the very kind of aggressive domination of much of Asia that we had fought Japan to prevent.

After the Geneva agreements, I am sure that Ho Chi Minh felt that he had again been negotiated out of a victory that he had considered won by his own efforts. When the French returned to North Vietnam in 1946 and when he himself went to negotiate with them at Fontainebleau, he undoubtedly thought he would end up as the master of a united Vietnam. He was, in fact, the only Communist who had achieved control of an anticolonial nationalist movement and become a kind of national hero. He was a rather remarkable individual. Not a great deal is known about his life. Ho Chi Minh is an alias meaning "he who enlightens." He was probably born Nguyen Tat Than on May 19, 1890. As a very young man he sailed as a mess boy on a French liner to Western Europe, lived and worked for many years in Paris, London and other Western European cities and became fluent in a number of languages. He was an early member of the French Socialist Party, and at a congress of the Party in 1920 accused France of "shamelessly exploiting and torturing" his homeland. When the Socialists subsequently split over colonial policy, Ho helped to found the French Communist Party. In 1922 he went to Moscow to join the Communist International, and worked in the Asian department of the Comintern apparatus for a good many years. He was jailed as a Comintern agent by the British in Hong Kong in the 1930s and by the Nationalist Chinese in China in the 1940s.

Another remarkable man came to power in the South. The ink was barely dry on the Geneva Accords when the French, with our encouragement, persuaded the Emperor Bao Dai to appoint as Prime Minister of South Vietnam another ardent but very different kind of nationalist, Ngo Dinh Diem. Diem was born in 1901 of a well-established Catholic family of mandarins in the region of Hué, the old imperial capital. His education, entirely in Vietnam but largely in French-influenced schools, was apparently a mixture of traditional Chinese classics and of Western culture, notably the French Humanist writers of the early nineteenth century. A serious student, he was capable of citing with pertinency and approval a Chinese legend or Thomas Jefferson or Sainte-Beuve. With this cultural background, Diem at an early age had followed his father into the service of the Emperor. He rose rapidly to the highest posts open to a Vietnamese. He came to realize, however, that he in fact wielded no power and was not long able to endure the state of colonial subservience into which the Vietnamese had fallen under the French. Consequently, Diem resigned in 1933 and thereafter, despite repeated appeals from the Emperor and others, refused to re-enter public service until he accepted the prime ministry. During his long retirement he was closely watched by the French authorities. In 1945 the Vietminh had struck at the Ngo family, raiding the house, burning Diem's library of ten thousand books and killing one of his five brothers, a former provincial governor. Diem himself was arrested and for a while kept under restraint by the Vietminh. In 1948 he left Vietnam on a world tour which took him to Japan, the Philippines, the United States, Belgium and France. He returned to Saigon on June 26, 1954, to take over the prime ministry. It is testimony to the mettle of the man that he should have chosen to take the great responsibility of government at what appeared to be the darkest hour in the history of Vietnam.

Diem was to have an uphill job. Despite the nominal grant of independence within the French Union in 1949 and the Geneva Accords themselves, the French continued to try to hold on to control of the country. It was some six months after Diem's acceptance of the prime ministry that the Vietnamese really began to get their hands on some of the levers of power. In December, 1954, they concluded an agreement in Paris giving them control of their own ports, customs, finances and foreign exchange, including the right to receive American aid directly. Gradually thereafter the Diem Government was able to take over from the French such instruments of sovereignty as the State Bank, the Foreign Exchange Office, Civil Aviation and the university. In the military field, the Vietnamese armed forces assumed regional commands and responsibility for security as the French withdrew to the South; but they remained under the over-all command of French General Paul Ely, at least nominally, until his departure in June, 1955; and the French expeditionary corps was not finally withdrawn and the French high command dissolved until April, 1956.

Meanwhile, Diem moved vigorously to defeat and disband the various private armies of several local sects which had been subsidized by the French. In this he met with some opposition from the absentee Emperor, who was living in France. Consequently, in October, 1955, Diem called upon the Vietnamese people to choose by referendum between the two. Overwhelmingly victorious, Diem proceeded to proclaim Vietnam a republic and was elected its first president. A constitution was worked out for the new Republic of Vietnam, which borrowed its basic structural concept from the United States and Philippine constitutions, with a strong executive and separation of executive, legislative and judicial powers.

Meanwhile, the Vietnamese armed forces were cut back from the high of about 230,000 which they had reached under the French during hostilities to about 150,000, mainly ground forces. They were reorganized with the help of a United States Military Assistance Advisory Group and equipped with American arms from the ample supplies still on hand from deliveries to the French. Also, during this time, regular internal security forces numbering roughly 100,000 were organized, equipped and trained with United States assistance. These forces included a provincial civil guard, a municipal police force, a village "self-defense" corps and a Vietnamese Bureau of Investigation. By the time I arrived in South Vietnam, in June, 1957, these internal security forces had already relieved the army of internal security responsibilities in twenty-five of the country's thirty-six provinces and were making good progress in terms of discipline, morale and skill. Sporadic skirmishes were still taking place with Vietminh and bandit remnants, mainly along the Cambodian border and in more remote parts of the Mekong Delta area, but internal security was pretty good and we were able to travel throughout the country without special protection.

On the economic side, United States aid was generous and the Vietnamese had worked feverishly to repair the ravages of eight years of war. Many observers were referring to the economic recovery as a "miracle," and members of our aid mission were calling South Vietnam a "showcase."

Meanwhile, frustrated in his wider ambitions, Ho Chi Minh set about consolidating Communist power in North Vietnam, where he set up what he called, in typically inverted Communist lingo, the Democratic Republic of Vietnam. Here he controlled about half the territory of the country and a population of about nineteen million, slightly higher than that of the South. Property was taken over by the state. Agriculture was collectivized. Religious institutions were subordinated. The remnants of the bourgeoisie—those who had not made the decision to flee to the South with their compatriots—were liquidated, and the late French Vietnamese specialist Bernard Fall estimated that nearly fifty thousand political opponents were killed outright. In contrast to the South, economic conditions deteriorated.

On the military side, the British, in their capacity as one of the Geneva Conference co-chairmen, had sent a note to the other co-chairman, the Soviets, in April, 1956, stating that "The Vietminh army has been so greatly strengthened by the embodiment and re-equipment of irregular forces that instead of the seven Vietminh divisions in existence in July, 1954, there are now no less than twenty." United States Assistant Secretary of State for Far Eastern Affairs Walter Robertson followed up in a speech on June 1, 1956, charging that "the Vietminh have imported voluminous quantities of arms across the Sino-Vietminh border and have imported a constant stream of Chinese Communist military personnel to work on railroads, to rebuild roads, to establish airports, and to work on other projects contributing to the growth of the military potential of the zone under Communist occupation."

As I noted above, the representatives of South Vietnam at Geneva had refused to sign the agreements reached there and had explicitly expressed reservations with regard to the projected elections. Indeed, that provision in the final declaration of the Geneva Conference issued on July 21, 1954, was so ambiguous and badly drafted that it could be the subject of varying interpretations. It seems advisable to take a look at the full text, since this has been a subject of controversy and of much spoken and written nonsense. It reads as follows:

The Conference declares that, so far as Vietnam is concerned, the settlement of political problems, effected on the basis of respect for the principles of independence, unity and territorial integrity, shall permit the Vietnamese people to enjoy the fundamental freedoms, guaranteed by democratic institutions established as a result of free general elections by secret ballot. In order to insure that sufficient progress in the restoration of peace has been made, and that all the necessary conditions obtain for free expression of the national will, general elections shall be held in July, 1956, under the supervision of an International Commission composed of representatives of the member states of the International Supervisory Commission, referred to in the agreement on the cessation of hostilities. Consultations will be held on this subject between the competent representative authorities from the two zones from July 20, 1955, onwards.

Some have argued that this provision called for a single nationwide election, with reunification assumed. The American interpretation was that what was meant was in effect a plebiscite as to whether reunification was desired, and this interpretation had strong support in reason and in the recollection of Geneva participants. In any case, in the circumstances developing after the Geneva Conference, President Diem was explicit, declaring that "the government considers the principle of really free elections as a peaceful and democratic instrument, but still it is necessary that conditions assuring freedom to live and to vote be established beforehand." At the same time, he proclaimed the government's dedication to the goal of "the unity of our country, but unity in freedom and not in slavery." During this post-Geneva period Diem had, in fact, gone a long way toward recapturing from Ho Chi Minh the banner of the "national cause." This fact, plus the increasing contrast between the progress being made in the South and the oppression in the North, undoubtedly had to do with the decision of Hanoi to resort again to the use of force to accomplish its aim of dominating the entire country.

While some thirty thousand combatants went from the South to the North after the Geneva Accords, it is estimated that a Vietminh cadre of some three thousand remained in the South to carry on terrorist activities, watch over the hidden stores of arms, ammunitions and other supplies, and generally provide a basis for possible future actions. During these early years the targets of the Vietminh cadres left behind were mainly provincial, district and village officials, teachers and administrators—some twenty thousand of whom were assassinated between

1954 and 1961. Beginning in about 1957, South Vietnamese included in the thirty thousand departees, after having been trained and indoctrinated in camps in North Vietnam, began to be infiltrated back into the South. They were carefully selected in order to give the impression that the "Vietcong," as the Communists' guerrillas were now called, were fighting a civil war in the South. By 1959 it was estimated that some ten thousand of them had come to the South and the flow was continuing. By 1964 there were no more indoctrinated Southerners in North Vietnam to infiltrate, so most of the infiltration since that date has been of regular North Vietnamese Army personnel.

In order to understand the developing situation it is now necessary to detour briefly into Laos. The Vietminh had never fulfilled the Geneva Accords with respect to Laos. Hanoi's Laotian puppet, Souphanouvong, had instead remained in the northeastern section of Laos, adjoining North Vietnam, and refused to join the central government in Vientiane. In 1959–60 Souphanouvong's forces collaborated with the Vietminh from Hanoi to attack westward deeply into Laos. They thus gained almost full control of eastern Laos, and this permitted them to activate the so-called Ho Chi Minh supply route through eastern Laos and Cambodia into South Vietnam.

So far as I know, this was the occasion of the first direct Soviet assistance to Hanoi. From December, 1960, to about the end of 1961 the Soviets assisted this military operation in Laos by flying supplies to the Communist forces in Soviet IL-14 transport planes. It seems quite possible to me that this help was given at the direct request of Ho Chi Minh, who may well have been getting somewhat uneasy about the extent of his dependence on Communist China.

In any case, the Vietminh drive into Laos and resultant opening of relatively easy supply routes to South Vietnam had portentous overtones which greatly bothered President Kennedy when he came into office in 1961. The situation in Laos was one of the main things he had on his mind when he met Khrushchev in Vienna, and was second only to Berlin in terms of the amount of discussion which took place there. Since Khrushchev was at this time tending to want to wash his hands of Southeast Asia as a result of his conflict with Mao Tse-tung, he agreed to the calling of a new conference on Laos, and this took place at Geneva in 1962. The resulting new agreement on Laos brought about the establishment of a "neutral" government there, under Laotian "neutralist" Prince Souvanna Phouma, and reaffirmed in stronger terms the provisions of the Geneva agreements of 1954 with respect to the end of foreign intervention in Laos. However, like the previous agreement, it was disregarded by the Vietminh, who maintained their positions in, and control of, eastern Laos.

In practice, then, President Kennedy failed to achieve what he had most hoped for in seeking a new agreement on Laos— the closing of the infiltration routes through the eastern pan-handle of that country. The Vietminh build-up continued and the scale of hostilities continued to intensify, including an increasing number of terrorist attacks on United States military installations and quarters. In 1960 President Eisenhower had doubled the size of the U.S. Military Assistance Advisory Group, from about 350 to around 700 members. In the fall of 1961, some six months after Vienna, President Kennedy took the decision to reinforce the group with further advisers, combat pilots and supporting military personnel, whose number was to rise gradually to a level of 25,000 in the next three years. This decision was the first major step toward substantial direct United States involvement in the fighting in Vietnam and was the natural precursor to the decisions taken by President Johnson in 1965 and later to introduce American combat personnel on a large scale. The later decisions to increase American commitments were also made more necessary by the deterioration of the internal political situation in Vietnam.

The fact that the French had left practically no adminis-trative structure in Indochina presented a major problem. Re-markable a man as he was, President Diem had inevitably inherited the authoritarian tendencies of the mandarin class. He tended consequently to concentrate all the authority in his own office, so that the presidency became a serious "bottleneck" inside the government. American aid officers and other American military and civilian officials in Vietnam reinforced this authoritarian tendency, instead of effectively combating it, since everyone tried to deal in his own field of interest with the President himself.

The great need for the development of an effective public administration in South Vietnam had been recognized, and in May, 1955, a group from Michigan State University was employed by the International Cooperation Administration (ICA) to undertake "improvement of governmental administration in Vietnam." The group established a National Institute of Administration, which started operating in Saigon in August, 1955, offering sixty-four courses in public administration. Unfortunately, the Institute was itself attached to the presidency. Our inspection team in 1957 challenged the university group with the question as to whether they were not, in violation of their professional standards, in fact institutionalizing an authoritarian regime. They replied that their recommendations had necessarily been influenced by emergency requirements and admitted that they had been further tempered to the President's proclivities in the interest of maintaining the group's acceptability and thus its effectiveness. They insisted, however, that their work had consistently stressed the need to reduce the work load of top personnel by delegation of responsibility and authority and had laid the basis for the development of a broad, decentralized organizational structure as soon as conditions permitted its effective implementation. These conditions of course never arrived, so that the net final effect of the program was to provide more efficient administrative machinery for the exercise of Diem's authoritarian tendencies, which came out strongly as he became more and more harassed with the increased aggression of the North Vietnamese and terrorism of the Vietcong inside the country. As he tried to bring more and more elements under tight control, his popularity waned and the military leadership was tempted to try to oust him. It finally succeeded, in November, 1963, when Diem and his brother were not only ousted but brutally assassinated.

For a year and a half after this South Vietnam wallowed in political confusion, and stability began to be restored only after

June, 1965, when political power finally passed, with the agreement of civilian political leaders, to a government headed by
General Nguyen Van Thieu and Marshal Nguyen Cao Ky. At
first this seemed just another turnover within the military junta
which ousted Diem. However, despite the raging war, the Thieu-
Ky leadership has moved ahead to re-establish constitutional
government in the country, a fact many of us tend to forget.
National elections were held in September, 1966, for a Constituent Assembly, with 532 candidates competing for 117 seats
and over 80 percent of the registered voters (over four million
people) casting their ballots. More than 500 foreign parliamentarians, journalists and diplomats were invited to observe
these elections and generally described them as effective, fair
and free. After much wrangling in the Constituent Assembly
and some charges of executive pressure, the new Constitution
was promulgated in April, 1967, on the basis of which Presidential elections were held in the following September, with an
even higher voter turnout—83.3 percent of the electorate or
nearly five million South Vietnamese.

It is true that the new Constitution concentrates more
power in the executive branch than would be normal by Western standards and that this probably reflects not only the
prevailing state of war in the country but the influence of the
military leaders. On the other hand, the elections were far from
being a single-list performance. There were many candidates
and opposition was vigorous. While Thieu and Ky won, running
on the same ticket for the posts of President and Vice President,
respectively, they did so only by a plurality of approximately a
third of the total votes cast. The increased number of voters in
1967 already represented an extension of the effective control of
the Saigon Government as a result of successful military operations against the Vietcong and reinvigoration of the so-called
"pacification program." The situation continued steadily to improve, and by August, 1969, nearly 90 percent—15.3 out of 17.3
million—of the population of South Vietnam was officially
considered to be living in at least "relative" security. And in the
previous year new elections for local officials had been held in
nearly 1,900 of the 2,300 villages in the country.

Another factor which has complicated the problem in Vietnam is the question of the organization and training of the Vietnamese armed forces. As I have noted, the French developed and left behind a purely professional mercenary army and our Military Advisory Group did not feel that it was possible, in the chaotic situation following the Geneva Accords, to start over again. Consequently, when I went there in 1957, I found that the annual per capita cost of native military personnel in Vietnam, including pay, allowances and benefits (such as clothing and medical care), but excluding equipment and overhead, amounted to $962. This compared with costs of $234 and $142 respectively in Korea and Taiwan, where the armed forces were basically conscriptees. The income status of the members of the Vietnamese armed forces was thus higher than the average of the civilian population, and the military operation was extremely costly.

My partner, James S. Killen of ICA, and I strongly recommended the conversion of these professional armed forces into conscript forces, in which national patriotism and civic duty should largely substitute for monetary inducement to service in the military ranks. Aside from the savings, we considered this a desirable end in itself, important to the nation-building process in a developing country. It seemed to us that the professional army without trained reserves was capable of only a one-shot performance. Moreover, with its high rates of pay and perquisites and abundance of facilities, relative to the civil sector, it tended to attract, develop and then monopolize a disproportionately high share of the country's scarce technical and administrative talents and skills. Thus, instead of serving as a major national educational institution plowing trained personnel back into the civilian economy, the armed forces constituted an obstacle to the development program by depriving it of existing human resources.

Our team was not authorized to inspect the military aid program as such, but we did feel our mandate required us to evaluate that program's relation to and impact on the problem of economic and social development in South Vietnam, in which the United States was making such a heavy investment. However, no action was taken on our recommendation, thanks to the relative quiescence of the military situation in Vietnam at the time and to bureaucratic reluctance to face the problem of overcoming Congressional opposition to increased military aid programs. The Diem Government did later decide to introduce conscription, but with the escalation of the attack from the North and the internal chaos after Diem's fall, the plan was not effectively implemented. It was not until 1967, after half a million American combat troops had been introduced into the battle and American casualty rates increased alarmingly, that President Johnson and the Thieu Government agreed to push ahead with the training and equipment of a national army in the Republic of Vietnam capable of taking over the main defense burden. President Nixon has greatly accelerated the program to "Vietnamize" the war and thus reduce the involvement and permit the gradual withdrawal of American combat forces.

As the Hanoi regime reverted to the use of force to accomplish its aims in Vietnam, it also took corollary political measures. In an article published in the Belgian Communist paper, *Drapeau Rouge*, on July 10, 1959, Ho Chi Minh stated: "We are building socialism in Vietnam, but we are building it in only one part of the country, while in the other part we still have to direct and bring to a close the middle-class democratic and anti-imperialist revolution." On September 20, 1960, the Congress of the Communist Party of North Vietnam issued a public appeal for the people in the South to establish a "national liberation front." It was not surprising, therefore, when some four months later Radio Hanoi announced and praised the establishment of the so-called National Front for the Liberation of South Vietnam (NFLSV). Many captured documents have since revealed the details of the setting up of the NFLSV in and by Hanoi, and Hanoi's direction of its activities.

The International Control Commission, set up to supervise observance of the Geneva Accords of 1954 and report to the British and Soviet co-chairmen of the conference, has never been very effective. Internally the Commission has been characterized by timidity on the part of the Indians and undeviating partisanship on the part of the Poles. Externally, it was able to establish its principal headquarters in Saigon and to have more or less free run in South Vietnam. However, while it was allowed to establish small offices in Hanoi and Haiphong, its movements around the countryside were restricted, on the pattern of the limitations imposed on foreigners in all Communist countries. As the guerrilla attacks escalated dramatically in 1961, President Diem repeatedly appealed to the ICC to investigate and finally goaded them into some action. In June, 1962, the Indian chairman and Canadian representative on the ICC, with the Pole abstaining, submitted an official report to the co-chairmen, stating, in part:

> There is evidence to show that arms, armed and unarmed personnel, munitions and other supplies, have been sent from the zone of the north to the zone of the south, with the objective of supporting, organizing and carrying out hostile activities, including armed attacks, directed against the armed forces and administration of the zone of the south. . . . There is evidence that the "People's Army of Vietnam" (the Vietminh) has allowed the zone of the north to be used for inciting, encouraging and supporting hostile activities in the zone of the south, aimed at the overthrow of the administration of the south.

As in previous but lesser cases, the Soviet side refused to accept the report as official, arguing that it was understood that the ICC would have to operate on a basis of unanimity. There was no such understanding, either written or verbal, so the British went ahead and published and circulated the report on their own. However, this Soviet attitude was a major factor frustrating any effective "control" by the International Control Commission.

During all this period of intense fighting in Southeast Asia, we were repeatedly talking about the situation with the Soviet officials, both in Moscow and in Washington, arguing that their responsibility as one of the co-chairmen of the Geneva Conferences of 1954 and 1962 placed an obligation on them to use their influence to restrain Hanoi from its aggressive moves. After the new agreement on Laos in 1962, we were particularly anxious to obtain their assistance in getting the Vietminh out of

Laos and thus closing the infiltration routes into South Vietnam. I frequently made representations to Soviet officials myself on the subject, and Ambassador Averell Harriman, who had been our delegate to the 1962 Geneva Conference, came to Moscow in April, 1963, when we had a long discussion about Laos with Khrushchev himself. But while the Soviets had continued to support Ho Chi Minh diplomatically and in their propaganda, it gradually became apparent that Moscow exercised no real influence in Hanoi at that time and that Khrushchev was beginning to wish that all of Southeast Asia would simply go away. This was even more apparent when Secretary Rusk came to Moscow, in July of 1963, to sign the partial Nuclear Test Ban Treaty and had long discussions on Southeast Asia, and particularly on Laos, with both Khrushchev and Foreign Minister Gromyko. The Soviet line was now that what was taking place in Laos, including the division of the country by Souphanouvong and his Pathet Lao forces, was purely an internal Laotian problem.

There were, however, indications that the Soviets wanted to head off a further build-up of American forces and would not be adverse to an end of the fighting. In April, 1964, they decided to support an appeal by Cambodian chief of state, Prince Norodom Sihanouk, for a reconvening of the Geneva Conference to work out specific guarantees for the neutrality and territorial integrity of Cambodia—a project which was generally considered to hold possibilities for corridor discussions aimed at bringing about a settlement in Vietnam itself. On February 26 a Tass statement had declared that conditions for a peaceful settlement in South Vietnam were maturing and warned against alleged American plans to expand the war. Again in May, *Pravda* indicated that Moscow approved not only a Laos conference but a new conference on all Indochina. And later that same month the Soviet Foreign Ministry officially proposed that a new conference on Laos be convened in June in Geneva. Then at the time of the Tonkin Gulf incident in August, 1964, when the Soviets might normally have been expected to come out with shrill charges of American aggression, Soviet public media reacted with surprising mildness. Unfortunately, none of these rather indirect efforts to seek an approach to a settlement in Vietnam came to anything. One of the main reasons was that the Chinese Communists were bitterly opposed; they were already describing the Soviet attitude as a betrayal of Communist interests in Southeast Asia, and Hanoi was going along with the Chinese.

It was precisely during this period that the polemical exchanges between Moscow and Peking reached a fever pitch. Khrushchev had just reached his decision to bring the conflict with the Chinese to a head and have a split in the world Communist movement. To this end, in August, 1964, he had summoned a preparatory conference of twenty-six Communist parties to meet in Moscow on the following December 15. This decision may well have been the trigger factor in his downfall in October, since most of his colleagues, appreciating the reluctance of most of the other Communist parties to formalize the break and have Moscow's central authority restored, thought that, come December 16, 1964, the whole Communist movement would be a shambles. In any case, Khrushchev had made his decision and clearly thought that Moscow would pick up most of the pieces, with only a few going to Peking, notably the countries of Southeast Asia. He was obviously prepared to leave Vietnam to the Chinese. It was a most unhandy place to reach from Moscow, and the Chinese predominant influence in Hanoi probably seemed unassailable to him. Besides, I think Khrushchev had in the back of his mind that the Americans could be counted on to contain the Chinese there.

The new Soviet leaders took an entirely different approach. They decided to avoid a formal break with Peking and promptly postponed the projected December meeting in Moscow. They dropped the polemics and decided not to give the Chinese Communists anything, but rather to vie with them in their own backyard. Consequently, the new Soviet Prime Minister, Kosygin, was sent off to Hanoi in February, 1965, to try to start the process of building up Soviet influence in Vietnam as against the Chinese influence. Finally, they decided to try to rally the Communist movement on the slogan of "Aid to Vietnam Against the Aggression of American Imperialism," and as a corollary to accept the deterioration in their relations with us. With the political chaos prevailing in Saigon after the fall of

Diem, it must have appeared to Moscow—as, indeed, it did to many world capitals—as though the politico-military base of the U.S. effort in South Vietnam would soon collapse.

The escalation of the American role in Vietnam made this road chosen by the new Soviet leadership much longer and much more uncertain as to destination than they had originally foreseen. It was also costly for them, involving a comparable escalation of Soviet military and economic aid to North Vietnam. Communist aid to Hanoi mounted from a pre-1964 annual level of about $100 million to a level of nearly $1 billion in 1967 and 1968. Total aid since the North Vietnamese launched their renewed offensive in 1958 has amounted to over $4 billion. This has been roughly half economic, half military, about 45 percent from the Soviet Union, 25 percent from Communist China and the balance from the smaller Communist-ruled countries.

The question of arms supplies to North Vietnam naturally arouses great emotions here at home. The arms situation in Vietnam has been complex. In the early years of the renewed struggle most of the equipment of the Vietminh and Vietcong was, in fact, American equipment captured from the French and government forces. In the mid-1960s the bulk of the Vietcong equipment was of Chinese origin, with Soviet supplies being a relatively minor component. The big Soviet military aid program from 1965 through 1968 consisted mainly of antiaircraft guns and missiles and radar and fighter planes, items which the Soviets insisted were "defensive," for the protection of North Vietnam against American bombing and shelling. Only in late 1968 and 1969 did Soviet arms begin showing up in substantial quantities in the South, notably mortars of a range and accuracy superior to those provided by the Chinese or made by the North Vietnamese themselves. There seems, in fact, to have been some Soviet restraint in arms assistance, perhaps regarded by Moscow as paralleling our own limited purposes in Vietnam. This consideration of not goading Moscow into a further escalation of its arms programs for Vietnam, both in quantity and in quality, has been, of course, one of the factors taken into account in our own politico-military planning, particularly as respects the controversial question of restrictions on bombardment of North Vietnam from air and sea.

Despite the unexpected complications of the situation in Vietnam, I believe the post-Khrushchev leaders, as they review the bidding, probably think their new course was the right one. I believe they consider their slogan of rallying Communists and other sympathizers against American imperialist aggression in Vietnam was an indispensable factor in enabling them to rally seventy-five of the world's Communist parties to the international conference in Moscow in June, 1969, and thus in accomplishing their principal objective of isolating the Chinese Communists, both within the world Communist movement and from the Afro-Asian countries.

On the other hand, I have thought since 1966 that the Kremlin leaders would be relieved to see a negotiated settlement, of course on the best terms that could be obtained for Hanoi. I am sure that they tried at least a couple of times to influence Hanoi toward negotiations, notably at the time of the visit of Politburo member Alexander Shelepin to Hanoi in January, 1966, and again when Soviet Prime Minister Kosygin visited London in February, 1967. However, they quickly desisted and fell back, when they ran into adamant opposition in the Vietnamese capital, to avoid giving any justification to Chinese charges of collusion with the United States or of selling out the North Vietnamese to the imperialists.

There are many who have disagreed with this analysis. They argue that Moscow has greatly profited by and even enjoyed the American loss of prestige throughout the world from the opposition of our friends, as well as our enemies, to our role in Vietnam. They conclude that Moscow feels the hostilities there are straining our political and military resources and draining our economy, and that the Kremlin would accordingly like to see the conflict continue.

I am sure this is not an accurate assessment. First of all, it leaves out the primary consideration. I think there is reason to believe that the Soviet leadership has continued to be uneasy about an irrational act on the part of Peking which would get the Chinese involved in this war. This would still present an impossible problem for them, in terms of their pretensions to leadership of world Communism. What would they do in such a case? Could they fail to honor their commitments under the

Treaty of Mutual Assistance? This is a problem they simply have not wanted and do not want to face.

On the question of resources, no Russian, knowing the difference in the economic base between the two countries—and most of them are keenly aware of this—thinks that Vietnam is draining our resources. Americans may think so, but I am sure Russians do not. As a matter of fact, a Russian probably considers that this war is enabling the United States to maintain a terrific military-industrial complex and thus to continue to stave off the economic collapse which Marxist dogma proclaims to be inevitable in capitalistic societies. This is more likely to be the line of thought in Moscow.

As for the military factor, we actually heard contrary views in Moscow from high Soviet military officers. They noted, with some envy, that our officer cadres and troops were getting battle experience in Vietnam that their troops have not had since World War II. They also consider that the United States has, in fact, made great progress in the development of improved and advanced conventional weaponry by using Vietnam as a testing and proving ground. In addition, after the beginning of the bombing of North Vietnam in February, 1965—which unfortunately coincided with the presence of Chairman Kosygin in Hanoi—Moscow was increasingly galled by the image this created of big Communist brother being unable or unwilling to protect little Communist brother. Finally, it is clear to me that the rapid and large-scale introduction of American combat forces into Vietnam in 1965 soon convinced the Soviet leaders that a Communist military takeover from the North was just not in the cards.

On the United States side, four successive administrations, including President Nixon's, have tried to dissociate Moscow as much as possible from the Vietnam picture, both because the Russians have been relatively restrained in their participation, and because, since they are a world power and one of the co-chairmen of the Geneva conferences, Soviet cooperation is eventually essential to a peaceful settlement. All four administrations have consistently reiterated the limited nature of United States objectives, sometimes against domestic opposition: no destruction of North Vietnam as a political entity, no reunification of Vietnam by force, no American bases or permanent American military presence in South Vietnam, simply the fulfillment of our pledge in 1954 to help South Vietnam defend its independence and assure its people of the right to determine freely their own future by demonstrating that aggression, whether direct or in the form of "guerrilla warfare, inspired by one nation against another," does not pay. These are the points repeatedly made by American Presidents over the years.

From the beginning resistance efforts have been accompanied by a search for the possibilities of finding a peaceful settlement. President Kennedy made his major but futile effort by getting Khrushchev in Vienna to agree to the convocation of the new conference on Laos in 1962. When he made his decision to up the American ante in 1965, President Johnson simultaneously launched and subsequently maintained a vigorous "peace offensive." The State Department and Congressional committees have published pamphlets about the many initiatives which were—or became—publicly known, and nongovernment writers have produced books in which they tried to probe even deeper.

From my personal point of view, the peace campaign involved me in making repeated representations to—and frequently in having long arguments with—top Soviet officials, and in a futile effort to establish a dialogue with the North Vietnamese representatives in Moscow. All these initiatives were consistently and hostilely rebuffed. The high point of the campaign—or, perhaps more accurately, the low point—was probably President Johnson's exchange of correspondence with Ho Chi Minh in 1967. In a personal letter to President Ho on February 8, coincident with a new suspension of the bombing of North Vietnam and with talks in London between the British and Soviet Prime Ministers, President Johnson proposed prompt negotiations on the basis of an end to the bombing and to the build-up of combat forces, on our side, and to Hanoi's infiltration of forces into the South, on the other side. In an abusive reply dated February 15, Ho Chi Minh rejected the proposal, charging the United States with aggression and with committing "war crimes, crimes against peace and against mankind" and calling for the withdrawal of "all U.S. and satellite troops" as the only "correct political solution to the Vietnam problem." Then, flouting established protocol, he published both the President's letter and his reply.

The breakthrough—not a very deep one—came with President Johnson's dramatic television address of March 31, 1968, in which he announced the end of the bombardment of North Vietnam, except in the immediate vicinity of the Demilitarized Zone, appealed to Ho Chi Minh to respond favorably and not to "take advantage of our restraint" and called on Great Britain and the Soviet Union as co-chairmen of the Geneva Conference to help get negotiations started. Then, to underscore his earnestness and seriousness of purpose, the President announced his own withdrawal from American political life.

This time, on April 3, Hanoi responded with a modified affirmative, saying that "further steps" were necessary but offering to send a representative to make contact with an American representative. After a few weeks of squabbling about the site, Paris was settled upon, and Ambassador Averell Harriman and North Vietnamese Minister Xuan Thuy held their first meeting on May 13, 1968. They agreed to meet weekly thereafter. During the first five months the North Vietnamese delegation held tenaciously to their immediate objective of getting the 90 percent suspension of bombardment replaced by a complete and, as they continued to say, "unconditional" cessation. It was clear from the Soviet press and other sources that they were encouraged in this posture by the Soviet leadership, to whom the bombing of the North was the most rankling aspect of the hostilities in Vietnam.

On October 31 President Johnson announced that, in view of some recent undisclosed but "hopeful" movement in the Paris talks, he was that day ordering a complete end to the bombing; then at the next meeting on November 6, representatives of the government of South Vietnam would be "free to participate." Representatives of the National Liberation Front would also be present, he continued, emphasizing "that their attendance in no way involves recognition . . . in any form."

Unfortunately, our diplomatic preparations in Saigon had not been completely buttoned up. President Thieu balked about having the representatives of the Republic of Vietnam appear to be equated with the Hanoi-organized political arm of the Vietcong. Some ten weeks of difficult negotiations ensued—ridiculous in some aspects but serious in essence—before the South Vietnamese were satisfied that the seating arrangements for the enlarged meetings in Paris would not, in fact, equate them with the representatives of the NFLSV. President Johnson was able to announce that this "procedural problem" had been solved only on January 16, 1969, just before his own departure from office. It was not until January 25, however, after President Nixon's inauguration and the replacement of Ambassador Harriman by Ambassador Henry Cabot Lodge, former U.S. envoy to Saigon, that the first of the new series of meetings was held in Paris with representatives of all four elements involved in attendance. How long these talks will continue before a political settlement is reached and the nature of that settlement will depend less on the efforts of our delegation in Paris than on what we and our allies do in Vietnam and in our own homelands.

The nature of Communist tactics and objectives was revealed in a speech by Politburo member and head of the Soviet trade unions Alexander Shelepin in a speech which received practically no notice in the Western press, probably because it was delivered to a Communist-oriented audience in a Communist country. Addressing a meeting of the Communist-dominated World Federation of Trade Unions in East Berlin on December 17, 1968, Shelepin said:

> The conflict in Vietnam has now entered upon a new stage, when, along with active military action, a struggle is being conducted for a political solution to the Vietnam problem. The commencement of talks in Paris and the results achieved in these talks are great victories for the heroic Vietnamese people, and the socialist countries, and all peace-loving forces. At the same time this is a new defeat for American imperialism.

> Of course, Vietnam's struggle does not end here. This is only the first step along the road toward ultimate victory over aggression.

Therefore we consider it impossible under any circumstances to weaken our support for the Vietnamese people's struggle; on the contrary, the interests of the working class and of the entire world demand the comprehensive mobilization of efforts to exert pressure on the U.S. ruling circles so as to make the American imperialists cease their aggressive war in Vietnam, withdraw all their troops and the troops of their satellites from South Vietnam, liquidate all military bases there, and achieve a complete political settlement of the Vietnamese question so that the South Vietnamese people can settle their own affairs, in accordance with the political program of the National Liberation Front of South Vietnam without foreign interference, and to make the United States abandon forever its infringement upon the sovereignty and security of the Democratic Republic of Vietnam.

Shelepin's general description of Communist intentions has been confirmed and supplemented by directives to political officers of the Vietcong subsequently captured in South Vietnam. These directives speak of "limited" or "piecemeal" victories designed to promote the "antiwar movement" in the United States and to push the Nixon administration "in our direction" at the Paris peace table. Moscow itself has vigorously promoted the campaign by every means at its command. Opposition to "American aggression in Vietnam" has been made the main theme of the entire Communist movement—of the International Communist Conference in Moscow in June, 1969, and of the World Peace Assembly in Berlin. "Solidarity with Vietnam" days, or weeks, or months are organized, and "antiwar" demonstrations are promoted throughout the world, and particularly in the United States itself.

There is nothing surprising in all of this to anyone familiar with Communist tactics, particularly to anyone who followed the course of the long negotiations that finally brought about the truce in Korea. In hailing the new four-element phase of the Paris talks starting in January, 1969, as a new North Vietnamese victory, the Soviet press warned that a "bitter struggle" still lies ahead. I agree. However, I am satisfied that Hanoi accepted President Johnson's offer in April, 1968, after rejecting all previous overtures, only because Ho Chi Minh had finally come around to sharing Moscow's earlier view that a military victory was impossible. If Ho Chi Minh, with his authentic "nationalist" image, unique prestige and personal charisma, realized that he could not continue to extract the enormous sacrifices required of the Vietnamese people by his costly effort to take over South Vietnam by force, then his little-known "collective" successors could not in sanity think they could do better. Hanoi was inevitably weakened by Ho's death, on September 3, 1969, not only because of the loss of a recognized and probably irreplaceable leader, but because of that basic flaw in the Communist system, the lack of an accepted and legitimate method of succession. The balance of power among the leading contenders in the Politburo—the heads of the Party, of the government (both reputedly pro-Moscow), of the Assembly and of the army (both reputedly pro-Peking)—was apparent in their agreement to designate an aged nonentity to be Ho's nominal replacement as President of the Democratic Republic of Vietnam. None of this was allowed to show publicly, of course. As usual in such circumstances, the top leaders huddled together to protect the system, while they assessed their personal chances. Invoking the alleged "Testament of Ho Chi Minh" produced and read at his funeral, they sounded even more bellicose than the master himself.

The Communist representations at the Paris talks likewise took an even harder line than before Ho's death. This more militant attitude may also have reflected, in some degree, both a relative increase in the Chinese Communists' influence in Hanoi after Ho's disappearance and an exaggerated evaluation of popular opposition to the war in the United States. But I believe it remains a simple fact that Hanoi without Ho cannot be as strong as Hanoi with Ho. And if we remain steady, and do not, on our side, weaken ourselves by undue dissension and division, then I am sure that a reasonable and honorable though probably not entirely satisfactory solution will eventually be reached.

The United States has certainly made some mistakes in Vietnam. I have suggested a couple that struck me as major ones when I visited there in 1957. If we had done a better job in the field of public administration and if we had started the building of a National Vietnamese Army in 1957 rather than ten years later, we might have avoided some later mistakes or at least some of the painful decisions necessitated by our earlier lack of foresight. We may well make more mistakes in our efforts to reach a settlement at the conference table. However, if we want to measure the results of our efforts, then I think we must look not only at Vietnam but outside and beyond the borders of that battle-scarred country. Without getting engaged in the fashionable academic debate as to the validity of the so-called "domino theory," I will say flatly that I think the American effort and the American presence in Vietnam, combined with our continued presence in Korea, have had a decisive influence on developments throughout the Pacific area.

After the Communist takeover of continental China and especially after the massive intervention of Chinese Communist forces in Korea in 1950, discouragement—almost fatalism—pervaded the Far East. The Chinese Communists had been temporarily checked by American power, but there was no confidence that this kind of protection could be counted on in the future. The Sino-Soviet bloc seemed monolithic and irresistible. It was a hardy Asian who would publicly challenge Communism's claim to be the wave of the future.

All this has changed. Around the periphery of mainland China, from Japan through Burma, discouragement and fear have been replaced with confidence and hope. Political stability is the rule rather than the exception. Prosperity is growing, mainly under a vigorous free enterprise system backed by public works and the development of economic infrastructure financed by the local governments and by outside aid. Japan has accomplished an economic miracle, to become the third greatest industrial nation on earth. Young nations like Korea, the Republic of China in Taiwan, the Philippines, formerly heavily dependent on American aid, now stand on their own economic feet. Indonesia crushed an imminent Communist takeover of its great population and rich resources and is recovering its political and economic health. National development plans are ambitious and are working. Agricultural research is developing new seeds and practical methods of cultivation which hold promise of reversing the dire predictions of Malthus. The Asian nations have themselves taken the initiative in developing a vast network of regional cooperation, with Japan—which will have to provide much of the technical know-how and a good deal of the finance—playing the leading role. An Asian Development Bank organized in 1966 and controlled by its eighteen Asian members is in operation. A project to develop the great Mekong River in Southeast Asia for power and agriculture is well under way. Other regional organizations have been formed to promote cooperation, not only in economic development but in education and social and cultural problems, and even—cautiously and hesitatingly—in the political field.

I do not want to suggest that there will not be troubles in the future. Even the Russians, in an article in the authoritative journal *Kommunist* in April, 1969, said: "It cannot be ruled out that after the conclusion of the war [in Vietnam] the Mao Tse-tung group would like to undertake attempts to extend its influence in other countries of Southeast Asia and would like to kindle military conflicts in various forms in this region." And what the Soviet leadership may itself do will depend on the evolution of developments in the Pacific area. We can be sure that Moscow is not really out to make life easier for us there. But if and when a reasonable settlement is reached in Vietnam, then we will find ourselves closer than at any time since World War II to the basic objectives we fought for in that war: a free Asia, economically healthy and politically stable.

CHAPTER XVI

The Middle East: Area of
Potential Confrontation

In his negotiations with Hitler's Foreign Minister in November, 1940, Soviet Foreign Minister Molotov handed the Germans a memorandum in which he described the territories adjoining the Black Sea as being "situated inside the security zone . . . of the Soviet Union," then went on to define "the area south of Batum and Baku in the general direction of the Persian Gulf . . . as the center of the aspirations of the Soviet Union." Molotov was defining not only the "aspirations" of the Soviet Government of 1940, but of the Czar's Government before that, and of Soviet Governments of today and in the future. While the projected deal with Hitler did not come off, Stalin demonstrated Soviet aims more concretely, after the war, by trying to hang on in Iran, by demanding that the Turks cede to the Soviet Union a base on the Turkish Straits and two Turkish provinces, and by supporting the Communist guerrillas in Greece. In September, 1945, Molotov had sent a chill down the spines of his Western allies by projecting Russian "aspirations" all the way across the Mediterranean. At a Council of Foreign Ministers meeting in London, he proposed the Soviet Union as an heir to part of the Italian Empire in North Africa, in the form of a Soviet trusteeship over Tripolitania (now part of Libya).

For three years after the war, first Great Britain and the United States, then the United Nations, struggled with the problem of the termination of the British mandate in Palestine, particularly in the light of the demands for the establishment of a Jewish "homeland" there. As no solution was reached and the British decided to go ahead and withdraw, fighting broke out between Arabs and Jews in Palestine. The Jews were soon in control of a secure base, and on May 14, 1948, the National Council of the Jewish population of Palestine and the General Zionist Council proclaimed the establishment of the State of Israel and set up a government in the territory they controlled. The United States recognized the new regime *de facto* two days later; former Secretary of State Dean Acheson has subsequently revealed that this was a personal decision of President Truman reflecting his sympathy for the Zionist cause. On the following day the Soviet Union granted *de jure* recognition.

It was clear to us in the embassy in Moscow at the time that the motivation of the Soviet action was not sympathy with the idea of a Jewish state per se, but the desire to confirm the removal of the British presence and influence from the eastern Mediterranean and to help implant in the area a permanent irritant in relations between the Arabs and the West. The Bolshevik leadership, including its Jewish members, had been anti-Zionist from the beginning, regarding Zionism as a force subverting Jews into a "dual loyalty." Stalin—and this has been confirmed by his daughter—was personally anti-Semitic, in his later years violently so. Early in his rule, most of the Jewish Bolsheviks, beginning with Trotsky, had been liquidated, and Soviet Jews had been eliminated from sensitive Party and government posts. At the very time of the recognition decision, in 1948, Stalin launched a new campaign against the Jewish population of the Soviet Union, liquidating some of the outstanding figures of the Jewish community and closing down the few remaining Yiddish publications and theaters. The campaign was intensified after the attendance of the first Israeli Ambassador—Mrs. Golda Meir, later to be Prime Minister—at a service in the Moscow synagogue aroused a mass turnout and enthusiastic demonstration by the capital's Jews. The Soviet police made even greater efforts than for the rest of us to isolate the new Israeli Embassy from the Soviet population—in this case, especially from contacts with the Jewish element—and the Ambassador was subjected to much abuse.

I was among a group talking with Mrs. Meir at a reception one evening, when the well-known Soviet-Jewish writer Ilya Ehrenburg approached. Mrs. Meir, who had been born in Russia but raised and educated in the United States, was speaking English. When she greeted Ehrenburg in the same language, he replied contemptuously in Russian that he was certainly not going to talk in any language but Russian with a "Kievan Jewess," then turned his back and walked away. The reaction of the group—and I think this would include Mrs. Meir—was one more of pity than of anger.

As the purges went on through 1948 and 1949 in the Soviet Union—and in the Eastern European satellites as well—we became accustomed to the charges of involvement in a "Zionist-imperialist espionage conspiracy" hurled against the victims; and we learned that the label "cosmopolitan" meant a Jew designated for suppression. Stalin's anti-Zionist and anti-Semitic mania reached a peak in the fabrication of the so-called "Doctors' Plot" in December, 1952, in connection with which the Soviet Union broke diplomatic relations with Israel.

Some months after Stalin's death, his successors restored relations with Israel, and in the next couple of years they turned their eyes more and more southward. They had been glancing with interest at the Algerian revolt against France, and were increasingly attracted by the possibilities presented by Nasser's revolution in Egypt. This interest was no doubt whetted by their uneasiness about the inroads the Chinese Communists had made with Nasser and other Afro-Asian leaders at the Bandung Conference in April, 1955. The editor of *Pravda*, Shepilov, who was about to succeed Molotov as Foreign Minister, headed a "good will" delegation to Cairo in July, and in the fall it was announced that arrangements had been made for Nasser to receive arms from Czechoslovakia.

In 1956, on the heels of an abrupt withdrawal of U.S. and British offers to help plan and finance the building of a high dam at Aswan on the Nile River, Nasser nationalized the Suez Canal (owned mainly by British and French stockholders). Then came the incredibly ill-considered invasion of Egypt by British, French and Israeli forces. The United States, which had been kept in the dark by its Western European allies, condemned the invasion, and our lead, both by direct action and through the UN, was certainly the major factor in compelling the withdrawal of the invading forces. However, Khrushchev also condemned and threatened, even proposed joint action with the United States to oust the invaders, and probably got the major credit in Arab eyes. The result was a complete collapse of British and French influence and the creation of a real power vacuum in the Middle East.

In a gesture toward filling the void, the Eisenhower Doctrine was promulgated under a Congressional resolution passed January 30, 1957, authorizing the President to extend economic and military aid to countries in the Middle East "desiring such assistance" and even "to employ the Armed Forces of the United States as he deems necessary to secure and protect the territorial integrity and political independence of any such nation or group of nations requesting such aid against overt armed aggression from any nation controlled by international communism." As the resolution was under discussion, Moscow attacked the proposal in terms designed for Arab eyes and ears. "It is known," an "authorized" Tass statement declared, "that the Soviet Union, unlike the United States, does not have and does not seek to have in the Near and Middle East any military bases or concessions with the object of extracting profits and does not strive to gain any privileges in this area." Later in 1957 a pro-

Soviet political turn in Syria led to rumors that Syria was
planning to attack her pro-Western neighbors, and then to other
rumors that Turkey was massing forces on the Syrian border.
The Soviets adopted and developed the latter story, charging
that the United States was pushing Turkey to attack Syria.
Moscow thundered against Ankara and then claimed its intervention had prevented aggression and forestalled a major
conflict.

All in all, the 1956–57 crisis in the Middle East was a
major setback for the West, a political and propaganda bonanza
for the Kremlin. Khrushchev's satisfaction was obvious, and it is
interesting to compare what actually happened with his version,
as given in an interview with the editor of the authoritative
Cairo paper *Al Ahram*. Responding to a request for his opinion
as to "the real reasons" for the tensions in the Middle East,
Khrushchev placed the blame on the desire of the "colonialists"
to suppress the "national liberation struggle in the area," then
went on more specifically:

> When Britain, France and Israel attacked Egypt, the ruling
> circles of the U.S.A. formally condemned the aggression. But it is
> absolutely clear that had they really condemned it, Britain and
> France, which in many respects are dependent on the U.S.A., and
> Israel even more, since it lives on American charity, would have
> come to attention, they would have been docile and obedient. . . .
> The Soviet Union declared to the United States that if its
> attitude was really one of condemning and halting the Anglo-Franco-
> Israeli aggression, then joint action should be taken against the
> aggressors. We knew, of course, that the ruling circles of the U.S.A.,
> in view of their actual role in the aggression of the three countries
> against Egypt, would turn down our proposal. But, by turning it
> down, they thereby revealed their insincerity. . . .
> When the French and British colonialists had discredited them-
> selves, the U.S.A. pretended that it was hastening to their [the
> Arabs'] aid, putting forward, among other things, the notorious
> "Dulles-Eisenhower doctrine." But this "support" on the part of the
> U.S. imperialist circles, calculated to retain imperialist influence in
> the Near and Middle East, is not unlike the support which the rope
> gives the man on the gallows. . . .
> So when the Arab countries, above all Egypt and Syria, offered

resistance to American imperialism, when the Dulles-Eisenhower doctrine was spurned, they resolved to overthrow the undesirable governments . . . aware that an Israeli attack against Syria would be extremely unpopular, though Israel would have willingly opted for the role of a gendarme. . . . They decided to use Turkey—a Moslem country—against Syria. This plan, however, came to grief, as you know, owing to the determination displayed by the peoples of the Arab countries, above all Syria and Egypt, and also because of the action taken by other peace-loving states, including the U.S.S.R.

The political pot continued to boil in the Middle East during the first half of 1958, and the subject became the main theme of the voluminous correspondence between Moscow and Washington in the early phase of Khrushchev's Sputnik diplomacy. Disorders broke out in still pro-Western Jordan and Lebanon. In May the Lebanese Government lodged a complaint with the UN Security Council, charging intervention by the United Arab Republic in its internal affairs. Then in July Lebanon asked for United States help under the Eisenhower Doctrine. On July 14 a violent nationalist military revolution in Iraq ousted and assassinated the King and Prime Minister and proclaimed the country a republic. On July 15 American Marines landed without opposition in Lebanon and British paratroopers in Jordan.

Outside these two countries, however, the situation was less quiet. Moscow's propaganda opened up full blast and polemical debates took place in the UN. In a letter to President Eisenhower on July 19, Khrushchev called for an immediate meeting "to stem the beginning military conflict" with top-level representatives of the four principal powers, plus India, as participants (thus apparently angering Peking, whither Khrushchev found it wise to repair for a four-day visit beginning July 31). In his reply, on July 22, the President said he saw no "factual basis for your extravagantly expressed fear of the danger of general war" and suggested the matter continue to be discussed in the Security Council, in which heads of government might represent their countries, if such were "generally desired." Calm having been restored in the area—and relative calm outside—the withdrawal of the American and British landing forces began on August 12 and was completed on October 25.

While major Soviet attention subsequently turned toward Berlin and finally Cuba and the conflict with Communist China, Soviet wooing of Nasser and the other Arabs continued persistently. Top-level official visits were made repeatedly in both directions between Moscow and Cairo and Algiers and other Arab capitals, and all kinds of Soviet and Arab delegations were exchanged at all levels. The Soviets picked up the Aswan Dam project which the West had so unceremoniously dropped, sending thousands of technicians and shiploads of equipment to the U.A.R. and receiving thousands of Egyptians for training in the Soviet Union.

It was in connection with this renewed interest in the regions south of its borders that the Soviets initiated and from 1955 onward developed their aid programs. The Arab countries have been the principal beneficiaries. Of the total of $9 billion in Soviet economic credits and grants between 1955 and 1968 over a third went to the Arab countries, and about 60 percent of this third went to the United Arab Republic alone. While a breakdown is not available, it is certain that during the same period the Arab countries, and Egypt in particular, received comparable, if not even higher, proportions of Soviet military aid, totaling about $5.5 billion in value. This Soviet military aid to the Arab countries was an especially unsettling factor in the Middle East; however, Moscow consistently rejected Western overtures for agreed limitations on military deliveries to the area or deflected such overtures by demanding the inclusion of Turkey, a NATO member, and Iran.

The Kremlin can thus not avoid a deep underlying responsibility for the events in the Middle East in June, 1967. Neither, I think, can it avoid a more immediate responsibility for the outbreak of the crisis. In the middle of May, high Soviet officials warned the Arab ambassadors in Moscow and a visiting Egyptian parliamentary delegation that Soviet intelligence indicated the Israelis were about to launch an all-out attack on Syria. A few days later, on May 18, Nasser demanded the immediate withdrawal of the United Nations forces supervising the armistice lines. As those contingents pulled out, he moved the Egyptian armed forces into the previously demilitarized Sinai Peninsula and closed the Strait of Tiran, thus cutting off Israel's outlet to the Red Sea through the Gulf of Aqaba. The United States tried frantically to organize the maritime powers to deal with the closure of this international strait and to restrain the Israelis from reacting militarily. A very smug Nasser was publicly proclaiming that any war would mean the destruction of Israel and that the "Soviet Union was pledged to block any American or Western" intervention. The Kremlin not only did not deny Nasser's assertion, but seemed to confirm it by ostentatiously reinforcing its fleet in the eastern Mediterranean. The Soviet representative in New York effectively prevented any Security Council action by insisting that the U.A.R. was within its rights and that there was no problem to discuss. He reflected Moscow's satisfied assumption during these few weeks that Nasser had, in fact, managed to get away with a *fait accompli*.

Then, on June 5, despite American restraining efforts, the Israelis struck. Within hours the Egyptian and Jordanian air forces were obliterated, within days the Egyptian and Jordanian armies. The official mood in Moscow turned to black despair. They saw their Middle East position completely lost. Soviet arms had been found wanting. Hundreds of millions of dollars' worth had been destroyed, even more captured. The Arabs were charging that the Soviet Union had betrayed them by not giving them the aid and protection they had been led to expect. This charge was made more embarrassing by Nasser's false assertion that the United States Air Force had helped the Israelis (in connection with which he and his Arab associates broke diplomatic relations with the U.S.). In their anxiety to contain the conflict, the Kremlin leaders had been on the "hot line" with Washington.

As the dust began to settle, Moscow saw that its worst fears had not been realized. The Israeli forces had stopped short of the neighboring Arab capitals. Nasser and the Syrian regime had survived the disaster and Iraq remained intact. The Soviets set about salvaging and restoring what they could out of the debris. They summoned a conference of Eastern European leaders in Moscow on June 9, which condemned Israeli "aggression" and proclaimed support for the Arabs. The next day the Soviet Union and all of the Eastern European countries except Rumania broke diplomatic relations with Israel. On June 13 the Soviet Foreign Minister called for an emergency special session of the General Assembly, at which Prime Minister Kosygin headed the delegation. While the Soviets were unsuccessful—as they must have expected—in passing their resolution demanding immediate and unconditional Israeli withdrawal to pre-June 5 positions, they effectively publicized their effort in a long series of violently anti-Israeli, pro-Arab pronouncements.

On the military side, beginning on June 23, Moscow launched a spectacular airlift, followed by a more massive sealift, to replace promptly a substantial portion of the aircraft, tanks and other military equipment lost by the Egyptians and the Syrians in the June war, and to strengthen the forces of other "progressive" Arab regimes. Deliveries of Soviet arms during the ensuing fifteen months were estimated to have reached a total value of about $2.5 billion. At the same time, the Kremlin undertook a significant build-up of Soviet naval strength in the Mediterranean. These forces, which before the mid-1960s had been limited to submarines and intelligence reconnaissance vessels, were converted into a self-sustaining naval squadron of about fifty units, including helicopter (but not aircraft) carriers, guided-missile frigates and auxiliaries, as well as submarines. In an interview with the Italian Communist Party paper L'Unità on May 12, 1968, Soviet Foreign Minister Gromyko declared that "being a Black Sea power and consequently a Mediterranean power, the Soviet Union is interested in peace and security in that area in direct proximity to the U.S.S.R.'s southern borders." Charging that the United States Sixth Fleet "exerts pressure on coastal Mediterranean states and attempts to hold in check national liberation movements in the Middle East and North Africa," Gromyko asserted that "the presence of Soviet ships in the Mediterranean is a factor safeguarding the security of the entire Mediterranean zone." The theme of the Gromyko interview has since been reiterated and elaborated by Soviet media and spokesmen. Pravda on November 27 strengthened the Gromyko formulation by saying that the Mediterranean is "vital to the security interests" of the U.S.S.R. and called on the United States to understand that the era of its "uncontrolled domination" was at an end.

The Soviet Mediterranean squadron, even considerably reinforced, is not likely to become a serious threat in the foreseeable future to the much more powerful U.S. Sixth Fleet, backed by the lesser naval forces of our NATO Allies bordering the Mediterranean and by NATO's newest Mediterranean command organized in 1968 to keep Soviet naval activities under surveillance. The Soviet squadron is strong enough, however, to have to be taken into account by the smaller Mediterranean countries. Its availability could mean, if there was a recurrence of such intraregional events as those which brought American Marines to Lebanon in 1958, that the Soviets would get there first and give us a new kind of game to play.

While the special session of the General Assembly ended inconclusively, the debates continued in the United Nations Security Council, which on November 22, 1967, unanimously adopted a British-sponsored "compromise" resolution. The compromise balanced the main Arab (and Soviet) demand for "withdrawal of Israeli armed forces from territories occupied in the recent conflict" (omitting "immediate and unconditional" from the original Soviet formula) with an indirectly worded provision calling on the Arab states to acknowledge and respect "the sovereignty, territorial integrity and political independence" of, and to end their declared "state of belligerency" with, Israel. Under the resolution's authority, the UN Secretary General appointed the Swedish Ambassador in Moscow, Gunnar Jarring, as his special representative to try to mediate between the parties and bring about a settlement.

Ambassador Jarring promptly initiated talks with both sides in the conflict, but was unable to make any headway. The Israelis were adamant in demanding direct negotiations and agreements with their Arab neighbors, to bring about adjusted and recognized frontiers and permanent peace settlements. They were unwilling to return to the insecure conditions prevailing before the conflict or to give up such territory as the Old City of Jerusalem—the traditional focus of Zionist aspirations—or the fortified Golan Heights in Syria—regarded as vital to Israel's security. On their part, the Arabs demanded Israeli withdrawal behind its June 5, 1967, frontiers as a first step before they would negotiate on anything and were noncommittal on such points as guaranteeing navigation rights through the Suez Canal and the Strait of Tiran. They flatly rejected any direct negotiations with Israel. After about a year of trying, Ambassador Jarring suspended his efforts and called for help.

Despite Israeli opposition, President Nixon early in 1969, responding to an appeal from France, agreed to United States participation in quadripartite talks—again the U.S., the U.S.S.R., the U.K. and France—in an effort to find a formula which would enable Ambassador Jarring to renew his mediation efforts with the influence of an agreed "big-four" position to back him up. When these talks got nowhere and were suspended, the United States and the Soviet Union continued bilateral discussions, likewise without result. Moscow's proposals in these exchanges have been cleared with Cairo. They have tended to be explicit in requiring Israeli withdrawal from and surrender of all occupied territory, vague as regards Arab concessions. The United States has sought a graduated plan, under which Israeli forces would be pulled back in stages related to performance on other points by the Arabs, the timing to be worked out by Ambassador Jarring.

While the negotiating process has been going on, Moscow has in a sense made itself a prisoner of the Arab governments involved in the conflict—in particular the U.A.R. and Syria—and they in turn are prisoners of the extremist Palestine guerrillas, whom they harbored, equipped and encouraged. The Soviets initially refrained from any public endorsement of the guerrilla activities as such, but they also refrained from condemning the raids in Israel and elsewhere (such as attacks on Israeli civilian aircraft abroad) and usually seemed to justify the guerrilla actions by linking them with Israeli "provocations." As guerrilla activities and influence increased, Moscow has veered toward open approval, with references to Palestine "patriots" and "partisans." A major article on the Middle East appearing in the authoritative Party journal *Kommunist* early in November, 1969, declared that "all the world's progressive and democratic forces are supporting the Palestinian resistance movement directed at eliminating the consequences of Israeli aggression, regarding this movement as a just, anti-imperialist, national liberation struggle."

During this same period, Soviet media have written favorably of the "growing combat-readiness of the Arab countries," improved morale and patriotism of their peoples and "ever-increasing coordination of their activities." On July 23, 1969, U.A.R. President Nasser, in a speech to his political party, the Arab Socialist Union, declared that the "liberation phase" of the war against Israel had begun. A week later, on August 2, the newspaper of the Soviet armed forces, *Red Star*, in a review of the Middle East situation, noted that "qualitative improvement" had been achieved in the U.A.R. military forces and that they had shifted to "active defense." Aside from the increasingly frequent forays and clashes of the regular forces of both sides, the activities of the Palestine guerrilla organizations have kept the whole area in an uproar. The guerrillas have been a particularly serious problem for the moderate governments of Lebanon and Jordan, as well as for Israel itself, their prime target.

Moscow propaganda has increasingly taken the line that the United States is the evil genius behind "Israeli aggression." It has attacked the American decision to supply fifty Phantom jet fighter aircraft to Israel (a decision taken by President Johnson before his departure from office as a small counter to the much greater number of MIG-21s and SU-7s supplied to the Arab countries). The visit of Prime Minister Golda Meir to the United States in the fall of 1969 was said to be for "confidential talks on additional armament of the Israeli aggressors with offensive weapons." A commentator in the Soviet Government newspaper *Izvestiya* on October 9, 1969, charged that "the United States is aspiring through the hands of the Israelis to struggle against the national liberation movement of the Arab peoples and for the restoration in this region of systems that suit the oil magnates and the military clique."

The Soviet Union has also continued to expand its presence

and influence around the periphery of the immediate area of conflict, from Algeria in the west to the new Republic of South Yemen—set up in 1968 when the British withdrew from Aden —in the east. The effort has featured economic and military aid programs, educational and cultural exchanges and top-level official visits. From March to June, 1968, a task force of the Soviet Pacific Fleet made an unprecedented cruise through the Indian Ocean, the Arabian Sea and the Persian Gulf, paying visits to India, Pakistan, Iran, Iraq and Somalia. The political overturn in Libya in September, 1969—following the Egyptian model of throwing out the King and setting up a republic run by a so-called Revolutionary Command Council—was hailed as a new blow against "imperialism," in this case against the U.S. Air Force base and American oil concessions in the country.

The still unsettled Middle East conflict of 1967 demonstrated again, as had the Cuba missile crisis, that the Soviet apparatus continues to be capable of making dangerous political and military miscalculations. The resumption of massive arms supplies to the Arabs and the Soviet naval build-up in the Mediterranean, as well as the nature of the continuing Soviet propaganda campaign, are not exactly encouraging indications that Moscow has learned from its past mistakes. It is true that in the crunch the episode also showed again that the Soviet Union does not want to risk a major confrontation with the United States at this stage. However, once this danger had clearly been averted, the Kremlin lost no time in making clear its longer-term interest in restoring and expanding its influence with the Arab states as an instrument for the reduction of Western influence and economic interests in the Middle East area. And the long-term prospect must be seriously pondered by all concerned, in the first instance by Israel itself, which must somehow find a way to live with its neighbors. Israel's skilled, literate and determined population of 2.6 million may be able to fend off attacks for some years to come. But these 2.6 million, huddled on 8,000 square miles of territory along the eastern Mediterranean, are surrounded by an Arab world numbering 106 million spread over 4.5 million square miles; and the governments ruling more than half this population consider themselves in a state of war with their small neighbor. These Arab masses are at present backward and illiterate, but they are struggling to emerge into the modern world. As they do, they may become more stable and understanding, and their governments may be guided more by reason and less by popular emotions and street mobs. But they will also learn how to run modern machinery and to handle modern arms.

Arabs themselves frequently argue that the religious teachings of Islam provide a barrier to the penetration of the materialistic and atheistic Marxist ideology. They also point out that Marx's revolutionary philosophy was based on and designed for relatively developed industrial societies. It is well to remember, however, that Marxism, as applied in actual practice by Lenin and Stalin, is a very different thing; and that the Russia of 1917, in which it was applied, was strikingly comparable to the Asian-African region today. There was the same frustrated group of revolutionary intellectuals, the same mass inferiority complex toward the West, the same backwardness and an entrenched religion (Russian Orthodox) which was similarly thought to constitute a barrier to political and social change. Moreover, the obvious material gains and increased power of the Soviet Union in the past fifty years inevitably leave their impress, particularly on backward neighbors. It is true that most of the Arab governments, including the "progressive, national revolutionary" regimes in the United Arab Republic, Algeria, Iraq and Yemen, have banned the Communist parties in their countries. However, they have set up their own single-party systems on the Russian model and call their programs "socialist." Moscow has noted this "socialist orientation" with approval. The article in the November issue of *Kommunist* declared that "The frequent references to the ideas of scientific socialism in the program documents of Arab revolutionary democracy . . . [provide] evidence that the very logic of the struggle for the people's interests leads to the adoption of the principles of scientific socialism."

Despite the similarities between revolutionary Russia and revolutionary Afro-Asia—and despite Moscow's obvious expectations—there is a significant difference. Russia—both Czarist and Soviet—was and continues to be imperialist and colonialist. This was not changed by the Russian Revolution, which was a struggle against *domestic* oppression. These emerging countries, on the other hand, were the victims of *outside* oppression. Their struggle was for freedom from foreign domination. Unless they are totally blinded by their hatred for Israel, they must in due course realize the risk they run of simply exchanging one subjection for another.

The basic lines of Soviet policy were pulled together (and, as a result, hardened) in a joint declaration on the Middle East, issued on November 26, 1969, by the Communist Parties and governments of the Soviet Union and of the other Eastern European countries, again except Rumania. Israel was accused of "organizing military provocations on a steadily increasing scale" and "pursuing a policy of colonial exploitation, oppression and coercion against the Arab population"—"acts . . . leading events toward a new military conflict" and placing "obstacles in the way of a just and stable peace." The declaration charged that "certain Western powers, U.S. imperialist circles above all . . . striving to regain their lost positions in the Middle East . . . are actively encouraging Israel's policy.

"The peoples of the world must compel Israel to withdraw its troops from the Arab territories it is occupying," the document continued, and a "solution must be found to secure the interests and legal rights of the Palestinian Arab people, fighting as they are for a heroic national liberation and fighting an anti-imperialist struggle." Since "the facts prove that the imperialists have not abandoned their attempts to overthrow the progressive Arab regimes and are using the Zionist ruling circles of Israel as instruments for the attainment of their aims . . . the socialist countries will give every assistance to the Arab states."

Pursuing an historic pattern of Russian "aspirations," Moscow has thus placed its stake on the Arabs. The Middle East is an area into which the Soviet Union can with relative ease project its influence and power and in which Western interests are both important and vulnerable. The region will certainly continue to be a problem area and a source of potential conflict.

Epilogue

Hundreds of books could be and probably will be written about hundreds of aspects of the Russian scene, of the Soviet political system, of Soviet-American relations and of the position and purposes of the two superpowers on a shrinking planet in an expanding universe. I have tried to look at the over-all picture, and my review of this vast and complex subject has necessarily been selective. I hope, however, that it has been sufficient to illustrate that some key forces at work in Russian society have been determinative in the past and can be expected to continue to operate in the future.

The contradictions in Soviet society, in particular the contrasts between the accomplishments of advanced science and the poverty of everyday life, are largely a result of deliberate policy decisions by the Soviet rulers. Under the command system of economy, Stalin could establish the priorities and they were simple—create a heavy-industry base: more oil, more coal, more electric power stations, more iron, more steel, more heavy machines and machine tools. The best of the country's limited human resources, its scientific and technical skills, and practically all investment funds went to these priority projects. The peasantry was milked for food and raw materials, and the consumer left to fend for himself. But inevitably, as the basic industrial plant was built up, and particularly after it was restored and expanded following World War II, the economy automatically became more complex and difficult to manage. Besides, the population had learned, during and after the war, that life was much better "outside"; and they began to demand more for themselves—better food, better clothing, better shelter. This imbalance in the economy goes far toward explaining some aspects of Soviet policies in their relations with the West: the desire to import industrial plants and machines incorporating advanced technology; the effort to establish agreements and arrangements for scientific and technological cooperation; and, indeed, the frequent recourse to industrial espionage. This desire for access to technical and scientific education and experience is also a factor in Soviet willingness to conclude broad "cultural" exchange agreements, despite the consequent penetration of the closed Soviet system.

In their millennial struggle for existence on the vast, flat, open Eurasian plains, the Russians have been attacked repeatedly and from all sides, by Mongols, by Turks, by Swedes, by Poles, by French, by Germans. The long Mongol occupation not only left its ethnic and political impress on the society, but also engendered a lasting antipathy toward the Mongol Chinese; two frightfully destructive invasions in the last half-century created a real fear of any resurgence of German might. The historic insecurity of their homeland is largely responsible for the Russian concept of "security-in-depth." This accounts not only for the "strategic retreat" and "scorched earth" policies followed during the Napoleonic invasion and World War II, but for the constant Russian drive to expand the country's borders, to create and control buffer states, and to reach outlets to and room for maneuver in "the warm seas." Herein lies the source of Czarist expansion into Siberia and Central Asia; of Soviet wartime demands for territorial concessions in the Far East and for a part of Mussolini's Italian Empire; of Stalin's postwar attempt to wrest lands from Iran and Turkey, of his takeovers in Eastern Europe, of his support of aggression in Greece and in Korea; of Khrushchev's effort to seize West Berlin; and of the Soviet drive into the eastern Mediterranean and the Middle East. It is little wonder that the Marxist doctrine of the inevitability of one Communist world fits like a glove this traditional Russian obsession with "security-in-depth."

This perpetual sense of insecurity is also a factor underlying the Russian concept of the relativity of power. The Soviet Union is stronger if its potential opponents are weaker—hence the development and support of foreign Communist parties, of pro-Soviet "front" organizations; the endless efforts to sow discord among the Western capitalist allies; the proposals for the liquidation of overseas bases and the withdrawal of U.S. forces stationed abroad (while Soviet forces on the great Eurasian land mass remain contiguous to a huge proportion of the world's population and riches).

Finally, the concept of the vulnerability of their sprawling domain to outside attack goes far to explain what we refer to as the "defense-oriented thinking" of Russian civil and military leaders. This outlook helps explain, for example, the priority they have given to radar systems and fighter aircraft, and their decision to develop and deploy an antiballistic missile (ABM) defense system at a time when the Pentagon's computers judged such an investment to be an unwarrantedly costly means of deterrence.

Marxism has been "Russified"—"Leninized"—to the point that as a political system it could be described as simply a more efficient and ruthless version of the authoritarian rule of the Czars. Yet Marxist-Leninist doctrine is essential to justify—to give "legitimacy" to—the rule of a minority political party holding a monopoly of political power. The consequence is a permanent dilemma in the decision-making process, between the promotion or protection of the national interests of the state and the pursuance of the messianic objectives of the Communist world revolution. There is no doubt that in the early days of Bolshevik rule the Utopian promises of Marxism, as interpreted by Lenin, made the doctrine an effective instrument of political power. But such Marxist concepts as "the withering away of the state" and "to each according to his need" have themselves withered away. Moreover, the ideology has not been able to prevail against the continuing influence of the great literature of the nineteenth-century "enlightenment," which exalted the individual, or against the growing awareness of the Soviet peoples —through wartime contacts, foreign radios, exchange programs —of a "better" world outside. The more the power of Marxist-Leninist ideology declines, the more frantically does the Kremlin leadership feel impelled to proclaim its validity and force its acceptance. Thus we witness the Kremlin's alarm and tragic decision to suppress the movement toward "liberalization" and "humanization" of Communism in Czechoslovakia, new efforts to suppress and control the intellectuals in the Soviet Union itself, and the launching of an ideological revival campaign which is to continue under forced draft through 1970 under the label of celebrations honoring the centennial of the birth of Lenin.

The narrowness of the Soviet human and material-resources base—the hard fact of a Gross National Product less than half that of the United States, with which they seek to compete—presents perhaps the most serious problem with which the Kremlin leaders have to cope on a day-to-day basis. Internally, this economic reality has pushed them toward new methods of industrial and agricultural management designed to improve labor productivity and total production, even toward the adoption of such un-Marxist concepts as monetary valuation of capital investment, depreciation, interest, profits and market prices. It has also stimulated the growth of special-interest groups in the country, rivaling each other and pressing the leadership for larger slices of an inadequate budgetary pie. In external affairs, the leadership's realization of Soviet financial, economic and technical limitations relative to the United States has been a major factor in making possible such developments as the treaty banning weapons of mass destruction in space and acceptance of bilateral strategic arms limitation talks.

The ups and downs in relations between the United States and the Soviet Union over the years reflect the interplay of these basic factors, conditioned by internal political developments in both countries and by events in the outer world beyond the control of either power.

Largely because of the preoccupation of the principal contenders for power in the Soviet Union after Stalin's death in 1953, there was a few years' break in the hostile confrontations of East and West. During this period we were able to end the Korean hostilities and the war in Indochina and to secure, at long last, an Austrian Peace Treaty. Then Soviet aggressiveness was revived in the form of Khrushchev's Sputnik diplomacy at the end of 1957, as Khrushchev set out to try to translate the new prestige and new power potential accruing to the Soviet Union from its space successes into concrete political and even territorial gains, particularly in Germany and Berlin. By the end of 1962 Khrushchev had been faced down in Berlin and Cuba, and a new element had entered the picture, in the form of Moscow's raging conflict with Peking. We thus had another period in which we could make some progress in bilateral relations between the United States and the Soviet Union. In 1963–64 we concluded the Nuclear Test Ban Treaty, negotiated and signed a bilateral Consular Convention, established a "hot line" for crisis communications between the White House and the Kremlin, concluded agreements for cooperation in the desalination of water and the exchange of satellite weather information by direct telegraph line between the two capitals, revived and reconfirmed the agreement for the establishment of civil airlines between Moscow and New York and substantially broadened our bilateral cultural exchange program.

The violent confrontations of the Stalin era and of the period of Khrushchev's Sputnik diplomacy, and now in Vietnam, have demonstrated that Communist attempts to expand their system by force can and will be contained by the determination of the free world. But by and large these responses have been reactive and defensive in nature. And these contests have also demonstrated that force is not a solution to the basic conflict between the political systems.

I am afraid that the full realization of this fact has not yet quite come home to the present Soviet leadership. While Khrushchev was ready to wash his hands of Southeast Asia, his successors, dominated by their concern over their conflict with Peking, decided instead to try to rally the world Communist movement and other sympathizers to Moscow by appealing for unity against "American imperialist aggression in Vietnam." There was thus a real deterioration in our relationship after the fall of Khrushchev. The new leadership took no new initiatives toward us and accepted no new initiatives from us. Negotiations were avoided, except in matters involving overwhelming Soviet interests, and even in such matters were preferably undertaken under multilateral cover, such as the United Nations (in the case of the treaty barring weapons of mass destruction in outer space), or the Geneva Disarmament Conference (in the case of the Nuclear Nonproliferation Treaty). This attitude began to moderate in mid-1968, as a result of three factors. The first was the cessation of the bombing of North Vietnam and the opening of the Paris talks. The second was the Kremlin's desire to screen and, so far as possible, to obliterate the militaristic and aggressive image left by their invasion of Czechoslovakia. And the third was the heating up of the Sino-Soviet conflict.

In July, 1968, the long-delayed inauguration of direct air services between Moscow and New York took place, the Supreme Soviet ratified the U.S.–U.S.S.R. Consular Convention signed back in 1964, and a new exchanges agreement for 1969–70 was belatedly signed. At the same time, the Kremlin leadership informed us they were ready at long last to accept our proposal of December, 1966, for bilateral talks about limiting the offensive and defensive missile race. There was some further delay, first on our side, due to Czechoslovakia and then to the need for the new Nixon administration to prepare itself, then again on the Soviet side. These strategic arms limitation talks—SALT, as they have come to be known—finally began in

November, 1969. They will inevitably be complex and long-drawn-out. However, I am sure there is an interest on the part of the Soviets, especially among the economic managers, as well as on our part, in seeking a means to avoid a new, costly but fruitless spiral in the missile race. Agreement was also reached on the text of a proposed treaty to ban the placement of nuclear weapons on the ocean floors.

Quadripartite and bilateral talks on the Arab-Israeli conflict have been continuing intermittently since early 1969. I would not expect, in view of the known attitudes of the Israelis and the Arabs, that a permanent settlement can be reached in the foreseeable future. However, ways may be found to take some of the heat out of the situation. Although Soviet representatives have taken the position that an arrangement to limit the shipment of arms to the Middle East could only be considered after the withdrawal of Israeli forces, I would not rule out an eventual change in this posture. I believe Moscow was shaken enough by the disastrous conflict of June, 1967, not to want that kind of thing to happen again; and however bleak the long-term prospect may be for the Israelis, they will for some years continue to be more than a match for their Arab neighbors.

If the international climate does not deteriorate from its present level of supportable tension, the United States and the Soviet Union might also move toward some further measures in the arms-control or disarmament field, such as mutual reduction in military budgets or agreed limitation of forces in Central Europe. We could probably also considerably increase our exchanges, including the reactivation of some projects which have been lying dormant, such as desalination of sea water and various cooperative ventures in the peaceful uses of atomic energy.

We might even eventually achieve some collaboration—or at least some division of labor—in such advanced new fields as exploration and exploitation of the oceans and of outer space, though the basic Soviet posture here is likely to remain one of rivalry. In this connection, it is well to remember that, despite its internal economic problems and popular demands for a higher standard of living, the Soviet system remains capable of concentrating its best scientific and productive resources on priority objectives in a way the United States can normally match only under conditions of wartime mobilization. And continued Soviet efforts to develop space vehicles and a world-wide maritime presence—on a scale disproportionate to the country's means—indicates a conviction in the Kremlin that new successes in these fields will restore the image of Soviet scientific and technical superiority originally achieved with the Sputniks.

I see little prospect for progress on the great political problems, such as the divided countries of Germany, Korea and Vietnam (assuming that a Vietnam settlement confirms the principle that these lines of partition are not to be altered by force—I dread to contemplate the disasters we would face if it shouldn't). These larger problems will have to await internal evolution in the Soviet Union and other Communist countries and some real change in the distribution of forces in the world.

But even if Vietnam is settled and international tensions are somewhat reduced, we should have no illusions that everything will suddenly be easy and rosy. The basic ideology which justifies Communist minority rule in the Soviet Union requires the existence of an outside capitalist-imperialist society to oppose and struggle against. There is no suitable candidate other than the United States of America. Thus, as long as Communism endures—and this is likely to be a long time—free societies will be faced with the direct challenge of a relentlessly hostile political system, established in the heartland of the great Eurasian land mass and reaching out from there to spread its ideology and its power to all parts of the earth. It behooves us to know and understand that system. Indeed, such knowledge and understanding may be a matter of freedom or slavery, or even of life and death.

In addition to this hostile political challenge, the world of the future will be exceedingly complex. The scientific and technological revolution of our times has already wrought vast changes and is still in full course. It has shrunk our planet physically to the point where man is already reaching out for the universe. The development of jet and rocket engines, the wonders of chemistry, the power of the atom and the miracles of electronics are changing and will continue to change the very nature of the physical environment in which we live. Through world-wide television we already see events as they happen in all parts of the globe. Electronic eyes peer down on us from outer space. Tomorrow it will not be seven hours across the Atlantic but three hours, and then thirty minutes. Electronic brains will make mathematical calculations previously undreamed of, will remove the last great obstacle to human communication by speedily translating the most difficult of foreign languages. Machines will be better and better, but who will use them—and for what? What about man? Can we say that we have produced or that we know how to produce a better man than, let us say, Plato of Athens or Jesus of Nazareth? On this score I would say that, while man today must understand science, the scientist must also understand man if life is to be good, or indeed if life is to be even tolerable on this earth for anyone, whether he call himself capitalist or Communist.

The second factor characterizing the world of today and tomorrow is usually referred to as the revolution of rising expectations. The development of the arts and sciences of communication has brought us far beyond the point where vast parts of the human family can live in isolation, ignorance and misery. Ease of travel, availability of radio communications, aided by the turbulence and turmoil arising from two world wars, have made the most backward populations aware of the fact that there is another way of life. They consider it a better way of life. They want that better life, better sanitation, better roads, better education, better justice. And they want to be free, to be their own masters. Too often they do not know how to go about reaching this new life. Too often they do not know the price in terms of sacrifice and hard work and consistent endeavor that must be paid. In the end, however, their consciousness of the new possibilities will impel them to find a way. The question that confronts them and confronts us is: what way? Their aspirations cannot be suppressed. If we are wise and generous, they can be guided.

This whole problem of the emergent peoples is complicated by the fact that the wonders of medical science, carried to the farthest reaches of the earth by missionaries and other people of good intent, have so reduced the toll of disease and lengthened the span of life as to produce almost literally an explosion of the world's population. What we in the past comfortably referred to as a total of two billion people has now passed three billion and is predicted to more than double—to over seven billion—by the end of the century. This simultaneous expansion of population and of wants brings up the most serious problems of production and distribution of goods, of education and of social organization. It may well involve fundamental reform of the world's trading and financial systems and a myriad of related problems. The solution of these problems will require not only the best technical skills that societies can develop but a deep and sympathetic understanding of the nature of the human beings involved.

Because of our wealth and power, much of the burden of coping with these looming problems will unavoidably fall upon the United States. But in tomorrow's world it will no longer be possible for anyone to live to himself and for himself alone. All will have to try to cope with these increasing complexities, and all will be affected by them. The Soviet leadership is already finding the Communist system inadequate to solve the social, industrial and agricultural problems of a relatively developed society. It has found that Communist ideology is diminishing in effectiveness as an instrument of political power, and that it does not provide adequate spiritual nourishment for a literate people. Internationally it has found that national interests are stronger than ideological ties. These trends, and the problems they create, are certainly not going to diminish in the future.

Demographers estimate that by the year 2000 the American and Soviet populations will roughly equalize, at about 325 million people. But at that time one-third of the Soviet population is likely to be non-Slav. The existence of such large minorities in the Soviet Union, quite apart from nationality differences among the Slavs themselves, that is, Russians, Ukrainians and Belorussians, cannot fail to raise difficult political and social issues. As Americans are all acutely aware, we already face those issues in our own free society. However, only one-sixth of *our* population will be nonwhite at the end of this century, a relatively more manageable problem, especially since we have already started trying to solve it.

On the economic side, experts predict that by the end of the century the United States Gross National Product will mount from its 1968 level of around $835 billion per year to $3.3 trillion and that in the same period the Soviet GNP will rise from $412 billion to $1.5 trillion. Per capita GNP will be roughly $10,000 and $4,750 respectively. The absolute gap in the respective GNPs would thus grow from the present $425 billion to $1.8 trillion, while the per capita gap would grow from about $2,500 to $5,300. Even so, both the United States and the Soviet Union would be strictly in the "have" class, and both, in varying degrees, would still have to cope with the fundamental problem of the ever-growing and even greater disparity between their own standards of living and the standard of living of the underdeveloped world. The demographers estimate, for example, that by the end of the century the Chinese population will have increased from its present 700-odd million to 1.2 billion. I know of no estimates on Chinese GNP, but it seems unlikely that production there can even keep level with the growth of population, let alone gain on it. In rough terms, the Chinese picture is probably valid for most of the underdeveloped world.

This picture of the future world may seem a little grim and frightening, but I believe that it is not beyond the powers of man to change the prospect for the better. We must think in bold terms—of population control, of pollution prevention, of desalination of sea water to make the deserts bloom, of farming and mining the seas, of weather control, of planetary exploration and colonization, of racial reconciliation, of mass education, of improved international organization. The magnitude of the problems facing us will create common interests not only among the developed free societies but with the Communist-ruled countries of Eastern Europe, including the Soviet Union. And this common interest in turn will have its influence on the evolution of those Communist societies. Then the "haves" must find a way to better the life of the "have-nots." If they are unwilling to share the wealth—and this seems to be a human characteristic—at least they must share their knowledge and skills and open their markets to enable the underprivileged to make a tolerable life for themselves.

Of one thing I am sure. The solution of these colossal problems will not be found through the system of political and social organization called "Communism," as developed and practiced in the Soviet Union or in Communist China. It will rather be found in the concepts of the American Revolution. I am not thinking here in the narrow terms of our War of Independence, inspiring as that event should be to other peoples who are today in the stage of development that we were two centuries ago. I am referring rather to the dynamic political, social and economic concepts which flowed from that great liberating movement and have been incorporated into our social organization. These concepts have given us what may, in truth, be called the permanent revolution. It is not an accident that each American generation insists on reviewing the state of our society and puts forward demands for the elimination of injustices and for reforms to correct old inequities or meet new conditions. Two generations ago this kind of agitation brought into being the antitrust laws and the progressive income tax. In my younger days it brought the economic reforms of the New Deal, recognizing the responsibility of government to prevent the recurrence of depressions, to ensure employment and to provide decent standards of social welfare. Today the demand is for equality of rights, of status and of opportunities for our black citizens and other minorities. These recurrent upheavals are indicators not of weakness but of strength.

Sometimes, in this process of review and change, we make some serious mistakes, especially as respects the world scene. When I was in school at the turn of the 1930s, a pacifist movement was sweeping the campuses, featured by demands for abolition of the ROTC, and a general mood was created which led the country toward isolationism and legislated "neutrality." At precisely the same time Hitler was making an aggressive military colossus of Germany, and the Japanese militarists were already moving through Asia toward their ultimate goal at Pearl Harbor. Our default in will and action thus jeopardized our national security and made us responsible in substantial measure for the tragedy of World War II, with its staggering total of eighteen million killed in battle, not to mention the wounded, and civilian losses beyond imagination—nearly fifteen million in the Soviet Union alone. In their frustration and introspection about Vietnam, many of our fellow citizens have made comparable mistakes. At a time when our efforts had finally brought our adversary to the negotiating table, they proposed that we throw our aces away. Whatever our differences of view as to the origins of the American involvement in Vietnam and however pure and noble the motives of the proponents, proposals for a unilateral cease-fire or abrupt withdrawal could only prolong the war they wished to stop and increase the casualty lists they wished to reduce.

We do have our problems and our confusion and our doubts. We do make mistakes. But as I look back at the progress we have made in emerging from the isolationism of the 1930s and adjusting to the world role that history has thrust upon us, I am optimistic.

Foreign policy begins at home. The most important thing we can do is to demonstrate, in response to the Communist challenge, that this permanent American revolution is the way to a better life for more and more of the earth's population. We must know our own country, its history, its traditions, its ideals. We must preserve and perfect the political institutions which provide the means for orderly change in conditions of freedom and justice. We must see to it that this system continues to meet the real wants of man by providing equality of opportunity and freedom of choice for all its citizens.

Sometimes I think the Russians are more conscious of our heritage and of the dynamics of our society than we are ourselves. Here, in fact, is a final contradiction. Soviet propaganda incessantly attacks the United States and portrays with malicious joy all our problems. And yet we have from the first days of Soviet power been held out as the standard of comparison, and thus as the object of envy, admiration and emulation. The Soviet peoples have been constantly exhorted to "overtake and surpass the Americans." It is up to us to keep this slogan valid.

Index

Abel, Rudolf, 269

Acheson, Dean, 279, 289, 295, 297, 300, 329, 399

Adenauer, Konrad, 313, 316, 330, 339

Adzhubei, Alexei, 135, 136, 335

Afghanistan, 118, 119, 138

Africa, 207, 210–12, 237, 239, 255, 256, 399

Agency for International Development (AID), 290

Agriculture, 2, 9, 145–47, 156, 245–46

in Asia, 396–97

under Khrushchev, 111, 116, 118, 124, 127, 136, 145–46, 248

under Lenin, 50, 51

Malenkov on, 111

under Stalin, 88, 122

state secrets on, 97, 98

See also Collective farming

Ahmed, Great Khan, 8

Akhmadulina, Bella, 125

Akhmatova, Anna, 125

Aksenov, Vasili, 126

Al Ahram, 402–3
Albania, 208, 239, 265, 278–79, 292, 364
Aleschin, Samuil, 126
Alexander I, 21–22
Alexander II, 22, 24–26
Alexander III, 27
Alexei, Patriarch, 261–62
Alliluyeva, Svetlana, 153, 158, 399
All-Russian Congress of Soviets, 41–42, 47
American Federation of Labor (AFL), 259–61
Amerika, 147
Amur River, 190, 193
Anders, General Wladyslaw, 78
Anzus Alliance, 302
Aptheker, Herbert, 259
Arbuzov, Alexei, 126
Armed forces, 10, 57, 245, 247–49, 415
    in Berlin, 306, 314, 323, 330, 335–36
    in Bolshevik Revolution, 43
    Comintern and, 168, 306
    in Eastern Europe, 273, 276, 283–84
    in February Revolution, 38–39
    in Khrushchev's ouster, 134, 248
    in Korea, 297
    in limited sovereignty actions, 232
    in Siberia, 215
    under Stalin, 73, 91, 102, 121, 123
    under Stalin purge, 58, 247
    White, 49
    in World War I, 36–37, 49
    in World War II, 67, 68, 72, 74, 80–85, 88, 91, 280
    See also Navy
Asian Development Bank, 397
Atlantic Charter, 76, 85, 305

Atom bomb, 92–93, 106, 201–2, 237, 266, 280
Attlee, Clement, 91
Australia, 302, 373
Austria, 129, 315, 417
Azerbaijan, 275

Baku, 52–53
Bakunin, Mikhail, 23, 41
Baltic States, 49, 61, 67, 68, 81
Bandung Conference, 210–11, 262, 401
Bao Dai, 370, 371, 374
Batu Khan, 7
Batum, 52
Belgium, 284, 289–90
Belinsky, Vissarion, *xvi*, 20, 73
Benelux, 284, 288–89
Beneš, Eduard, 283, 284
Beria, Lavrenti, 93, 108–10, 116, 137
Berlin, 269, 305–6, 319, 321–23, 325, 328–38, 348
    blockade and airlift in, 285–88, 301, 308, 309, 333
    division of, 308–10
    riots in, 313
    wall in, 333, 336
    World Peace Assembly in, 259, 262, 394
Bevin, Ernest, 91
Black Partition, 26, *see also* Social Democrats
Black Sea, 3
Blake, George, 269
Bloody Sunday, 33
Bolivia, 354, 358, 362, 363
Bolshevik (magazine), 83–84, 103
Bolshevik Revolution (October, 1917), *xv*, 43–44, 43*n*, 90, 154, 155, 161, 355
Bolsheviks, 47–49, 54, 57
    as anti-Zionist, 399–400

beginnings of, 31, 33, 34, 39, 41, 54
in Constituent Assembly, 47–48
Kerensky on, 42
membership of, 43
program of, 47, 50–51
right to rule of, *xvii*, 43, 90
on socialism, 57
Bonn Agreements (1952), 312–13
Boris Godunov (opera), 9, 15–16
Bosch, Juan, 350
Bosporus, 69
Brandt, Willy, 333–34, 339
Brest-Litovsk, Treaty of, 49
Brezhnev, Leonid, 133, 134, 214, 264
on China, 235–36
in Czechoslovakian crisis, 220, 222, 223, 229–30
at 50th Anniversary, 155, 243–44
on Germany, 338
on military power, 248
on NATO, 293
in power, 139, 140,156
on Soviet-American relations, 157
youth of, 137–38
Brezhnev Doctrine, 229–32
British Trade Union Congress (BTUC), 259–61
Brussels, Treaty of, 288–89, 314
Bulganin, Nikolai, 108–9, 111, 118–19, 129–30, 317–18
Bulgaria, 69, 81, 92, 278–79
Bundy, McGeorge, 331
Burgess, Guy, 268–69
Byrnes, James, 92, 278, 311

Cahiers du Communisme, Les, 243
Cambodia, 129, 302, 369, 371–73, 376, 379, 386

Canada, 265–66
Candia, General Ovando, 363
Carr, Sam, 266
Caspian Sea, 2, 3, 191
Castro, Fidel, 344, 345, 348–55, 358–61, 364
Castro, Raúl, 356
Ceaucescu, Nicolae, 222, 238
Censorship, 14, 147, 149–52
under Czars, 18–21, 25, 27, 34
in Czechoslovakia, 221, 223, 226–28, 233
under Khrushchev, 124–28
under Lenin, 48
inside Party, 54
of scientists, 151
under Stalin, 56, 95, 98–99
Central Intelligence Agency (CIA), 270, 320, 326, 331
Central Treaty Organization (CENTO), 302
Cernik, Oldrich, 225
Chandra, Romesh, 259
Charles XII (Sweden), 14
Chechen Republic, 102
Cheka, 49–50, 58
Chekhov, Anton, *xvi*, 15, 20, 73
Chernyshevsky, Nikolai, 25, 73
Chiang Kai-shek, 170, 192, 196, 294
Chicherin, Boris, 161
Chile, 350, 352, 362
China, 60, 137, 175, 186–217, 255, 294–95, 371, 396, 423
aid to, 196–98
atomic weapons in, 201–2, 205–7, 216
Brezhnev on, 235–36
Cuba and, 345, 349, 350, 354, 364
cultural revolution in, 206, 211
in embassy demonstrations, 213–14

China (cont'd)
    at Indian border, 203–4
    in Korea, 299–301, 396
    on Nuclear Test Ban Treaty,
        204–6
    Russian attitudes toward, xv,
        187, 196, 414
    Stalin on, 170, 196, 301
    trade with, 196–97
    Vietnam and, 370, 372–73,
        377, 387–89
    in World War II, 76, 82
Chinese Communist Party, 237–
    41, 294, 387, 389
Chou En-lai, 214, 241
Churchill, Sir Winston, 70, 72,
    76, 79–81, 86, 91, 247, 273,
    276
Cisar, Cestmir, 221, 222, 225
Civil rights, xvi, 14, 151, 271
    under Duma, 38–39
    in Germany, 307
    under Lenin, 50
    under Nicholas II, 34
    under Stalin, 56
Clay, General Lucius, 306, 333–
    34
Climate, xv, xviii, 1–5
Colby, Bainbridge, 60
Cold War, 87–105, 176, 273, 301
    Khrushchev on, 111
    revisionists on, 103–5
    inside Soviet Union, 95–104
Collective farming, xiv, 109,
    116, 145
    under Stalin, 55, 72, 82–83
    in Yugoslavia, 182
Colombia, 263, 358, 363
Cominform, see Communist In-
    formation Bureau
Comintern, see Communist In-
    ternational, Third
Communes, 8–9, 23, 36, 43
Communist Information Bureau
    (Cominform), 172–75, 181,
    283

Communist International, First,
    23
Communist International, Third
    (Comintern), 60, 81, 161–
    72, 174, 183–85, 210, 237,
    264–67
    democratic centralism in, 161,
        162, 164, 183, 185
    dissolution of, 75
    in East Germany, 170, 306
    front organizations of, 164,
        171–172, 258, 267, 415
    in trade unions, 164, 171, 266
Communist Party, 56, 57, 160,
    241, 255
    on assassination, 26
    conferences of, 58–59
    Congress, 7th, of, 226
    Congress, 14th, of, 54, 59
    Congress, 19th, of, 107
    Congress, 20th, of, 112, 119–
        22, 136, 156, 316
    Congress, 21st, of, 136, 198–
        200
    Congress, 22nd, of, 136, 199–
        200, 208
    Congress, 23rd, of, 154–155,
        265, 351
    Congresses of, 58–59
    economy and, 144–45
    international, 198–200, 205–
        13, 218–20, 234–41, 264–
        65, 345–46, 349, 361, 389,
        394, 396, see also Commu-
        nist Internationals
    Khrushchev and, 124, 135–37
    leadership of, xvii–xviii, 107,
        137, 395
    legitimacy of, 105, 107, 282
    limited sovereignty in, 229–
        30, 233, 236, 241
    membership in, xvii, 83, 84,
        90, 239
    polycentrism in, 123
    Presidium of, 107–8, 110–12,
        133–34, 154

propaganda of, 153–57, 164, 266, 268, 271
public opinion and, 103
purges of, 57–59
Secretariat of, 108, 110, 112
after Stalin's death, 107–9
Congress of Industrial Organizations (CIO), 260–61
Constitutional Democrats (Kadets, KD), 35, 48
Constitutions, 271
demands for, 22, 27, 39
under Nicholas II, 34
Soviet, 56, 151
Cossacks, 8, 9, 190
Council for Economic Mutual Aid (COMECON), 181, 218
Council of Foreign Ministers (CFM), 77, 92, 95–96, 308, 311, 371, 399
Council of Working Men's Representatives, 34
Crimean Tatar Republic, 102
Crimean War, 24
Cuba, 248, 252, 337, 340–65
Tricontinental Conference in, 262–64, 350–52, 360
Cuban Communist Party, 347, 356
Custine, Astolphe de, 10–15
Czars, xvi, 13–14
legitimacy of, xvii, 90
overthrow of, xv, 9
Romanov dynasty of, 9
Czechoslovakia, 184, 219, 401
in Marshall Plan, 281
rebellion (1968) in, 148, 151, 157, 159, 220–38, 261, 293, 359–60
takeover (1948) of, 283–84
in World War II, 62, 64–65

Dairen, 81, 85, 192
Daniel, Yuli, 149–51
Dardanelles, 69
Davies, Joseph, 86

Debray, Régis, 352, 354, 358
Decembrists, 21–22, 41
Diem, Ngo Dinh, 274–75, 378, 380–81, 385
Dimitrov, Georgi, 170
Disarmament, 130, 158, 202, 258–59, 318, 320, 321, 329, 336
Dobrynin, Anatoly, 336
Dominican Republic, 348, 350
Donskoy, Dmitri, xvii, 7–8, 73
Dostoyevsky, Feodor, 20, 23
Drapeau Rouge, 384
Dubcek, Alexander, 220, 225–28
Dudintsev, Vladimir, 125, 152
Dulles, Allen, 326
Dulles, John Foster, 129, 130, 317, 319–23
Duma, 34–35, 37–44
Dyomin, Mikhail, 152

Economy, 141–47, 198–200, 245–47, 414, 416
under Khrushchev, 124, 136, 142, 143
of postwar Germany, 308, 338
in satellite countries, 177–81, 218–19
Stalin on, 88, 282, 283
See also Agriculture; Industry
Eden, Anthony, 91, 129, 276
Ehrenburg, Ilya, 124–25, 400
Eisenhower, General Dwight D., 129, 202, 317–20, 323–25
Khrushchev on, 119, 327–28
on Middle East, 401–3
on U-2, 327, 328
on Vietnam, 380
Eisenstein, Sergei, 15
Ely, General Paul, 375
Engels, Friedrich, 23, 24, 44
England, see United Kingdom
Ercoli, Palmiro, 168
Escalante, Aníbal, 356
Espionage, 171, 265–70, 294

Espionage (*cont'd*)
    U-2 incident of, 131, 269,
        325–28
European Coal and Steel Com-
    munity, 313
European Community of Atomic
    Energy (Euratom), 317
European Defense Community,
    312–13
European Economic Community
    (Common Market), 317
Exchange programs, 147, 154,
    157, 414, 417
    under Khrushchev, 127–28,
        130, 131, 343, 344

Fall, Bernard, 377
Faure, Edgar, 129
February Revolution, *xv*, 38–39,
    43*n*
Finland, 49, 68–69, 81
First International, 23
Foreign aid, 254–57, 404, 406
    to China, 196–98, 201–2
    to Cuba, 356–57, 361
    to Vietnam, 379, 386–88
Foreign relations, 11, 59–62,
    242–45, 253–57, 279–80
    during Cold War, 97–98
    Comintern and, 161, 168–69
    under Khrushchev, 118, 128–
        31, 243, 254
    propaganda in, 245, 253, 257–
        59
    with satellite countries, 178–
        79
Formosa, *see* Taiwan
Fowler, Henry (Joe), 331
France, 64–67, 258, 269
    in Berlin blockade, 286–87
    on German remilitarization,
        311–13
    on Israel, 408
    in Marshall Plan, 281, 283–84
    in Vietnam, 368–75, 380
Franklin, Benjamin, 18

French Communist Party, 238,
    239, 243, 282–83
Furtseva, Yekaterina, 118, 343

Galanskov, Yuri, 150
Gapon, Father, 33
García Peláez, Raúl, 357
Gaulle, General Charles de, 327,
    330, 335, 370
Geneva Conferences, 129–30,
    258–59, 315–16, 321, 324–
    25
    on Vietnam, 372, 377–80,
        385–86
Genghis Khan, 188
Geography, 1–4
Germany, 49, 59–60, 64–70, 81,
    92, 219, 232, 305–16, 318
    conferences about, 129, 130,
        315
    elections in, 315–16
    Khrushchev on, 136, 321
    reunification of, 318, 324, 339
    Stalin on revolution in, 170
    See also Berlin
Germany, East (Democratic Re-
    public), 170, 237, 309,
    332–33, 337–39
    recognition of, 259, 316, 339
    remilitarization in, 312–13
    Soviet military forces in, 249,
        306
Germany, West (Federated Re-
    public), 237, 285, 288, 292,
    310, 316
    elections in, 313–14
    in Marshall Plan, 284–85
    remilitarization of, 311–14
Ginsburg, Alexander, 150
Gitlow, Benjamin, 165, 166
Gogol, Nikolai, *xvi*, 15, 19
Gorky, Maxim, 15, 20, 73
Gottwald, Klement, 169–70, 281,
    284
Gray, General David, 331

Grechko, Marshal Andrei, 139, 222
Greece, 92, 94–95, 274, 276–79, 292, 399, 415
Gregory, Dick, 259
Gromyko, Andrei Andreyevich, 213, 230–31, 253–54, 386
    on Germany, 334–36
    on Greece, 278
    on Mediterranean, 406
    in UN, 254, 256, 294, 334
Gross National Product, xviii, 141, 199, 253, 416, 423
Guerrilla warfare, 352, 358, 379, 385, 391, 408–9
Guevara, Che, 337, 352, 354, 358
Guzenko, Igor, 265

Hamilton, Alexander, 18
Hammer, Armand, 51
Harriman, Averell, 51, 74, 75, 270, 386, 392–93
Hart, Armando, 351–52
Herter, Christian, 323, 325–27
Herzen, Alexander, xvii, 21–23, 25, 41
Hitler, Adolf, 2, 61, 62, 64–67, 70–73, 76, 82
Ho Chi Minh, 184, 369–70, 373–74, 376–79, 384, 391–92, 394–95
Hoffer, Eric, 117
Hoover Relief Commission, 50
Hopkins, Harry, 74, 75, 80
Hot line, 131, 344, 405, 417
Hull, Cordell, 76, 84, 275–76
Hungary, 81, 92, 123, 130, 219, 232
Husak, Gustav, 225–28

Ilyichev, Leonid, 126, 127
India, 68, 118, 119, 138, 191, 203–4, 239, 255, 410
Indonesia, 239, 315, 396
Industry, xiv, 10, 26, 61, 141–45, 156, 245–47
    Five-Year Plans in, 55, 88, 98, 124, 246
    under Khrushchev, 111, 124, 127, 135
    nationalization of, 48, 51, 60, 178
    in satellite countries, 178, 180
    state secrets on, 97
    under Witte, 31–32
International Red Cross, 79, 259
Iran, 129, 138, 274–75, 302, 399, 404, 410, 415
Iraq, 319, 403, 405, 410, 411
Iskra (The Spark), 30–31
Israel, 316, 399–412, 419
Italian Communist Party, 238, 239, 282–83
Ivan III, 8
Ivan IV (the Terrible), 9, 15, 58
Izvestiya, 153, 206, 409

Japan, 32–33, 193, 195, 239, 274, 302, 396–97
    in World War II, 81, 85, 86, 368, 369
Jarring, Gunnar, 407–8
Jews, 35, 84, 102–3, 126, 152, 399–400
Johnson, Lyndon B., 158, 333–34
    on Israel, 409
    on Vietnam, 380, 384, 391–93

Joliot-Curie, Frédéric, 258
Jordan, 319, 403, 405, 409

Kaganovich, Lazar, 108, 111–14, 116
Kaplan, Fanny, 50
Katyn massacres, 78–79
Kazakhstan, 3, 138, 140, 145–46
Kazakov, Yuri, 126
Kennan, George, 101
Kennedy, John F., 26, 329–35, 337, 348, 379–80, 391

Kerensky, Alexander, 37–39, 41–43, 47
Kerensky, Feodor, 28
Khrushchev, Nikita Sergeyevich, 108–34, 175, 207–9, 317
  art under, 118, 124–28
  on Beria, 110
  on Berlin, 321, 323, 325, 328–30, 332, 334, 335, 338
  on China, 192, 193, 198, 201–3, 387, 403
  on Communism, 347
  conspiracy against, xvii, 133–37
  on Cuba, 341–44, 347–49
  foreign relations under, 118, 128–31, 243, 254
  at Geneva Conference, 129–30
  on Kennedy's assassination, 26
  Lin Piao on, 213
  on Middle East, 401–3
  on military power, 247–48, 252
  personality of, 116–19
  in power struggle, 108–13, 116, 128, 156, 316
  as revisionist, 208, 213
  rise in Party of, 114–16
  on satellites, 181
  secret speech on Stalin of, 112, 119–23, 125, 156
  Sputnik diplomacy of, 130–31, 202, 252, 317, 318, 403, 417
  on Stalin, 114, 115, 316, 317
  on Svoboda, 221
  with Tito, 174–75
  on U-2, 326–28
  in U.S., 116, 119, 131, 203, 246–47, 325
  at Vienna meeting with Kennedy, 330, 348, 379–80, 391
  on Vietnam, 386, 387
  during World War II, 115
  youth of, 113–14

Kiev, xvi, 3, 6–7, 14, 114, 116, 126, 152, 187
Killen, James S., 383
Kim Il Sung, 297
Kochetov, Vsevolod, 125
Kommunist, 147, 189, 206–7, 362, 397, 409, 411
Komsomol, 121, 122, 140, 141
Komsomolskaya Pravda, 152
Korea, 237, 239, 256, 258, 296–302, 312, 371, 373, 383, 396, 415
  armistice negotiations on, 128, 301, 315
  Russian ambitions in, 32, 85
Kornilov, General Lavr, 42–43
Kościuszko, Tadeusz, 78
Kosygin, Alexei Nikolayevich, 134, 135, 140, 157, 214, 222, 241, 406
  in Cuba, 354
  on economy, 143, 144, 156
  at Glassboro meeting, 157
  on military power, 248
  Vietnam and, 387, 389, 390
  youth of, 138–39
Kozlov, Frol, 131, 134–35, 324–25
Krupskaya, Nadezhda, 29, 30, 39
Krylov, Viktor, xvi, 4
Kuchum, 188, 190
Kurile Islands, 81, 85
Kutuzov, Mikhail, xvii, 73
Kuznetsov, Anatoly V., 126, 152
Kuznetsov, Vasili, 344
Ky, Air Marshal Nguyen Cao, 382

Labor, 56, 144, 145
  forced, 55, 83, 102, 141
  under Stalin, 55–56, 96, 100, 101, 148
Land reform, 24–25, 35–36, 47

Laos, 129, 302, 369, 371–73, 379–80, 385, 386, 391
Latin America, 207, 210, 212, 237, 239, 263–64, 345–65
League of Nations, 61, 76, 85, 260
Lebanon, 319, 403, 407, 409
Lend-Lease, 2, 74–76, 100, 104, 280
Lenin, Vladimir Ilyich, 87,
  April theses of, 41, 353
  assassination attempt on, 50
  centenary of, 238, 240
  Chernyshevsky read by, 25
  on Comintern, 161–62
  on Constituent Assembly, 47–48
  death of, *xvii*, 51
  democratic centralism of, *xvii*, 58, 161, 162, 183
  on ends and means, 244
  in exile, 39, 42
  on government titles, 46–47
  illness of, 51, 106
  on Kornilov revolt, 42–43
  on Marxism, 29–30
  political power used by, 31, 35, 57, 58, 62–63
  on power, 43, 46, 353
  return to Russia of, 40–41, 43
  on revolution, 31, 34, 47, 160, 161, 198, 236, 242–43, 353
  on Russo-Japanese War, 32
  Stalin and, 51–54, 73, 122, 242–43
  on Stolypin's policies, 36
  on world outlook, 242
  writings of, 29–31, 39–40, 43
  youth of, 27–29
Leningrad (Petrograd, St. Petersburg), 33–34, 40, 49, 53–54
  founding of, 10, 14
  during World War I, 37–38
  during World War II, 72, 84

Lermontov, Mikhail, 19
Liberman, Yevsey, 143
Libya, 399, 410
Lin Piao, 212–13
Litvinov, Maxim, 61, 65, 66
Liu Shao-chi, 192
Lodge, Henry Cabot, 393
Lunik I, 130, 253
Lvov, Prince Georgi, 38

MacArthur, General Douglas, 299, 300
McCarthy, Joseph, 295
Maclean, Donald, 268–69
Macmillan, Harold, 330
McNamara, Robert, 248, 251, 331
Malenkov, Georgi, 108–12, 116, 128, 129
Malinovsky, Marshal Rodion, 134, 139, 214
Manchuria, 32, 82, 196–97, 297
Manuilsky, Dmitri, 277
Mao Tse-tung, 109, 136, 186, 187, 196, 207–9, 216, 294–95, 298, 380
  on atomic weapons, 210–2, 205–7
  "cultural revolution" of, 206, 211
  deification of, 189
  on Outer Mongolia, 192
  rural revolution of, 212
  on Turkestan, 193
Marshall, General George C., 280–81, 294, 296
Marshall Plan, 104, 173, 174, 261, 280–285, 371
Marx, Karl, *xvii*, 23, 28, 44–45, 52
Marxism, 42, 221, 271, 411, 416
  in China, 187
  in Russia, 29–31, 57, 415–16
Marxism-Leninism, *xvii*, 120,

Marxism (cont'd)
166, 169, 223, 239, 240, 243, 353, 354, 415–16
Masaryk, Jan, 221, 222, 284
Masaryk, Thomas G., , 221, 222
Matthews, Herbert, 354
Meir, Golda, 400, 409
Menon, V. K. Krishna, 259
Mensheviks, 31, 33–35, 41, 48
in Petrograd Soviet, 39
Michael, Grand Duke, 38
Middle East, 255, 259, 318, 398–412, 415, 419, see also specific countries
Mikoyan, Anastas, 108, 118, 131, 133, 214, 344
Minin, Kuzma, xvii, 73
Molotov, Vyacheslav, 66–70, 76, 85, 91, 128, 173, 276
on Berlin, 286, 310
at Geneva Conference, 129–30
on Germany, 311, 314
on Greece, 278
on Marshall Plan, 281
memorandum of, 69–70, 77, 94, 274, 398–99
on peace, 243
after Stalin's death, 108, 111–12
Mongol-Tatar invasions, xv, xvi, 2, 7–8, 187, 414
Mongolia, Outer, 60, 81, 191–192, 210, 215
Moscow, 3–4, 7–9, 49, 72, 91
Mott, Newcomb, 157–58
Murmansk, 2, 49, 68
Murphy, Robert, 287–88, 325
Mussorgsky, Modest, 9, 15–16

Nagibin, Yuri, 126
Napoleon, xvi, 2, 14, 21
Narodnaya Volya (Will of the People), 26–29, 41
Narodniks (Populists), 29

Nasser, Gamal Abdul, 316, 400–1, 404–5, 409
Navy, 10, 247–49, 410
in revolt against Lenin, 50
in Mediterranean, 406, 410
Nechaev, Sergei, 23, 41
Nevsky, Alexander, xvii, 15, 73
New Times, 87
New Zealand, 302, 373
Nicholas I, 12, 13, 22, 24, 25
Nicholas II, 9, 33, 34, 37–38, 50
Nikodim, Metropolitan, 261–62
Nitze, Paul, 331
Nixon, Richard M., 116, 131, 159, 251, 324, 338, 384, 408
NKVD, 58, 79, 81, 121, 269
North Atlantic Treaty Organization (NATO), 233–34, 237, 250, 300, 318
espionage in, 269, 294
formation of, 289–94, 301
Germany and, 292, 311, 312, 314–15, 322, 331, 336
in Mediterranean, 407
Soviet memo on, 291–94
Novgorod the Great, 3
Novikov, V. N., 361
Novosti, 257
Novotny, Antonin, 219–21
Novy Mir, 125–27, 152
Nuclear Test Ban Treaty, 131, 204–5, 344, 386, 416

Ob River, 4, 190
Odessa, 49
Official Gazette, 98
Ogarëv, Nikolai, 21–23
Ogonyok, 152
Okhotsk, 190
Okhrana, 58, see also Police
Oktyabr, 125, 152
Olivares Sánchez, Carlos, 341
Organization of American States (OAS), 263–64
Organization of Latin-American

Solidarity (OLAS), 354, 360
Orwell, George, 135
Ostrovsky, Alexander, 20

Pakistan, 119, 239, 312, 373
Papandreou, George, 277–78
Pares, Sir Bernard, 5
Pasternak, Boris, 125
Paustovsky, Konstantin, 125
Peasants, 4, 5, 8, 25, 26, 29, 32, 36, 50, 145
    under Stalin, 55, 56, 101, 142, 146, 414
    voting of, 35
Penkovsky, Oleg, 157, 270
People's Daily, 212, 234
Perm, 190
Persian Gulf, 69, 399, 410
Peru, 263, 363
Peter the Great, 10, 14, 55
Petrograd, see Leningrad
Philby, Harold, 268–69
Philippines, 302, 373, 396
Pieck, Wilhelm, 170, 288
Pistrak, Lazar, 113
Plekhanov, Georgi, 29, 30, 47, 73
Podgorny, Nikolai Viktorovich, 139, 140, 156
Poland, 49, 59, 92, 115, 219
    under Khrushchev, 123, 130
    during World War II, 65–67, 75–81
Police, 14, 147–48
    in atom bomb work, 93, 266, 268
    under Beria, 109–10
    of Comintern, 164
    under Czars, 18–19, 22, 24, 27, 265
    espionage by, 265, 270
    under Khrushchev, 123, 124, 140
    in Khrushchev's ouster, 134
    Kuznetsov on, 152
    political, 57–58

in satellites, 178, 180, 182
    under Stalin, 98–99, 148
    See also Cheka; NKVD
Polyansky, Dmitri, 131, 147
Ponomarev, Boris, 259
Population, xviii, 84, 144, 145, 422
Port Arthur, 85, 192
Potsdam Conference, 77, 91–93, 292, 307–8, 313
Powers, Francis Gary, 269
Pozharsky, Prince Dmitri, xvii, 73
Pravda
    April theses in, 41
    on art under Khrushchev, 126
    on Bandung Conference, 210–211
    on Beria, 109–10
    Brezhnev Doctrine in, 229–30
    on China, 206, 219
    on Cominform, 173, 181
    on culture, 82
    on Germany, 336
    on Khrushchev, 115
    on Latin America, 352, 361–62
    on Mediterranean, 407
    propaganda in, 153
    on religion, 262
    on Stalin's daughter, 153
    on Vietnam, 386
    on Voskhod launch, 132–33
Pushkin, Alexander, xvi, 14–15, 18, 19, 73

Radio Moscow, 257
Radzinsky, Edvard, 126
Rashidov, Sharaf, 263
Rasputin, Grigori, 37
Red International of Trade Unions (Profintern), 260
Red Star, 83, 409

Religion
  beginnings of, 6–7
  churches restored as monuments of, 16
  in foreign policy, 261–62
  Marxism and, 411
  Petrograd Soviet on, 38
  under Stalin, 74, 261
  subjugation under Czars of, 14
Reuter, Ernst, 309
Revisionists, 103–5, 176, 177, 188, 208, 213, 222, 240, 350
Revolution, 17, 240, 255
  Brezhnev on, 236, 243–44
  Castro on, 345, 349, 350, 352–53, 358, 360–61
  Comintern in, 165, 166, 169, 170, 183
  Ho Chi Minh on, 384
  Khrushchev on, 110, 243
  Lenin on, 31, 34, 47, 160, 161, 198, 236, 242–43, 353
  Mao Tse-tung on, 211, 212
  Marx on, 45, 271
  Narodniks on, 29
  propaganda about, 21, 25
  societies for, 22, 25
  Stalin on, 54, 160–61, 198
  See also Bolshevik Revolution; February Revolution; Decembrists
Rhee, Syngman, 296
Ribbentrop, Joachim von, 66–68, 77, 274
Robertson, Walter, 377
Robeson, Paul, 172
Roosevelt, Franklin D., 60, 74–76, 79, 81, 84, 86, 172, 273, 275, 276, 370
Rose, Fred, 266
Rozhdestvensky, Robert, 125
Rozov, Viktor, 126
Rude Pravo, 184–85
Rumania, 24, 65, 68, 81, 92, 184, 218, 406, 412
  on Czechoslovakian rebellion, 222, 234, 238
Rusk, Dean, 329–31, 334, 336, 341, 386

St. Petersburg, see Leningrad
Sakhalin, 69, 81, 85, 211
Sakharov, Andrei, 151
Satellite countries, 177–82, 218–219, 228, 291, 296
  limited sovereignty in, 232
  in Marshall Plan, 281–83
  See also Warsaw Pact; and specific satellites
Schroeder, Louise, 309
Schulenberg, Werner von der, 66
Scinteia, 185
SEATO, 302, 373
Sechenov, Ivan, 73
Second International, 161
Semenov, Vladimir, 336
Semichastny, Vladimir, 134, 140, 141
Serfdom, xvi, 8–9, 19–20, 22, 24–25
Shelepin, Alexander, 134, 140, 389, 393–94
Shepilov, Dmitri, 113, 118, 401
Siberia, 3, 4, 145, 188, 194, 211, 215, 415
  exile to, 14, 55, 81, 93, 99, 102, 115
  settlement of, 9, 190, 215
Sihanouk, Norodom, 386
Simon, Abbot, 172
Sinyavsky, Andrei, 149–50
Smith, Adam, 18
Smith, General Walter Bedell, 11, 62, 103, 286, 372
Smolensk, 78–79
Social Democrats, 38
  beginnings of, 26, 29–31, 41
  Comintern on, 164, 183, 237
  in Duma election, 35

Social Revolutionaries, 26, 39, 41, 47–48
Socialism, 56–57, 89, 175–76, 198–200
  in Arab countries, 411
  Brezhnev on, 229–31, 244
  Ho Chi Minh on, 384
  Soviet aid and, 255–56
  Stalin on, 54, 88–90, 170, 282
Sokolovsky, Marshal Vasili, 103
Soldatov, Alexander, 357
Solzhenitsyn, Alexander, 126, 150, 152
Souphanouvong, 379, 386
Souvanna Phouma, 380
Soviet of Workers' and Soldiers' Deputies, 38–39, 41, 43, 48, 56
Spaak, Paul Henri, 233
Space programs, 130, 131, 249, 252–53, 317, 318, 320, 417, 419
Sputnik I, 130, 253, 317
Stalin, Joseph, 12–13, 51–59, 62–63, 91, 155–56, 184, 291
  as anti-Semitic, 399–400
  on Balkans, 276
  on Berlin, 286–88, 306
  on China, 170, 196, 301
  in Cold War, 95, 103–5, 273
  in Communist International, 75, 165, 166, 168, 170, 171
  death of, xvii, 15, 106–7
  despotism of, 10, 13, 120
  on Doctors' Plot, 106, 122, 400
  Ehrenburg on, 124
  on foreign policy, 61, 242–43
  Germany and, 66–70, 247
  on government titles, 98
  on Iran, 398–99
  on Japan, 32–33
  Khrushchev's secret speech on, 112, 119–23, 125, 156
  on Korea, 297, 301
  Lenin and, 51–54, 73, 122, 242–43
  on military power, 247
  peasants under, 55, 56, 101, 142, 146, 414
  on Poland, 80–81
  at Potsdam conference, 91
  rehabilitation of, 148, 154
  on socialism, 54, 88–90, 170, 282
  Suslov on, 183
  at Teheran conference, 86
  terror used by, 57–58, 156, 166
  on World War II, xvii, 71–74, 87–89, 121
  at Yalta conference, 81, 86
  youth of, 52–53
Stalina, Nadya Alliluyeva, 53
Stalingrad, 91
Stolypin, Peter, 35–36
Strang, William, 66
Strategic arms limitation talks (SALT), 251, 418–19
Strikes
  during Red Terror, 50
  in St. Petersburg, 33–34
  during World War I, 37, 38
Strong, Anna Louise, 13
Suslov, Mikhail, 157, 183–84, 259
Suvorov, Alexander, xvii, 73
Svoboda, General Ludvik, 220–21, 225
Svyatoslav, Vladimir, 6
Syria, 402–6, 408

Taiwan (Formosa), 203, 295, 297, 383, 396
Tannu Tuva, 191, 192
Tarsis, Valery, 149
Tass, 257–58
Taylor, General Maxwell, 331
Teheran conference, 77, 86, 274
Tendryakov, Vladimir, 126

Thieu, General Nguyen Van, 382, 384, 393
Third International, see Communist International, Third
Thompson, Llewellyn, 335
Thorez, Maurice, 170
Thuy, Xuan, 392
Tito, Josip Broz, 174–75, 181–82, 278, 279
Tobolsk, 190
Togliatti, Palmiro, 123, 209
Tolstoy, Leo, xvi, 15, 19–20, 26, 73
Tomsk, 190
Trade, 158–59, 275, 282
    with Cuba, 356–57, 361
    with Latin America, 349, 354, 363
    from satellites, 180
    with U.S., 301
Trade unions, 32, 259–61
    Comintern in, 164, 171, 266
    Lenin on, 30, 32
Trapeznikov, Vadim, 143
Trotsky, Leon, 48, 49, 51, 52, 161
    arrest of, 34
    in Bolshevik Revolution, 43
    on dictatorship, 63
    expulsion of, 55, 59, 156, 166, 399
    on Lenin, 27, 46–47
    on Stalin, 54, 62
Truman, Harry S., 80, 91–92, 95, 182, 291, 300, 306
Truman Doctrine, 95, 173, 174, 274, 279
Turgenev, Ivan, 15, 19
Turkestan, 191, 193
Turkey, 94–95, 129, 274, 292, 302, 343, 402–4, 415
Turkish Straits, 69, 94, 274, 399
Tvardovsky, Alexander, 125, 127, 152

U-2 affair, 131, 269, 325–28
Ukraine, 3, 232
    Germans in, 49, 82–83
    Khrushchev in, 114–16, 118
    Party purge in, 109, 115
Ulbricht, Walter, 136, 170, 184, 288, 335, 339
Ulyanov, Alexander, 27–28
Ulyanov, Ilya, 27
Ulyanov, Vladimir Ilyich, see Lenin, Vladimir Ilyich
Ulyanovsk, 27
Unification Congresses, 31, 33–35
Union of Societies of Friendship, 258
Unità, L', 406
United Arab Republic (Egypt), 130, 255, 316, 400–8, 411
United Kingdom, 60, 64–68, 72, 73, 75, 76, 273–76, 280
    in Berlin blockade, 286–87
    in CENTO, 302
    espionage in, 266, 268–69
    Khrushchev on, 118–19
    in Marshall Plan, 281, 283–84
    in Middle East, 399–404, 407–8, 410
United Nations, 76, 81, 84–85, 98, 262–63, 269, 275
    on aggression, 231–32
    in Cuba, 343–44
    on Czechoslovakia, 224–25, 230–31, 233, 284
    on Germany, 287, 313, 330
    on Greece, 277–79
    Khrushchev at, 347–48
    on Korea, 296, 298–300
    on Middle East, 318, 399, 401, 403–7
    Red China and, 298, 300
    Truman on, 95
U.S.S.R. in, 129, 256–57, 262–63, 277–78, 283, 298, 305, 318, 349, 406, 418

United Nations Relief and Rehabilitation Administration (UNRRA), 104, 280
United States, 50, 59–61, 70–76, 86, 141, 196, 201, 207, 273–76, 279
    in Berlin blockade, 285–88
    China and, 213–14, 216–17, 294–95
    in Cold War, 104–5, 273
    Cuba and, 337, 345, 347–48, 353, 359–60, 364–65
    espionage in, 266, 268–70
    imperialism of, 174, 176, 205, 219, 235–37
    Korea and, 296, 298–302
    in Middle East, 399, 401–10, 412
    military strength of, 250–53
    in NATO, 289–94, 301
    treaties of, 301–3
    Vietnam and, 370–73, 376, 379–81, 383–97
United States Information Agency (USIA), 291, 322, 331
Ussuri River, 191, 194

Vandenberg, Arthur, 291
Varga, Eugene, 283
Venezuela, 263, 353, 358, 362
Vietnam, 157–59, 219, 237–39, 248, 302, 366–97, 417–18
    Castro on, 345, 352, 364
    Paris Peace talks on, 392–93
    Soviet aid to, 379, 386–88
Vladivostok, 1, 49
Voice of America, 101, 127, 291
Volsky, Viktor, 361–62
Voroshilov, Marshal Kliment, 66, 108, 111
Voskhod, 132–33, 135
Voznesensky, Andrei, 150, 187–88
Vyshinsky, Andrei, 4

Warsaw, 79–80
Warsaw Pact, 218–19, 222–26, 228, 292–94, 315, 318, 336
Wedemeyer, General Albert C., 294
Welles, Sumner, 70–71
Werth, Alexander, 92
White, Andrew Dickson, 24–25
Wilson, Woodrow, 48
Witte, Sergei, 31–32, 34, 35
Wolfe, Bertram, xviii, 45, 118–19, 271
World Council of Churches, 261
World Federation of Trade Unions (WFTU), 260–261, 393
World Marxist Review, 353
World Peace Council, 258–59, 394
World War I, 36–37, 39, 40, 47–49, 59–60
World War II, 61–62, 64–86, 93, 102, 273–76, 307
Writers Union, 125–26, 150, 152

Yalta conference, 77, 81, 86, 93, 105, 192, 273, 292, 305–6, 318
Yelyutin, Vyacheslav, 197–98
Yemen, South, 410, 411
Yepishev, General Alexei, 134
Yermak, 188, 190
Yevtushenko, Yevgeny, 125, 126, 194–95
Yugoslavia, 81, 174–75, 177, 181–82, 184, 208, 229, 232, 234, 239, 278–79

Zemstvos, 26, 27
Zhdanov, Andrei, 99, 106, 108
Zhukov, Georgi, 91, 108–10, 113, 119, 130, 139, 195, 216, 306
Zinoviev, Grigory, 51
Zorin, Valerian, 206, 284

ABOUT THE AUTHOR

Foy D. Kohler, a native Ohioan, entered the United States Foreign Service in 1931, the year he was graduated from Ohio State University. On a variety of assignments he has served in Yugoslavia, Rumania, Greece, Egypt, Turkey and Canada. He has been Director of the Voice of America, Assistant Secretary of State for European Affairs and Deputy Under Secretary of State for Political Affairs. He was a resident of Moscow for nearly seven years, in 1947–49 as Counselor of Embassy, and from 1962 until November, 1966, as Ambassador to the U.S.S.R. Ambassador Kohler retired from the Foreign Service in 1967. Since 1968 he has been connected with the University of Miami as Professor at the Center for Advanced International Studies.

70 71 72 73 10 9 8 7 6 5 4 3 2 1